The Best of
Chinese
Cooking

The Best of
Chinese
Cooking

Cecilia Au-yeung
Photography by Wilson Au-yeung

D
DEALERFIELD

Printed in 1991 for Reed Books

This edition specially printed in 1995 for Dealerfield
Glaisdale Parkway, Glaisdale Drive, Notts NG8 4GA

Illustrated by Joyce Tuhill

ISBN 1 85927 055 7

Photoset in Linotron 202 Times
by Wyvern Typesetting Limited, Bristol

Produced by Mandarin Offset
Printed and bound in China

Useful Facts and Figures

Notes on metrication

In this book quantities are given in metric and Imperial
measures. Exact conversion from Imperial to metric measures
does not usually give very convenient working quantities and so
the metric measures have been rounded off into units of 25
grams. The table below shows the recommended equivalents.

Ounces	Approx g to nearest whole figure	Recommended conversion to nearest unit of 25
1	28	25
2	57	50
3	85	75
4	113	100
5	142	150
6	170	175
7	198	200
8	227	225
9	255	250
10	283	275
11	312	300
12	340	350
13	368	375
14	396	400
15	425	425
16 (1 lb)	454	450
17	482	475
18	510	500
19	539	550
20 (1¼ lb)	567	575

Note When converting quantities over 20 oz first add the appropri-
ate figures in the centre column, then adjust to the nearest unit of
25. As a general guide, 1 kg (1000 g) equals 2.2 lb or about 2 lb 3 oz.
This method of conversion gives good results in nearly all cases,
although in certain pastry and cake recipes a more accurate conversion is necessary to produce a balanced recipe.

Liquid meausres The millilitre has been used in this book and the following table gives a few examples.

Imperial	Approx ml to nearest whole figure	Recommended ml
¼ pint	142	150 ml
½ pint	283	300 ml
¾ pint	425	450 ml
1 pint	567	600 ml
1½ pints	851	900 ml
1¾ pints	992	1000 ml (1 litre)

Spoon measures All spoon measures given in this book are level unless otherwise stated.

Can sizes At present, cans are marked with the exact (usually to the nearest whole number) metric equivalent of the Imperial weight of the contents, so we have followed this practice when giving can sizes.

Oven temperatures

The table below gives recommended equivalents.

	°C	°F	Gas Mark
Very cool	110	225	¼
	120	250	½
Cool	140	275	1
	150	300	2
Moderate	160	325	3
	180	350	4
Moderately hot	190	375	5
	200	400	6
Hot	220	425	7
	230	450	8
Very hot	240	475	9

Notes for American and Australian users
In America the 8 fl oz measuring cup is used. In Australia metric measures are now used in conjunction with the standard 250-ml measuring cup. The Imperial pint, used in Britain and Australia, is 20 fl oz, while the American pint is 16 fl oz. It is important to remember that the Australian tablespoon differs from both the British and American tablespoons; the table below gives a comparison. The British standard tablespoon, which has been used throughout this book, holds 17.7 ml, the American 14.2 ml, and the Australian 20 ml. A teaspoon holds approximately 5 ml in all three countries.

British	American	Australian
1 teaspoon	1 teaspoon	1 teaspoon
1 tablespoon	1 tablespoon	1 tablespoon
2 tablespoons	3 tablespoons	2 tablespoons
3½ tablespoons	4 tablespoons	3 tablespoons
4 tablespoons	5 tablespoons	3½ tablespoons

An Imperial/American guide to solid and liquid measures

Imperial	American
Solid measures	
1 lb butter or margarine	2 cups
1 lb flour	4 cups
1 lb granulated or caster sugar	2 cup
1 lb icing sugar	3 cups
8 oz rice	1 cup

Liquid measures	
¼ pint liquid	⅔ cup liquid
½ pint	1¼ cups
¾ pint	2 cups
1 pint	2½ cups
1½ pints	3¾ cups
2 pints	5 cups (2½ pints)

NOTE When making any of the recipes in this book, only follow one set of measures as they are not interchangeable.

Contents

Introduction

This cookery book offers a collection of authentic recipes from all over China, including traditional dishes which may be cooked as part of daily meals or as celebration dishes. Soups, dim sum, roasts and vegetarian dishes are featured and there are sweet dishes too. At the back of the book there is an extensive glossary of ingredients and a section which explains the Chinese kitchen equipment. To help you plan a meal there are also menu suggestions.

I have chosen famous recipes which are popular among Chinese people. Many of the unusual ingredients are available from Chinese supermarkets, ethnic shops, health food shops and delicatessens. The colour photographs which accompany all the recipes will show you what the finished dish should look like and, in some cases, they will help you to identify some of the less common ingredients.

From the different regions of China come many different types of cooking. For example, Cantonese and Southern Chinese cooking techniques are considered to be the most subtle and sophisticated in China. In these areas the food is always marinated and the dish usually has a sauce or gravy. The sauces or gravies are quite individual to complement the wide variety of recipes and rice is always served with the meal. The cooking of Shanghai and Szechuan is richer and spicier: these foods usually contain chillies, dark soy sauce and tabasco. The people from this region consume a great deal of pasta, flour and various other doughs. Noodles and buns are generally served with a meal. Pekinese cooking has less variety but it is world famous for its Peking duck and deep fried foods coated in light egg white batters. Pekinese dishes are simple to prepare and easier to handle.

If you are unfamiliar with authentic Chinese food you may be surprised to find recipes for casseroles. There are many different recipes for Chinese casseroles and they are usually made with meat. Traditionally cooked in decorative earthenware pots, the meat develops a fluffy texture and it becomes soft and tender. Rice and congee (rice soups) can also be cooked in this way.

Many of the traditional dishes have been passed on from generation to generation and are prepared particularly for the Chinese New Year or other festivals and special occasions such as weddings or the birth of a child. The Chinese New Year, which is around mid-January to mid-February according to the Julian calendar, is the most important time of the year for Chinese people. Not only does the festival symoblise a fresh start to a year full of resolutions, but it is also a celebration of togetherness and unity for the whole family. Often, during this time, all members of the family gather together (this gathering may include several generations) to celebrate for as long as twenty days. During this time many delicious dishes are prepared for friends and relatives and, due to the natural superstition of our ancestors, these are named after different signs of luck; the names are still used today to uphold the spirit of the old fashioned feast.

Dim sum, the famous Chinese snacks which originated in Guangzhou (Canton) a region of Southern China, are traditionally served at tea houses. I have included some dim sum which are very simple to prepare and others which are more difficult to make. You may have difficulty in ordering some of these rarer dim sum dishes in many Chinese restaurants. What is simpler than to make these dishes yourself to solve this problem?

Most people are afraid to attempt Chinese cookery because of the elaborate preparation, ingredients and utensils which are required. If you try these recipes you will find that they are easy to follow and they can be prepared in any Western kitchen. All the recipes have been tested and retested by myself, my assistants and my students in our fully-equipped kitchen. They are workable recipes and they are all illustrated with tempting colour pictures as it is my firm belief that seeing is better than reading. So why not make these mouth-watering dishes yourself, to be served steaming hot from your own kitchen, at your own table and you will save money at the same time!

Dried Scallop Chowder

50 g/2 oz dried scallops
25 g/1 oz dried squid
50 g/2 oz mushrooms
50 g/2 oz carrots
2 spring onions
50 g/2 oz cooked ham
50 g/2 oz canned bamboo
  shoots (optional)
2 tablespoons oil
1 teaspoon dry sherry
1.15 litres/2 pints plus 2
  tablespoons water
1 teaspoon salt
pinch of pepper
2–3 teaspoons sugar
½ teaspoon soy sauce
1 tablespoon cornflour
1 egg, beaten

Soak the scallops and squid in cold water to cover for 1 hour. Drain off the water and cut the seafood into fine shreds, then place these on a large plate and steam them over boiling water for 20 minutes. Meanwhile, clean and shred the mushrooms, carrots and spring onions. Shred the ham and bamboo

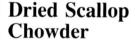

shoots (if used) into similar sized pieces.

Heat the oil in a large saucepan. Add the sherry, then pour in the water and bring to the boil. Stir in the scallops, squid, mushrooms and carrots and simmer, covered, for 10 minutes.

Add the ham, bamboo shoots, salt, pepper, sugar and soy sauce, then continue to simmer the soup for a further 5 minutes. Blend the cornflour to a smooth cream with the 2 tablespoons water, then gradually pour this into the soup, stirring vigorously, and simmer for 2 minutes until thickened. Taste the soup and adjust the seasoning if necessary.

Finally stir in the beaten egg, pouring it in a thin steady stream into the simmering soup. Remove the pan from the heat, sprinkle the spring onions over the soup and serve at once in individual bowls. *Serves 4–6*

Congee with Fishballs and Lettuce

225 g/8 oz round-grain rice
2 bean curd sheets
20 ginkgo nuts
450 g/1 lb lettuce
4.5 litres/8 pints plus 2
  tablespoons water
25 g/1 oz dried shrimps
450 g/1 lb white fish fillet (for
  example, cod or haddock)
salt and pepper
¼ teaspoon sugar
1 teaspoon cornflour
3 tablespoons oil
1 teaspoon sesame oil
2 tablespoons finely shredded
  fresh root ginger
2 tablespoons finely shredded
  spring onion

Wash and drain the rice. Rinse the bean curd sheets under running water, then tear them into small pieces. Shell, peel and crush the ginkgo nuts. Wash and shred the lettuce, then set it aside.

Pour the water into a very large saucepan. Add the rice, bean curd and ginkgo nuts.

Bring to the boil over medium heat, lower the heat and simmer gently, uncovered, for 2 hours. Soak the dried shrimps in cold water for 30 minutes

Skin the fish fillets, remove any bones, then finely mince or pound the flesh until smooth. Mash the drained shrimps and add them to the minced fish. Stir well with ½ teaspoon salt, the sugar, a pinch of pepper, the cornflour and 2 tablespoons water. Pound the mixture with a wooden spoon until it becomes quite elastic. Dampen your hands and shape spoonfuls of the fish into balls about the size of walnuts; arrange these on a greased plate.

When the congee has turned milky, add the fishballs and shredded lettuce, then continue simmering for 3–5 minutes, or until the fishballs are cooked. Season to taste and stir in the oils. Serve hot, in small bowls with the shredded ginger and spring onion sprinkled on top.
Serves 6

Congee with Minced Beef

100 g/4 oz round-grain rice
3 tablespoons oil plus oil for
  deep frying
salt and pepper
10 ginkgo nuts
3.5 litres/6 pints plus 6
  tablespoons water
350 g/12 oz minced beef
3 teaspoons soy sauce
1 teaspoon each of sugar
  sherry and cornflour
50 g/2 oz rice vermicelli
1 tablespoon very finely
  chopped fresh root ginger
2 tablespoons chopped chives
1 teaspoon sesame oil
parsley sprig to garnish
TO SERVE
50 g/2 oz fresh root ginger,
  finely shredded
4 spring onions, shredded
Twisted Doughnuts (page 210)

Wash and drain the rice, then place it in a bowl with 1 tablespoon of the oil and 2 teaspoons salt. Shell and blanch the ginkgo nuts.

Bring the water to the boil in a large saucepan. Add the rice and nuts and simmer gently for 1 hour.

Mix the beef with the soy sauce, sugar, sherry, cornflour, a pinch of pepper, 6 tablespoons water and remaining oil. Set aside for 30 minutes.

Heat the oil for deep frying to 190 c/375 f, then fry the vermicelli until puffed up. Drain on absorbent kitchen paper, crush into small pieces, then stir into the beef with the ginger and chives. Shape the meat into small meatballs and add them to the congee. Alternatively, the minced meat can be stirred in as it is. Simmer for about 5 minutes, or until cooked. Add seasoning with the sesame oil. Serve, garnished with a parsley sprig, with the suggested accompaniments.
Serves 6

Prawn Ball and Winter Melon Soup

275 g/10 oz peeled cooked prawns (defrosted if frozen)
salt and pepper
pinch of sugar
2 teaspoons cornflour
1 teaspoon plus a few drops sesame oil
5 canned water chestnuts
2 teaspoons finely chopped chives
450 g/1 lb winter melon or marrow
2 tablespoons oil
3 medium-thick slices fresh root ginger
1 teaspoon dry sherry
1.4 litres/2½ pints water
pinch of monosodium glutamate
parsley sprig to garnish

Mash the prawns into a paste and mix in a pinch each of salt, pepper and sugar, the cornflour, and a few drops of sesame oil. Pound the mixture with a wooden spoon until it becomes firm and elastic.

Mince or very finely chop the water chestnuts and mix them into the prawns with the chives. Pound the mixture until it is thoroughly mixed. Chill for 1 hour.

Peel the winter melon or marrow and discard any seeds. Cut the flesh into small pieces. If you like, the vegetable can be sliced, then cut into shapes using a small biscuit cutter.

Shape the chilled paste into small balls. Use two oiled spoons or wet your hands to prevent the mixture sticking. Set aside.

Heat the oil in a large saucepan. Sauté the ginger until it gives off its strong aroma. Stir in the winter melon or marrow and continue to fry for a few minutes. Add the sherry and pour in the water. Bring to the boil, drop in the prawn balls and reduce the heat; simmer for 10 minutes.

Stir the monosodium glutamate and 1 teaspoon sesame oil into the soup, then taste it and adjust the seasoning. Serve hot, garnished with a parsley sprig. *Serves 6*

Chicken and Pea Chowder

175 g/6 oz boneless chicken breast, minced
1 teaspoon Ginger Juice (page 227)
3 teaspoons dry sherry
salt and pepper
5 egg whites
½ teaspoon sesame oil
225 g/8 oz shelled peas
1.15 litres/2 pints chicken stock
4 tablespoons oil
2 medium-thick slices fresh root ginger
2 shallots, grated
¼ teaspoon monosodium glutamate
1 tablespoon cornflour
2 tablespoons water
2 glacé cherries to garnish

Mix the chicken with the ginger juice, 1 teaspoon sherry, ¼ teaspoon salt and a pinch of pepper, then set aside for 10 minutes.

Whisk the egg whites with ¼ teaspoon salt, a pinch of pepper and the sesame oil. Stir them into the chicken.

Mash and sieve the peas.

Weigh 40 g/1½ oz of the chicken and stir this into the pea purée. Stir in 300 ml/½ pint stock. Stir another 300 ml/½ pint stock into the white chicken.

Heat half the oil in a saucepan, and fry 1 slice of ginger and half the shallot, until fragrant. Discard. Stir in 1 teaspoon sherry, the white chicken and 300 ml/½ pint chicken stock. Bring to the boil, stirring continuously. Add half the monosodium glutamate and salt. Blend the cornflour with the water, then pour half into the soup, whisking. Simmer for 2 minutes, then keep hot. Heat the remaining oil and fry the remaining ginger and shallot. Discard. Stir in the remaining sherry and stock. Add the pea and chicken mixture and bring to the boil. Whisk in the remaining monosodium glutamate, salt and cornflour mixture. Simmer for 2 minutes.

To serve, ladle the two soups into a bowl to form the shape of a *Yin-Yang*. Decorate and serve immediately. *Serves 4–6*

Chicken and Sweet Corn Chowder

50 g/2 oz uncooked boneless chicken meat
1½ teaspoons dry sherry
1 teaspoon Ginger Juice (page 227)
salt and pepper
3½ teaspoons cornflour
1 egg, separated
2 tablespoons oil
900 ml/1½ pints plus 2 tablespoons water
1 (326-g/11½-oz) can sweet corn, drained
¼ chicken stock cube
a few drops of sesame oil
½ teaspoon sugar
parsley sprigs to garnish

Mince the chicken meat, then mix it with 1 teaspoon of the sherry and the ginger juice. Stir in a pinch of pepper, ½ teaspoon of the cornflour and half the egg white, then set aside to marinate for 10 minutes.

Heat the oil in a large saucepan, sprinkle in the remaining sherry and pour in the 900 ml/1½ pints water, then bring to the boil. Stir in the sweet corn and crumbled stock cube with seasoning to taste. Add a few drops of sesame oil and the sugar.

Blend the remaining cornflour to a smooth cream with the 2 tablespoons water. Stirring continuously, slowly mix the minced chicken into the simmering soup. Still stirring, pour in the cornflour mixture, then continue to simmer for 2 minutes. Beat the remaining egg white and yolk together and swirl this into the soup; remove the pan from the heat. Serve immediately, in individual bowls, garnished with parsley sprigs. *Serves 4*

Pork Slice and Cabbage Soup

100 g/4 oz lean, boneless pork
1 teaspoon soy sauce
½ teaspoon sugar
½ teaspoon cornflour
3 tablespoons oil
1.4 litres/2½ pints plus 2 tablespoons water
1 teaspoon dry sherry
salt and pepper
450 g/1 lb Chinese cabbage or Swiss chard
3 medium-thick slices fresh root ginger
¼ teaspoon monosodium glutamate
½ teaspoon sesame oil

Cut the pork into fine slices. Mix the soy sauce, sugar, cornflour, 1 tablespoon of the oil, the 2 tablespoons water, ½ teaspoon of the sherry and a pinch of pepper until smooth. Pour this mixture over the pork and toss the pieces well to coat them thoroughly. Set aside to marinate for 20 minutes.

Meanwhile, wash and thoroughly drain the Chinese cabbage or Swiss chard and cut it into large chunks. Chop the ginger very finely. Blanch the marinated pork for 1 minute, then drain it and set aside. (To do this, bring a small amount of water to the boil, add the pork and bring it back to the boil, then cook for 1 minute before draining the meat.)

Heat the remaining oil in a large saucepan, add the ginger and fry until it gives off its aroma. Quickly brown the pieces of meat on both sides, then remove them from the pan. Add the cabbage or chard and fry for 1 minute. Add the remaining sherry and pour in the water. Bring to the boil, then reduce the heat and simmer for 10 minutes.

Stir the monosodium glutamate, sesame oil and seasoning to taste into the soup. Add the pork and continue to simmer for 5 minutes. Serve the soup hot, in individual bowls. *Serves 6*

Soups

Duck Bone and Melon Soup

meaty bones from Peking Duck (page 82)
450 g/1 lb winter melon or cabbage
50 g/2 oz Virginia ham
2 tablespoons oil
2 medium-thick slices fresh root ginger
1 teaspoon dry sherry
1.4 litres/2½ pints water
salt

Chop the duck bones into small pieces. Peel and cut the melon into big chunks. Shred the cabbage (if used) and the ham.

Heat the oil in a saucepan. Sauté the ginger, melon or cabbage, ham and bones for a while, pour in the sherry and water. Bring to the boil, then cover and reduce the heat to simmer the soup for 30 minutes.

Season to taste and serve in one large bowl or in individual soup bowls. *Serves 4*

Virginia Ham: True ham is smoked or cured meat taken from the leg of the pig. Many types of ham sold today are taken from the shoulder of the pig, a cut which gives more fat and less flavour.

Virginia ham, from the United States of America, is sweet and smoked, with an excellent flavour but gammon can be substituted.

Roast Duck and Bean Thread Soup

100 g/4 oz pickled vegetable
salt and pepper
225 g/8 oz bean thread
175 g/6 oz Peking Duck (page 82)
4 tablespoons oil
1 medium-thick slice fresh root ginger
2 teaspoons dry sherry
1.15 litres/2 pints stock
1 shallot, sliced
1 clove garlic, sliced
1 tablespoon sugar
2 teaspoons cornflour
1 tablespoon water
1 teaspoon light soy sauce
1 teaspoon sesame oil

Soak the pickled vegetable in salted water for 1 hour. Drain, wash and cut into 1-cm/½-in sections. Cook over a low heat in a dry wok or frying pan until very dry. Set aside.

Cut the bean thread into 10-cm/4-in lengths. Soak these in water until required. Shred the roast duck meat and place it on a platter.

Heat 2 tablespoons of the oil in a saucepan. Sauté the ginger until fragrant, then add 1 teaspoon of the sherry and 600 ml/1 pint of the stock, bring to the boil and season to taste. Stir in the bean thread, then simmer for 5 minutes.

Meanwhile, heat the remaining oil in a saucepan, sauté the shallot and garlic until fragrant; discard. Add the pickled vegetables and fry these with the sugar, then stir in the roast duck and mix evenly. Pour in the remaining 1 teaspoon sherry and add the remaining stock. Bring to the boil. Blend the cornflour to a smooth paste with the water, then stir it into the duck and simmer for 1 minute.

To serve, stir the soy sauce and sesame oil into the bean thread soup and pour it into a bowl. Ladle the duck on top. Serve hot. *Serves 4–6*

Double Meatball Soup

450 g/1 lb peeled cooked
prawns (defrosted if frozen)
salt and pepper
½ egg white
175 g/6 oz pork fillet
4 water chestnuts
1 teaspoon soy sauce
1 teaspoon sugar
1.15 litres/2 pints plus 2
tablespoons water
1 teaspoon cornflour
a few drops of sesame oil
2 tablespoons oil
1 teaspoon dry sherry
¼ chicken stock cube
1 lettuce, washed and
separated into leaves

Mash the prawns to a paste.
Add ¼ teaspoon salt, a pinch
of pepper and the egg white.
Pound the mixture thoroughly
so that it binds together, then
chill it for 1 hour.

Meanwhile mince the pork
with the water chestnuts. Mix
the soy sauce, sugar, 2
tablespoons water and the
cornflour into the meat. Add
the sesame oil and set aside to

marinate for 30 minutes.

Using wet hands, shape the
prawn mixture into small
balls. Shape the marinated
meat into similar-sized balls
and set aside.

Heat the oil in a large
saucepan and pour in the
sherry. Add the 1.15 litres/2
pints water and crumble in the
stock cube, then bring to the
boil. Add the meatballs,
prawnballs and lettuce leaves.
Season the soup to taste and
simmer for 5 minutes or until
the meatballs are thoroughly
cooked. Serve immediately,
ladled into individual bowls.
Serves 4–6

Minced Beef Chowder

150 g/5 oz lean minced steak or
beef
1 teaspoon soy sauce
½ teaspoon sugar
6½ teaspoons cornflour
2 tablespoons oil
1–1.15 litres/1¾–2 pints plus 4
tablespoons water
1 teaspoon dry sherry
1 chicken stock cube
1 tablespoon finely shredded
fresh root ginger
1 tablespoon finely shredded
spring onion
a few flat-leafed parsley sprigs
salt
2 egg whites
parsley sprigs to garnish

Place the meat in a bowl. Add
the soy sauce, sugar, ½
teaspoon of the cornflour, half
the oil and 2 tablespoons of
the water, then mix
thoroughly and set the mince
aside to marinate for 20
minutes.

Heat the remaining oil in a
large saucepan. Sprinkle in
the sherry, then add the

crumbled stock cube and pour
in the bulk of the water. Bring
to the boil and add the mince,
then simmer for 5 minutes.

Meanwhile, put the
shredded ginger, spring onion
and parsley sprigs into one
large soup bowl or individual
bowls. Blend the remaining
cornflour to a smooth cream
with the remaining 2
tablespoons water. Gradually
pour this mixture into the
simmering soup, stirring
continuously to prevent lumps
forming. Simmer for 1 minute.

Before serving, taste the
soup and add seasoning. Stir
in the egg whites and pour
into the prepared soup bowl
or bowls. Serve garnished with
sprigs of parsley. *Serves 4–6*

Hot and Sour Soup

15 g/½ oz black fungus
4 Chinese dried mushrooms
50 g/2 oz fresh squid
50 g/2 oz cooked ham
75 g/3 oz carrots
100 g/4 oz bean curd
2 tablespoons oil
1 teaspoon dry sherry
1.15 litres/2 pints chicken stock
salt and pepper
1 teaspoon sugar
3 tablespoons white vinegar
1 teaspoon soy sauce
chilli sauce to taste
2 tablespoons cornflour
2 tablespoons water
1 egg, beaten
a little sesame oil
2 spring onions, shredded, to
    garnish

Soak the fungus in hot water to cover for 1 hour. Soak the mushrooms in hot water for 30 minutes. Meanwhile, prepare the squid according to the instructions given at the end of this recipe. Shred all the prepared squid.

Shred the ham and carrots and cut the bean curd into small strips. Finally, drain and shred the fungus and blanch it in boiling water for 1 minute. Drain the shreds and rinse them under cold running water. Shred the drained mushrooms.

Heat the oil in a large saucepan, then add the sherry and pour in the stock. Bring to the boil before adding all the prepared ingredients. Reduce the heat and simmer for 10 minutes, then add seasoning to taste, the sugar, vinegar, soy sauce and chilli sauce.

Blend the cornflour to a smooth cream with the water, then slowly stir this mixture into the simmering soup. Continue to cook for 2 minutes before pouring in the egg in a slow steady stream.

To serve, pour a little sesame oil into a large soup bowl or tureen, add some pepper, then pour in the soup. Garnish with shredded spring onion and serve immediately. *Serves 4–6*

To clean squid: Rub your hands with a little salt to enable you to grip the squid. Hold the body of the squid in one hand, then grasp the tentacles in the other. Pull the head and tentacles away from the body, then reach inside the body and remove the transparent bone-like strip which runs down the back. Cut the body into thin slices.

Cut the head off the tentacles and remove the ink sac which is not required for this recipe. Discard the head and cut up the tentacles ready for use.

HOT AND SOUR SOUP

This is one of the best known Chinese soups and it can be made from various ingredients; however, to retain its essential character it must be thickened, and well flavoured. As its title suggests, this soup must be both hot (a flavour derived in this recipe from the addition of chilli sauce) and sour (contributed by the addition of vinegar).

If you are unused to cooking with chilli sauce add it carefully and taste the soup to make sure you do not make it too hot for your taste.

Coconut Consommé

50 g/2 oz Chinese dried
  mushrooms
salt
½ teaspoon sugar plus a little
  for seasoning
1 tablespoon oil
2 large fresh coconuts
1.15 litres/2 pints boiling water
2 medium-thick slices fresh
  root ginger
½ teaspoon dry sherry
1 teaspoon sesame oil
GARNISH
a few carrot slices, decoratively
  cut
a few Chinese dried
  mushrooms, soaked and
  steamed

Wash and soak the
mushrooms in hot water to
cover for 30 minutes. Remove
and discard the stalks from
the drained mushrooms, then
marinate the mushroom caps
in 1 teaspoon salt, the ½
teaspoon sugar and the oil for
about 30 minutes.

Pierce two of the eyes in
the top of each coconut, then
drain all the liquid from the
inside – this is the coconut
water and must not be
confused with coconut milk.
Saw the tops off the coconuts.
Pour away any remaining
coconut water and pour the
boiling water into the nuts.
Replace the tops on the
coconuts and stand them in a
steamer, or two steamers.

Cook the nuts over boiling
water for 1 hour. Remember
to top up the boiling water in
the saucepan below the
steamer if necessary during
cooking. Add the marinated
mushrooms and ginger to the
soup in the coconuts and
continue to steam for a
further 20 minutes.

Carefully stir in the sherry,
sesame oil, salt and sugar to
taste, then serve it straight
from the coconuts. Add a
garnish of carrot shapes and
cooked dried mushrooms, if
you like, as shown in the
picture. *Serves 4–6*

Note: If you have no other use
for the coconut water but if
you do not want to throw it
away, then it can be used to
make a refreshing cold drink.

Bean Thread and Vegetable Soup

50 g/2 oz mung bean thread
50 g/2 oz preserved mustard
50 g/2 oz carrots
225 g/8 oz courgettes
10 deep fried bean curd balls
  (page 136)
4 Chinese dried mushrooms
2 tablespoons oil
2 medium-thick slices fresh
  root ginger
1 teaspoon dry sherry
1.15 litres/2 pints chicken
  stock
salt and pepper
pinch of sugar
½ teaspoon sesame oil

Soak the bean thread in hot
water to soften it, then cut the
threads into shorter pieces.
Set aside for later use.

Rinse and slice the
preserved mustard and slice
the carrots. If you like, cut
the carrot slices into
decorative shapes. Remove
strips of peel from the
courgettes to form a
decorative pattern on the skin,
then slice them into thick
pieces. Halve each bean curd
ball.

Rinse the mushrooms and
soak them in water to cover
for 30 minutes. Drain the
soaked mushrooms, place
them on a greased plate and
steam them over boiling water
for 10 minutes. Slice the
mushrooms and set them
aside.

Heat the oil in a large
saucepan, add the ginger and
fry the slices for a few minutes
until they give off their
aroma. Add the sherry, stock,
mushrooms and carrot and
continue to cook for a few
minutes. Bring to the boil,
then stir in the courgettes,
preserved mustard and bean
curd balls and simmer for 2
minutes. Finally, stir in the
bean thread, seasoning to
taste, sugar and sesame oil.
Cook for 1 minute before
serving hot. *Serves 4–6*

Sweet Corn and Bean Curd Chowder

12 canned straw mushrooms or
button mushrooms
6 Chinese dried mushrooms
salt and pepper
1 teaspoon sugar
generous 1 tablespoon oil
275 g/10 oz bean curd
1 tomato
50 g/2 oz shelled peas
50 g/2 oz carrots
1 teaspoon dry sherry
1.75 litres/3 pints chicken stock
1 (326-g/11½-oz) can sweet
corn, drained
1 tablespoon light soy sauce
3 tablespoons cornflour
2 tablespoons water
½ teaspoon sesame oil

Soak the straw mushrooms in cold water to cover for 30 minutes, then drain them and blanch them in boiling water for 1 minute. Drain and rinse the mushrooms in cold water, then dice them.

Soak the dried mushrooms in cold water to cover for 30 minutes. Drain and dice them, then transfer them to a small heatproof bowl and add a little salt, half the sugar and a few drops of the oil. Set aside to marinate for 10 minutes, then steam the mushrooms for 10 minutes.

Dice the bean curd and tomato, then blanch these with the peas in boiling water for 1 minute. Drain, rinse under cold water and set aside. Dice and blanch the carrots in the same way.

Heat the remaining oil in a saucepan, then add the sherry and stock. Bring to the boil, stir in the carrots, steamed mushrooms and straw mushrooms. Simmer for 8 minutes. Add the sweet corn, bean curd mixture, remaining sugar and light soy sauce. Simmer for 6 minutes.

Blend the cornflour to a smooth cream with the water. Stirring continuously, gradually pour the cornflour mixture into the soup and bring back to the boil. Simmer for 1 minute, then add salt to taste. Pour the soup into a serving bowl or tureen and top with pepper and sesame oil before serving. *Serves 6*

Vegetable and Salted Egg Soup

450 g/1 lb mustard cabbage or
Chinese cabbage
2 or 3 Salted Eggs (page 226)
3 tablespoons oil
2 medium-thick slices fresh
root ginger, grated
½ teaspoon dry sherry
1.75 litres/3 pints water
salt
½ teaspoon sugar

Wash and cut the mustard cabbage or Chinese cabbage into 5-cm/2-in chunks. Crack the salted eggs into a bowl.

Heat 2 tablespoons of the oil in a wok or frying pan. Sauté the ginger until fragrant, then stir in the cabbage and fry for a while. Remove and set aside.

Heat the remaining oil in a large saucepan, add the sherry and pour in the water, then bring to the boil. Add the cabbage to the pan. Simmer, uncovered, for 10 minutes, then carefully slide in the salted eggs and season to taste with salt. Simmer gently for a further 5 minutes, or until the eggs are cooked. Stir in the sugar, then pour the soup into one large bowl or individual bowls to serve. *Serves 4–6*

Congee with Salted Pork and Preserved Egg

100 g/4 oz round-grain rice
1 tablespoon oil
salt and pepper
20 ginkgo nuts
2 Salted Eggs (page 226)
6–12 dried oysters
2.25 litres/4 pints water
225 g/8 oz salted pork or
*   gammon*
a little chopped parsley
*   (optional)*
TO SERVE
Twisted Doughnuts (page 210)

Wash and drain the rice, then mix it with a little of the oil and a little salt. Shell and peel the ginkgo nuts. Boil the salted eggs for 6 minutes then remove their shells. Wash the dried oysters and soak them in boiling water until soft.

Bring the measured water to the boil in a large saucepan. Add the rice,

ginkgo nuts, eggs, dried oysters and pork or gammon. Lower the heat and simmer for 2 hours.

Remove the lid and season to taste, then serve hot, with a little pepper, oil and chopped parsley sprinkled over. Offer twisted doughnuts or a similar crisp accompaniment with the soup. *Serves 4–6*

Bean Curd Chop Suey Chowder

225 g/8 oz bean curd
1 chicken liver
25 g/1 oz canned straw
*   mushrooms*
1 small carrot
2 teaspoons dry sherry
1 teaspoon Ginger Juice (page
*   227)*
25 g/1 oz peeled cooked
*   shrimps*
2 tablespoons cornflour
salt and pepper
25 g/1 oz shelled peas
2 tablespoons oil
1.15 litres/2 pints plus 2
*   tablespoons water*
1 chicken stock cube
½ teaspoon sugar
a few drops of sesame oil
1 egg, beaten
2 spring onions, chopped, to
*   garnish*

Dice the bean curd, chicken liver, straw mushrooms and carrot. Marinate the chicken liver in half the sherry and the ginger juice for 30 minutes. Coat the shrimps with a little of the cornflour and pepper.

Blanch the shrimps, chicken liver, straw mushrooms, carrot and peas in boiling water for 1 minute, then drain and rinse the ingredients under cold water.

Heat the oil in a saucepan, then add the remaining sherry and 1.15 litres/2 pints water. Crumble in the stock cube and bring to the boil, then add seasoning to taste, the sugar and sesame oil. Stir in all the prepared ingredients and simmer the soup for a few minutes.

Blend the remaining cornflour to a smooth cream with the 2 tablespoons water, then pour it slowly into the soup, stirring continuously. Continue to simmer for 2 minutes.

Finally, stir in the egg and pour the soup into a serving bowl or tureen. Top with the spring onions and serve immediately. *Serves 4–6*

Fish Rolls in Egg Batter

8 canned or frozen asparagus
  spears
8 plaice fillets, skinned
1 teaspoon light soy sauce
¼ teaspoon sugar
salt and pepper
½ teaspoon cornflour
3 tablespoons oil
2 cloves garlic, sliced
flour for dusting
2 eggs, beaten
1 teaspoon dry sherry
½ teaspoon vinegar
a few drops of sesame oil
GARNISH
flat-leafed parsley sprigs
3 spring onions, shredded

Place one asparagus spear at
the head end of each fish fillet
and roll up into a cylinder
shape. Lay the fish rolls in a
shallow dish, then sprinkle
over the soy sauce, sugar, a
pinch of pepper and the
cornflour. Set aside to
marinate for 10 minutes.

Heat the oil in a large
frying pan, add the garlic and
sauté until fragrant. Coat the
fish rolls thoroughly in flour,
then dip them in the beaten
egg and arrange them in the
frying pan. Fry over a medium
heat until golden, then turn
and fry the other side.

Sprinkle the sherry and
seasoning over and cook for a
further 2 minutes. Sprinkle
the vinegar and sesame oil
over the fish and remove the
rolls from the pan. Cut each
roll in half, then arrange the
halves on a serving plate and
garnish the fish with parsley
and spring onions if you like.
Serve immediately. *Serves 4*

Fish Strips in Egg White Batter

275 g/10 oz white fish fillets
  (for example, plaice)
1 teaspoon soy sauce
¼ teaspoon sugar
½ teaspoon sesame oil
pinch of monosodium
  glutamate
1 teaspoon finely chopped
  fresh root ginger
1 teaspoon chopped spring
  onion
salt and pepper
oil for deep frying
4½ teaspoons plain flour
4½ teaspoons cornflour
8 egg whites
tomato ketchup (optional)
GARNISH
2 (5-cm/2-in) pieces cucumber
½ tomato
1 green glacé cherry
TO SERVE
Spicy Salt (page 229)

Cut the fish fillets into small
fingers about 5 cm/2 in long.
Mix the soy sauce, sugar,
sesame oil and monosodium
glutamate, then stir in the
ginger and spring onion and
add a generous pinch each of
salt and pepper. Coat the fish
strips in the seasonings.
Marinate for 10 minutes.

For the garnish, slice the
cucumber lengthways. Cut the
tomato into four wedges and
cut back the peel off each
wedge. Halve the cherry.

Heat the oil for deep frying
to 190 c/375 F. Meanwhile,
sift the flour and cornflour
together. In a large bowl,
whisk the egg whites until
they stand in stiff peaks, then
gradually fold in the flour
until a light batter is formed.

Coat the pieces of fish
generously in the batter, then
deep fry them, a few at a
time, until crisp and golden.
Drain the fish on absorbent
kitchen paper, then arrange
the pieces to one side, or on
opposite sides of a serving
plate. Arrange the ingredients
for garnish on the plate as
shown in the picture.

Serve the spicy salt in a
small bowl to accompany the
fish. Add a little tomato
ketchup to the top of the
garnish if you like and serve
at once. *Serves 4–6*

Deep Fried Fish Fritters

175 g/6 oz white fish fillet (for example, cod or haddock)
2 teaspoons light soy sauce
1 teaspoon Ginger Juice (page 227)
¼ teaspoon sugar
pepper
4 teaspoons cornflour plus cornflour for dusting
½ teaspoon finely chopped fresh root ginger
1 teaspoon chopped spring onion
100 g/4 oz plain flour
1 teaspoon baking powder
3 tablespoons oil plus oil for deep frying
¼ teaspoon salt
100–150 ml/4–5 fl oz water
GARNISH
1 red chilli
1 small tomato, sliced
parsley sprigs
TO SERVE
Spicy Salt (page 229)

Cut the fish fillet into bite-sized pieces. In a bowl, mix the soy sauce, ginger juice and sugar with a pinch of pepper, 1 teaspoon of the cornflour, the ginger and spring onion. Add the fish and toss the pieces in the seasonings to coat them thoroughly. Marinate for 10 minutes.

Prepare the garnish: slit the chilli several times to make strips attached at the stalk end like a tassel. Place this in ice-cold water until the strips curl.

Sift the flour, remaining cornflour and baking powder into a mixing bowl. Stir in the 3 tablespoons oil, salt, a pinch of pepper and enough of the water to mix the dry ingredients into a batter. Set aside to rest for 30 minutes.

Heat the oil for deep frying to 190 c/375 F. Drain off any excess marinade from the fish and coat each piece lightly in cornflour. Dip the fish in the batter, then deep fry the pieces in the hot oil until crisp and golden brown. Drain on absorbent kitchen paper.

To serve, arrange the fish on a serving plate and add the garnish ingredients as shown in the picture. Serve a small bowl of spicy salt to accompany the fish. *Serves 4*

Deep Fried Fish in Sweet Corn Sauce

225 g/8 oz white fish fillet, skinned (for example, cod, haddock or plaice)
1 teaspoon soy sauce
1 teaspoon Ginger Juice (page 227)
50 g/2 oz plus 2 teaspoons cornflour
¼ teaspoon sugar
salt and pepper
2 eggs, separated
2 tablespoons oil plus oil for deep frying
1 teaspoon dry sherry
100 ml/4 fl oz chicken stock
1 (326-g/11½-oz) can sweet corn, drained
1 tablespoon water
a few drops of sesame oil
flat-leafed parsley sprigs to garnish

Cut the fish into small slices. Mix the soy sauce, ginger juice, 1 teaspoon of the cornflour, sugar, a pinch of pepper and 1 egg white to make a batter. Coat the fish slices in this mixture and set aside to marinate for 20 minutes.

Beat the egg yolks in a bowl. Lift the fish out of the marinade, then coat them first in beaten yolk then in the 50 g/2 oz cornflour. Heat the oil for deep frying to 190c/375 F, then deep fry the fish slices until golden. Drain them on absorbent kitchen paper and arrange on a platter. Keep hot.

Heat the 2 tablespoons oil in a wok or a small saucepan. Add the sherry, then pour in the stock and season to taste. Add the sweet corn and bring to the boil.

Blend the remaining cornflour with the water, then add it to the sauce stirring continuously. Bring to the boil, add the sesame oil and remaining egg white, stir well before pouring the sauce over the fish. Serve immediately, garnished with parsley. *Serves 4*

Fish Kung Po

225 g/8 oz white fish fillet (for
  example, cod, haddock or
  plaice)
½ beaten egg
2 tablespoons cornflour
salt and pepper
4 dried red chillies
3 cloves garlic
1 spring onion
1 tablespoon oil plus oil for
  deep frying
2 medium-thick slices fresh
  root ginger
1 tablespoon sugar
2 teaspoons light soy sauce
1 tablespoon dry sherry
1½ teaspoons vinegar

Cut the fish into bite-sized
pieces. Gradually beat the egg
into the cornflour to make a
small amount of batter. Add
¼ teaspoon pepper and beat
well. Place the fish in the
batter and toss well to coat all
the pieces evenly.
  Halve the chillies, remove
their seeds and stalks, then
finely shred the rest. Slice the
garlic and shred the spring
onion. Heat the oil for deep
frying to 190 c/375 F, then
deep fry the pieces of fish
until golden brown. Drain on
absorbent kitchen paper and
keep hot.
  Heat the 1 tablespoon oil in
a wok or frying pan, then
sauté the chillies, garlic and
ginger for a few minutes. Stir
in the sugar and soy sauce,
then add a pinch of salt. Add
the fish and stir-fry for a
while, then pour in the sherry
and mix in the shredded
spring onion. Pour the vinegar
round the edge of the wok or
pan, then serve immediately.
Serves 4

Sautéed Fish with Green Vegetables

175 g/6 oz cod fillet, cut into
  chunks
1½ teaspoons cornflour
2 teaspoons light soy sauce
3¼ teaspoons sugar
salt and pepper
4 tablespoons oil plus oil for
  deep frying
175 g/6 oz broccoli
3 teaspoons dry sherry
2 teaspoons Ginger Juice (page
  227)
½ teaspoon monosodium
  glutamate
1 large carrot, sliced
2 teaspoons water
4 medium-thick slices fresh
  root ginger
2 cloves garlic, crushed
2 tablespoons chicken stock
a few drops of sesame oil
¼ teaspoon dark soy sauce
2 spring onions

Marinate the fish in 1
teaspoon each of cornflour,
light soy sauce and sugar, and
a pinch of pepper for 10
minutes. Heat the oil for deep
frying to 190 c/375 F. Fry the
fish for 1–2 minutes. Drain
thoroughly.
  In a medium-sized
saucepan, boil enough water
to blanch the broccoli. Add 2
teaspoons each of salt, sugar,
sherry and ginger juice, the
monosodium glutamate and 2
tablespoons of the oil, boil
and add the broccoli. Boil for
1 minute, drain and rinse.
Blanch the carrot for 1
minute. Drain and rinse.
Blend the remaining cornflour
with the water.
  Heat the remaining 2
tablespoons oil in a wok or
large frying pan, add the
ginger and garlic and cook
until they give off their strong
aroma. Stir in the carrot,
broccoli and fish, then
sprinkle in the remaining
sherry, add the stock,
remaining sugar, light soy
sauce and a few drops of
sesame oil. Toss all the
ingredients together, then stir
in the cornflour mixture and
dark soy sauce. Bring to the
boil and cook for 1 minute,
then stir in the spring onions.
Serve at once. Serves 4

Fishball and Bean Curd Casserole

1 (450-g/1-lb) mackerel, gutted and head removed
2 tablespoons cornflour
4 tablespoons water
1 large open mushroom
1 teaspoon mashed dried shrimps
salt and pepper
1 tablespoon chopped spring onion
2 teaspoons sugar
450 g/1 lb bean curd
2 tablespoons oil plus oil for deep frying
a few crisp lettuce leaves
2 medium-thick slices fresh root ginger
2 shallots
1 teaspoon dry sherry
150 ml/¼ pint chicken stock
1 teaspoon light soy sauce
1 tablespoon oyster sauce
1 teaspoon sesame oil

Bone the mackerel, then scrape all the flesh off the skin and place it in a mixing bowl. Blend the cornflour to a smooth cream with the water. Dice the mushroom and add it to the fish. Marinate the mashed shrimps with a little pepper for a few minutes, then add them to the fish with the spring onion. Add a pinch each of salt and pepper and ½ teaspoon of the sugar.

Pound the mixture thoroughly until it becomes firm and elastic enough to bind together. As you pound the fish, gradually add 3–4 tablespoons of the cornflour mixture. Take heaped teaspoonfuls of the mixture and squeeze them out to form small fishballs. If you dampen your hands first, then you will find that it is easier to make smooth fishballs. Set these aside on a greased platter.

Cut the bean curd into small cubes. Heat the oil for deep frying to 190 c/375 f, then add the cubes and deep fry them until golden brown. Drain the bean curd on absorbent kitchen paper. Blanch the lettuce in boiling salted water. Mince or very finely chop the ginger and shallots together.

Heat the 2 tablespoons oil in a wok or deep frying pan, then add the ginger and shallot and cook until fragrant. Stir in the fishballs and roll them evenly in the oil. Add the bean curd and sherry. Pour in the stock and simmer for 8 minutes.

Stir the lettuce into the stock and add seasoning to taste, then the soy sauce, oyster sauce and remaining sugar. Bring to the boil, then pour in the remaining cornflour mixture, stirring continuously to prevent the sauce from becoming lumpy.

Lastly, stir in the sesame oil and serve hot. *Serves 4*

To bone fish: Mackerel and similar fish are very easy to bone because they have large, quite prominent bones.

When the fish is gutted and the head has been removed, lay the body flat with the flesh down on a clean board or surface. Run your hand firmly down the skin side of the backbone, pressing down evenly along the length of the bone. Press lightly all over the skin, then turn the fish over.

The bones should lift off in one piece, but make sure that there are no stray bones left on the flesh before it is used.

Fishballs with Chrysanthemum

*275 g/10 oz white fish fillet (for
    example, cod, haddock or
    coley)*
4 teaspoons cornflour
salt and pepper
1 white chrysanthemum flower
*1 tablespoon oil plus oil for
    deep frying*
2 teaspoons water
*2 medium-thick slices fresh
    root ginger*
1 shallot, chopped
1 clove garlic, sliced
*1 carrot, sliced lengthways and
    cut into 2.5-cm/1-in pieces*
*4 sticks celery, cut into 2.5-cm/
    1-in strips*
1 teaspoon dry sherry
50 ml/2 fl oz chicken stock
1 teaspoon soy sauce
1 teaspoon sugar
3 spring onions, shredded

Cut the fish into chunks. Then
coat them in 3 teaspoons of
the cornflour and add pepper
to taste. Wash the
chrysanthemum, remove the
petals and set aside. Discard
the rest.

Heat the oil for deep frying
to 190 c/375 F. Add the fish
and cook lightly, then drain
the pieces on absorbent
kitchen paper. Blend the
remaining cornflour to a
smooth cream with the water.

Heat the 1 tablespoon oil in
a wok or frying pan. Add the
ginger, shallot and garlic and
stir-fry until the ingredients
give off their aroma. Discard
the fried ingredients and add
the carrot, celery and fish to
the oil remaining in the pan.
Toss well, then pour in the
sherry, stock, soy sauce, sugar
and seasoning to taste.

Heat through to boiling
point then pour in the
cornflour mixture and cook
for 1 minute, stirring
continuously. Stir in the spring
onions and serve immediately,
sprinkled with the flower
petals. *Serves 4*

Fishballs with Lettuce

2 Chinese dried mushrooms
450 g/1 lb white fish fillet,
　skinned
2 spring onions, chopped
15 g/½ oz pork fat
salt and pepper
½ teaspoon sugar
1 teaspoon light soy sauce
2 tablespoons cornflour
2 tablespoons oil
1 teaspoon dry sherry
100 ml/4 fl oz fish stock or
　chicken stock
450 g/1 lb lettuce
a few drops of sesame oil
green part of 1 spring onion,
　shredded, to garnish

Soak the mushrooms in cold
water for 15 minutes, then
drain and dice them. Mince
the fish, place it in a bowl,
then stir in the mushrooms
and spring onions.
　Place the piece of pork fat
in a small saucepan, pour in
water to cover and bring to
the boil. Cook for a minute,
then drain and dice the fat
before adding it to the fish.

Stir in salt and pepper to
taste, the sugar and soy sauce.
Shape generous teaspoonfuls
of the fish mixture into balls
about the size of walnuts. Roll
these fishballs in the
cornflour.
　Heat the oil in a large
frying pan, add the fishballs
and cook them, frequently
rolling them over, until lightly
browned all over. Remove
from the pan with a slotted
spoon. Pour in the sherry and
stock and bring just to the
boil before replacing the
fishballs, then simmer for a
few minutes.
　Meanwhile, separate the
lettuce leaves, wash and drain
them. Add them to the
fishballs and continue to
simmer for a further 5
minutes. Stir in the sesame oil
and transfer to a serving dish,
arranging the lettuce under
the fish if possible. Sprinkle
the shredded spring onion
over and serve hot. *Serves 4*

Egg White with Fish Slice

100 g/4 oz white fish fillet,
　skinned and shredded
salt and pepper
12 egg whites
2 teaspoons cornflour
1 tablespoon oil plus oil for
　deep frying
½ teaspoon finely chopped fresh
　root ginger
2 spring onions, finely
　chopped
1 teaspoon dry sherry
100 ml/4 fl oz fish stock
1 teaspoon milk
1 tablespoon water
1 egg yolk
1 teaspoon each of chopped
　parsley, light soy sauce and
　wine vinegar
½ teaspoon sesame oil
GARNISH
4 tomatoes, sliced
flat-leafed parsley sprigs
a few red and green glacé
　cherries, sliced

Mix the fish with salt and
pepper, 1 tablespoon egg
white and 1 teaspoon
cornflour. Marinate for 10

minutes. Heat the 1
tablespoon oil in a small
saucepan and add the ginger
with half the spring onions.
Pour in the sherry, stock and
milk. Add seasoning to taste,
then bring to the boil. Blend
the remaining cornflour with
the water and stir this into the
sauce. Simmer for 1 minute,
then keep hot.
　Lightly whisk the egg
whites, add seasoning to taste
and the fish mixture, then stir
to combine thoroughly. Heat
the oil for deep frying to 190 c/
375 f and pour in the egg
white and fish. It should cook
almost immediately and
separate into pieces. Remove
the pieces of cooked egg and
fish with a draining spoon as
they float.
　To serve, mix the fried egg
and fish into the sauce on a
serving dish. Make a small
hollow in the middle for the
egg yolk. Mix the chopped
parsley, remaining spring
onion, soy sauce, vinegar and
sesame oil to serve with the
dish. Garnish and serve.
Serves 4

Deep Fried Spicy Mackerel

1(450-g/1-lb) mackerel, gutted
and head removed
7 teaspoons sugar
1 tablespoon Ginger Juice
(page 227)
½ teaspoon plus a few drops
sesame oil
1 tablespoon light soy sauce
salt and pepper
2 star anise
small piece of cinnamon stick
2 tablespoons oil plus oil for
deep frying
2 cloves garlic, crushed
2 medium-thick slices fresh
root ginger
2 spring onions
1 tablespoon dry sherry
150 ml/¼ pint chicken stock
1 tablespoon dark soy sauce
1 teaspoon vinegar
GARNISH
carrot flowers
watercress sprigs

Cut the fish across into steaks about 2.5 cm/1 in thick. Mix 1 teaspoon of the sugar, the ginger juice, the ½ teaspoon sesame oil, light soy sauce and seasoning. Coarsely crush the star anise and cinnamon, then add them to the mixture before pouring it over the fish. Turn the steaks to coat them thoroughly and set aside to marinate for 30 minutes.

Heat the oil for deep frying to 190 c/375 f, then remove the fish from its marinade (reserve the liquid) and deep fry the steaks until they are golden. Drain on absorbent kitchen paper and set aside.

Heat the 2 tablespoons oil in a wok or a frying pan which has a lid, add the garlic, ginger and spring onions and stir-fry until fragrant. Pour in the sherry, fish marinade and stock and bring to the boil. Stir in the dark soy sauce and remaining sugar, then slide the fish into the pan. Cover and simmer gently for 5–6 minutes by which time most of the sauce should have evaporated. Sprinkle in the vinegar and a few drops of sesame oil, mix well and remove from the heat. Allow to cool.

To serve, arrange the cold fish steaks on a platter and add a garnish of carrot flowers and watercress. *Serves 4*

Shallow Fried Fish in Soy Sauce

2 (350-g/12-oz) mackerel,
gutted
2 tablespoons Ginger Juice
(page 227)
2 tablespoons oil
3 medium-thick slices fresh
root ginger
3 tablespoons fish or chicken
stock
2 tablespoons light soy sauce
1 tablespoon sugar
pepper
1 teaspoon dry sherry
1 teaspoon lemon juice
1 teaspoon sesame oil
GARNISH
1 tablespoon finely shredded
fresh root ginger
1 tablespoon shredded spring
onion
flat-leafed parsley sprigs
1 red chilli, deseeded and
finely shredded

Rinse and dry the fish. Sprinkle the ginger juice over and leave to marinate for 20 minutes.

Heat the oil in a wok or frying pan. Add the sliced ginger and sauté it, rubbing it round the pan to give off its flavour and aroma. Add the fish to the wok and fry it over a low heat, turning once, until golden on both sides.

Mix the stock, soy sauce, sugar and pepper to taste. Pour the sherry in a thin trickle around the edge of the pan, then stir in the soy sauce mixture. Cook for 2 minutes, turn the fish over and cook for a further 3 minutes; by this time most of the juices should have dried up. Sprinkle in the lemon juice and sesame oil.

To serve, transfer the fish to a heated serving dish and sprinkle the shredded ginger, spring onion, parsley and chilli on top. Serve at once. *Serves 4*

Fish with Ginger and Spring Onion

1 (1-kg/2-lb) red or grey
    mullet, or any other whole
    fish, gutted
salt and pepper
1 teaspoon minced or finely
    chopped fresh root ginger
2 spring onions
2 tablespoons plain flour
50 ml/2 fl oz oil
2 eggs, beaten
2 cloves garlic, sliced
pinch of sugar
2 tablespoons shredded fresh
    root ginger
a few drops of sesame oil
2 teaspoons dry sherry
50 ml/2 fl oz chicken stock
GARNISH
2 tomatoes
flat-leafed parsley sprigs

Rinse and dry the fish; make
three cuts on each side of the
body. Mix ½ teaspoon salt with
the minced ginger. Chop one
spring onion and add it to the
ginger. Press this mixture into
the cuts in the fish and leave
to marinate for 20 minutes.

Sift the flour over both sides
of the fish. Heat the oil in a
large frying pan. Dip the fish
in the beaten egg, then place
it in the pan and fry until crisp
and brown on the underneath.
Repeat on the other side, then
lower the heat and add the
sliced garlic. Fry for a further
2 minutes, turn the fish and
fry the other side for another
2 minutes.

Shred the remaining spring
onion and add it to the fish
with the sugar, seasoning to
taste, the shredded ginger,
sesame oil, sherry and stock.
Continue to cook for a further
2 minutes.

Cut the tomatoes into
wedges. Cut the peel away
from the fruit on most of the
wedges and cut the other
wedges into thin slices.
Transfer the fish to a serving
dish. Arrange the tomatoes
round the sides of the dish
and sprinkle the parsley over
the top of the fish. Serve at
once. *Serves 4–6*

Sweet and Sour Steamed Fish

2 Chinese dried mushrooms
1 (1-kg/2-lb) carp, gutted and
    descaled
salt and pepper
1 large carrot
50 g/2 oz canned bamboo
    shoot
3 tablespoons oil
1 teaspoon finely chopped
    fresh root ginger
1 teaspoon finely chopped
    spring onion
1 tablespoon dry sherry
250 ml/8 fl oz fish or chicken
    stock
1 red or green pepper,
    deseeded and shredded
1½ tablespoons sugar
1 tablespoon light soy sauce
1½ teaspoons dark soy sauce
2 tablespoons red wine vinegar
¼ teaspoon monosodium
    glutamate
1 teaspoon cornflour
1 tablespoon water
parsley sprigs to garnish

Soak the mushrooms in water
for 30 minutes. Rinse and dry
the fish. Cut slits into the skin

at intervals with a sharp knife.
Sprinkle with salt and pepper,
then place in a steamer or on
a large plate and steam over
boiling water for 12 minutes.
Drain and steam the
mushrooms with the fish for
10 minutes of the cooking
time. Keep the fish hot. Cook
the carrot and bamboo shoot
in boiling water for 5 minutes.
Drain, rinse and shred finely.
Shred the mushrooms.

Heat 2 tablespoons of the
oil in a small saucepan. Add
the ginger and spring onion,
sprinkle in the sherry, then
pour in the stock. Stir in the
shredded pepper and other
vegetables, sugar, light and
dark soy sauce, vinegar,
monosodium glutamate and
seasoning to taste. Bring to
the boil. Blend the cornflour
to a smooth cream with the
water, then pour it into the
pan and bring to the boil
stirring continuously. Simmer
for 2 minutes, stir in the
remaining oil and pour this
sauce over the fish. Garnish
with parsley sprigs and serve
immediately.
Serves 4

Sweet and Sour Fried Fish

1 (1-kg/2-lb) red or grey
  mullet, or any other whole
  fish, gutted
salt and pepper
1 Chinese dried mushroom
1 onion, chopped
1 dessert apple, peeled, cored
  and diced
1 large carrot, diced
1 green pepper, deseeded and
  diced
1 green chilli, deseeded and
  diced
50 g/2 oz plain flour
4 teaspoons cornflour
½ teaspoon baking powder
25 g/1 oz lard, melted
1 egg, beaten
2 tablespoons oil plus oil for
  deep frying
2 cloves garlic, sliced
1 teaspoon sugar
1 tablespoon dry sherry

1 teaspoon soy sauce
1 teaspoon sesame oil
1 quantity Sweet and Sour
  Sauce (page 227)
1 tablespoon water

Rinse and dry the fish. Cut off
the head, then remove the
main bone snipping it at the
tail end to leave the tail in
place. Traditionally the fish
head should be cut through,
flattened and cooked
separately to serve with the
fish. Score the fish flesh in a
criss-cross pattern, then
season it on both sides.

Soak the mushroom in
water for 30 minutes, then
steam it on a plate over
boiling water for 10 minutes.
Remove the stalk and dice the
cooked mushroom. Mix it
with the onion, apple, carrot,
green pepper and chilli.

Sift the flour, 3 teaspoons of
the cornflour and the baking
powder into a bowl. Make a

well in the middle and pour in
the lard. Add the egg, then
gradually beat in the dry
ingredients to make a smooth
batter.

Heat the oil for deep frying
to 190 c/375 F. Dip the fish in
the batter, then deep fry it
until golden brown. Drain on
absorbent kitchen paper, then
transfer to a serving dish and
keep hot.

Heat the 2 tablespoons oil
in a saucepan. Add the garlic
and cook until fragrant. Stir in
the diced ingredients and stir-
fry for a few minutes. Add
seasoning to taste, the sugar,
sherry and soy sauce. Sprinkle
in the sesame oil and pour in
the sweet and sour sauce, then
heat through to boiling point.

Meanwhile, blend the
remaining cornflour to a
smooth cream with the water.
Pour this slowly into the
sauce, stirring continuously,
and simmer for 2 minutes.

Pour this sauce over the fish
and serve immediately.
Serves 4

Note: If you prefer, you can
use white fish fillets to make
this dish. For example,
haddock, cod, plaice or
whiting fillets can all be used
to make a delicious sweet and
sour dish.

Braised Fish with Ginger and Spring Onion

450 g/1 lb cod steak in one
   piece
pepper
25 g/1 oz fresh root ginger
2 large cloves garlic
25 g/1 oz shallots
4 tablespoons oil
1 teaspoon dry sherry
150 ml/¼ pint water
2 tablespoons light soy sauce
1¼ teaspoons dark soy sauce
pinch of monosodium
   glutamate
2 tablespoons sugar
1 teaspoon sesame oil
2 spring onions, shredded
1 red chilli, deseeded and
   shredded
1 tablespoon finely shredded
   fresh root ginger to garnish
GARNISH
lemon slices
flat-leafed parsley sprigs

Make cuts into the skin of the
fish at 1-cm/½-in intervals.
Season with pepper. Mince
and mix half the ginger, 1
clove of garlic and 1 shallot.

Press this mixture into the
cuts in the fish. Slice the
remaining ginger, garlic and
shallot and set aside for later
use.

Heat the oil in a wok or
large frying pan. Add the
ginger slices and rub them
round the pan. Add the fish
and fry it over a fairly low
heat until both sides are
golden. Add the sliced garlic
and shallot and continue to fry
for 4 minutes. Pour in the
sherry, water, light and dark
soy sauce, sugar, monosodium
glutamate, sugar, pepper to
taste and the sesame oil.
Sprinkle in half each of the
spring onions and chilli.
Continue to cook for 3
minutes.

Transfer the fish to a heated
serving platter, sprinkle the
remaining spring onion, chilli
and shredded ginger over,
then garnish with lemon slices
and parsley. Serve
immediately. *Serves 4*

Steamed Fish in Soy Sauce

1 (675–900-g/1½–2-lb) whole
   fish (for example, carp or
   mullet), gutted, or tail steak
   of cod
5 spring onions
7 tablespoons oil
3 medium-thick slices fresh
   root ginger
1 teaspoon dry sherry
2 tablespoons light soy sauce
1 tablespoon dark soy sauce
3 tablespoons sugar
1 tablespoon sesame oil
pepper
GARNISH
2 tablespoons finely shredded
   fresh root ginger
flat-leafed parsley

Rinse and dry the fish. Place 2
of the whole spring onions on
a plate with 2 tablespoons of
the oil. Lay the fish on the
plate and add the sliced
ginger. Cook the fish in a
steamer for 12–15 minutes,
then transfer it to a serving
plate, discarding the spring
onions, ginger and the
cooking juices, and keep hot.

Heat the remaining oil in a
wok or large frying pan. Add
the sherry and remove the pan
from the heat before stirring
in the light and dark soy
sauce, sugar, sesame oil and
pepper to taste. Shred the
remaining spring onions.

To serve, pour the sauce
over the fish and garnish with
the shredded spring onions,
shredded ginger and parsley
sprigs. Serve hot. *Serves 4*

Note: If the thought of
steamed fish suggests bland,
tasteless invalid food, then try
some of these deliciously full-
flavoured Chinese steamed
fish ideas. By steaming, the
delicate flavour of the fish is
brought out to the full and
enhanced by the spicy
ingredients.

Steamed Fish in Black Bean Sauce

1 whole plaice, gutted
pepper
1 teaspoon Ginger Juice (page 227)
4½ teaspoons Black Bean Paste (page 229)
1 tablespoon minced or finely chopped fresh root ginger
2 cloves garlic, crushed
1 teaspoon sugar
2 teaspoons light soy sauce
½ teaspoon sesame oil
3 tablespoons oil
4 spring onions
GARNISH
2 spring onions, shredded
1 tablespoon shredded fresh root ginger
1 red chilli, deseeded and shredded

Rinse and dry the fish. Season with pepper and the ginger juice and set aside for 20 minutes.

Mix the black bean paste, minced or chopped ginger, garlic, sugar, soy sauce and oils, then pour the mixture over the fish to coat it evenly.

Place the 4 whole spring onions on a platter and lay the plaice on top. Cook the fish in a steamer, or over a saucepan of boiling water, for 5 minutes.

Serve immediately, garnished with the shredded spring onion, ginger and chilli. *Serves 4*

To steam fish: If you do not have a steamer large enough to hold a sizeable platter, then lay the fish on a large plate – choose one which is as deep as possible. Cover with a second plate, or with a sheet of cooking foil crumpled firmly around the rim of the plate.

Stand the plate over a saucepan of simmering water and regulate the heat so that it cooks gently for the required length of time. If the water boils too rapidly it will boil over, if it does not simmer steadily, then the fish will not cook.

Poached Fish in Hot Oil

1 (450–675-g/1–1½-lb) garoupa or carp, or other whole fish, gutted
2 tablespoons oil plus oil for deep frying
25 g/1 oz fresh root ginger, shredded
1 teaspoon dry sherry
3 tablespoons dark soy sauce
1 tablespoon light soy sauce
2–3 tablespoons sugar
pepper
GARNISH
3 spring onions, shredded
flat-leafed parsley

Rinse and dry the fish. Heat the oil for deep frying to 190 c/375 F, lower the heat and fry the fish gently for 10–12 minutes. Drain on absorbent kitchen paper, then transfer the fish to a warmed serving plate. Keep hot.

Heat the 2 tablespoons oil in a wok or frying pan. Add half the ginger and cook until fragrant. Pour in the sherry, dark and light soy sauce, sugar and pepper to taste.

Bring to the boil, then pour this sauce over the fish. Serve at once, garnished with the remaining shredded ginger, spring onions and parsley. *Serves 4*

Flat-leafed parsley: Sometimes sold as French parsley, this must not be confused with coriander, a spicy herb which looks very similar. The easiest, although not always the safest, way of distinguishing between the two is to look at the stalk ends; coriander is usually sold with the roots intact, whereas flat-leafed parsley does not have roots on when it is cut into bunches.

This variety of parsley has more flavour than the common curled variety and it looks more delicate for certain garnishes. However, if you cannot find any, then use the common curled-leaf parsley.

Cod with Bean Curd

450–675 g/1–1½ lb tail cod steak
salt and pepper
1 tablespoon plus 1 teaspoon
  (optional) cornflour
3 Chinese dried mushrooms
150 ml/¼ pint oil
3 medium-thick slices fresh
  root ginger
225 g/8 oz bean curd, cut into
  small cubes
2 shallots, sliced
2 teaspoons dry sherry
450 ml/¾ pint fish or chicken
  stock
1 teaspoon light soy sauce
1 teaspoon dark soy sauce
1 teaspoon oyster sauce
2 teaspoons sugar
1 tablespoon water (optional)
GARNISH
1 small red chilli, deseeded
  and finely shredded
1 tablespoon shredded fresh
  root ginger
1 tablespoon shredded spring
  onion
flat-leafed parsley sprigs

Rinse and dry the fish. Season it on both sides with pepper and dust with the 1 tablespoon cornflour. Soak the mushrooms in water for 30 minutes, then steam them over boiling water for 10 minutes. Remove the stalks, shred the caps and set aside.

Heat the oil in a fairly deep frying pan. Add the sliced ginger and cook for a few minutes. Add the cod and fry until golden, turn and cook the second side. Remove the fish from the pan and drain it on absorbent kitchen paper.

Fry the bean curd in the oil remaining in the pan until golden. Remove and drain on absorbent kitchen paper. Remove the pan from the heat and allow to cool slightly.

Pour away all but 2 tablespoons of the oil from the pan. Return the pan to the cooker to heat the reserved oil.

Add the shallots and cook for a few minutes without browning the pieces. Pour in the sherry and stock. Lay the fish in the liquid and add the mushrooms and bean curd. Simmer, uncovered, until the stock is reduced by half – about 30 minutes.

Stir in the light and dark soy sauce, oyster sauce, sugar and seasoning to taste, then continue to cook, uncovered, until the liquid is further reduced by about half. If you like, the remaining sauce can be thickened with the 1 teaspoon cornflour blended with the water.

To serve, transfer the fish to a heated serving dish and scatter the garnish on top, or to one side. *Serves 4*

To make fish stock: Fish stock can be made from all the trimmings from any fish. The bones, skin and head of a fish can be cooked in simmering water in a covered saucepan for at least 45–60 minutes.

If you are preparing a dish which does not offer any fish trimmings, then use about 450 g/1 lb of a cheaper fish (for example coley or any unusual fish can be used). There is no need to spend a great deal of time on the preparation of the fish, simply chop it into chunks and put it in a pan with water to cover and plenty of seasoning. Strain the cooled stock, then use it as required.

Red Mullet in Tomato Sauce

1 (450-g/1-lb) red mullet, gutted
pepper
2 tablespoons Ginger Juice (page 227)
4 medium-thick slices fresh root ginger
3 tablespoons oil
1 clove garlic, crushed
1 small onion, quartered
350 g/12 oz tomatoes, peeled and quartered
1 teaspoon dry sherry
50 ml/2 fl oz fish or chicken stock
3 tablespoons tomato ketchup
1 teaspoon light soy sauce
1 teaspoon sugar
1 teaspoon sesame oil
GARNISH
parsley sprig
2 spring onions, shredded

Rinse and dry the red mullet. Season the fish with pepper, then sprinkle with the ginger juice and marinate for 20 minutes. Finely shred 2 slices of the ginger.

Heat the oil in a wok or frying pan, add the ginger slices and rub them round the pan. Slide in the fish and shallow fry over medium heat, turning once, until both sides are golden. Remove and drain on absorbent kitchen paper. Discard the ginger slices. Add the shredded ginger and garlic to the oil remaining in the pan. Add the onion and stir-fry for a while. Stir in the tomatoes and return the fish to the pan.

Sprinkle in the sherry and pour in the stock, tomato ketchup, soy sauce, sugar and pepper. Sprinkle in the sesame oil and cook for 5 minutes. Transfer to a warmed serving dish and add a garnish of parsley and spring onions. Serve at once. *Serves 4*

To peel tomatoes: Place the tomatoes in a bowl and pour in enough boiling water to cover them completely. Leave for 30–60 seconds, then drain and rinse them under cold water. Slit the peel and carefully remove it from the tomatoes.

Steamed Snapper

1 (350–450-g/12–16-oz) red snapper, gutted
4 spring onions
15 g/½ oz fresh root ginger
3 tablespoons oil
1 tablespoon dark soy sauce
1 tablespoon light soy sauce
1 tablespoon sugar
pepper
1 teaspoon sesame oil
1 red chilli, deseeded and shredded, to garnish

Rinse and dry the snapper. Cut 2 spring onions in half and finely shred the remainder. Reserve the shredded onion for garnish. Finely slice half the ginger and shred the remainder for the garnish.

Arrange the halved spring onions and ginger slices on a plate and lay the fish on top. Place the fish in a steamer and cook over a high heat for 5 minutes. Transfer the fish to a warmed serving dish and keep hot. Discard the cooked spring onions and liquid.

Heat the oil in a wok or frying pan and stir in the dark and light soy sauce, sugar, pepper and sesame oil. Heat through, then pour this sauce over the fish and serve immediately, garnished with the shredded ginger, spring onion and chilli. *Serves 4*

Red snapper: Fished in southern Atlantic waters, red snapper is available spasmodically from good fishmongers. It can be frozen for a few months, so it is worth buying this fish and storing it in your freezer for later use.

However if you have problems finding a snapper, then try using red or grey mullet (if you can buy a small one) instead.

Trout with Ginger

6 small trout, gutted
2 tablespoons Ginger Juice
  (page 227)
2 shallots
1 clove garlic
3 tablespoons oil
3 medium-thick slices fresh
  root ginger
1 teaspoon dry sherry
2 tablespoons water
1 tablespoon light soy sauce
1½ teaspoons sugar
1 teaspoon sesame oil
pepper
flat-leafed parsley sprigs to
  garnish

Season the trout on both sides with pepper. Pour the ginger juice over the fish and set aside to marinate for 20 minutes. Meanwhile, mince the shallots with the garlic.

Swirl the oil all around the inside of a wok or large frying pan, then heat it and rub 2 slices of the ginger around the pan. Add the minced shallot mixture and fry until fragrant. Arrange the fish in the pan, then continue to fry until golden and crisp underneath. Turn the trout over and cook until crisp on the second side. Shred the remaining ginger.

Sprinkle the sherry, water, soy sauce, sugar, sesame oil and pepper to taste into the pan. Heat through, then transfer the trout to a warmed serving platter. Garnish with the shredded ginger and parsley and serve at once. *Serves 6*

Bean Curd with Fish Paste

225 g/8 oz bean curd
100 g/4 oz peeled cooked
  shrimps
100 g/4 oz white fish fillet,
  skinned
1 teaspoon salt
1 teaspoon sugar
¼ teaspoon monosodium
  glutamate
¼ teaspoon pepper
½ teaspoon sesame oil plus a
  little for sprinkling
1 egg white
2 tablespoons chopped spring
  onion
1 tablespoon chopped fresh
  root ginger
2 teaspoons cornflour
a little light soy sauce
parsley sprigs to garnish

Rinse and mash the bean curd. Reserve a few shrimps for garnish, then mash the remainder to make a paste. Mince the fish, then mix it with the shrimp paste. Add the salt, sugar, monosodium glutamate, pepper and sesame oil, then mix in the egg white.

Pound the mixture until firm, then add the chopped spring onion and ginger, mixing thoroughly. Stir this fish and shrimp paste into the mashed bean curd, adding the cornflour. Continue to stir until well mixed.

Transfer the mixture to a greased dish. Lightly smooth the surface and garnish with the reserved shrimps. Place in a steamer and cook over boiling water for 12 minutes.

Serve at once, sprinkled with a little sesame oil and light soy sauce. Add a sprig of parsley to garnish. *Serves 4*

Fish and Seafood

Seafood Casserole

175 g/6 oz fresh squid
1 teaspoon cornflour plus cornflour for coating
6 scallops, cleaned
salt and pepper
175 g/6 oz peeled uncooked prawns
100 g/4 oz white fish fillet
½ egg white
1½ teaspoons light soy sauce
1½ teaspoons sugar
1½ teaspoons sesame oil
50 g/2 oz mung bean sheet
1 crisp lettuce
2 shallots
2 tablespoons oil plus oil for deep frying
2 medium-thick slices fresh root ginger
1 tablespoon dry sherry
250 ml/8 fl oz fish stock
1 tablespoon water
spring onion curls to garnish (see below)

Clean the squid according to the instructions given in the recipe for Hot and Sour Soup on page 16. Score a criss-cross pattern on the inside of the squid, then dust each piece with cornflour.

Thoroughly wash and dry the scallops, then toss them in cornflour and pepper to coat each one evenly.

Devein the prawns and dust them all over with a little cornflour and pepper. Rinse and finely slice the fish, then place it in a bowl with the egg white, ½ teaspoon of the light soy sauce, ½ teaspoon of the sugar, pepper to taste and ½ teaspoon of the sesame oil. Set aside to marinate for 10 minutes.

Soak the mung bean sheet in cold water for 30 minutes, then drain and blanch it in boiling water for 1 minute. Drain and cut the sheet into strips. Wash and trim the lettuce. Chop the shallots.

Heat the oil for deep frying to 190 c/375 f. Lightly cook the squid, scallops and prawns separately without allowing them to brown. Drain each batch on absorbent kitchen paper. Lightly fry the marinated fish without allowing it to brown, then drain it in the same way.

Heat the 2 tablespoons oil in a flameproof casserole. Add the ginger and shallots and fry until fragrant. Stir in the half-cooked seafood and fry for a while. Pour in the sherry and stock and simmer for 3 minutes, then add the mung bean sheet and lettuce. Blend the 1 teaspoon cornflour with the water and stir into the sauce. Add salt and pepper, the remaining soy sauce and sugar. Simmer for a few minutes until thickened, then sprinkle in the remaining sesame oil and serve, garnished with the spring onion curls. *Serves 4–6*

To make spring onion curls: Use large spring onions; cut short lengths off the green and white parts, then shred both ends into thin strips. Place in a bowl of ice cold water and leave for at least 30 minutes to curl.

Chinese Savoury Pancake

275 g/10 oz plain flour
½ teaspoon bicarbonate of soda
2 teaspoons shrimp paste
600 ml/1 pint water
½ teaspoon salt
1 teaspoon sugar
3 tablespoons melted lard
½ teaspoon sesame oil
150 g/5 oz Cha Shiu (page 225)
1 small leek
1 carrot, cooked
150 g/5 oz peeled cooked
   shrimps
pepper
oil for cooking

Sift the flour and bicarbonate of soda into a mixing bowl. Put the shrimp paste in the water, mix well and add the salt, sugar and lard. Stir until well blended, then pour this liquid into the dry ingredients. Add the sesame oil and beat to make a smooth batter.

Finely chop the Cha Shiu and leek; dice the carrot; rinse and chop the shrimps. Add all these prepared ingredients to the batter, stir in pepper to taste and mix well.

Heat a large frying pan or griddle and brush it with a little oil. Pour a ladleful of the batter on to the pan and cook until golden on the underside. Turn and cook the second side until golden. Transfer to a warmed serving dish and keep hot until the remainder of the batter is cooked in the same way. Serve hot. *Serves 6*

Stuffed Twisted Doughnuts

50 g/2 oz fat pork (optional)
275 g/10 oz peeled cooked
   prawns (defrosted if frozen)
1 tablespoon chopped spring
   onion
1 teaspoon cornflour
salt and pepper
pinch of sugar
1 teaspoon sesame oil
2 pieces Twisted Doughnuts
   (page 210)
oil for deep frying
Spicy Salt (page 229) to serve

Blanch the pork (if used) in boiling water for 1 minute, then drain, rinse and finely dice it. Mash the prawns and mix in the pork, spring onion, cornflour, salt and pepper, sugar and sesame oil. Pound the mixture until it is thoroughly blended and firm.

Cut the twisted doughnuts into 5-cm/2-in lengths, then cut each piece in half. Fill the pieces of doughnut with the prawn mixture, pressing it in well.

Heat the oil for deep frying to 190 c/375 f, then cook the stuffed doughnuts until golden brown. Drain them on absorbent kitchen paper and serve hot with spicy salt. *Serves 6*

Oriental garnishes: Elaborate carved garnishes are difficult to make. The one in this picture, a chrysanthemum, is carved from the thick end of a large carrot. A slightly less elaborate carrot flower is illustrated on page 75 with carving instructions.

If you do want to have a go at making some of these superb decorations, use a small, fairly sharp, pointed knife and allow plenty of time to sit down with the task. Work slowly and very carefully, cutting out each petal to resemble the shape in the picture. Work from the base upwards, in a spiral direction. You can also try making shapes from a potato before you attempt to carve a carrot.

Plain Boiled Crayfish

1 kg/2 lb crayfish
2 teaspoons salt
2 chicken stock cubes
100 ml/4 fl oz dry sherry
50 g/2 oz fresh root ginger,
  sliced
50 g/2 oz shallots, chopped
DIPPING SAUCE
1 tablespoon oil
2 medium-thick slices fresh
  root ginger
2 shallots, chopped
1 teaspoon sherry
100 ml/4 fl oz dark soy sauce
1 tablespoon sugar
1 teaspoon chopped red chilli
¼ teaspoon pepper
1 tablespoon sesame oil
1 tablespoon chopped parsley

Wash the crayfish under
running water, then drain
them thoroughly. Bring a
large saucepan of water to the
boil, stir in the salt and
crumbled stock cubes. Add
the sherry, ginger and
shallots, then bring back to a
full boil. Drop in the crayfish,
cover the pan and boil for 5
minutes. Drain thoroughly,
then transfer to a warmed
serving dish and keep hot.
  To make the dipping sauce,
heat the oil in a small
saucepan. Add the ginger and
shallots, then cook until
fragrant. Remove these
ingredients from the pan and
discard them before adding
the sherry, soy sauce and
sugar. Heat through, then add
the chilli, pepper, sesame oil
and parsley. Transfer to a
small bowl and serve with the
crayfish. *Serves 4*

Spicy Prawns

450 g/1 lb frozen uncooked
  king prawns
cayenne pepper
1 tablespoon salt
3 tablespoons oil
3 medium-thick slices fresh
  root ginger, shredded
2 cloves garlic, sliced
1 teaspoon dry sherry
1 teaspoon sugar
pinch of pepper
2 teaspoons sesame oil
GARNISH
3 spring onions, shredded
1 lemon, sliced
2 red chillies, shredded to
  make tassels (see page 45)

Do not peel the prawns –
leave them whole, remove any
roe, then rinse and dry the
prawns on absorbent kitchen
paper.
  Heat the cayenne to taste
with the salt in a wok or
frying pan. Arrange the
prawns on the salt and fry for
a few minutes. Turn and fry
until the prawns change
colour. Transfer to kitchen
paper and wipe off the excess
seasoning.

Heat the oil in the wok or
frying pan. Add the ginger
and garlic and fry until
fragrant. Pour in the sherry,
sugar, pepper and sesame oil.
Replace the prawns in the
pan, toss them in the
seasonings so that they are
thoroughly coated. Serve the
prawns at once, garnished
with the spring onions, halved
lemon slices and chilli tassels.
Serves 4

Battered Prawns

8 frozen uncooked king
   prawns (defrosted)
½ teaspoon finely chopped or
   minced fresh root ginger
salt and pepper
1 teaspoon light soy sauce
½ teaspoon sugar
½ teaspoon sesame oil
5 egg whites
1 tablespoon plain flour
2 tablespoons cornflour
oil for deep frying
GARNISH
1 lemon
parsley sprigs
1 glacé cherry

Shell and devein the prawns,
leaving the tail end intact.
Make a slit down the back of
each prawn, then press lightly
to flatten the flesh. Sprinkle
the minced ginger and pepper
to taste over, then marinate
for 10 minutes.

Mix the soy sauce, sugar,
sesame oil and a little pepper,
then sprinkle this over the
prawns and leave to marinate
for another 10 minutes.

Whisk the egg whites until
stiff. Sift the flour,

1 tablespoon of the cornflour
and a pinch of salt together.
Add the dry ingredients to the
egg whites, whisking until the
mixture stands in stiff peaks.

Coat the prawns in the
remaining cornflour. Heat the
oil for deep frying to 190 c/
375 f, then dip the prawns
into the batter and deep fry
them until golden.

Drain on absorbent kitchen
paper and transfer to a
warmed serving dish. Keep
hot.

Using a sharp pointed knife,
cut the lemon in half, making
equal zig-zag cuts into the
middle of the fruit. Garnish
the prawns with parsley, one
lemon half and a cherry.
Serve at once. *Serves 2–4*

Prawns with Preserved Vegetables

75 g/3 oz Chinese preserved
   vegetable
2 tablespoons oil
1 chilli, deseeded and shredded
25 g/1 oz fresh root ginger,
   thinly sliced
2 shallots, sliced
1 clove garlic, sliced
50 g/2 oz canned bamboo
   shoot or par-cooked carrot,
   shredded
450 g/1 lb unpeeled cooked
   prawns
1 teaspoon dry sherry
2 tablespoons chicken stock
1 teaspoon light soy sauce
2 teaspoons sugar
pepper

Soak the preserved vegetable
in salted water for 1–2 hours,
then drain and rinse it.
Squeeze out all the excess
water and cut the vegetable
into 2.5-cm/1-in pieces. Dry
the pieces in a hot wok or
heavy-based frying pan,
turning them to prevent them
from sticking. Set aside.

Heat the oil in a wok or
frying pan, then add the chilli,
ginger, shallots and garlic and
fry until fragrant. Add the
preserved vegetable and
bamboo shoot or carrot. Fry
for a few minutes before
stirring in the prawns, sherry,
stock, soy sauce and sugar.
Stir well and heat through to
boiling point. Add pepper to
taste and cook for a few
minutes before serving.
Serves 4

Note: If you cannot obtain the
Chinese preserved vegetable,
then mange tout peas (snow
vegetables) can be used
instead. Trim off the ends of
the mange tout and slice them
crossways into fairly narrow
pieces. Add them to the pan
with the bamboo shoot or
carrot.

Prawn and Cabbage Roll

450 g/1 lb peeled cooked
  prawns (defrosted if frozen)
salt and pepper
½ teaspoon sugar
6 teaspoons cornflour
15 g/½ oz black fungus or black
  moss
3 large cabbage leaves
3 celery sticks
2 tablespoons oil
1 clove garlic, crushed
1 shallot, chopped
1 teaspoon dry sherry
100 ml/4 fl oz chicken stock
1 tablespoon water
1 teaspoon oyster sauce
1 egg white
½ teaspoon sesame oil
celery leaves to garnish

Mash the prawns and mix
them with seasoning to taste,
sugar and 3 teaspoons of the
cornflour. Pound the mixture
until it becomes firm and
elastic, then chill it for 1 hour.

Meanwhile, soak the fungus
or black moss for 15 minutes,
then blanch it in boiling water
for 2 minutes. Drain and dry
the fungus or moss and set
aside. Blanch the cabbage
leaves in boiling water for 2
minutes, then drain
thoroughly and lay the leaves
flat on a clean surface.

Use a further 2 teaspoons of
the cornflour to sprinkle over
the cabbage leaves. Top each
leaf with a layer of the
mashed shrimp mixture,
spreading it evenly. Arrange a
layer of fungus or black moss
over the mixture, then top
each leaf with a celery stick.
Roll up each leaf and press
well to make sure the filling is
firmly enclosed.

Steam the cabbage rolls on
a plate in a steamer, or over a
saucepan of hot water, for 7
minutes.

While the rolls are cooking,
heat the oil in a small
saucepan. Add the garlic and
shallot; sauté these for a few
minutes or until they give up
their flavour, then discard
them. Sprinkle in the sherry
and pour in the stock, then
bring to the boil. Blend the
remaining 1 teaspoon
cornflour with the water and
stir it into the stock. Stir in
the oyster sauce and seasoning
to taste. Simmer for a few
minutes.

To serve, cut the cabbage
rolls into slices and arrange
them on a warmed serving
plate. Stir the egg white and
oil into the simmering sauce
and pour this over the
cabbage roll slices. Serve
immediately, garnished with
celery leaves if you like.
Serves 4

Note: Fine strips of parboiled
carrot can be used instead of
the black fungus or black
moss in this recipe. If you
have a local health food shop
which sells dried purple
seaweed, then you can also
substitute this for the black
moss.

Prawns in Sweet Sauce

1 tablespoon oil
1 clove garlic, sliced
1 tablespoon shredded fresh root ginger
1 tablespoon shredded spring onion
450 g/1 lb peeled cooked prawns (defrosted if frozen)
1 teaspoon dry sherry
½ teaspoon salt
1 teaspoon sugar
2 tablespoons tomato ketchup
4 tablespoons chicken stock
1 teaspoon cornflour
1 tablespoon water
½ teaspoon white vinegar
½ teaspoon sesame oil
GARNISH
1 small lemon, sliced
1 small tomato, cut into wedges
parsley sprigs

Heat the oil in a wok or frying pan. Add the garlic, ginger and spring onion and cook until fragrant. Stir in the prawns and mix well. Pour in the sherry, salt, sugar, ketchup, and stock.

Blend the cornflour to a smooth cream with the water, then stir this into the prawns and bring to the boil. Sprinkle in the vinegar and sesame oil and toss well.

Transfer the prawns to a heated serving dish and add a garnish of halved lemon slices, tomato wedges and parsley. Serve at once. *Serves 4*

To shred fresh root ginger:
First cut the ginger into very fine slices. It is easier to remove the outer peel from each of the slices than to peel a large piece of ginger. When the slices are peeled, cut them into very fine, fairly short, strips and use as required.

Stuffed Peppers with Golden Corn

450 g/1 lb very small red and green peppers
450 g/1 lb peeled cooked prawns (defrosted if frozen)
50 g/2 oz fat pork
salt and pepper
½ teaspoon sugar
2 teaspoons cornflour plus extra for coating
3 red or green chillies (or a mixture of both)
1 carrot, diced
3 tablespoons oil
1 shallot, chopped
1 (326-g/11½-oz) can sweet corn, drained
1 teaspoon dry sherry
175 ml/6 fl oz chicken stock
1 teaspoon light soy sauce
2 tablespoons water

Cut the tops off the peppers, remove their seeds and coat the inside of each with a thin layer of cornflour. Mash the prawns to a paste. Blanch and dice the pork, then mix well with the prawn paste. Add seasoning to taste, the sugar and 1 teaspoon of the cornflour. Pound the mixture until firm. Deseed and dice the chillies and parboil the diced carrot. Stuff the peppers with the prawn paste, pressing it firmly into the vegetables.

Heat 2 tablespoons of the oil in a wok or large frying pan, then add the peppers, standing them neatly with the filling downwards. Cover and cook gently until golden. Turn the peppers and cook for a few minutes.

While the peppers are cooking, heat the remaining oil in a separate saucepan. Add the shallot and cook for a few minutes, then stir in the chillies, carrot, sweet corn and seasoning to taste.

To make the sauce, stir the sherry, stock and soy sauce together in a separate saucepan. Blend the remaining cornflour with the water and stir this into the sauce. Bring to the boil and simmer for 2 minutes.

To serve, spoon the sweet corn on to a warmed serving plate and arrange the peppers on top. Pour the sauce over and serve at once. *Serves 4–6*

Shrimp-stuffed String Beans

350 g/12 oz peeled cooked
shrimps
20 string beans, runner beans
or French beans
¼ teaspoon salt
1 teaspoon sugar
pinch of pepper
2 teaspoons cornflour plus
extra for coating
½ teaspoon sesame oil
8 teaspoons water
50 g/2 oz fat pork, diced
1 tablespoon chopped spring
onion
oil for cooking
1 clove garlic, crushed
1 shallot, grated
1 teaspoon dry sherry
3 tablespoons chicken stock
1 teaspoon light soy sauce
1 teaspoon oyster sauce

Mince the shrimps. Blanch the beans in boiling salted water for a few minutes, then drain and rinse them under cold water. Drain thoroughly.

Mix the salt, half the sugar, a pinch of pepper, 1 teaspoon cornflour, the sesame oil and 1 teaspoon water into the minced shrimps. Add the diced pork and spring onion. Pound until blended.

Take a bean, then twist and knot it to form a ring, tucking in the ends neatly. Continue knotting the beans until they are all shaped into circles.

Dust a bean ring with cornflour, then use a teaspoon to press a small amount of the shrimp mixture on to it. Press well to form a neat cake. Continue until all the beans and shrimp mixture have been used. Dust the stuffed beans with a little cornflour.

Heat a little oil in a wok or frying pan, add the garlic and shallot and fry until fragrant. Add the stuffed beans to the pan and cook until golden brown on both sides. Transfer to a serving platter. Keep hot.

Blend the remaining cornflour with the remaining water, sherry, stock, light soy sauce, oyster sauce and remaining sugar. Pour this mixture into the pan and heat through to boiling point. Simmer for 2 minutes, then pour this sauce over the string beans and serve. *Serves 4–6*

Shrimps with Diced Vegetables

1 Chinese dried mushroom
1 broccoli floret
1 (227-g/8-oz) can water
chestnuts, drained and diced
1 carrot, diced
1 large red chilli, deseeded and
chopped
salt and pepper
pinch of monosodium
glutamate
2 tablespoons oil
1 clove garlic, sliced
1 shallot, sliced
275 g/10 oz peeled cooked
shrimps (defrosted if frozen)
½ teaspoon sugar
¼ chicken stock cube, finely
crumbled
1 teaspoon dry sherry
1 teaspoon light soy sauce
175 ml/6 fl oz chicken stock
¾ teaspoon cornflour
1 tablespoon water
a few drops of sesame oil
parsley sprigs to garnish

Soak the mushroom in cold water for 15 minutes, then drain and dice it. Cut the broccoli into small pieces, then mix it with the water chestnuts, carrot, chilli and mushroom.

Bring a small quantity of water to the boil. Add a pinch each of salt and monosodium glutamate. Add the diced ingredients and simmer for 5 minutes, then drain and set aside.

Heat the oil in a wok or frying pan. Add the garlic and shallot, fry for a few minutes to extract their flavour, then discard these ingredients. Add the diced mixture to the oil and stir-fry for a few minutes. Stir in the shrimps, seasoning to taste, the sugar and crumbled stock cube. Sprinkle in the sherry, then pour in the soy sauce and stock; bring to the boil.

Blend the cornflour with the water and pour this mixture into the pan. Re-boil, stir in the sesame oil and transfer to a warmed serving plate. Serve at once, garnished with parsley sprigs. *Serves 4*

Fried Shrimps with Cashew Nuts

225 g/8 oz peeled cooked shrimps (defrosted if frozen)
about ½ egg white
1 teaspoon cornflour
salt and pepper
100 g/4 oz unroasted cashew nuts
2 tablespoons oil plus oil for deep frying
100 g/4 oz cauliflower florets
50 g/2 oz carrot, diced
100 g/4 oz red and green chillies, deseeded and diced
1 clove garlic, sliced
1 shallot, chopped
1½ teaspoons sweet paste
1½ teaspoons ground yellow bean paste
1 teaspoon dry sherry
½ teaspoon sugar
½ teaspoon sesame oil

Marinate the shrimps with the egg white, cornflour and a pinch of pepper for 10 minutes. Meanwhile, cook the cashew nuts in boiling water for 5 minutes; drain.

Heat the oil for deep frying

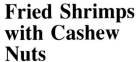

to 190 c/375 F. Add the prawns and cook until golden. Drain on absorbent kitchen paper and set aside. Deep fry the cashew nuts until golden; drain on absorbent kitchen paper and set aside.

Break the cauliflower into small pieces, then soak these in salted water for 10 minutes. Parboil the carrot and chillies together, then drain.

Heat the 2 tablespoons oil in a wok or frying pan. Add the garlic and shallot and cook until fragrant. Remove the pan from the heat and stir in the sweet paste and yellow bean paste. Stir in the nuts, vegetables and chillies and stir-fry for a few minutes over high heat.

Lastly, add seasoning to taste, the sherry and sugar. Stir in the shrimps and stir-fry for a few minutes. Stir in the sesame oil and serve at once. *Serves 4*

Prawn and Vegetable Salad

225 g/8 oz potatoes, cooked
225 g/8 oz carrots, cooked
1 cucumber
2 celery sticks
100 g/4 oz shelled peas (defrosted if frozen)
salt and pepper
3 eggs, hard-boiled
2 dessert apples, peeled, cored and cubed
1 teaspoon sugar
450 g/1 lb peeled cooked prawns (defrosted if frozen)
GARNISH
150 ml/¼ pint mayonnaise
1–2 tablespoons single cream
2 tomatoes
2 lemon slices
parsley sprigs
1 black olive, stoned and halved

Cut the potatoes and carrots into dice and mix them in a bowl. Dice about two-thirds of the cucumber and the celery and mix these into the other vegetables. Blanch the peas in boiling salted water for 2 minutes, then drain and add

them to the vegetables.

Cut two slices from the eggs, then roughly chop the remainder and add them to the salad with the apples, seasoning to taste and sugar. Toss well, then arrange the salad in a fish shape on a large oval platter. Top with the prawns.

To finish the salad, add a garnish of mayonnaise. Thin the mayonnaise with cream, then pipe or trickle it over the salad as shown in the picture.

Cut the reserved cucumber in half, then thinly slice the halves, leaving the slices attached at one side. Fold alternate slices as shown in the picture, then arrange the cucumber around the salad. Add the tomatoes, halved lemon slices and parsley. Place the slices of egg in position for eyes and top each with an olive half. Lightly chill before serving. *Serves 4*

Prawns in Tomato Sauce

*8 frozen uncooked king
  prawns (defrosted)
1 medium-thick slice fresh root
  ginger
2 shallots
1 spring onion
2 tablespoons oil
1 clove garlic, sliced
½ teaspoon dry sherry
100 ml/4 fl oz chicken stock
3 tablespoons tomato ketchup
salt and pepper
2 teaspoons sugar
1 teaspoon vinegar
1 teaspoon cornflour
1 tablespoon water
a few drops of sesame oil
a few crisp lettuce leaves to
  serve*

Wash and peel the prawns (if
necessary). Devein them and
cut each lengthways into
three. Place the pieces of
prawn in a sieve or colander
and scald them with boiling
water. Finely chop the ginger,
slice the shallots and finely
shred the spring onion.
  Heat the oil in a wok or
saucepan. Add the ginger,
spring onion and garlic and
stir-fry for a few minutes.
Sprinkle in the sherry and
pour in the stock. Bring to the
boil, then add the ketchup
seasoning to taste, the sugar
and vinegar. Add the prawns
and cover the pan, then
simmer for 4 minutes.
  Blend the cornflour to a
smooth cream with the water
and stir this into the prawns.
Bring back to the boil and
simmer for 2 minutes.
Sprinkle in the sesame oil just
before serving.
  Arrange the lettuce leaves
in a dish and pile the prawns
in the middle. Serve at once.
Serves 4

Prawn Cutlets

*20 frozen uncooked king
  prawns (defrosted)
salt and pepper
plain flour for coating
3 eggs, beaten
100 g/4 oz dry white
  breadcrumbs
oil for deep frying
watercress sprigs to garnish*

Shell the prawns, leaving their
tails intact. Devein and toss
them in salt, then wash, drain
and dry the prawns on
absorbent kitchen paper.
Make a slit down the back of
each one, open out the flesh
and press it lightly to flatten.
Coat the prawns in seasoned
flour, then dip them in the
beaten egg and cover them
completely in breadcrumbs.
  Heat the oil for deep frying
to 190 c/375 f. Deep fry the
prawns until golden brown,
then drain them on absorbent
kitchen paper.
  To serve, arrange the
prawns on a serving platter
and add a garnish of
watercress sprigs. Serve at
once. *Serves 6*

King prawns: Uncooked king
prawns are available from
good fishmongers and Chinese
supermarkets. Sometimes
known as Mediterranean
prawns, these are significantly
larger than the small
commonly available prawns.
When you find a source of
uncooked king prawns, either
fresh or frozen, it is well
worth buying some for your
freezer as the flavour achieved
by cooking them from the raw
state is far superior to that
obtained by using ready-
cooked prawns.

Szechuen Prawns

450 g/1 lb frozen uncooked king prawns (defrosted)
½ teaspoon salt
2 red chillies, deseeded
5 tablespoons oil
2 shallots, shredded
1 clove garlic, chopped
2 medium-thick slices fresh root ginger, shredded
1 tablespoon broad bean paste
1 tablespoon dry sherry
1 tablespoon tomato ketchup
1 teaspoon sugar
2 teaspoons soy sauce
1 teaspoon sesame oil
1 teaspoon cornflour
3 tablespoons water
3 spring onions, shredded, to garnish

Wash, peel and devein the prawns, if necessary, leaving their heads and tails intact. Dry and sprinkle with the salt. Slice the chillies into rings.

Heat 3 tablespoons of the oil in a wok or frying pan. Lay the prawns in the pan and fry for 3 minutes on each side. Remove from the pan and drain on absorbent kitchen paper.

Discard the oil from the pan and add the remaining 2 tablespoons of fresh oil. Fry the shallots, garlic, ginger and chillies until fragrant. Stir in the broad bean paste and replace the prawns in the wok.

Stir in the sherry, ketchup, sugar, soy sauce and sesame oil. Blend the cornflour to a smooth paste with a little of the water, then add it to the sauce with the remaining water.

Bring to the boil and simmer for a few minutes before serving, garnished with the spring onions. *Serves 4*

Szechuen: This is the largest province of China and one of the most fruitful. In this area, quantities of rice, corn, wheat and cotton are produced. Silk is also produced in Szechuen. Even though this is not a coastal region, there are many rivers and lakes and there is certainly no shortage of freshwater fish or even prawns.

During the summer months, this area of China becomes very hot and, like many tropical countries, the climate is reflected in the diet. To encourage a cooling of the body, the food is often quite hot and spicy. The idea is that the hot food encourages the body to perspire and therefore lose heat.

Here is a recipe which lives up to the reputation of Szechuen cooking: these prawns are flavoured with various ingredients, among them are fresh root ginger, chillies and broad bean paste (see glossary) which all contribute to the hot taste of the cooked dish. The other ingredient used in a comparatively large quantity is salt, and this too is typical of the recipes from this region, where salt is used to its full advantage to emphasise the flavour of fresh foods.

If you are unfamiliar with hot flavoured foods, then do take a little care when serving these prawns and offer plenty of plain cooked rice to eat with them. Then, if you do find that the sauce is a little spicier than you had anticipated, the rice will help to absorb some of the hot flavour.

Chop Suey with Prawns

3 Chinese dried mushrooms
100 g/4 oz broccoli
1 (425-g/15-oz) can whole
  baby corn, drained
1 carrot, sliced
8 canned water chestnuts,
  sliced
1 red chilli, deseeded and
  sliced
salt and pepper
3 tablespoons oil
1 clove garlic, crushed
2 shallots, chopped
3 medium-thick slices fresh
  root ginger
100 g/4 oz bean sprouts
275 g/10 oz peeled cooked
  prawns (defrosted if frozen)
1 teaspoon dry sherry
½ teaspoon sugar
1 teaspoon light soy sauce
2 teaspoons oyster sauce
½ teaspoon sesame oil
3 tablespoons chicken stock
1 teaspoon cornflour
1 tablespoon water

Soak the mushrooms in cold
water for 15 minutes, then
drain and steam them over
boiling water for 10 minutes.
Slice the cooked mushrooms.

Slice the broccoli and corn
then mix both with the carrot,
water chestnuts and chilli.
Blanch these ingredients in
boiling salted water for 2–3
minutes. Drain.

Heat the oil in a wok or
frying pan. Add the garlic,
shallots, and ginger and fry
until fragrant, then remove
from the pan and discard.
Quickly stir-fry the
beansprouts for a few seconds,
then remove them from the
pan.

Add the vegetable mixture
to the pan and stir-fry for a
few minutes. Stir in the
prawns and sprinkle in the
sherry. Add seasoning to
taste, the sugar, soy sauce,
oyster sauce, sesame oil and
stock. Bring to the boil. Blend
the cornflour to a smooth
paste with the water, then stir
this into the chop suey and
simmer for 2 minutes.

Lastly, stir in the
beansprouts and transfer the
chop suey to a warmed dish.
Serve at once. *Serves 4*

Shrimp and Pea Omelettes

5 eggs
salt and pepper
50 g/2 oz shelled peas
175 g/6 oz peeled cooked
  shrimps (defrosted if frozen)
1 tablespoon chopped spring
  onion
1 tablespoon chopped parsley
½ teaspoon sesame oil
oil for cooking
flat-leafed parsley to garnish

Beat the eggs with seasoning
to taste. Blanch the peas in
boiling water for 2 minutes,
then drain and add to the eggs
with the shrimps, spring onion
and parsley. Stir in the sesame
oil.

Heat a little oil in a frying
pan and add a large spoonful
of the egg mixture. Fry until
golden, then turn and cook
the second side. Continue in
this way until all the egg
mixture is cooked. As the
omelettes are cooked, transfer
them to a warmed serving
dish, cover and keep hot until
they are all prepared. Serve
the omelettes as soon as they
are all ready and add a
garnish of flat-leafed parsley.
Serves 6

Note: You can use canned
shrimps for this recipe: use 1
(200-g/7-oz) can drained of
liquid.

For speed, the omelette
mixture can be cooked as two
large omelettes rather than
making small omelettes. This
is not traditional and not as
attractive to serve, but the
flavour will be the same. Cut
the large omelettes into
wedges to serve, then arrange
the pieces on a warmed
platter with a garnish of
parsley.

Mussels in Hot Sauce

1 kg/2 lb mussels
a little oatmeal
3 tablespoons oil
2 teaspoons finely grated fresh
    root ginger
1 shallot, chopped
2 cloves garlic, crushed
1 green pepper, deseeded and
    chopped
2 red chillies, deseeded and
    chopped
2 teaspoons dry sherry
3 tablespoons Garlic Chilli
    Paste (page 229)
2 tablespoons sweet paste
1 tablespoon light soy sauce
1½ teaspoons sugar
¼ teaspoon monosodium
    glutamate
salt and pepper
1 teaspoon sesame oil
chilli tassel to garnish (below)

Place the mussels in a large bowl or bucket of water, add a handful of oatmeal and leave them to stand overnight. This way they will be cleaned of any sand.

Drain and thoroughly scrub the mussels, discarding any open shells which do not shut when tapped firmly. It is most important that any mussels which are to be cooked are very fresh and still alive, as harmful toxins quickly build up in the dead shellfish.

There are two ways of deciding whether the mussels are edible: the first is to make sure they are firmly shut when they are cleaned (or that they shut quickly when tapped) and the second is to make sure that they have all opened when they are cooked. On no account use any shellfish which do not conform to these rules. It goes without saying that fresh mussels should not

be collected from just any beach or seaside area because they could well be polluted. Always buy fresh mussels from a reputable fishmonger and use them as soon as they have been cleaned of sand.

Heat the oil in a heavy-based saucepan, add the ginger, shallot and garlic and cook until fragrant. Stir in the green pepper and chillies and fry until softened but not browned. Add the prepared mussels, sherry, chilli paste and sweet paste. Cook, stirring occasionally, until all the mussels are opened. Discard any mussels which do not open.

Stir in the light soy sauce, sugar, monosodium glutamate and seasoning to taste. Sprinkle the sesame oil over the mussels and serve at once, garnished with the chilli tassel.
Serves 4–6

To make chilli tassels: Shred as many chillies as you require, working from the stalk end towards the point, leaving the strips attached at the stalk. Rinse away any loose seeds and place the chillies in a bowl of iced water. Leave for at least 30 minutes or several hours. The strips of chilli will curl to make an attractive garnish.

Lobster with Spicy Sauce

1 cooked lobster
2 tablespoons oil
2 shallots, sliced
2 cloves garlic, sliced
1 teaspoon dry sherry
250 ml/8 fl oz chicken stock
salt and pepper
2 teaspoons sugar
2 tablespoons tomato ketchup
1 teaspoon chilli oil (page 228)
a few drops of vinegar
50 g/2 oz fresh root ginger,
    shredded
3 spring onions, shredded
a few crisp lettuce leaves to
    serve

Twist the claws and legs off
the lobster and crack these
with nut crackers or with a
hammer. Set aside. To split
the lobster use a large sharp
knife: cut from the shoulder
down through the head,
tapping the knife with a
weight to crack the shell if
necessary. Next split the body
in the same way. Separate the
halves and remove all the
edible white flesh.

Heat the oil in a wok or
large frying pan. Add the
shallots and garlic and fry
until they are fragrant. Add
the lobster meat, cracked
claws and legs and cook for a
few minutes. Sprinkle in the
sherry and stock and bring to
the boil. Stir in seasoning to
taste, the sugar, ketchup and
chilli oil. Sprinkle in the
vinegar, then add the ginger
and spring onions. Toss well
and serve at once, spooned on
to a bed of crisp lettuce
leaves. *Serves 2–4*

Abalone in Oyster Sauce

1 (454-g/1-lb) can abalone,
    drained
1 Iceberg lettuce
2 tablespoons oil
1 teaspoon dry sherry
150 ml/¼ pint chicken stock
3 tablespoons oyster sauce
1 teaspoon sugar
a few drops of sesame oil
1 teaspoon cornflour
1 tablespoon water

Slice the abalone into thin
pieces. Wash and trim the
lettuce, then blanch it in
boiling water for just a few
seconds. Drain thoroughly.
Arrange the lettuce in a
serving dish and keep hot.
    Heat the oil in a wok or
frying pan, pour in the sherry
and stock and bring to the
boil. Add the abalone. Stir in
the oyster sauce, sugar and
sesame oil. Blend the
cornflour with the water, stir
this into the sauce and simmer
for 2 minutes. Serve hot,
poured over the lettuce.
Serves 4

Abalone: These are white
shellfish, with a slightly oval
shell. Canned abalone is a
good substitute for the fresh
shellfish which is not readily
available. When fresh, the
abalone does in fact require
extensive beating or very
lengthy simmering to make
the flesh tender. Dried
abalone (which may be
available from certain
specialist stores) is not worth
the effort involved in the very
lengthy soaking which it
requires.

Crab in Spring Onion and Ginger Sauce

1 cooked crab
3 tablespoons oil
2 cloves garlic, crushed
100 g/4 oz fresh root ginger,
grated
1 bunch spring onions,
shredded
2 teaspoons dry sherry
salt and pepper
2 teaspoons sugar
1 teaspoon light soy sauce
100 ml/4 fl oz chicken stock

Prepare the crab as for Hot and Sour Crab (page 48), but leave the brown meat in the shell. Crack this shell into two or three pieces.

Heat the oil in a wok or saucepan. Add the garlic and ginger and cook until fragrant. Stir in half the spring onions with the prepared crab (and the shell) and stir-fry for a few minutes. Sprinkle in the sherry, seasoning to taste, sugar and soy sauce, then pour in the stock.

Bring to the boil, cover the pan and reduce the heat, then simmer for 5 minutes. Sprinkle with the remaining spring onions and serve hot.
Serves 4–6

Hot and Sour Crab

1 cooked crab
50 g/2 oz shallots
1 bulb garlic, separated into
* cloves and peeled*
40 g/1½ oz fresh root ginger
3 tablespoons oil
2 tablespoons broad bean paste
2 tablespoons tomato ketchup
2 teaspoons dry sherry
250 ml/8 fl oz plus 1 tablespoon
* water*
3 tablespoons vinegar
2–3 tablespoons sugar
1 teaspoon cornflour
4–5 spring onions

To prepare the crab, hold the shell firmly in one hand and the body, with the claws attached, in the other. Pull the two apart. Remove the stomach bag – which lies just below the head – from the shell. Scrape out all the brown meat.

Remove the legs from the body, discard the tiny claws and crack the rest with a nut cracker. Discard the greyish-white 'dead men's fingers'

from the body and remove the white flesh.

Finely chop 1 shallot, crush 1 clove garlic and grate one-third of the ginger. Heat the oil in a wok or large saucepan, add the prepared shallot, garlic and ginger and cook until fragrant. Stir in the broad bean paste and ketchup, stir until well mixed, then add all the prepared crab and cracked claws.

Slice the remaining ginger and add it to the pan with the remaining whole shallots and garlic cloves. Stir-fry for a while, then pour in the sherry, the 250 ml/8 fl oz water and the vinegar. Stir in the sugar, then cover and simmer for 6–8 minutes.

Before serving, blend the cornflour with the 1 tablespoon water and stir into the sauce. Simmer for 1 minute, then sprinkle in the spring onions and serve.
Serves 4–6

Crab Claws with Shrimps

450 g/1 lb peeled cooked
* shrimps (defrosted if frozen)*
100 g/4 oz fat pork (optional)
½ egg white
1 teaspoon chopped spring
* onion*
salt and pepper
¼ teaspoon sugar
½ teaspoon sesame oil
1 tablespoon cornflour plus
* cornflour for coating*
10 crab claws
1 egg, beaten
100 g/4 oz fine white
* breadcrumbs*
oil for deep frying
GARNISH
1 lemon
1 glacé cherry
1 bunch watercress
Spicy Salt (page 229) to serve

Mash the shrimps to make a paste. Cook the pork (if used) in boiling water for 10 minutes, then rinse it under cold water. Finely chop the cooked meat and add it to the shrimps with the egg white, spring onion, seasoning to

taste, sugar, sesame oil and the 1 tablespoon cornflour. Pound the mixture with a wooden spoon to thoroughly bind all the ingredients.

Crack the crab claws and remove all the meat. Reserve this for another use. Dust the claws with a little cornflour, then mould a little of the shrimp mixture around each. Press the mixture firmly on to the claws and mould it into an even shape. Coat the mixture first in cornflour, then in beaten egg and lastly press on the breadcrumbs.

Heat the oil for deep frying to 190 c/375 f, then deep fry the claws until golden brown. Drain on absorbent kitchen paper and transfer to a heated serving plate.

Cut the lemon in half: use a sharp pointed knife and cut in a zig-zag pattern all around the middle of the fruit. Separate the halves and top one with a cherry. Garnish the crab claws with finely shredded watercress, the lemon half and cherry. Serve hot with spicy salt.
Serves 4–6

Lobster with Mung Bean Thread

1 cooked lobster
4 Chinese dried mushrooms
100 g/4 oz mung bean thread
2 tablespoons oil
25 g/1 oz fresh root ginger, sliced
1 clove garlic, crushed
1 shallot, chopped
2 teaspoons dry sherry
450 ml/¾ pint chicken stock
2 teapoons light soy sauce
salt and pepper
1 teaspoon sugar
1 teaspoon sesame oil
2 spring onions, shredded, to garnish

Remove and reserve the legs and claws from the lobster. Crack these with nut crackers so that they can be included in the dish. Crack the lobster down the back, working first from the shoulder to the head, then from the shoulder towards the tail. Remove all the white meat and break it into chunks.

Soak the mushrooms in cold water for 15 minutes, then drain and steam them over boiling water for 10 minutes. Remove the stalks and shred the mushroom caps. Wash the bean thread under cold water, then soak it in fresh water for about 10 minutes.

Heat the oil in a heavy-based saucepan or flameproof casserole. Add 1 slice of the ginger, the garlic and shallot and cook until brown; remove and discard. Sprinkle in the sherry and pour in the stock. Season with the light soy sauce, salt and pepper to taste, the sugar and sesame oil.

Bring to the boil, add the drained bean thread and mushrooms, then reduce the heat and simmer for 2 minutes, stirring occasionally.

Meanwhile, shred the remaining ginger and set aside. Add the lobster meat, legs and claws to the pan, then simmer for a further 3 minutes. Stir in the remaining ginger and serve at once, garnished with the shredded spring onions. *Serve 4*

To Split a Lobster

1 *Use a sharp, heavy knife to cut from shoulder to head. Tap the knife gently but firmly with a mallet or rolling pin if necessary.*

2 *Work from the shoulder towards the tail to completely split the lobster.*

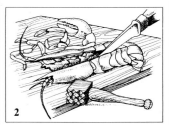

Scallops with Chicken Livers

2 chicken livers, sliced
1 teaspoon Ginger Juice (page 227)
4 teaspoons dry sherry
2 teaspoons cornflour
350 g/12 oz shelled fresh or frozen scallops (defrosted if frozen)
3 celery sticks
100 g/4 oz carrots
2 tablespoons oil
2 cloves garlic, crushed
3 medium-thick slices fresh root ginger
4 tablespoons chicken stock
1 teaspoon light soy sauce
1 teaspoon oyster sauce
½ teaspoon sugar
salt
1 tablespoon water
2 spring onions, shredded

Place the chicken livers in a bowl with the ginger juice, 1 teaspoon of the sherry and half the cornflour. Set aside to marinate for 30 minutes.

Meanwhile prepare the other ingredients: rinse and slice the scallops; cut the celery into finger-length pieces; pare ridges from the carrots, then slice them.

Bring a pan of water to the boil, add the chicken livers and scallops. Bring the water rapidly back to the boil, then drain and dry the livers and scallops.

Heat the oil in a wok or frying pan. Add the livers and scallops, stir for a minute, then remove from the pan. Add the garlic and ginger to the oil and stir-fry until fragrant. Stir in the celery and carrot and cook for a few minutes.

Return the livers and scallops to the pan, pour in the remaining sherry, stock, light soy sauce, oyster sauce, sugar and salt to taste, then bring to the boil. Blend the remaining cornflour with the water and stir the mixture into the sauce. Simmer for 2 minutes, then stir in the spring onions and serve. *Serves 4–6*

Sautéed Scallops with Celery

50 g/2 oz fresh root ginger
2 teaspoons dry sherry
1 teaspoon cornflour
450 g/1 lb shelled fresh or frozen scallops (defrosted if frozen)
1 small carrot
2 celery sticks
2 tablespoons oil
1 clove garlic, crushed
1 shallot, chopped
3 or 4 small broccoli florets
100 ml/4 fl oz chicken stock
½ teaspoon sugar
1 teaspoon oyster sauce
salt and pepper
1 tablespoon water
3 spring onions, shredded

Grate half the ginger, then mix it with half the sherry and half the cornflour. Toss the scallops with this mixture and set them aside to marinate for 20 minutes.

Slice the remaining ginger. Pare ridges down the length of the carrot, then slice it. Parboil the carrot in salted water; drain. Cut the celery sticks in half lengthways, then across into short pieces.

Heat the oil in a wok or frying pan. Add the scallops and cook for 1 minute, then remove and drain them on absorbent kitchen paper. Add the garlic, shallot, remaining ginger, carrot, celery and broccoli. Stir-fry for a few minutes, then replace the scallops in the pan, sprinkle in the remaining sherry, add the stock, sugar, oyster sauce and seasoning to taste. Bring to the boil; blend the remaining cornflour with the water and stir this mixture into the sauce. Stir in the spring onions, then simmer for 2 minutes before serving. *Serves 4–6*

Fish and Seafood

Deep Fried Oysters

2 tablespoons oil plus oil for
  deep frying
25 g/1 oz fresh root ginger,
  sliced
1 bunch spring onions,
  chopped
3 tablespoons dry sherry
1.15 litres/2 pints water
450 g/1 lb shelled oysters
1 tablespoon Ginger Juice
  (page 227)
½ teaspoon sugar
½ teaspoon sesame oil
salt and pepper
BATTER
100 g/4 oz plain flour
2 teaspoons cornflour plus
  extra for coating
2 teaspoons baking powder
¼ teaspoon salt
100 ml/4 fl oz water
3 tablespoons oil

GARNISH
1 chilli tassel (page 45)
watercress sprigs
TO SERVE
Worcestershire sauce
Spicy Salt (page 228)

Heat the 2 tablespoons oil in a wok or saucepan. Add the ginger and spring onions and cook until fragrant. Pour in the sherry and water and bring to the boil. Drop the oysters into the water, bring rapidly back to the boil, then drain them immediately. Dry the oysters on absorbent kitchen paper. Marinate the oysters in the ginger juice, sugar, sesame oil and seasoning to taste for 20 minutes. Meanwhile, make the batter. Sift the flour, cornflour, baking powder and salt into a bowl, then gradually beat in the water and oil to make a smooth batter.

Heat the oil for deep frying to 190 c/375 f. Coat the oysters with cornflour, dip them in the batter and deep fry until golden. Drain on absorbent kitchen paper and pile them on a serving plate. Garnish with a chilli tassel and watercress sprigs, then serve at once with Worcestershire sauce and spicy salt as accompaniments. *Serves 6*

Fresh oysters: As with all shellfish it is of prime importance that oysters are very fresh when they are cooked. They must also come from clean areas which are unpolluted. Some of the finest European oysters are taken from the oyster beds of Britain. They are not available in the summer months and are at their best in the late autumn and winter when they are not spawning. If you have any doubts about the freshness of an oyster, then discard it rather than risk being poisoned.

If the oysters have not been opened by the fishmonger for you, then you will need a strong knife or special oyster-shucking knife to open the shells. Hold the oyster firmly, then insert the knife at the hinge in the shell. Hold the shell very firmly and twist the knife in the hinge to break it apart.

Carefully open the oyster and cut through the muscle which is attached to the lifted shell. To free the oyster from the shell, carefully slide the knife underneath it and lift it out. The effort involved is well worth it as the reward is superb, and deep fried oysters are quite delicious, particularly if you do not like the thought of swallowing the raw shellfish.

Cuttlefish in Oyster Sauce

675 g/1½ lb cuttlefish or fresh squid
1 teaspoon soy sauce
1 teaspoon Ginger Juice (page 227)
2 teaspoons dry sherry
2 teaspoons cornflour
1 (213-g/7½-oz) can button mushrooms, drained
3 tablespoons oil
1 clove garlic, crushed
1 cucumber, roughly chopped
3 tablespoons oyster sauce
1 teaspoon sugar
a few drops of sesame oil
salt and pepper
3 tablespoons water
GARNISH
3 Chinese dried mushrooms, soaked until soft
1 tomato, sliced and halved
1 lettuce heart, shredded

Clean the cuttlefish or squid as described in the recipe for Hot and Sour Soup on page 16. Cut the fish into pieces, then marinate them in 1 teaspoon each of soy sauce, ginger juice, sherry and cornflour for 30 minutes.

Blanch the marinated fish for a few seconds, then drain and rinse it under cold water. Reserve a few of the button mushrooms for garnish and score a criss-cross pattern on them. Heat the oil in a wok or large frying pan. Add the garlic and fry until fragrant, then stir in the cucumber and button mushrooms. Toss in the cuttlefish and stir-fry until well cooked.

Sprinkle in the remaining sherry, the oyster sauce, sugar, sesame oil and seasoning to taste. Blend the remaining cornflour to a smooth cream with the water, stir into the sauce and simmer for 2 minutes.

Transfer the cooked fish to a warmed serving dish and add a garnish of the reserved button mushrooms, with the sliced Chinese mushrooms and tomatoes, arranged in a rose pattern on the shredded lettuce. Serve at once.
Serves 4–6

Cuttlefish Balls with Mange Tout Peas

450 g/1 lb cuttlefish or squid
5 canned water chestnuts
4 cloves garlic, 2 crushed and 2 halved
salt and pepper
1 teaspoon sugar
3 teaspoons cornflour
4 tablespoons water
3 tablespoons oil
2 medium-thick slices fresh root ginger, finely shredded
2 shallots, sliced
100 g/4 oz mange tout peas, roughly shredded
2 red chillies, deseeded and shredded
1 teaspoon dry sherry
100 ml/4-oz fish or chicken stock
1 teaspoon light soy sauce
1 teaspoon sesame oil
a few drops of dark soy sauce

Wash and prepare the cuttlefish or squid according to the instructions on page 16. Finely mince the seafood, or grind it in a food processor. Mince the water chestnuts and add them to the cuttlefish with the crushed cloves of garlic. Mix in salt to taste, ½ teaspoon of the sugar, 2 teaspoons of the cornflour, a pinch of pepper and 2 tablespoons of the water. Pound the mixture thoroughly until well bound together and elastic. Chill thoroughly.

Heat the oil in a wok. Add the fishballs and cook until golden brown, turning them frequently. Drain on absorbent kitchen paper and set aside. Add the halved cloves of garlic, ginger and shallots to the pan and fry until fragrant. Stir in the mange tout peas, and chillies and fry for a while, then return the fishballs to the pan.

Pour in the sherry, stock, light soy sauce, remaining sugar, pepper to taste, sesame oil and dark soy sauce. Blend the remaining cornflour and water together until smooth, then pour into the sauce and bring to the boil. Simmer for 2 minutes, stir well and serve at once. *Serves 4*

Squid with Green Pepper

450 g/1 lb fresh squid
1 teaspoon Ginger Juice (page 227)
2 teaspoons dry sherry
2 teaspoons cornflour
2 tablespoons oil
3 cloves garlic, crushed
2 green peppers, deseeded and cut into chunks
½ teaspoon sugar
½ teaspoon vinegar
a few drops of sesame oil
1 spring onion, chopped
salt and pepper
50 ml/2 fl oz chicken stock
1 tablespoon water

Prepare the squid according to the instructions in the recipe for Hot and Sour Soup on page 16. Cut the inside of the squid into a criss-cross pattern. Place in a bowl and sprinkle with the ginger juice, half the sherry and half the cornflour. Set aside to marinate for 20 minutes, then blanch in boiling water for a few seconds, rinse and thoroughly drain.

Heat the oil in a wok or large frying pan. Add half the garlic and fry until fragrant. Stir in the squid and green peppers. Pour in the remaining sherry, sugar, vinegar and sesame oil. Stir thoroughly before adding the last of the garlic, the spring onion, seasoning to taste and the stock. Blend the remaining cornflour to a smooth cream with the water, then stir this into the squid and simmer for about 2 minutes. Serve hot.
Serves 4–6

Garlic Eel Casserole

450 g/1 lb eel
salt and pepper
100 g/4 oz Roast Belly Pork (page 88)
2 small leeks
small piece of tangerine peel
2 tablespoons oil
2 shallots, sliced
12 cloves garlic, crushed
2 teaspoons dry sherry
250 ml/8 fl oz chicken stock
2 teaspoons light soy sauce
1½ teaspoons sugar
1 teaspoon cornflour
2 tablespoons water

First skin the eel: cut off the head and pull back the skin to peel it off. Chop the eel into 2.5-cm/1-in sections. Season these with pepper
Cut the pork into 8-mm/⅓-in thick pieces. Wash the leeks and cut them into 3.5-cm/1½-in sections. Soak the tangerine peel in hot water until soft, then shred it finely.
Heat the oil in a flameproof casserole, then add and sauté the shallots and garlic. Stir in

the eel and stir-fry quickly, then add the pork, leeks and tangerine peel and mix thoroughly. Pour in the sherry, stock, light soy sauce, salt and pepper to taste, and sugar. Bring to the boil, reduce the heat, cover and simmer for 30 minutes.
Blend the cornflour with the water, then pour this into the casserole and simmer for 2 minutes. Serve at once.
Serves 4

Sautéed Squid with Red Chillies

450 g/1 lb fresh squid
2 tablespoons Ginger Juice
   (page 227)
3½ teaspoons cornflour
2 tablespoons oil plus oil for
   deep frying
15 g/½ oz fresh root ginger,
   sliced
2 shallots, sliced
2 cloves garlic, sliced
50 g/2 oz red chillies
1 teaspoon dry sherry
2 tablespoons water
2 teaspoons soy sauce
1 teaspoon sugar
½ teaspoon sesame oil
salt and pepper
1 tablespoon water
3 spring onions, shredded
GARNISH
1 orange, sliced
1 cucumber, carved into
   seafood shapes (optional)

Clean the squid according to the instructions in the recipe for Hot and Sour Soup (page 16). Score a criss-cross pattern on the inside of squid, then marinate it with the ginger juice and 3 teaspoons of the cornflour for 20 minutes.

Heat the oil for deep frying to 190 c/375 F. Cook the squid until it curls up. Remove and drain on absorbent kitchen paper.

Heat the 2 tablespoons oil in a wok or frying pan. Sauté the ginger, shallots and garlic until fragrant. Put in the chillies and squid and stir-fry quickly. Add the sherry, water, soy sauce, sugar, sesame oil and seasoning. Blend the remaining cornflour with the water, then stir this into the sauce and simmer for 2 minutes to thicken.

Stir the spring onions into the squid and serve hot. Garnish with orange slices and cucumber, if you like.
Serves 4–6

Cucumber Prawns

1 Cut a 10-cm/4-in length of cucumber in half horizontally.

2 Use a small pointed knife. Cut five 2.5-cm/1-in slits at one end of the cucumber to make the head. Make a few short slits into the side, from head to tail. Trim the slits to make the fin-like features.

3 Cut the tail and make a zig-zag pattern along the edge. Carve a few notches down the back.

4 Trim the slits at the head end, carving the middle piece in a zig-zag shape. Trim the cucumber flesh from underneath. Add tiny balls of red-coloured flour and water dough for eyes.

Steamed Eel in Fermented Black Bean Sauce

450 g/1 lb eels
3 medium-thick slices fresh
  root ginger, shredded
2 cloves garlic, crushed
2 tablespoons fermented black
  bean paste
1 tablespoon light soy sauce
2 tablespoons sugar
1 teaspoon sesame oil
3 tablespoons oil
pepper
2 spring onions, shredded
3 red chillies, deseeded and
  shredded
flat-leafed parsley sprigs to
  garnish

Cut the heads off the eels (or eel if you have one large one), then peel back and discard the skin (this is preferable although not essential). Thoroughly wash the fish in salted water, then cut it into 2.5-cm/1-in lengths.

Mix half the ginger and the garlic into the black bean paste. Stir in the soy sauce, sugar and both types of oil.

Add a pinch of pepper, then use this seasoning mix to coat the pieces of eel. Place them on a plate and stand the plate in a steamer. Cook over boiling water for 1 hour, topping up the water as necessary with more boiling water.

Sprinkle the cooked eel with the shredded spring onions, chillies and remaining ginger. Add a garnish of parsley and serve hot.
Serves 4–6

Steamed Shrimps with Dark Soy Dip

450 g/1 lb whole uncooked
  shrimps
DIPPING SAUCE
2 tablespoons oil
2 tablespoons grated fresh root
  ginger
2 shallots, grated
4 tablespoons dark soy sauce
3 tablespoons sugar
¼ teaspoon pepper
1 tablespoon sesame oil
GARNISH
1 chilli, deseeded and shredded
2 spring onions, shredded

Thoroughly wash the shrimps. Place them in a steamer and cover tightly. Cook over rapidly boiling water for 3–5 minutes or until the shrimps are pink.

While the shrimps cook, prepare the dipping sauce: heat the oil in a wok or frying pan and sauté the ginger and shallot until fragrant; discard. Stir in all the remaining dipping ingredients and mix well, then bring to the boil.

Pour into small bowls and scatter the chilli and spring onions on top.

Remove the steamer from the wok or saucepan and serve the shrimps straight from it. The steamer can be stood on a serving platter to take to the table. Each person helps themself to the shrimps. Have a bowl ready to take the peelings from the shellfish. The shelled shrimps are dipped in the prepared sauce as they are eaten. *Serves 4*

Scallops with Asparagus

*450 g/1 lb green asparagus, cut
into 5-cm/2-in pieces*
salt and pepper
*2 tablespoons oil plus oil for
deep frying*
*1 tablespoon sugar plus 1
teaspoon*
*1 teaspoon monosodium
glutamate*
*275 g/10 oz fresh or frozen
shelled scallops (defrosted if
frozen)*
*2 tablespoons grated fresh root
ginger*
2 shallots
2 cloves garlic
2 teaspoons dry sherry
4 tablespoons water
2 teaspoons light soy sauce
1 teaspoon sesame oil
1 teaspoon oyster sauce

GARNISH
1 orange, sliced
1 lemon, sliced
2 tomatoes, sliced

Cook the asparagus in
simmering salted water for 5
minutes, then drain it
thoroughly. Heat the oil for
deep frying to 190 C/375 F.
Mix 1 tablespoon salt, the 1
tablespoon sugar and the
monosodium glutamate with
the asparagus, then deep fry it
for a few minutes. Drain on
absorbent kitchen paper.

Meanwhile, coat the
scallops with pepper and
cornflour, then deep fry them
for 2–3 minutes. Drain on
absorbent kitchen paper.

Heat the 2 tablespoons of
oil in a wok or frying pan and
sauté the ginger, shallots and
garlic until fragrant; discard.
Stir in the asparagus and fry
for a while. Add the scallops
and sherry.

Pour in 3 tablespoons of the
water, the remaining sugar,
light soy sauce, sesame oil and
oyster sauce. Simmer the
sauce for 2 minutes with the
cornflour blended to a cream
with the remaining water.
Serve at once, garnished with
the halved orange, lemon and
tomato slices. *Serves 6*

To prepare fresh scallops: If
the fishmonger has not already
removed the scallops from the
shell, then this is quite a
simple operation. Hold the
scallop with the rounded shell
uppermost. Slip a strong knife
between the upper and lower
shells, then prize them apart.

As the shells open, cut the
scallop away from the
rounded shell. The easiest way
to cut the scallop away from
the flat shell is with a pair of
kitchen scissors. Discard the
grey flesh which surrounds the
white part. Cut away the dark

intestine and all attached
organs.

The part which is eaten is
the white muscle. Attached to
this is the red coral and this
too should be saved.

When you have removed
the scallop from its shell, rinse
it thoroughly under cold
water, taking care not to
damage any of the flesh. Pat
dry on absorbent kitchen
paper and use as required.

Shrimps in Chilli Sauce

2 tablespoons oil
25 g/1 oz onion, chopped
15 g/½ oz fresh root ginger, grated
15 g/½ oz shallot, grated
4 cloves garlic, crushed
1 stick celery, finely chopped
3 chillies, deseeded and finely chopped
350 g/12 oz peeled cooked shrimps
1 teaspoon dry sherry
2 tablespoons broad bean paste
2 tablespoons tomato ketchup
1½ tablespoons sugar
2 teaspoons light soy sauce
1 teaspoon sesame oil
1 teaspoon cornflour
2 tablespoons water

Heat the oil in a wok or frying pan, add and sauté the onion, ginger, shallot, garlic and celery until fragrant. Stir in the chillies and shrimps, then fry for a while. Pour in the sherry, broad bean paste, tomato ketchup, sugar, light soy sauce and sesame oil and heat through.

Blend the cornflour to a smooth paste with the water, then stir this into the shrimps and simmer for a further 2 minutes, or until thickened. Serve at once. *Serves 4*

Steamed Prawns in Black Bean Sauce

12 whole uncooked king prawns
5 teaspoons black bean paste
5 teaspoons light soy sauce
1 tablespoon sugar
pinch of pepper
3 cloves garlic, crushed
2 tablespoons corn oil
1 spring onion, shredded
1 parsley sprig
1 teaspoon sesame oil (optional)
GARNISH
1 spring onion
½ red pepper
2 thin slices fresh root ginger
1 teaspoon sesame oil (optional)

Peel, devein and rinse the prawns. Cut each prawn in half and arrange the pieces on a platter.

Mix the black bean paste, light soy sauce, sugar, pepper and garlic. Coat the prawns evenly with this mixture, then add the corn oil and mix thoroughly. Place the prawns in a steamer and cook them over boiling water for 5–6 minutes.

For the garnish, cut the spring onion in half widthways, then cut it in half again lengthways. Place the cut side down on a board and finely shred both pieces. Remove any stalk and seeds from the pepper, then cut away any pith. Cut the pepper into very fine strips and cut across these to make short pieces. Cut the ginger into fine shreds.

Mix all the shredded garnishing ingredients and sprinkle them down the middle of the prawn mixture. Sprinkle with sesame oil if you like and serve immediately. *Serves 4*

Sautéed Shrimps with Peas

100 g/4 oz shelled peas
2 tablespoons oil
½ teaspoon finely shredded
    fresh root ginger
1 shallot, sliced
1 clove garlic, sliced
275 g/10 oz peeled cooked
    shrimps
1 teaspoon dry sherry
½ teaspoon salt
pinch of pepper
1 teaspoon sugar
1 teaspoon soy sauce
½ teaspoon sesame oil
1 teaspoon cornflour
2 tablespoons water

Blanch the peas in boiling salted water for 2 minutes. Drain and rinse under cold water, then set aside in a bowl of iced water until required.

Heat the oil in a wok and sauté the ginger, shallot and garlic until fragrant. Stir in the peas and shrimps and stir-fry quickly. Pour in the sherry, salt and pepper, sugar, soy sauce and sesame oil. Blend the cornflour with the water,

then pour it into the pan and bring to the boil. Simmer for 2 minutes, toss the ingredients to make sure they are well mixed and serve at once. *Serves 4*

Note: If shrimps are not easily available then peeled cooked prawns can be used instead. Use fresh or frozen prawns but do not allow frozen prawns to defrost before cooking.

Although fresh peas give by far the best flavour, frozen peas can be used instead. Again, they should not be defrosted before cooking.

Deep Fried Fishballs

350 g/12 oz white fish fillet
½ teaspoon salt
½ teaspoon sugar
1 teaspoon light soy sauce
pinch of pepper
½ teaspoon sesame oil
1 teaspoon cornflour plus extra
    for coating
2 tablespoons water
2 Chinese dried mushrooms
15 g/½ oz dried shrimps
50 g/2 oz pork fat
1 tablespoon chopped parsley
1 tablespoon chopped chives
oil for deep frying
TO SERVE
1 small lettuce, shredded
1 large carrot, shredded
flat-leafed parsley

Skin the fish and mince it finely (a food processor is useful for this). Place the minced fillets in a mixing bowl, add the salt and sugar, then pound the ingredients so that they are thoroughly mixed. Mix in the soy sauce, a pinch of pepper, the sesame oil, 1 teaspoon cornflour and

the water. The ingredients should be well bound together.

Soak the mushrooms in cold water for 10 minutes, then drain them and steam them over boiling water for 15 minutes. Remove the stalks, then dice the mushroom caps. Soak, drain and chop the dried shrimps.

Blanch the pork fat in boiling water for 2 minutes, then drain and dice it. Mix the pork into the fish, add the chopped herbs, mushrooms and shrimps.

Mould the fish mixture into small balls about the size of walnuts. Coat these generously in cornflour.

Heat the oil for deep frying to 190 c/375 f, then drop in the fishballs and deep fry until golden. Drain on absorbent kitchen paper. Serve the hot fishballs on the mixed lettuce and carrot, topped with a leaf of parsley. *Serves 4*

Fishballs in Satay Sauce

2 tablespoons oil
2 cloves garlic, crushed
1 teaspoon finely shredded
  fresh root ginger
175 g/6 oz Fishballs (page 224)
1 small onion, chopped
1 green pepper, deseeded and
  cut into cubes
2 red chillies, deseeded and
  chopped
2 tablespoons Satay Sauce
  (page 228)
1 teaspoon cornflour
50 ml/2 fl oz water
1 teaspoon dry sherry
1 teaspoon light soy sauce
1 teaspoon sugar
pinch of pepper
a few drops of sesame oil
parsley sprigs to garnish

Heat the oil in a wok or frying pan, then add the garlic and ginger and sauté until fragrant. Stir in the fishballs, onion, green pepper and chillies and stir-fry until lightly cooked. Stir in the satay sauce and cook until well mixed.

Mix the cornflour with the water and all the remaining ingredients. Pour this mixture into the pan and bring to the boil, stirring continuously. Simmer for 2 minutes, until thickened, give the ingredients a good stir, then serve at once, garnished with parsley sprigs. *Serves 4*

Poached Chicken

2 tablespoons dry sherry
salt
2 tablespoons Ginger Juice
(page 227)
4 teaspoons sugar
1 (1.5-kg/3-lb) chicken
sesame oil for brushing
25 g/1 oz fresh root ginger
1 bunch spring onions,
chopped
2 tablespoons hot oil

Bring a large saucepan of water to the boil. Add the sherry, 2 tablespoons salt, the ginger juice and 3 teaspoons of the sugar. Lower the chicken into the pan and bring back to the boil. Simmer for 1 hour, then allow to cool for 20 minutes in the pan.

Drain the chicken and refresh it under cold running water. Drain thoroughly and dry the bird on absorbent kitchen paper. Brush the bird all over with a little sesame oil and chop it into pieces. Arrange the chicken back into its original shape on a serving platter.

Mix the ginger, spring onions, remaining sugar, hot oil and salt to taste. Serve this dip with the cold chicken. *Serves 4–6*

Note: This is the traditional way in which whole cooked chickens are served. The cooked bird is chopped with a meat cleaver, without removing any of the bones, then re-formed to resemble its original shape.

However, if you prefer to serve the meat off the bone, simply slice it off when the chicken is cool enough to handle. Cut it into bite-sized pieces and arrange these on a platter to serve.

Stewed Chicken in Oyster Sauce

450 g/1 lb chicken thighs
2 tablespoons plus ½ teaspoon
dark soy sauce
10 small Chinese dried
mushrooms
100 g/4 oz carrots
2 tablespoons oil plus oil for
deep frying
a few slices fresh root ginger,
grated
2 shallots, finely chopped
2 cloves garlic, crushed
250 ml/8 fl oz chicken stock
2 teaspoons dry sherry
1 teaspoon light soy sauce
2 tablespoons oyster sauce
1 teaspoon sugar
pepper
2 teaspoons cornflour
2 tablespoons water
parsley sprigs to garnish

Coat the chicken with 2 tablespoons of the dark soy sauce and set aside. Soak the mushrooms in cold water for 15 minutes, then drain and steam them for 10 minutes. Carve pieces out of the carrots in a decorative pattern and score the sides, then slice them fairly thinly.

Heat the oil for deep frying to 190 c/375 f, add the chicken and deep fry until golden brown. Drain on absorbent kitchen paper. Heat the 2 tablespoons oil in a wok, add the ginger, shallots and garlic and cook until fragrant. Pour in the stock, sherry, light soy sauce and oyster sauce, sugar, remaining dark soy sauce and a pinch of pepper.

Add the chicken to the sauce with the mushrooms and carrots. Simmer for 5 minutes, then remove the chicken. Chop the portions into chunks and arrange them on a warmed serving platter. Keep hot.

Blend the cornflour with the water, pour the mixture into the sauce and simmer for 2 minutes. Pour the sauce over the chicken, add a garnish of parsley and serve at once. *Serves 4–6*

Chicken and Mushrooms in Yunnan Pot

*50 g/2 oz small Chinese dried
  mushrooms*
salt
½ teaspoon sugar
1 tablespoon oil
1 small chicken, skinned
*2 medium-thick slices fresh
  root ginger*

Soak the mushrooms in hot water until soft. Drain them and reserve the liquid. Cut off the stalks, then marinate the caps with ½ teaspoon each of salt and sugar and the oil. Chop the chicken in half. Blanch the bird in boiling water for 1 minute, then drain and refresh it under cold water.

Place the chicken in a yunnan pot, or a large heatproof casserole with a lid. Pour in the reserved mushroom stock and enough boiling water to cover the chicken. Add the ginger and stand the pot over a saucepan of boiling water. Cover closely and steam for 1½ hours. Top up the boiling water in the saucepan as necessary during cooking.

Add the mushrooms to the chicken to cook for a further 30 minutes. Add seasoning to taste and serve straight from the pot. *Serves 4–6*

Chicken with Abalone

1 small chicken, skinned
225 g/8 oz pork, trimmed of fat
3 red dates
*1 (454-g/1-lb) can abalone,
  drained*
*3 medium-thick slices fresh
  root ginger, finely chopped*
1 teaspoon dry sherry
1¼ teaspoons salt

Blanch the chicken in boiling water for 1 minute, then drain and refresh it under cold water. Cut the pork into slices, discarding any bone. Slit the dates and remove their seeds.

Place the chicken in a large heatproof casserole or mixing bowl (see note below). Add the abalone, pork, dates and ginger. Pour in enough boiling water to cover the bird, then stand the pot over a saucepan of boiling water. Simmer for 1½ hours.

At the end of the cooking time stir in the sherry and salt, then serve straight from the pot. *Serves 4–6*

Note: The vessel used to cook the chicken in this recipe must be large enough to hold the whole chicken as well as the other ingredients and enough boiling water to cover them. A very large heavy mixing bowl is ideal and you will need a big saucepan over which to stand the bowl. Cover the bowl with a double thickness of cooking foil to prevent loss of heat during cooking.

If you really do not have a suitable vessel for holding the chicken, then it can be simmered very gently in a heavy-based saucepan.

Herbal Chicken Pot

½ chicken, skinned
50 g/2 oz boiling bacon
25 g/1 oz red berries (kei chi)
50 g/2 oz wai san
15 g/½ oz dried longan
2 teaspoons salt

Blanch the chicken in boiling water for 2 minutes. Drain and refresh under cold water. Blanch and slice the bacon. Wash the red berries, wai san and longan.

Place the chicken with all the other ingredients in a yunnan pot or heatproof casserole. Pour in enough boiling water to cover the chicken. Cover and place on top of a saucepan of boiling water. Steam for 2 hours remembering to top up the water in the saucepan as necessary. Add salt to taste to the cooked chicken and serve hot. *Serves 4*

Yunnan Pot: A yunnan pot is shown in the picture. It is a type of casserole which has a funnel-shaped inlet into the middle of the container. The covered pot is put over a saucepan of boiling water to cook. Steam flows up through the funnel and into the pot, so increasing the heat which reaches the food. This method of cooking is a way of steaming moist, casserole-type dishes.

Chicken and Taro Casserole

350 g/12 oz chicken thighs
2 tablespoons Ginger Juice (page 227)
4 tablespoons dry sherry
2 tablespoons cornflour
2 tablespoons light soy sauce
275 g/10 oz taro or potatoes
4 tablespoons oil plus oil for deep frying
50 ml/2 fl oz coconut milk (page 68)
100 ml/4 fl oz chicken stock
2 medium-thick slices fresh root ginger
2 cloves garlic, crushed
salt and pepper
1 teaspoon sugar
1 teaspoon sesame oil
3 tablespoons canned evaporated milk
1 spring onion, roughly chopped, to garnish

Chop the chicken into pieces. Marinate them with the ginger juice, 2 tablespoons sherry, cornflour and light soy sauce for 30 minutes.

Peel the taro or potatoes and cut it into thick slices. Heat the oil for deep frying to 190 c/375 f and deep fry the vegetable until golden. Drain on absorbent kitchen paper. Deep fry the chicken pieces until just cooked but not well browned. Drain on absorbent kitchen paper and set aside.

Heat 2 tablespoons of the oil in a flameproof casserole. Add half the remaining sherry, the coconut milk, taro or potato and half the stock. Simmer for a few minutes.

In a separate wok or frying pan, heat the remaining 2 tablespoons oil, then sauté the ginger and garlic until fragrant. Stir in the chicken and cook until browned. Sprinkle in the remaining sherry and add the rest of the stock. Stir in seasoning to taste, the sugar and the sesame oil. Transfer to the casserole and mix well. Cook until the pieces of taro or potatoes are tender.

Stir in the evaporated milk and simmer for a while. Serve the casserole hot, garnished with the spring onion. *Serves 4*

Chicken Thigh and Mushroom

50 g/2 oz Chinese dried
  mushrooms
2 tablespoons oil plus oil for
  marinating and deep frying
salt and pepper
2 teaspoons sugar plus a little
  for marinating
4 chicken thighs
2 tablespoons Ginger Juice
  (page 227)
3 tablespoons dry sherry
2½ teaspoons light soy sauce
2 teaspoons cornflour
¼ teaspoon monosodium
  glutamate
1 teaspoon sesame oil
15 g/½ oz fresh root ginger,
  grated
2 shallots, sliced
2 cloves garlic, sliced
1 (213-g/7½-oz) can button
  mushrooms, drained
1 teaspoon oyster sauce
2 tablespoons water
1 spring onion, roughly
  chopped, to garnish

Rinse, then soak the dried
mushrooms until soft – about
15 minutes. Drain the
mushrooms and squeeze them
dry. Reserve the liquid, then
marinate the mushrooms for
10 minutes with a little oil,
salt and sugar. Steam the
mushrooms for 12 minutes,
then blanch them for 2
minutes and refresh them
under cold water.

Chop the chicken thighs
into bite-sized pieces.
Marinate with 2 tablespoons
each of ginger juice and
sherry for 30 minutes. Mix in
1½ teaspoons light soy sauce, 1
teaspoon each of sugar and
cornflour; ¼ teaspoon each of
pepper and monosodium
glutamate and the sesame oil.
Set aside to marinate for a
further 30 minutes.

Heat the oil for deep frying
to 190 c/375 f. Add the
marinated chicken and fry
until half cooked. Remove
and drain on absorbent
kitchen paper.

Heat the 2 tablespoons oil
in a wok or heavy-based
saucepan. Sauté the ginger,
shallots and garlic until
fragrant. Stir in the chicken
and fry thoroughly. Add the
Chinese mushrooms and
remaining sherry. Pour in the
reserved water. Cover and
simmer for 10 minutes.

Mix in the button
mushrooms and add the
remaining light soy sauce,
oyster sauce, remaining sugar
and salt to taste. Blend the
remaining cornflour to a
smooth cream with the water,
then stir it into the sauce.
Simmer for a further 2
minutes and serve hot,
sprinkled with the spring
onion. *Serves 4*

Chinese casseroles: Casseroles
such as this one are especially
popular in winter. Many hot
Cantonese dishes are
casseroles which are kept hot
in the traditional thick clay
pots.

Terracotta pots with curved
bottoms are used, as too are
coarse clay pots with glazed
interiors. Many of the pots are
beautifully decorated and
most attractive for serving
food, as you will see from the
picture on page 63.

Chicken in Rich Soy Sauce

1 chicken
3 tablespoons Ginger Juice
* (page 227)*
50 ml/2 fl oz dry sherry
2 tablespoons cornflour
3 tablespoons oil plus oil for
* deep frying*
5 medium-thick slices fresh
* root ginger*
2 shallots, chopped
50 ml/2 fl oz dark soy sauce
3 tablespoons sugar
pepper
a few drops of sesame oil
1 spring onion, shredded, to
* garnish*

Cut the chicken into small portions. Marinate these with the ginger juice and 2 tablespoons each of the sherry and cornflour for 30 minutes.

Heat the oil for deep frying to 190 c/375 F then fry the chicken pieces until lightly cooked.

Heat the remaining oil in a heavy-based saucepan or flame-proof casserole. Add the ginger and shallots and sauté for a while. Stir in the chicken, then sprinkle in the remaining sherry, dark soy sauce, sugar and pepper. Stir in the sesame oil, then cover the pan and serve hot, sprinkled with the spring onion. *Serves 4–6*

To cut up the chicken: For this recipe the chicken should be chopped into pieces on the bone. If you have a heavy meat cleaver and a very thick chopping board, then these are ideal utensils.

Alternatively, use a good sharp knife and a steak mallet or heavy rolling pin to tap the blade through the bones. A pair of poultry scissors is also useful.

Chicken Casserole with Mushrooms and Bamboo Shoots

350 g/12 oz chicken thighs
1 tablespoon Ginger Juice
* (page 227)*
5 teaspoons dry sherry
1 tablespoon cornflour
50 g/2 oz Chinese dried
* mushrooms*
2 tablespoons oil plus a little
* for marinating*
salt and pepper
1 teaspoon sugar
1 (227-g/8-oz) can bamboo
* shoots*
3 medium-thick slices fresh
* root ginger, finely chopped*
3 shallots, finely chopped
2 cloves garlic, crushed
1 teaspoon oyster sauce
½ teaspoon dark soy sauce
a few drops of sesame oil
2 spring onions, roughly
* chopped*

Chop the chicken joints into bite-sized pieces. Marinate these for 30 minutes in the ginger juice, 1 tablespoon of the sherry and the cornflour.

Wash and soak the mushrooms in enough boiling water to cover for 1 hour. Trim off the stalks. Squeeze the excess water from the mushrooms and reserve it with all the liquid from soaking. Marinate the mushrooms with a little oil, salt to taste and a little of the sugar. After about 10 minutes steam the mushrooms for 12 minutes over boiling water.

Cut the bamboo shoots into wedges. Heat the 2 tablespoons oil in a flameproof casserole, then sauté the ginger, shallots and garlic until fragrant. Add the chicken and fry for 2 minutes. Stir in the mushrooms and bamboo shoots. Pour in the remaining sherry, mushroom liquid, oyster sauce, dark soy sauce, sesame oil, remaining sugar and seasoning to taste. Bring to the boil. Cover and simmer for 10 minutes. Serve hot, garnished with the spring onions. *Serves 4*

Che Che Chicken

350 g/12 oz chicken thighs
4 teaspoons cornflour
4 teaspoons ground bean paste
4 teaspoons Ginger Juice (page 227)
6 teaspoons dry sherry
75 g/3 oz pig's liver
3 Chinese dried mushrooms
2 tablespoons oil
75 g/3 oz shallots
3 tablespoons grated fresh root ginger
2 cloves garlic, crushed
100 ml/4 fl oz chicken stock
salt
1 tablespoon sugar

Chop the chicken into bite-sized pieces. Mix 1 tablespoon each of cornflour, ground bean paste, ginger juice and the sherry. Pour this over the chicken, mix well and set aside to marinate for 30 minutes.

Slice the liver and marinate it with the remaining cornflour and ginger juice and 1 teaspoon of the remaining sherry. Set aside for 30 minutes.

Blanch the liver in boiling water for a few seconds, then refresh under cold water. Soak the mushrooms in cold water for 15 minutes, then drain and steam them for 15 minutes. Remove the stalks and slice the caps.

Heat the oil in a flameproof casserole. Add the shallots, ginger and garlic and cook until fragrant. Stir in the chicken and sprinkle in the last of the sherry. Pour in the stock, remaining ground bean paste, salt to taste and the sugar. Bring to the boil, then simmer for 10 minutes. Stir in the liver, spring onions and mushrooms and cook for a further 5 minutes. Serve at once. *Serves 4–6*

Chicken in Sweet Wine

1 small chicken
50 ml/2 fl oz plus 1 teaspoon Ginger Juice (page 227)
600 ml/1 pint medium-dry white wine
2½ teaspoons cornflour
100 g/4 oz pig's liver
100 g/4 oz lean boneless pork, sliced
1 teaspoon light soy sauce
2 tablespoons water
100 g/4 oz unsalted peanuts
25 g/1 oz black fungus
2 tablespoons oil
1 clove garlic, crushed
2 shallots, chopped
225 g/8 oz fresh root ginger, grated
1 teaspoon sugar
salt

Chop the chicken into pieces and marinate them for 30 minutes with 50 ml/2 fl oz of the ginger juice, 50 ml/2 fl oz of the wine and 1 teaspoon of the cornflour.

Slice the liver and marinate it with the 1 teaspoon ginger juice, 1 teaspoon of the wine and 1 teaspoon of the cornflour for 30 minutes.

Marinate the pork with the light soy sauce, ½ teaspoon of the cornflour and the water for 10 minutes. Soak the peanuts in cold water for 30 minutes. Wash and soak the black fungus for a similar time.

Heat the oil in a heavy-based saucepan, add the garlic and shallots and fry for a while. Add the ginger, then the chicken and nuts and sauté for 5 minutes. Pour in the remaining wine and bring back to the boil. Add the fungus and simmer for 10 minutes.

Blanch the pork and liver in boiling water for a minute, then add them to the chicken with the sugar and salt to taste and continue simmering for 5 minutes. Serve hot. *Serves 6*

Steamed Chicken in Yellow Wine

1 (1.5-kg/3-lb) chicken
2 teaspoons salt
450 ml/¾ pint yellow wine or
 sweet sherry
2.5-cm/1-in piece fresh root
 ginger, grated
3 shallots, grated
2 star anise, ground
cayenne pepper
450 ml/¾ pint chicken stock
2 spring onions
3 tablespoons sugar
1 teaspoon Ginger Juice (page
 227)

Rub the chicken both inside and out with 1 teaspoon of the salt and 2 tablespoons of the sherry. Mix the ginger, shallots and ground anise and put the mixture inside the chicken. Set aside to marinate for 30 minutes. Steam the bird on a deep plate in a steamer over a saucepan of boiling water for 1 hour.

Remove the chicken from the steamer, reserve the liquid on the plate and from inside the bird, but discard the ground ingredients from inside, scraping them out with a spoon.

Heat a wok or frying pan and add a generous sprinkling of cayenne pepper with the remaining salt. Dry cook for a few minutes, then rub this seasoning over the chicken. Set aside for 1 hour.

In a large bowl, mix the remaining sherry, stock, reserved chicken liquid, spring onions, sugar and ginger juice. Chop the chicken into joints then add these to the wine mixture and set aside to soak for 24 hours. Serve lightly chilled. *Serves 4–6*

Spicy Chicken in Pumpkin

1 (1.75-kg/4-lb) pumpkin
1 medium-thick slice fresh root
 ginger, chopped
2 spring onions, chopped
½ teaspoon spicy salt
1 tablespoon sugar
¼ teaspoon monosodium
 glutamate
1 tablespoon red wine
1 tablespoon fermented red
 bean curd
1½ teaspoons dark soy sauce
50 g/2 oz rice flour
1 small chicken, chopped into
 bite-sized pieces
3 tablespoons oil
GARNISH (optional)
1 lemon, sliced
2 tomatoes, sliced
1 white radish flower
a few canned straw
 mushrooms

Cut the top off the pumpkin in a decorative way to form a pot with a lid as shown in the picture. Remove all the seeds.

Mix the ginger and spring onions with spicy salt, sugar, monosodium glutamate, red wine, fermented red bean curd, soy sauce and the rice flour. Coat the pieces of chicken in this mixture and marinate for 15 minutes.

Heat the oil in a frying pan, add the chicken and cook until lightly browned. Transfer the chicken with its juices to the pumpkin and cover with the lid. Steam for 40 minutes over boiling water, then serve hot with plain rice. If you like, the pumpkin can be served with an oriental garnish of halved lemon and tomato slices, arranged to represent roses, a carved flower and straw mushrooms. In the picture the pumpkin is surrounded by crisp fried shredded seaweed. *Serves 6*

CHINESE TITLE

The Chinese title of this traditional recipe, passed on from generation to generation, means A Long Life to Everyone. *This dish is a symbol of something good.*

Steamed Chicken with Mushrooms

2 chicken joints
1 teaspoon Ginger Juice (page 227)
1½ teaspoons dry sherry
salt and pepper
1 teaspoon sugar
2 tablespoons oyster sauce
1 teaspoon soy sauce
1 teaspoon cornflour
25 g/1 oz Chinese dried mushrooms
½ teaspoon sesame oil
7 g/¼ oz black fungus
2 tablespoons water
1 tablespoon oil
GARNISH
1 tablespoon shredded fresh root ginger
1 tablespoon shredded spring onion
flat-leafed parsley sprigs

Chop the chicken into bite-sized pieces. Marinate these with the ginger juice and 1 teaspoon of the sherry for 20 minutes. Mix in seasoning to taste, the sugar, remaining sherry, oyster sauce, soy sauce and cornflour, then set aside to marinate for another 20 minutes.

Soak the mushrooms in boiling water for 30 minutes. Squeeze out the excess water and mix it with the sesame oil. Soak the black fungus in water until soft.

Place the marinated chicken, mushrooms and fungus on a deep platter. Add the water and oil. Put into a steamer and cook over boiling water for 30 minutes, or until thoroughly cooked. Serve the chicken hot, sprinkle with the shredded ginger, spring onions and parsley. *Serves 4*

Chicken Kung Po

2 boneless chicken breasts
1 tablespoon Ginger Juice (page 227)
2 tablespoons dry sherry
salt and pepper
2 teaspoons cornflour
½ egg white
2 tablespoons oil plus oil for deep frying
50 g/2 oz unroasted peanuts
3 medium-thick slices fresh root ginger, shredded
2 cloves garlic, chopped
10 dried red chillies, deseeded and chopped
3 tablespoons water
1 tablespoon light soy sauce
1½ teaspoons vinegar
1 teaspoon sugar
½ teaspoon sesame oil
a few glacé cherries, roughly chopped, to garnish (optional)

Dice and marinate the chicken with the ginger juice, 1 tablespoon of the sherry, a pinch each of salt and pepper, 1 teaspoon cornflour and the egg white for 30 minutes.

Heat the oil for deep frying to 190 c/375 F and fry the chicken until lightly browned. Drain on absorbent kitchen paper and set aside.

Heat a wok or heavy-based frying pan, then dry fry the peanuts until brown. Remove from the pan and set aside. Add the 2 tablespoons oil and sauté the ginger, garlic and chillies together until fragrant. Stir in the chicken, then pour in the remaining sherry, 2 tablespoons of the water, soy sauce, vinegar and sugar.

While the mixture is heating, blend the remaining cornflour with the remaining water, then pour it into the pan and bring to the boil. Simmer for 2 minutes, toss in the sesame oil and serve at once, sprinkled with the cherries if you like. *Serves 4*

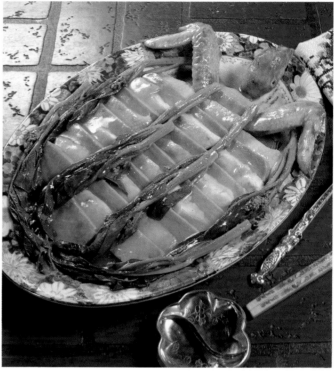

Curried Chicken

1 (1.5-kg/3-lb) chicken
*2 tablespoons Ginger Juice
  (page 227)*
2 tablespoons dry sherry
2 tablespoons cornflour
2–3 tablespoons curry powder
*5 tablespoons oil plus oil for
  deep frying*
2 large onions, grated
1 clove garlic, crushed
*2 teaspoons blachan (shrimp
  paste)*
1 tablespoon ground coriander
1 teaspoon turmeric
10-cm/4-in piece lemon grass
450 g/1 lb potatoes, cooked
300 ml/½ pint water
1 teaspoon salt
1 tablespoon sugar
*½ teaspoon monosodium
  glutamate*
300 ml/½ pint coconut milk

Chop the chicken into chunks and marinate these in 1 tablespoon each of ginger juice, sherry, cornflour and curry powder for 30 minutes.

Heat the oil for deep frying to 190 c/375 f, then quickly fry the chicken pieces. Drain and set aside.

Mix 2 tablespoons of the oil into the rest of the curry powder and stir into a thick paste. Sauté the grated onions in the remaining oil until fragrant, then add the curry paste. Mix well. Pound the garlic and blachan into a smooth paste. Mix this into the sautéed curry paste and onion. Add the coriander and turmeric. Stir-fry until mixed.

Put in the chicken pieces and lemon grass; stir and sprinkle in the remaining sherry. Add the potatoes, water, salt, sugar and monosodium glutamate, then simmer for 20 minutes. Stir in the coconut milk and bring to the boil again. Serve at once. *Serves 4–6*

To make coconut milk: This can either be purchased in cans or in the form of a block, both for diluting according to the instructions on the packet, or it can be made from grated fresh coconut or desiccated coconut. Put the coconut in a bowl, cover with boiling water; cool. Drain, squeezing out all the liquid – this is the coconut milk.

Boneless Chicken with Ham

salt and pepper
3 teaspoons dry sherry
*3 medium-thick slices fresh
  root ginger*
3 teaspoons chopped chives
2 star anise
1 (1.75-kg/3½-lb) chicken
*100 g/4 oz Chinese ham or
  Virginia ham in one piece*
*275 g/10 oz Chinese green
  vegetables, spring greens or
  broccoli*
2 tablespoons oil
2 shallots
150 ml/¼ pint chicken stock
½ teaspoon sugar
1 teaspoon light soy sauce
½ teaspoon sesame oil
2 teaspoons cornflour
2 tablespoons water

Rub 1 teaspoon each of salt and sherry over the chicken skin. Mix a further 1 teaspoon salt, 1 slice of ginger, 1 teaspoon chives and 1 star anise. Place this mixture inside the chicken. Place the chicken on a deep plate in a steamer and cook over boiling water for 50–60 minutes. Top up the boiling water as necessary during cooking. Leave to cool.

Remove all the meat from the chicken bones and cut it into bite-sized pieces.

Blanch the ham in boiling water for a minute. Refresh and drain. Cut into pieces about the same size as the chicken. Arrange the ham and chicken alternately on an oval platter.

Blanch the green vegetables in boiling salted water for 1 minute. Drain thoroughly and arrange round the chicken and ham. Keep hot.

Heat the oil in a wok or frying pan. Sauté the shallots until browned then remove and discard. Pour in the last of the sherry and the stock and season to taste. Stir in the sugar, soy sauce and sesame oil, bring to the boil, then reduce the heat. Blend the cornflour with the water, stir into the sauce and simmer for 2 minutes. Pour this over the meat and vegetables and serve. *Serves 4–6*

Shredded Ham in Chicken Wing

750 ml/1¼ pints water
3 medium-thick slices fresh
    root ginger
5 teaspoons dry sherry
12 chicken wings
350 g/12 oz Chinese ham or
    Virginia ham, shredded
12 carrots, grated
1 tablespoon oil
1 shallot, chopped
1 clove garlic, crushed
½ teaspoon salt
½ teaspoon sugar
1 teaspoon light soy sauce
pepper
½ teaspoon sesame oil
225 g/8 oz Chinese vegetables
    or spring greens
1 teaspoon cornflour
1 tablespoon water

Heat the water, 1 slice of the
ginger and 3 teaspoons sherry
to boiling point. Put the
chicken wings into the boiling
water and cook for 5–6
minutes. Drain and rinse
under cold water. Reserve the
stock. Cut both ends off the

wings. Remove the two bones
from the middle part of the
wings. Fill the holes with ham
and carrot. Arrange on a deep
plate. Heat the oil in a wok or
frying pan. Add the remaining
ginger, shallot and garlic and
fry until fragrant. Sprinkle
with the remaining sherry,
then add 100 ml/4 fl oz of the
reserved stock, the salt, sugar,
soy sauce, pepper and sesame
oil and bring to the boil. Pour
this stock on to the wings,
then steam for 20 minutes
over boiling water.

Meanwhile cook the
Chinese vegetables or spring
greens in boiling salted water
for just a few minutes. Drain
thoroughly and arrange on a
serving platter. Keep hot.

Heat the remaining stock
from cooking the chicken.
Blend the cornflour with the
water, stir this into the stock,
then bring to the boil and
simmer for 2 minutes. Season
to taste.

Arrange the chicken wings
on the serving platter, pour
over the sauce and serve at
once. *Serves 6*

Rice Crisp with Assorted Meat

3 slices canned abalone
3 slices cooked ham
2 chicken joints, cooked
50 g/2 oz peeled cooked
    shrimps (defrosted if frozen)
1 egg white
3 tablespoons cornflour
3 Chinese dried mushrooms
1 piece canned bamboo shoot
100 g/4 oz cooked long-grain
    rice
2 tablespoons dry sherry
750 ml/1¼ pints chicken stock
50 g/2 oz shelled peas
1½ teaspoons salt
1 teaspoon sugar
½ teaspoon monosodium
    glutamate
2 tablespoons dark soy sauce
½ teaspoon sesame oil
2 tablespoons water
oil for deep frying

Dice the abalone, ham and
chicken. Mix the shrimps with
the egg white and 1
tablespoon of the cornflour.
Soak the mushrooms in cold
water for about 15 minutes,
then drain and dice them.

Dice the bamboo shoot.

Press the rice into a baking
tin and cook in a moderately
hot oven (200 c, 400 f, gas 6)
for 30 minutes, or until lightly
browned.

Heat the sherry and stock,
then bring to the boil. Add all
the diced ingredients, the
shrimps and peas, then boil
for a few minutes. Stir in the
salt, sugar, monosodium
glutamate, soy sauce and
sesame oil. Blend the
remaining cornflour with the
water, then stir it into the
soup and simmer gently,
covered, for about 15–20
minutes.

Heat the oil for deep frying
to 190 c/375 f, add pieces of
the pressed rice and deep fry
until golden. Drain on
absorbent kitchen paper and
place in a bowl. Pour the
mixed meat into a serving
bowl. The crisp rice is served
in bowls with the meat
mixture poured over.
Serves 4–6

Sautéed Chicken with Ginger and Pineapple

175 g/6 oz boneless chicken
  breast
1 tablespoon Ginger Juice
  (page 227)
2 tablespoons dry sherry
salt and pepper
pinch of monosodium
  glutamate
1 teaspoon sugar
1½ teaspoons cornflour
¼ egg white
3 tablespoons oil
50 g/2 oz Pickled Ginger (page
  226)
50 g/2 oz fresh or canned
  pineapple
1 teaspoon grated fresh root
  ginger
1 shallot, sliced
2 cloves garlic, sliced
2 red or green chillies,
  deseeded and chopped
  (optional)
½ teaspoon light soy sauce
2 tablespoons chicken stock
1 teaspoon sesame oil
2 teaspoons water
2 spring onions, shredded

Slice the chicken. Marinate it
with 1 tablespoon each of
ginger juice and sherry; a
pinch each of salt and
monosodium glutamate; ¼
teaspoon sugar, 1 teaspoon
cornflour and ½ egg white. Set
aside for 30 minutes. Mix in 1
tablespoon oil and marinate
for a further 30 minutes.
   Slice the pickled ginger and
pineapple. Meanwhile, heat
the remaining 2 tablespoons
oil in a wok or frying pan.
Sauté the grated ginger,
shallot and garlic until
fragrant. Add the chillies and
fry for a while. Stir in the
pickled ginger, pineapple and
chicken. Sauté rapidly, then
pour in the remaining sherry.
Stir in seasoning to taste, the
remaining sugar, light soy
sauce, stock and sesame oil.
   Blend the rest of the
cornflour with the water. Stir
this into the sauce and bring
to the boil. Cook for 2
minutes. Serve hot, garnished
with the spring onions.
Serves 2–4

Diced Chicken with Sweet Paste

salt and pepper
1 teaspoon sugar
1 teaspoon cornflour
1 tablespoon dry sherry
1 teaspoon Ginger Juice (page
  227)
1 egg white
generous 2 tablespoons oil plus
  oil for deep frying
2 boneless chicken breasts,
  diced
50 g/2 oz unroasted cashew
  nuts
1 clove garlic, sliced
4½ teaspoons sweet paste
1 tablespoon soy sauce
½ teaspoon sesame oil
GARNISH
3 pineapple rings (fresh or
  canned), halved and
  trimmed to resemble
  butterfly wings
1 glacé cherry, quartered
a few shreds of green pepper

Mix ¼ teaspoon salt, ¼ teaspoon sugar, the cornflour, 1
teaspoon of the sherry, the
ginger juice, the egg white
and 1 teaspoon oil. Marinate

the chicken in the prepared
mixture for 20 minutes.
   Blanch the cashew nuts in
boiling water for 3 minutes,
then drain and set aside. Heat
the oil for deep frying to 190 C/
375 F. Add the chicken and
fry until half cooked. Drain
on absorbent kitchen paper
and set aside.
   Heat the 2 tablespoons oil
in a wok or frying pan. Sauté
the garlic and sweet paste for
a while, then stir in the diced
chicken. Pour in the
remaining sherry, soy sauce,
sugar and sesame oil. Stir in
the nuts and continue to sauté
for a few minutes.
   Serve hot, garnished with
the pineapple, cherry and
pepper in the shape of
butterflies. *Serves 4*

Sautéed Chicken in Preserved Black Bean Sauce

½ chicken
2 tablespoons Ginger Juice
  (page 227)
4 tablespoons dry sherry
2 tablespoons cornflour
3 tablespoons oil plus oil for
  deep frying
10 shallots, peeled
2 cloves garlic, crushed
1 tablespoon grated fresh root
  ginger
2 tablespoons preserved black
  bean paste
2 green peppers, deseeded and
  cut into chunks
2 red chillies, deseeded and
  chopped
100 ml/4 fl oz chicken stock
salt
2 teaspoons sugar
1 teaspoon dark soy sauce

Chop the chicken into bite-sized pieces. Marinate these with the ginger juice, 2 tablespoons of the sherry and the cornflour for 20 minutes.

Heat the oil for deep frying to 190 c/375 f, then deep fry the chicken until half cooked. Drain the pieces on absorbent kitchen paper and set aside.

Heat 2 tablespoons of the oil in a wok or frying pan. Sauté the shallots, garlic, ginger and black bean paste until fragrant. Add the peppers, chillies and chicken and quickly stir-fry until lightly browned.

Pour in the remaining sherry and stock, then simmer for 5 minutes. Season to taste, add the sugar and dark soy sauce, then pour in another 1 tablespoon of oil. Mix thoroughly and serve hot.
Serves 4–6

Sautéed Chicken with Shallot and Onion

1 large chicken portion (about 275 g/10 oz in weight)
1 tablespoon Ginger Juice (page 227)
5 teaspoons dry sherry
2½ teaspoons cornflour
salt and pepper
2 teaspoons sugar
50 ml/2 fl oz plus 8 teaspoons water
3 tablespoons oil
100 g/4 oz shallots
1 onion, cut into chunks
25 g/1 oz fresh root ginger, sliced
1½ teaspoons light soy sauce
1 teaspoon oyster sauce
GARNISH *(optional)*
½ large carrot
parsley sprigs

Remove the bones and score a criss-cross pattern on the chicken, then cut it into bite-sized pieces. Marinate these with the ginger juice and 1 tablespoon sherry, 1½ teaspoons of the cornflour, a pinch of salt, ½ teaspoon sugar

and 2 tablespoons water for 10 minutes. Add 1 tablespoon of the oil, mix well and allow to stand for a further 30 minutes. Cook the marinated chicken in boiling water for 3–4 minutes, then drain and set aside.

Heat the remaining oil in a wok or frying pan. Sauté the shallots, onion and ginger until fragrant. Add the chicken and fry until browned. Pour in the remaining sherry, add the 50 ml/2 fl oz water and season to taste. Stir in the light soy sauce, remaining sugar and oyster sauce.

Blend the last of the cornflour with 2 teaspoons water, stir this solution into the chicken and bring to the boil. Simmer for 2 minutes, then serve hot. Garnish the dish, if you like, with a halved carrot carved into the shape of a rose, and sprigs of parsley.
Serves 4–6

Shredded Chicken with Bamboo Shoots

75 g/3 oz canned bamboo shoot
75 g/3 oz carrot or canned baby corn
175 g/6 oz boneless chicken breast
salt and pepper
1 teaspoon sugar
1 teaspoon Ginger Juice (page 227)
2 teaspoons dry sherry
2 teaspoons cornflour
2 tablespoons oil plus oil for deep frying
2 cloves garlic, sliced
2 shallots, sliced
2 medium-thick slices fresh root ginger
50 ml/2 fl oz chicken stock
1 teaspoon oyster sauce
1 teaspoon light soy sauce
a few drops of sesame oil
2 teaspoons water
parsley sprigs to garnish

Slice the bamboo shoot and carrot if used. Blanch the

carrot in boiling water for a minute, then drain and rinse under cold water. Drain thoroughly. Shred and marinate the chicken with a pinch each of salt and sugar; 1 teaspoon each of ginger juice, sherry and cornflour for 30 minutes.

Heat the oil for deep frying to 190 C/375 F, add the chicken and deep fry until half cooked. Drain on absorbent kitchen paper and set aside. Heat the 2 tablespoons oil in a wok or frying pan. Sauté the garlic, shallots and ginger until fragrant. Add the bamboo shoot, carrots or corn and chicken, then sauté for a while. Pour in the remaining sherry, stock, oyster sauce, soy sauce, sesame oil and remaining sugar. Bring to the boil.

Blend the remaining cornflour with the water, stir this solution into the chicken and simmer for 2 minutes, or until thickened. Serve hot, garnished with parsley.
Serves 4

Sautéed Chicken with Green Pepper

½ chicken
1 tablespoon Ginger Juice (page 227)
4 teaspoons dry sherry
1 tablespoon cornflour
2 tablespoons oil plus oil for deep frying
2 cloves garlic, crushed
1 red chilli, deseeded and roughly chopped
2 medium-thick slices fresh root ginger
100 ml/4 fl oz chicken stock
salt and pepper
1 teaspoon sugar
2 teaspoons soy sauce
½ teaspoon sesame oil
2 spring onions, shredded

Chop the chicken into bite-sized pieces. Marinate these with 1 tablespoon each of ginger juice, sherry and cornflour for 30 minutes.

Heat the oil for deep frying to 190 c/375 f, then add the chicken and fry until half cooked. Drain on absorbent kitchen paper and set aside.

Heat the remaining 2 tablespoons oil in a frying pan. Sauté the garlic, chilli and ginger until fragrant, stir in the chicken and fry for a while. Sprinkle with the remaining sherry, pour in the stock, seasoning, sugar and soy sauce. Mix well. Cover and simmer over a low heat for 5 minutes or until the liquid has almost dried up.

Add the green pepper and fry for a few seconds. Drop in the sesame oil and spring onions, then serve hot.
Serves 4–6

Note: There are many different types of chillies; some are very hot, others quite mild. Red chillies tend to be quite hot and the seeds are particularly hot so these should be removed. If you like, try using a plump, smooth, small green chilli instead of the hot red one.

Shredded Chicken with Sesame Sauce

2 boneless chicken breasts
1 tablespoon Ginger Juice (page 227)
1 tablespoon dry sherry
3 tablespoons light soy sauce
½ Iceberg lettuce, shredded
100 g/4 oz carrots, shredded
1 cucumber, sliced
2 teaspoons chilli oil
1 teaspoon sesame oil
1 tablespoon sugar
pinch of pepper
50 ml/2 fl oz chicken stock
3 tablespoons sesame paste
1 teaspoon finely shredded fresh root ginger
1 teaspoon finely shredded spring onion

Marinate the chicken in the ginger juice, sherry and 1 tablespoon light soy sauce for 30 minutes. Cook the marinated chicken over boiling water for 15 minutes, then leave to cool.

Arrange the shredded lettuce, carrot and the cucumber on a serving platter.

Finely shred the cooked chicken, then arrange it on the prepared ingredients. Mix all the other ingredients apart from the shredded ginger and spring onion, then pour the mixture over the chicken. Top with the ginger and spring onion and serve lightly chilled.
Serves 4

Salt-baked Chicken Wings

10 chicken wings
2 tablespoons Ginger Juice (page 227)
2 tablespoons dry sherry
1 tablespoon grated fresh root ginger
1 tablespoon finely chopped spring onion
1 tablespoon ground star anise
1 teaspoon Spicy Salt (page 229)
1 teaspoon sugar
2 teaspoons light soy sauce
1 teaspoon ground ginger
a little dark soy sauce
greaseproof paper
3.5 kg/8 lb sea salt
parsley sprigs to garnish

Make a few cuts into each side of the chicken wings. Marinate them with the ginger juice and sherry for 30 minutes. Mix in the grated ginger, spring onion, star anise, spicy salt, sugar, light soy sauce and ground ginger. Brush each chicken wing with dark soy sauce.

Cut the greaseproof paper into 30-cm/12-in squares, allowing one for each chicken wing. Brush each square generously with oil. Place a wing in each piece of paper and wrap up securely.

Heat the salt in a wok or large flameproof casserole until very hot. Using a wooden spoon, make a well in the middle and place the chicken packets in it. Cover up with hot salt. Remove from the heat, or turn it off, and leave to bake for 15–20 minutes. Unwrap the chicken and wipe each with absorbent kitchen paper. Brush with sesame oil and serve, garnished with parsley.
Serves 6

Chicken Wings with Ginger and Spring Onions

450 g/1 lb chicken wings
5 teaspoons dry sherry
1 tablespoon Ginger Juice (page 227)
5 teaspoons cornflour
salt and pepper
1 teaspoon sugar
2 teaspoons light soy sauce
3 tablespoons oil
50 g/2 oz fresh root ginger, sliced
2 shallots, sliced
2 cloves garlic, sliced
1 bunch spring onions, shredded
150–250 ml/5–8 fl oz chicken stock
a few drops of dark soy sauce
1 teaspoon sesame oil
1 tablespoon water

Chop the chicken into bite-sized pieces, then marinate these with 1 tablespoon each of sherry, ginger juice and cornflour; ¼ teaspoon salt, and 1 teaspoon each of sugar and light soy sauce for 30 minutes.

Parboil the marinated chicken in boiling water for 2–3 minutes. Drain thoroughly.

Heat 2 tablespoons of the oil in a wok or frying pan, then sauté the ginger, shallots and garlic until fragrant. Add the chicken, half the spring onions and stir-fry for a while. Sprinkle in the remaining sherry; pour in the stock, remaining light and dark soy sauces, remaining sugar, a pinch of pepper and the sesame oil. Bring just to the boil, then reduce the heat, cover the pan and simmer for 5–10 minutes.

Blend the remaining cornflour with the water, then stir this mixture into the chicken and simmer for 2 minutes. Finally, stir in the last 1 tablespoon of oil and the remaining spring onions. Serve hot. *Serves 4–6*

Chicken Wings in Rich Salt Sauce

1 kg/2 lb chicken wings
4 star anise
6 medium-thick slices fresh
    root ginger
50 g/2 oz salt
1 chicken stock cube
50 g/2 oz sugar
50 ml/2 fl oz dry sherry
2 teaspoons sesame oil
5 spring onions, roughly
    chopped
parsley sprigs to garnish

Cook the chicken wings in boiling water for 10 minutes, then drain them thoroughly and soak them in iced water for 30 minutes.

Bring a large saucepan of water to the boil. Add the star anise, ginger, salt, stock cube, sugar, sherry, half the sesame oil and spring onions. Simmer gently for 20 minutes, then turn the heat off and add the chicken wings (drained thoroughly) to the hot liquid. Leave to soak for 30 minutes.

To serve, remove the chicken wings from the liquid, brush them lightly with the remaining sesame oil and serve garnished with parsley sprigs. *Serves 6*

Chrysanthemum Carrot

1 Use a large peeled carrot. Pare away a little carrot from the wide part to make the centre higher.

2 A wood carving knife can be obtained from hobby shops, otherwise use a small, pointed knife. Cut out a star shape from the middle of the carrot.

3 Working outwards, carve four pointed petals between the star points. Then carve a third and fourth row of petals.

4 Discard all the unwanted carrot and neaten the petals. Cut the flower off the carrot.

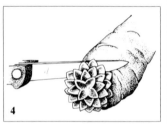

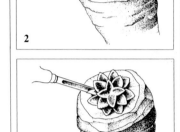

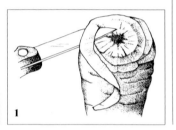

Stuffed Chicken Wing Casserole

15 chicken wings
2 tablespoons Ginger Juice
(page 227)
3 tablespoons dry sherry
50 g/2 oz carrots
2 sticks celery
2 tablespoons oil
3 medium-thick slices fresh
root ginger, grated
1 shallot, grated
1 clove garlic, crushed
1 (213-g/7½-oz) can button
mushrooms
100 ml/4 fl oz chicken stock
1 teaspoon cornflour
salt and pepper
1 teaspoon sugar
1 teaspoon light soy sauce
1 teaspoon oyster sauce
½ chicken stock cube
¼ teaspoon dark soy sauce
2 tablespoons water
1 teaspoon sesame oil

Cook the chicken wings for 5 minutes in boiling water seasoned with 2 tablespoons each of the ginger juice and sherry. Drain thoroughly, then chop off both ends of the wings and remove the bones from inside.

Cut the carrot and celery into matchstick pieces, then stuff these into the holes left by the bones in the chicken. Fill one gap with the celery, the other with carrot.

Heat the oil in a flameproof casserole. Sauté the ginger, shallot and garlic until fragrant, then add the chicken wings and mushrooms and fry for a while. Pour in the remaining sherry and the stock. Blend the cornflour with all the remaining ingredients and pour the mixture into the casserole, stirring it into the liquid around the chicken. Bring to the boil and cover, then simmer for a few minutes before serving. *Serves 4*

Chicken Wings in Black Bean Sauce

450 g/1 lb chicken wings
3 tablespoons Ginger Juice
(page 227)
4 tablespoons dry sherry
4½ teaspoons cornflour
pinch of monosodium
glutamate
3 tablespoons fermented black
bean paste
2 tablespoons oil
15 g/½ oz fresh root ginger,
sliced
25 g/1 oz shallots, finely
chopped
3 cloves garlic, crushed
1 large geen pepper, deseeded
and cut into chunks
50 g/2 oz red chillies, deseeded
and roughly chopped
250 ml/8 fl oz chicken stock
1 tablespoon light soy sauce
pinch of pepper
1½ teaspoons sugar
1 teaspoon sesame oil
2 spring onions, shredded

Chop each chicken wing into three portions. Marinate these for 30 minutes with the ginger juice, 3 tablespoons of the sherry, the cornflour and a pinch of monosodium glutamate. Add the black bean paste, mix thoroughly and continue to marinate for 30 minutes. Parboil the chicken and drain.

Heat the oil in a wok or frying pan. Sauté the ginger, shallots and garlic until fragrant. Stir in the peppers, chillies and chicken wings. Pour in the remaining sherry, stock, light soy sauce, pepper, sugar and sesame oil. Cover and simmer for 8 minutes. Stir in the spring onions and serve hot. *Serves 4*

Deep Fried Chicken Chops

1 (1.5-kg/3½-lb) chicken
1 tablespoon finely grated fresh root ginger
1 tablespoon grated shallot or onion
2 cloves garlic, crushed
2 tablespoons Ginger Juice (page 227)
3 tablespoons dry sherry
½ teaspoon salt
3 tablespoons sugar
2 tablespoons dark soy sauce
½ teaspoon pepper
1 teaspoon sesame oil
cornflour for coating
oil for deep frying
GARNISH
chilli tassel (page 45)
carrot flower (page 75)
parsley sprigs

Chop the chicken into small pieces: about eight pieces in all. Mix all the remaining ingredients apart from the cornflour and pour the mixture over the chicken. Allow to marinate for 30 minutes.

Drain the marinated chicken, reserving the marinade, and coat each piece generously in cornflour. Heat the oil for deep frying to 190 c/375 f, then add the chicken and cook until golden brown. Drain on absorbent kitchen paper and arrange on a heated serving dish.

Pour all the reserved marinade into a small saucepan and bring to the boil, then cook for a few minutes and pour into a small bowl to serve with the chicken. Add the garnish of a chilli tassel, carrot flower and parsley sprigs. If you like, keep the garnish simple and use just the chilli tassel with parsley. Serve at once.
Serves 4

Deep Fried Spicy Chicken

4 chicken thighs
2 tablespoons Ginger Juice (page 227)
2 tablespoons dry sherry
3 tablespoons five-spice powder
½ teaspoon pepper
2 tablespoons grated fresh root ginger
2 tablespoons grated shallot or onion
4 large cloves garlic, crushed
¼ teaspoon salt
3 tablespoons sugar
3 tablespoons light soy sauce
2 teaspoons sesame oil
1 egg
50 g/2 oz cornflour
oil for deep frying
parsley sprigs to garnish

Cut each thigh in half. Slash three or four cuts into each piece of chicken and hit firmly with the side of a meat cleaver or rolling pin. Marinate the chicken for 20 minutes in the ginger juice and sherry. Mix the five-spice powder, pepper, ginger, shallot, garlic, salt, sugar, light soy sauce and sesame oil. Pour over the chicken and marinate for another hour, turning the chicken every 15 minutes.

Beat the egg and add it to the chicken marinade; mix well. Dust each marinade-coated chicken portion generously with cornflour.

Heat the oil for deep frying to 190 c/375 f. Add the coated chicken and deep fry until golden. Drain on absorbent kitchen paper and serve hot, garnished with parsley. *Serves 4–6*

Chicken Wings in Cha Shiu Sauce

10 chicken wings
2 tablespoons Ginger Juice (page 227)
3 tablespoons dry sherry
1 teaspoon cornflour
3 medium-thick slices fresh root ginger
2 shallots
2 cloves garlic
2 tablespoons ground bean paste
2 tablespoons sweet paste
1 tablespoon sesame paste
1 teaspoon light soy sauce
2 tablespoons sugar
2 tablespoons oil
250 ml/8 fl oz chicken stock

Chop the chicken wings into large chunks, then blanch them in boiling water for 2–3 minutes. Refresh and drain thoroughly. Marinate these with the ginger juice, 2 tablespoons sherry and the cornflour for 30 minutes.

Mince the ginger, shallots and garlic together. Mix the ground bean paste, sweet paste, sesame paste, soy sauce and sugar with half the ginger, shallot and garlic mixture. Stir about one-third of this paste into the chicken marinade and mix well. Continue to marinate for 30 minutes.

Heat the oil in a wok or frying pan. Sauté the remaining ginger mixture until fragrant. Pour in the chicken wings with their marinade and sauté thoroughly. Stir in the remaining sherry and stock and simmer, covered, for 10 minutes. Remove the lid then stir-fry until the sauce nearly dries. Serve hot. *Serves 6*

Chicken in Hot Sesame Paste

275 g/10 oz boneless uncooked chicken, cut into chunks
1 tablespoon sesame paste
1 tablespoon hot mustard
salt and pepper
1 teaspoon sugar
2 teaspoons Ginger Juice (page 227)
1 teaspoon dry sherry
1 teaspoon soy sauce
1 egg, beaten
100 g/4 oz plus 1 teaspoon cornflour
oil for deep frying
GARNISH
1 carrot, carved into a flower shape (page 75)
parsley sprigs

Marinate the chicken in the sesame paste, mustard, seasoning, sugar, ginger juice, sherry and soy sauce for 30 minutes.

Stir in the beaten egg, mixing well. Coat the individual pieces of chicken, slightly drained of excess marinade, evenly and thickly with cornflour.

Heat the oil for deep frying to 190 c/375 F. Deep fry the chicken until golden brown – approximately 5 minutes. Drain on absorbent kitchen paper and leave to cool. Deep fry the chicken again for 1 minute. Drain off the excess oil, again on absorbent kitchen paper.

Serve at once, garnished with the carrot and parsley sprigs. *Serves 4–6*

Paper-wrapped Chicken and Prawns

225 g/8 oz boneless uncooked chicken
1 teaspoon sugar
½ teaspoon salt
½ teaspoon ground mixed spice
1 teaspoon Ginger Juice (page 227)
2 teaspoons dry sherry
1 teaspoon light soy sauce
2 teaspoons cornflour
a few drops of sesame oil
2 tablespoons water
1 tablespoon oil plus oil for deep frying and greasing
225 g/8 oz peeled cooked prawns (defrosted if frozen)
cellophane paper
100 g/4 oz carrots, finely shredded
6 spring onions, cut into 2.5-cm/1-in pieces
parsley sprigs

Slice the chicken into small thin pieces. Mix the sugar, salt and spice, ginger juice, sherry, light soy sauce, cornflour and sesame oil with the water and 1 tablespoon oil. Pour half of this over the chicken and set aside to marinate for 15 minutes. Marinate the prawns in the remaining seasonings.

Cut the cellophane paper into 15-cm/6-in squares; grease each with oil. Blanch the carrots in boiling water for a minute, then drain.

Place a slice of chicken on a piece of cellophane paper and add some spring onion. Wrap up and seal like an envelope. Place a prawn, parsley and shredded carrot on cellophane and wrap up in the same way as chicken. Continue until all the chicken and prawns are wrapped. Reserve the remaining shredded carrots and spring onions for garnish.

Heat the oil for deep frying to 190 c/375 F. Deep fry the packages, allowing about 3 minutes for the prawns and 7 minutes for the chicken. Arrange the cooked packages on a plate and garnish them with the shredded vegetables. Serve immediately.
Serves 4–6

Deep Fried Chicken in Lemon Sauce

2 boneless chicken breasts
1 tablespoon Ginger Juice (page 227)
4 teaspoons dry sherry
salt and pepper
2 tablespoons sugar
100 g/4 oz plus ½ teaspoon cornflour
1 teaspoon light soy sauce
1 egg, beaten
juice of 1 lemon
3 tablespoons vinegar
2 tablespoons custard powder
3 tablespoons water
2 tablespoons oil plus oil for deep frying
150 ml/¼ pint chicken stock
½ teaspoon sesame oil
GARNISH
1 small lemon, sliced
watercress sprigs
1 glacé cherry

Slice the chicken horizontally into thin fillets. Mix the ginger juice, 4 teaspoons of the sherry, ¼ teaspoon each of salt and sugar, 1 teaspoon cornflour and the light soy sauce. Marinate the chicken in this prepared mixture for 30 minutes.

Toss the marinated chicken in beaten egg, then coat it evenly and thickly with cornflour. Set aside.

Mix the lemon juice with the vinegar. Blend the custard powder with the ½ teaspoon cornflour and the water. Heat the 2 tablespoons oil in a saucepan. Sprinkle in the remaining sherry, add the stock, vinegar mixture, remaining sugar, and a pinch each of salt and pepper. Bring to the boil, reduce the heat and thicken the gravy with the custard and cornflour solution. Cover, leave over a very low heat and cook the chicken.

Heat the oil for deep frying to 190 c/375 F, add the chicken and fry until golden brown. Drain on absorbent kitchen paper and arrange on a heated serving plate. Stir the sesame oil into the sauce and pour it over the chicken.

Serve at once, garnished with twists of lemon, watercress and a cherry.
Serves 4

Bundled Duck with Ham and Mushrooms

1 (1.75-kg/4-lb) duck
1 tablespoon Ginger Juice
   (page 227)
6 tablespoons dry sherry
4 teaspoons cornflour
salt and pepper
2 teaspoons sugar
4 medium-thick slices fresh
   root ginger, finely chopped
5 spring onions
175 g/6 oz Chinese ham or
   Virginia ham
1 (227-g/8-oz) can bamboo
   shoots, drained
50 g/2 oz Chinese dried
   mushrooms
2 tablespoons oil
100 g/4 oz preserved vegetable
2 teaspoons soy sauce
50 ml/2 fl oz chicken stock
275 g/10 oz Chinese green
   vegetable or broccoli
2 cloves garlic
½ teaspoon sesame oil
1 tablespoon water

Blanch the duck in boiling water for 5 minutes. Drain and rinse under running water, then chop it into pieces. Marinate the chunks with 1 tablespoon each of ginger juice and sherry, and 3 teaspoons of the cornflour. Add salt to taste and the sugar. Leave for 30 minutes.

Half fill the saucepan with water. Add the ginger, spring onions and another 3 tablespoons of the sherry. Bring to the boil, put in the duck and blanch again for a few minutes. Drain.

Cut the ham into pieces about the same size as the duck, then blanch them in boiling water for a few minutes; drain.

Slice the bamboo shoots in the same way. Soak the mushrooms in cold water for 30 minutes, then squeeze out the excess. Marinate the mushroom caps with 1 tablespoon of the oil, salt and the remaining sugar. Cut each in half.

Put 1 piece each of duck, ham, bamboo shoot and mushroom together and tie up with the torn preserved vegetable. Arrange these bundles in a double boiler or on a deep plate in a steamer. Add seasoning to taste, the soy sauce and stock. Cover closely, then cook over boiling water for 30 minutes.

Cook the green vegetables in boiling salted water, then drain and arrange round the edge of a serving dish. Drain the duck bundles, reserving the stock, and arrange them in the middle of the dish. Keep hot.

Heat the remaining oil in a small saucepan. Sauté the garlic until fragrant then remove and discard. Sprinkle in the remaining sherry, the stock from the duck and the sesame oil. Blend the remaining cornflour with the water, stir this into the sauce and bring to the boil. Simmer for 2 minutes, then pour the sauce over the duck and serve at once. *Serves 4–6*

Sesame Chicken

175 g/6 oz boneless uncooked
  chicken, minced
1 teaspoon Ginger Juice (page
  227)
1 teaspoon dry sherry
2 tablespoons cornflour plus
  extra for coating
2 egg whites
salt and pepper
½ teaspoon sugar
½ teaspoon sesame oil
275 g/10 oz fat pork
75 g/3 oz sesame seeds
oil for deep frying
GARNISH
½ carrot, carved into a flower
  shape (page 75)
parsley sprigs
cayenne pepper to serve

Marinate the chicken for 10
minutes with the ginger juice,
sherry and cornflour, 1 of the
egg whites and a pinch of
pepper. Mix in seasoning to
taste, the sugar and sesame
oil.
  Blanch the pork in boiling
water for 5 minutes, then
drain and rinse it under cold
water. Drain thoroughly. Cut
the cold pork into 3.5 × 2.5-
cm/1½ × 1-in pieces. Dust
each piece with a little
cornflour, brush with the
remaining egg white, lightly
whisked, then coat thoroughly
in a layer of the minced
chicken. Coat in sesame
seeds, pressing them on very
firmly.
  Heat the oil for deep frying
to 190 c/375 f, then cook the
chicken shapes until golden
brown. Drain on absorbent
kitchen paper and arrange on
a serving dish. Garnish with a
carved carrot flower and
parsley sprigs. Serve with
cayenne. *Serves 6*

Bean sprouts with Roast Duck

225 g/8 oz bean sprouts
225 g/8 oz roasted duck (page
  83)
25 g/1 oz white part of leek
1 spring onion
2 tablespoons oil
1 clove garlic, crushed
½ teaspoon grated fresh root
  ginger
salt
pinch of sugar
1 teaspoon dry sherry
1 teaspoon light soy sauce
½ teaspoon sesame oil

Rinse and drain the bean
sprouts. Sort through them
and discard any which are
slightly discoloured. Cut all
the meat off the duck bones
and shred it finely. Cut the
white leek and spring onion
into fine strips.
  Heat the oil in a wok or
frying pan. Add the garlic and
cook until fragrant. Stir in the
bean sprouts and cook for a
few seconds, then remove
them from the pan. Add the
ginger and duck, cook for
several minutes, until the duck
is almost reheated, then
replace the bean sprouts.
Continue to cook, stirring,
add salt to taste, the sugar,
sherry, soy sauce, sesame oil
and leek. Toss well over fairly
high heat until all the
ingredients are hot, then
transfer the mixture to a
warmed serving dish and serve
at once. Plain boiled rice
should be served to
accompany the prepared dish.
Serves 4

Note: Sautéed Shrimps with
Peas (page 58) can be served
with this dish to make a light
meal for four people.

Peking Duck

*1 large duck (about 2.75 kg/
6 lb in weight)*
*3 tablespoons Ginger Juice
(page 227)*
4 tablespoons dry sherry
*3 tablespoons Spicy Salt (page
229)*
*½ teaspoon monosodium
glutamate*
250 ml/8 fl oz vinegar
40 g/1½ oz sugar
a little red food colouring
TO SERVE
*2 tablespoons bean paste,
ground*

Cut a 1-cm/½-in opening into
the skin at the back of duck's
neck. Blow through a drinking
straw between the skin and
the body until the skin
separates from the flesh and
the whole duck is swollen up.

Mix the ginger juice and 2
tablespoons of the sherry,
then pour this into the duck
through both openings. Put in
the spicy salt and monosodium
glutamate, then marinate for
20 minutes.

Blanch the duck for 1
minute in boiling water, then
drain it thoroughly. Bring the
vinegar and remaining sherry
to the boil. Stir in the sugar
and a little red food colouring.
Pour this evenly over the
duck, then hang it up to dry
for 8–10 hours, in a cool
place.

Roast the duck on a rack in
a hot oven (230 C, 450 F, gas
8) for 20 minutes. Turn the
bird and roast for a further 20
minutes. Remove from the
oven and slice the skin and
flesh to serve separately.
Serve with bean paste. Keep
the duck bones for soup, if
you like. *Serves 6*

Cantonese Roast Duck

1 large duck (about 2.75 kg/
6 lb in weight)
2 tablespoons Ginger Juice
(page 227)
2 tablespoons Spicy Salt (page
229)
4 shallots, grated
2 cloves garlic, crushed
2 star anise, ground
50 g/2 oz sugar
3 tablespoons ground bean
paste
2 tablespoons sweet paste
2 tablespoons sesame paste
1 tablespoon light soy sauce
1 teaspoon sesame oil
2 tablespoons dry sherry
250 ml/8 fl oz vinegar
pinch of red food colouring

Make a 1-cm/½-in cut at the
back of the duck's neck. Blow
between the skin and the flesh
(use a drinking straw for this)
until the skin is all separated
from the flesh. Rub the inside
of the duck with the ginger
juice and spicy salt. Set aside
to marinate for 20 minutes.
Mix the shallots, garlic,
ground star anise, half the
sugar, the three pastes, light
soy sauce, sesame oil and
sherry. Mix thoroughly, then
spoon the mixture into the
duck and secure the openings
with a skewer. Pour boiling
water over the outside of the
duck to tighten skin.

Bring the vinegar to the
boil. Add the remaining sugar
and red food colouring, and
stir until dissolved. Pour this
over the duck to coat it
evenly, then hang the bird to
dry for 10 hours. Cook the
duck in a hot oven (230 c,
450 f, gas 8) for 20 minutes.
Turn the duck over and roast
for another 15–20 minutes.
Remove and chop it into bite-
sized pieces, then serve hot.
Serves 6

Phoenix Cold Meat Combination

10 Chinese dried mushrooms
225 g/8 oz lamb's liver
2 tablespoons oil
4 boneless chicken breasts
450 g/1 lb pickled vegetable
450 g/1 lb Chinese ham or
Virginia ham, sliced
1 (425-g/15-oz) can abalone,
drained and sliced
2 large carrots
1 small cucumber
1 egg, hard-boiled
a few glacé cherries
a few peas
225 g/8 oz peeled cooked
prawns (defrosted if frozen)
parsley sprigs

Soak the mushrooms in cold
water for 30 minutes, then
steam for 15 minutes, slice
and set aside.

Sauté the liver in the oil,
turning once until cooked
through – about 20 minutes.
Remove and slice thinly.

Poach the chicken in boiling
water until cooked – about 30
minutes. Remove the skin,
then shred the meat. Arrange
some of the pickled vegetable
on a platter in the shape of
the phoenix's head. Add the
shredded chicken in the shape
of the neck, piling it on top of
the vegetable. Cut a small
piece of mushroom to
represent an eye.

Arrange more pickled
vegetable for the phoenix's
body. Arrange the liver, ham,
abalone and mushroom to
form the rows of the right
wing, then arrange rows of
liver, abalone and mushrooms
for the left side of the body.

Continue to arrange the
ingredients in this way to form
the shape of a phoenix as
shown in the picture.

Cut the carrots and
cucumber into long phoenix
feathers and arrange them at
the side of tail. Slice the egg
and cherries, then add these
with the peas to decorate each
piece of cucumber.

Lastly, arrange the prawns,
parsley and any remaining
chicken to form the garnish
above the head. Cover and
chill until served. *Serves 6–8*

Roast Duck with Lychees

24 fresh or canned lychees
100 ml/4 fl oz French dressing
½ roast duck (page 83)
a few drops of sesame oil

Shell, stone, wash and dry the fresh lychees. Drain canned lychees. Fill each piece of fruit with French dressing.

Cut all the roast duck off the bones and slice it into small pieces. Arrange these neatly on a platter and sprinkle the sesame oil on top.

Arrange the lychees on the duck, cover and chill lightly before serving. *Serves 3*

Fresh lychees: These are small and round, about the size of a damson, with slightly hairy, bright pink to red coloured knobbly skin. Cut in half, a shiny brown stone is revealed, surrounded by translucent white flesh. The lychees should be plump and not at all shrivelled or they will have darkening flesh which has lost its delicate flavour.

The lychees should be peeled and stoned for use. Their slightly tangy-sweet flavour is most complementary with rich meats and poultry – as in this recipe with duck. They also go very well with pork.

If you can find fresh lychees (they are sold in many good greengrocers and some supermarkets) they are better than the canned fruits.

Steamed Duck with Yam

1 (1.75-kg/4-lb) duck
2 tablespoons Ginger Juice (page 227)
4 tablespoons dry sherry
1 teaspoon Spicy Salt (page 229)
3 tablespoons dark soy sauce
4 tablespoons oil
3 tablespoons minced or finely chopped fresh root ginger
3 tablespoons finely chopped shallot
9 cloves garlic, crushed
1 kg/2 lb yam, washed and peeled
Duck Paste (see note)
2 tablespoons sugar
3 tablespoons water
100 g/4 oz button mushrooms

Wash and dry the duck. Coat the inside with the ginger juice and 2 tablespoons of the sherry. Marinate for 30 minutes. Rub the spicy salt thoroughly inside the duck. Brush the skin with the dark soy sauce.

Heat the oil in a wok or large frying pan then fry the ginger, shallot and garlic until fragrant. Add the duck and fry until golden brown on all sides. Remove from the pan.

Roughly chop the yam and sauté it in the oil in the pan, then add half the paste. Remove and set aside. Pour in the remaining sherry, add the remaining duck paste, sugar and the water and bring to the boil. Put the duck in the pan, turning it over to coat it thoroughly with sauce. Remove, then spoon the remaining sauce into the duck on a deep platter and steam it for 1½ hours.

Arrange the yam and mushrooms round the duck, then continue to steam for a further 30 minutes. The duck can be served whole or it can be chopped into pieces before serving and it should be hot when taken to the table. *Serves 4–6*

Duck paste: Mix the following: 1 tablespoon each of bean paste, hoisin paste and mashed red bean curd; 2 teaspoons sesame paste and 1½ teaspoons dark soy sauce.

Sautéed Duck with Pineapple

2 duck portions
1 teaspoon Ginger Juice (page 227)
4 teaspoons light soy sauce
2 teaspoons cornflour
3 teaspoons dry sherry
½ teaspoon meat tenderiser
2½ teaspoons sugar
3 tablespoons water
1¾ teaspoons sesame oil
1 small ripe pineapple
2 tablespoons oil
3 medium-thick slices fresh root ginger, grated
2 shallots, grated
2 cloves garlic, crushed
1 green pepper, deseeded and roughly chopped
2 red chillies, deseeded and roughly chopped
150 ml/¼ pint chicken stock
pinch of pepper
a few drops of dark soy sauce
2 spring onions, shredded

Slice the duck meat off the bones and cut it into large thin pieces. Marinate these with the ginger juice, 1 teaspoon each of the light soy sauce, cornflour and sherry; the meat tenderiser, ½ teaspoon sugar, 2 tablespoons of the water and ¾ teaspoon of the sesame oil.

Trim, peel and cut the pineapple into bite-sized pieces. Heat the oil in a wok or frying pan. Add the duck, cook for a few minutes then remove. Sauté the ginger, shallots and garlic until fragrant. Stir in the pepper and chillies and fry for a while, then add the pineapple and replace the duck to sauté until thoroughly cooked.

Pour in the remaining sherry, light soy sauce and sugar, the stock, pepper and dark soy sauce. Mix well. Blend the cornflour with the remaining water and pour it into the sauce. Simmer for 2 minutes. Sprinkle in the remaining sesame oil and spring onion, toss well and transfer to a warmed serving platter. Serve hot. *Serves 4*

Note: The platter of duck with pineapple makes a colourful dish in itself but it can be further enhanced by the addition of a simple garnish.

For example, why not add halved orange slices (as shown in the picture) or a few sprigs of parsley. Prepare the chosen garnish in advance – cut the orange slices or wash and separate the parsley sprigs – so that the finished dish will not have time to become cold once it is transferred to the serving platter.

Mock Bean Curd with Diced Duck

250 ml/8 fl oz egg whites (from
    about 8 eggs)
300 ml/½ pint water
½ teaspoon salt
pinch of pepper
1 teaspoon sugar
½ teaspoon sesame oil
150 g/5 oz roast duck
2 tablespoons oil
1 clove garlic, crushed
1 teaspoon dry sherry
150 ml/¼ pint chicken stock
½ teaspoon light soy sauce
1 teaspoon oyster sauce
2 teaspoons cornflour
2 tablespoons water
2 tablespoons chopped spring
    onion

Whisk the egg white and
water with the salt, pepper,
½ teaspoon sugar and sesame
oil. Strain through a sieve into
a heatproof dish. Cook the
egg white in a steamer over
boiling water for 8 minutes, or
until set firmly. Remove.
    Dice the roast duck,
removing all the bones. Heat
the oil in a wok or frying pan.
Sauté the garlic until fragrant,
then discard. Stir in the roast
duck and fry for a while. Pour
in the sherry and stock and
bring to the boil. Add the soy
sauce, oyster sauce and
remaining sugar to taste.
Blend the cornflour with the
water, then pour into the
sauce and simmer until
thickened.
    Lastly, mix in the chives
and pour this sauce over the
egg white. Serve at once.
Serves 6

Multi-flavoured Chicken

2 chicken thighs
2 teaspoons Ginger Juice (page
    227)
2 teaspoons dry sherry
pinch of monosodium
    glutamate
50 g/2 oz unsalted peanuts
½ cucumber, diced
1 teaspoon shredded fresh root
    ginger
1 tablespoon chopped spring
    onion
2 teaspoons light soy sauce
1 teaspoon sesame oil
¾ teaspoon rice vinegar or cider
    vinegar
2 tablespoons sesame paste
1 teaspoon chilli paste
½ teaspoon salt
1 teaspoon sugar

Marinate the chicken thighs
with the ginger juice, 1
teaspoon dry sherry and a
pinch of monosodium
glutamate for 30 minutes.
Steam the chicken over
boiling water for 20 minutes,
or until cooked.
    Cut all the meat off the
chicken bones and discard any
skin. Cut the reserved meat
into small pieces.
    Roast the peanuts under a
moderately hot grill until
brown – the grill must not be
too hot or the nuts will burn.
Turn them frequently during
cooking so that they become
evenly coloured.
    Place the diced cucumber,
chicken meat, peanuts,
shredded ginger and spring
onion in a mixing bowl. Mix
all the remaining ingredients,
then pour on to the chicken
mixture and toss to coat all
the pieces. Chill lightly before
serving. *Serves 2–4*

Jumbo Won Tons with Assorted Meat

100 g/4 oz won ton wrappers
FILLING
100 g/4 oz boneless pork, diced
100 g/4 oz peeled cooked shrimps, diced
1 teaspoon soy sauce
½ teaspoon sugar
salt and pepper
pinch of monosodium glutamate
½ teaspoon cornflour
½ teaspoon sesame oil
1 egg yolk
beaten egg for brushing
25 g/1 oz carrot, grated
1 teaspoon chopped chives
ASSORTED MEAT
100 g/4 oz boneless cooked chicken
100 g/4 oz roast duck (page 82)
100 g/4 oz Cha Shiu (page 225) or cooked ham

75 g/3 oz fresh squid or cuttlefish
1 teaspoon Ginger Juice (page 227)
2 teaspoons cornflour plus extra for coating
1 egg white
75 g/3 oz peeled cooked prawns
2 tablespoons oil plus oil for deep frying
2 medium-thick slices fresh root ginger
2 shallots, sliced
2 cloves garlic, sliced
1 onion, cut into wedges
1 green pepper, deseeded and roughly chopped
2 red chillies, deseeded and chopped
1 teaspoon dry sherry
450 ml/¾ pint Sweet and Sour Sauce (page 227)
½ teaspoon sugar
¼ teaspoon monosodium glutamate
1 teaspoon sesame oil
1 tablespoon water

Handle the wrappers carefully so as not to split them. Mix the pork and shrimps with the soy sauce, sugar, a pinch each of pepper and monosodium glutamate, the cornflour, sesame oil and egg yolk. Marinate for 10 minutes, then add the carrot and chives and pound until firm. Place a little filling in each won ton, brush the edge with beaten egg, then press the dough around the filling.

For the assorted meat, chop the chicken and duck into bite-sized pieces. Slice the Cha Shiu or ham. Prepare the squid according to the instructions on page 16. Marinate the squid with the ginger juice and 1 teaspoon cornflour for 20 minutes then blanch and drain.

Lightly whisk the egg white, then dip the prawns in it, season with pepper and coat with cornflour. Heat the oil for deep frying to 190 c/375 F. Fry the prawns until golden. Drain and set aside.

Add the won tons to the hot oil and deep fry them until golden. Drain thoroughly and keep hot.

Heat the 2 tablespoons oil in a saucepan. Add the ginger, shallots and garlic and cook until fragrant. Stir in the onion, green pepper and chillies; fry until softened. Stir in the sherry and sauce; boil. Add seasoning, the sugar, monosodium glutamate and the sesame oil. Stir in the Cha Shiu, fried prawns and squid.

Blend the remaining cornflour with the water, then stir into the sauce and simmer for 2 minutes. Top with the poultry. Serve with the won tons. *Serves 6*

Pork

Roast Belly Pork

1.25 kg/2½ lb belly pork
250 ml/8 fl oz cider vinegar
2 tablespoons honey
red food colouring
2 tablespoons Spicy Salt (page 229)
watercress sprigs to garnish (optional)

The pork must first be cooked in boiling water for 4–5 minutes. Drain the meat thoroughly.

Heat the vinegar with the honey and add just a little food colouring (make sure it is a true red, not pink), then pour it over the rind of the pork. Rub the spicy salt all over the rind and the meat and hang the pork, or leave it on a rack over a roasting tin, to dry for a few hours.

Prick the skin all over, then place the pork in the roasting tin. Baste it thoroughly with the juices and cook in a hot oven (230 C, 450 F, gas 8) for about 30 minutes, or until the rind has thoroughly browned and become crisp. Reduce the oven temperature to moderate

(180 C, 350 F, gas 4) and roast the pork for a further 40 minutes, or until thoroughly cooked.

Serve the pork hot, placed on a warmed serving platter and garnished with sprigs of watercress if you like. Alternatively allow the meat to cool, then use as required.
Serves 4–6

Note: Roast belly pork is an essential ingredient for many of the dishes throughout this book, so it's a good idea to perfect the art of cooking pork to achieve a good colour and a crisp golden skin. If you prefer, remove all the bones from the pork before it is cooked.

Roast Pork with Carrots and Bamboo Shoots

350 g/12 oz Roast Belly Pork (recipe left)
1 (227-g/8-oz) can bamboo shoots, drained
175 g/6 oz carrots
2 tablespoons oil
2 shallots
2 cloves garlic, crushed
2 tablespoons grated fresh root ginger
salt and pepper
1 teaspoon sugar
1 teaspoon dry sherry
100 ml/4 fl oz chicken stock
1 tablespoon oyster sauce
¼ teaspoon dark soy sauce
a few drops of sesame oil
1½ teaspoons cornflour
2 tablespoons water
2 spring onions, shredded, to garnish

Cut the roast pork into strips about 3.5 × 2.5 × 0.5 cm/1½ × 1 × ¼ in. Cut the bamboo shoots and carrots into wedges. Blanch in boiling water, then refresh under cold water and drain.

Heat the oil in a wok or frying pan. Sauté the shallots, garlic and ginger until fragrant. Add the bamboo shoots and carrots. Sprinkle in seasoning to taste and the sugar and mix well. Stir in the roast pork, then add the sherry, stock, oyster sauce, soy sauce and sesame oil. Cover and simmer for 5–6 minutes.

Blend the cornflour with the water, then stir the mixture into the pork and simmer for 2 minutes. Serve garnished with the spring onion.
Serves 4–6

Roast Pork and Bean Curd Casserole

*175 g/6 oz Roast Belly Pork
(page 88)*
450 g/1 lb bean curd
2 tablespoons oil
*2 medium-thick slices fresh
root ginger*
5 cloves garlic, sliced
4½ teaspoons shrimp paste
1 teaspoon dry sherry
50 ml/2 fl oz chicken stock
1 tablespoon sugar
1 teaspoon light soy sauce
¼ teaspoon pepper
½ teaspoon cornflour
1 tablespoon water
*75 g/3 oz green leek or Chinese
broccoli*

Prepare the roast pork according to the recipe instructions, then set it aside until it is cool enough to handle.

Cut the cooled pork and the bean curd into bite-sized pieces, removing any bones from the meat as you do so.

Heat the oil in a flameproof casserole. Add the ginger, garlic and shrimp paste, then sauté these ingredients until fragrant. Stir in the pork, then sprinkle in the sherry and add the stock. Stir thoroughly. Gently mix in the bean curd, then add the sugar, light soy sauce and pepper. Bring to the boil, then reduce the heat and simmer gently for 5 minutes.

Blend the cornflour with the water, then stir it into the casserole. Add the leek or broccoli and simmer for a further 2 minutes, or until thickened. Serve hot. *Serves 4*

Roast Pork with Chestnuts

*275 g/10 oz Roast Belly Pork
(page 88)*
*50 g/2 oz Chinese dried
mushrooms*
generous 2 tablespoons oil
salt and pepper
generous 1 teaspoon sugar
450 g/1 lb chestnuts
2 shallots
2 cloves garlic
1 teaspoon dry sherry
300 ml/½ pint chicken stock
1 teaspoon oyster sauce
1 teaspoon dark soy sauce
a few drops of sesame oil
1 teaspoon cornflour
1 tablespoon water
2 spring onions to garnish

Cut the pork into strips about 3.5 × 2.5 × 0.5 cm/1½ × 1 × ¼ in. Soak the dried mushrooms for about 15 minutes or until soft. Squeeze out the excess water, then sprinkle them with a little oil, salt and sugar and steam them over boiling water for 10 minutes.

Cook the chestnuts in boiling water for 10 minutes, then drain and peel them. Heat the oil in a flameproof casserole. Sauté the shallots and garlic until fragrant. Stir in the chestnuts, mushrooms and roast pork and fry for a while. Pour in the sherry and stock, and oyster sauce, soy sauce, sesame oil, seasoning and sugar. Cover and simmer for 30 minutes.

Blend the cornflour with the water, then stir this mixture into the casserole and simmer for a further 20 minutes. Serve garnished with the spring onions. *Serves 4–6*

Pork

Oyster and Pork Casserole

3 Chinese dried mushrooms
150 g/5 oz Roast Belly Pork
  (page 88)
2 medium-thick slices fresh
  root ginger
2 tablespoons oil
1 clove garlic, sliced
1 (100 g/4 oz) can oysters
2 teaspoons dry sherry
50 ml/2 fl oz chicken stock
1 teaspoon oyster sauce
½ teaspoon dark soy sauce
salt and pepper
1 teaspoon sugar
a few drops of sesame oil
1 teaspoon cornflour
1 tablespoon water
3 spring onions, shredded

Soak the mushrooms in hot
water for 30 minutes, then
drain and slice them,
removing their woody stalks.
Slice the pork and shred the
ginger.
  Heat the oil in a flameproof
casserole. Sauté the ginger
and garlic until fragrant, then
add the oysters, pork and
mushrooms, mixing well. Pour

in the sherry, stock, oyster
sauce, dark soy sauce,
seasoning to taste, sugar and
sesame oil.
  Blend the cornflour with the
water, then stir this into the
pork and simmer for a further
2 minutes. Serve hot,
sprinkled with the spring
onions. *Serves 4*

Note: This dish should be
made with fresh oysters. If
they are available, use 6–10
and scrub and prepare them
according to the instructions
on page 50. Blanch the shelled
oysters in boiling water for 1
minute, then drain them
thoroughly and rinse them
under cold water. Use as
directed in the recipe.

Double-cooked Pork

225 g/8 oz Roast Belly Pork
  (page 88)
2 medium-thick slices fresh
  root ginger
2 spring onions
4 teaspoons dry sherry
2 tablespoons oil
2 shallots, sliced
2 cloves garlic, sliced
2 tablespoons hot broad bean
  paste
2 green peppers, deseeded and
  chopped
2 chillies, deseeded and
  chopped
100 g/4 oz winter cabbage,
  shredded
1 tablespoon water
1 teaspoon light soy sauce
½ teaspoon sesame oil
1 teaspoon sugar
½ teaspoon cayenne pepper
2 leeks, shredded

Bring half a saucepan of water
to the boil. Add the pork,
ginger, spring onions and 3
teaspoons of the sherry, then
simmer for 30–40 minutes.
Drain and rinse under running

water. Drain thoroughly, then
chill until firm. Slice thinly.
  Heat the oil in a wok or
frying pan. Sauté the shallots,
garlic and broad bean paste
until fragrant. Stir in the
peppers, chillies, cabbage and
sliced pork and fry for a
while.
  Pour in the remaining
sherry, water, soy sauce,
sesame oil, sugar and cayenne
pepper. Bring to the boil,
then stir in the leeks and serve
hot. *Serves 4*

Pork with Preserved Vegetable

350 g/12 oz belly pork
coarse salt
3 tablespoons dry sherry
4 medium-thick slices fresh
    root ginger
4 shallots, sliced
2 tablespoons dark soy sauce
150 g/5 oz preserved vegetable
5 tablespoons oil plus oil for
    deep frying
2 cloves garlic, sliced
1½ teaspoons sugar
100 ml/4 fl oz chicken stock
1 teaspoon light soy sauce
pinch of pepper
a few drops of sesame oil
1½ teaspoons cornflour
2 tablespoons water
GARNISH
1–2 carrots, cooked, sliced and
    cut into leaf shapes
a few shelled peas, cooked

Rub the pork rind all over with coarse salt, then rinse it off. Place the meat in a saucepan with 2 tablespoons of the sherry, 2 slices of the ginger and 2 shallots. Pour in enough water to cover the pork and bring to the boil. Cover the pan, reduce the heat and simmer for about 40 minutes. Drain and coat the pork with the dark soy sauce. Meanwhile soak the preserved vegetable for 20 minutes.

Heat the oil for deep frying to 190 c/375 F. Carefully lower the pork into the pan and deep fry it until it is well browned. Drain on absorbent kitchen paper and allow to cool until it can be handled. Cut into 1-cm/½-in slices.

Drain and dice the preserved vegetable, then dry it out thoroughly in a wok or heavy-based frying pan over a medium heat. Set aside for later use.

Heat 3 tablespoons of the oil in a wok and sauté half the remaining ginger and shallot and half the garlic; discard when browned. Put in the preserved vegetable and sprinkle in 1 teaspoon sugar, then sauté for a few minutes. Transfer to a flameproof casserole and arrange the sliced pork on top.

Heat the remaining oil in the pan. Put in the remaining ginger, shallot and garlic and sauté until fragrant. Sprinkle in the remaining sherry and pour in the stock together with the light soy sauce, remaining sugar, pepper to taste and sesame oil.

Bring to the boil. Blend the cornflour with the water, then stir this mixture into the sauce and simmer for 2 minutes.

Pour the sauce over the pork and cook gently, covered, for 30 minutes. Garnish and serve. *Serves 4*

Note: Attractive carrot shapes can be made quite simply by using aspic cutters. Parboil the carrot first, then slice it lengthways to give the largest slices. Cut out small shapes and use these as a garnish. If you do not have any small cutters, then use a small, sharp pointed knife to cut out leaf or diamond shapes.

Steamed Pork with Taro

225 g/8 oz belly pork
3 tablespoons dry sherry
2 medium-thick slices fresh
*   root ginger*
2 spring onions
1 tablespoon dark soy sauce
*   plus extra for coating*
oil for deep frying
225 g/8 oz taro or potatoes
2 tablespoons fermented red
*   bean curd*
3 tablespoons sugar
100 ml/4 fl oz plus 1 tablespoon
*   water*
pinch of pepper
1 teaspoon grated shallot
1 teaspoon crushed garlic
1 teaspoon grated fresh root
*   ginger*
1 Iceberg lettuce
1 teaspoon cornflour
a few drops of sesame oil

Place the pork in a saucepan with 2 tablespoons of the sherry, the sliced ginger and spring onions. Boil, then cover and simmer for 30 minutes. Drain and coat in soy sauce.

Heat the oil for deep frying to 190 c/375 f, then fry the pork until browned. Drain on absorbent kitchen paper and cut into 5-mm/¼-in slices.

Peel, wash and slice the taro or potatoes. Deep fry these until golden. Drain.

Mix the fermented red bean curd, 1 tablespoon soy sauce, sugar, remaining sherry, 100 ml/4 fl oz water and pepper. Stir in the shallot, garlic and grated ginger; use to coat the pork and taro. Place the pieces alternately in a bowl with any remaining mixture. Steam over boiling water for 1 hour. Drain off and reserve the sauce.

Arrange the lettuce on a platter, then invert the bowl on to it. Heat the sauce. Blend the cornflour with 1 tablespoon water, stir into the sauce and simmer for 2 minutes. Stir in the sesame oil and pour over the pork. Serve hot. *Serves 4*

Pork and Garlic Vegetable Stew

350 g/12 oz belly pork
¼ teaspoon dark soy sauce
100 g/4 oz preserved vegetable
1 tablespoon oil
2 medium-thick slices fresh root ginger, shredded
2 shallots, sliced
1 clove garlic, sliced
1 (227-g/8-oz) can bamboo shoots, drained and cut into wedges
1 teaspoon dry sherry
300 ml/½ pint chicken stock
2 teaspoons light soy sauce
2 teaspoons sugar
¼ teaspoon salt
1 teaspoon cornflour
1 tablespoon water
flat-leafed parsley sprigs to garnish

Cut the pork into bite-sized pieces. Blanch these in boiling water for a few seconds. Refresh under cold running water. Dry and brush with the dark soy sauce.

Wash and dry the preserved vegetable. Heat the oil in a flameproof casserole. Sauté the ginger, shallots and garlic until fragrant. Stir in the pork and sauté for a while. Add the bamboo shoots and preserved vegetable. Pour in the sherry, stock, light soy sauce, sugar and salt. Bring to the boil, then reduce the heat and simmer for 30 minutes.

Blend the cornflour with the water, then stir into the casserole and simmer for 2 minutes. Serve hot, garnished with parsley sprigs. *Serves 4*

Farmhouse Stew

450 g/1 lb belly pork
175 g/6 oz dried soya beans
75 g/3 oz preserved vegetable
175 g/6 oz gluten (page 225)
1 tablespoon oil plus oil for deep frying
2 medium-thick slices fresh root ginger
2 shallots, sliced
1 clove garlic, sliced
1 teaspoon dry sherry
600 ml/1 pint chicken stock
1 tablespoon light soy sauce
½ teaspoon sesame oil
1½ teaspoons sugar
¼ teaspoon pepper

Cut the pork into large chunks. Wash the soya beans and soak them in cold water to cover for 3 hours. Drain. Soak the preserved vegetable for about 15 minutes, then drain and squeeze dry.

Meanwhile, cut the gluten into pieces. Heat the oil for deep frying to 190 c/375 f, then add the pieces of gluten and fry until puffed and golden brown. Drain on absorbent kitchen paper and set aside.

Heat the 1 tablespoon oil in a flameproof casserole. Fry the ginger, shallots and garlic until fragrant, then add the pork. Sprinkle in the sherry and stir well. Add the soya beans, gluten and preserved vegetable. Pour in the stock, bring to the boil, then cover and simmer for about 1 hour, or until the beans are tender. Add more water if necessary to prevent the liquid drying up.

Stir in the remaining ingredients, seasoning the stew to taste, and serve hot. *Serves 6*

Steamed Belly Pork with Shrimp Paste

275 g/10 oz belly pork
2 shallots, or 1 small onion, grated
2 cloves garlic, crushed
1 tablespoon grated fresh root ginger
3 teaspoons shrimp paste or anchovy essence
1 teaspoon sugar
1 teaspoon dry sherry
2 teaspoons cornflour
3 tablespoons water
pinch of pepper
parsley sprigs to garnish

Remove all the bones from the pork, then slice it widthways into fairly thin pieces. Mix the shallots, garlic, ginger, shrimp paste or anchovy essence, sugar, sherry, cornflour, water and pepper to taste. Coat the sliced pork thoroughly in this paste, rubbing it over the skin, fat and meat to cover the whole joint. Set aside to marinate for 30 minutes.

Arrange the pork on a greased heatproof platter (select one which will fit into a steamer) and place it in a steamer. Cook the pork over boiling water for 20–30 minutes, or until thoroughly cooked.

Serve hot, garnished with parsley sprigs. Offer plain boiled or steamed rice as an accompaniment. *Serves 4*

Note: Belly pork is a cut of pork which is quite commonly used in Chinese cooking. The layer of fat keeps this meat moist and gives a good flavour. However it may be unacceptable to some people. If you select the pork carefully you will find that some joints have only a thin layer of fat. On the other hand you can always use a leaner cut if you prefer; try pork shoulder for example.

Assorted Meat with Bean Sprouts

2 Chinese dried mushrooms
50 g/2 oz uncooked boneless chicken
½ egg white
2 teaspoons dry sherry
1 teaspoon Ginger Juice (page 227)
1 teaspoon light soy sauce
1 teaspoon cornflour
½ teaspoon sugar
pinch of pepper
4 tablespoons oil plus oil for deep frying
2 cloves garlic, sliced
2 shallots, sliced
175 g/6 oz bean sprouts
1 chilli, deseeded and shredded
50 g/2 oz Chinese ham or Virginia ham, shredded
75 g/3 oz roast duck (page 82), shredded
¼ teaspoon dark soy sauce
½ teaspoon sesame oil
25 g/1 oz white part of leek or spring onion, shredded

Soak the mushrooms in cold water for 30 minutes, then steam them over boiling water for 15 minutes.

Shred and marinate the chicken with the egg white, 1 teaspoon each of sherry and ginger juice; ½ teaspoon each of light soy sauce and cornflour; ¼ teaspoon sugar and a pinch of pepper for 20 minutes.

Heat the oil for deep frying to 190 c/375 f, then deep fry the chicken until very lightly cooked. Drain on absorbent kitchen paper.

Heat 2 tablespoons of the oil in a wok or frying pan. Sauté half the garlic and shallots until fragrant. Stir in the bean sprouts and fry for a few seconds. Remove.

Add another 2 tablespoons oil and sauté the remaining garlic and shallots with the chilli. Stir in the chicken, ham and duck; bean sprouts and mushrooms. Sprinkle in the remaining sherry, sugar, remaining light and dark soy sauce, pepper and sesame oil.

Blend the cornflour with the water, stir in and simmer for 2 minutes. Serve, garnished with the leek or spring onion.
Serves 4

Assorted Meat and Vegetable Casserole

25 g/1 oz dried scallops or 4
  fresh scallops, shelled
25 g/1 oz Chinese dried
  mushrooms
50 g/2 oz bean thread
100 g/4 oz loin of pork
2 teaspoons light soy sauce
1 teaspoon sugar
1½ teaspoons cornflour
1.75 litres/3 pints plus 2
  tablespoons water
4–5 tablespoons oil
1 teaspoon Ginger Juice (page
  227)
1 teaspoon dry sherry
salt and pepper
100 g/4 oz boneless uncooked
  chicken, sliced
1 shallot, sliced
a few slices canned bamboo
  shoot

a few slices carrot, blanched
  and drained
100 g/4 oz cooked ham, sliced
2 squares bean curd, cut into
  triangles
225 g/8 oz Chinese cabbage, or
  Swiss chard, roughly
  shredded
1 chicken stock cube
½ teaspoon sesame oil

Soak the dried scallops and mushrooms in boiling water. Break up the bean thread and soak it thoroughly. Wash and slice the pork loin.

Mix 1 teaspoon of the light soy sauce, ¼ teaspoon of the sugar, ½ teaspoon of the cornflour, 2 tablespoons water and 1 teaspoon of the oil. Pour this over the pork, mix well and set aside to marinate for 10 minutes.

Blanch the pork in boiling water for a few seconds. Drain the meat, then rinse it under cold water, drain it

again and set aside.

Mix the ginger juice, sherry and remaining cornflour with a pinch of salt, ¼ teaspoon sugar and 1 tablespoon oil. Spread this mixture evenly over the chicken slices, then set them aside to marinate for 10 minutes.

Blanch the chicken in boiling water for 1 minute, rinse and drain.

Heat 3 tablespoons oil in a saucepan. Sauté the shallot until fragrant, then discard. Pour in the 1.75 litres/3 pints water and bring to the boil. Stir in the soaked or fresh scallops, mushrooms, bamboo shoots and carrot, then simmer for 20 minutes. Add the chicken, ham, bean curd and pork, then simmer for another 10 minutes.

Finally add the cabbage and bean thread and simmer for a few minutes, until the bean thread is cooked. Stir in the

crumbled stock cube, sesame oil, remaining soy sauce and sugar, and simmer for a few minutes. Serve the casserole hot. *Serves 6*

Braised Bean Curd with Shredded Pork

450 g/1 lb bean curd
salt and pepper
2 tablespoons oil plus oil for deep frying
2 teaspoons light soy sauce
2 teaspoons cornflour
1½ teaspoons sugar
1½ teaspoons dry sherry
100 ml/4 fl oz plus 2 tablespoons water
a few drops of sesame oil
100 g/4 oz loin of pork
3 Chinese dried mushrooms
2 medium-thick slices fresh root ginger
2 shallots, sliced
1 clove garlic, crushed
100 g/4 oz shelled peas
1 teaspoon oyster sauce
1 tablespoon shredded spring onion
1 red chilli, deseeded and cut into fine strips

Cut the bean curd into 3.5-cm/1½-in squares which are 1 cm/½ in thick. Season with salt. Heat the oil for deep frying to 190 c/375 F. Deep fry the bean curd until golden brown. Drain on absorbent kitchen paper. Set aside.

Mix half the light soy sauce with half the cornflour, ½ teaspoon each of the sugar and sherry; 1 tablespoon water, a few drops of sesame oil and a pinch of pepper. Cut the pork into fine strips and marinate them in this mixture for 20 minutes.

Soak the mushrooms in hot water for 30 minutes, then drain and slice them. Cut the ginger slices into fine strips.

Heat the oil in a wok. Add the pork and cook until lightly browned. Remove and then add the ginger, shallots and garlic. Cook for a few minutes then add the bean curd and replace the pork. Stir in the peas and mushrooms, pour in the 100 ml/4 fl oz water, remaining soy sauce and sherry, the oyster sauce and the remaining sugar. Blend the rest of the cornflour with the remaining water, then pour this into the pan, stirring, and boil. Simmer for 2 minutes. Stir in the spring onion and chilli. Serve. *Serves 4*

Pork Loin in Garlic Sauce

450 g/1 lb loin of pork, rind removed
2 medium-thick slices fresh root ginger
1 spring onion
1 cucumber
8 cloves garlic, finely chopped
¼ teaspoon salt
1 teaspoon sugar
1 teaspoon dry sherry
1 tablespoon soy sauce
¾ teaspoon vinegar
1 teaspoon sesame oil
¼ teaspoon monosodium glutamate
100 ml/4 fl oz chicken stock
100 ml/4 fl oz sweet soy sauce

Place the pork in a saucepan with the ginger and spring onion. Pour in enough water to cover the pork and bring to the boil. Simmer gently for 50–60 minutes, then drain and rinse under cold water. Dry and chill the meat for 30 minutes. Slice the pork and arrange it round a platter.

Place the garlic in a bowl with all the remaining ingredients. Mix well, then pour over the pork.

Trim the ends off the cucumber and cut it into three pieces. Trim off both sides of each piece, then slice the cucumber lengthways into very thin pieces. Soak the slices in cold water for about 15 minutes, then drain thoroughly, mop them with absorbent kitchen paper and place in the middle of the platter. Serve at once, before the cucumber weeps. *Serves 4*

Sweet and Sour Pork

275 g/10 oz loin of pork
½ teaspoon sugar
2 teaspoons dry sherry
salt and pepper
1 teaspoon soy sauce
50 ml/2 fl oz plus 1 tablespoon
water
3 tablespoons oil plus oil for
deep frying
50 g/2 oz plus 2 teaspoons
cornflour
1 clove garlic
3 medium-thick slices fresh
root ginger
1 onion, quartered
2 green peppers, deseeded and
roughly chopped
2 chillies, deseeded and
chopped
150 ml/¼ pint Sweet and Sour
Sauce (page 227)
2 pineapple rings (fresh or
canned), cut into pieces
2 spring onions, shredded

Chop the pork into bite-sized
pieces. Mix the sugar, half the
sherry, seasoning to taste, soy
sauce, 50 ml/2 fl oz water, 1
tablespoon oil and 1 teaspoon
cornflour. Add the pork;
marinate for 30 minutes.

Coat the pork completely
with cornflour, pressing it on
well. Heat the oil for deep
frying to 190 c/375 F, then
deep fry the pork until lightly
browned. Drain on absorbent
kitchen paper.

Heat the 2 tablespoons oil
in a saucepan. Add the garlic
and ginger and fry until
fragrant. Add the onion,
peppers and chillies and sauté
for a few minutes. Stir in the
remaining sherry and sweet
and sour sauce, then boil.

Blend the remaining
cornflour with the
1 tablespoon water. Stir
this into the sauce with the
pineapple. Simmer for 2
minutes.

Deep fry the pork again
until crisp. Drain and toss
with the sauce. Serve,
garnished with spring onions.
Serves 4

Rice with Roast Pork

275 g/10 oz pork fillet
2 teaspoons ground bean paste
2 teaspoons hoisin paste
1 teaspoon sesame paste or
* peanut butter*
1 teaspoon Chinese rose wine
* or dry sherry*
1 clove garlic, crushed
1 grated shallot
50 g/2 oz sugar
50 ml/2 fl oz soy sauce
sesame oil to taste
3 tablespoons honey
225 g/8 oz long-grain rice,
* boiled or steamed to serve*
Chinese cabbage to garnish

Cut the pork into two thick
strips. Score a cross-cross
pattern on each. Mix all the
remaining ingredients apart
from the rice and honey. Pour
this marinade over the pork,
rubbing it in well. Leave for
about 1 hour.

Remove the meat from the
marinade (reserve the liquid)
and place it in a roasting tin.
Cook in a moderately hot
oven (200 c, 400 f, gas 6) for
15 minutes. Brush the pork all
over with honey, then
continue to roast for a further
15–20 minutes, or until
cooked through. Allow to
cool.

Slice the cold pork and
arrange it on the freshly
cooked rice. Heat the
marinade and pour over to
serve. Garnish with Chinese
cabbage. *Serves 4*

Broccoli with Sliced Pork

450 g/1 lb broccoli
5 tablespoons oil plus oil for
* deep frying*
6 teaspoons dry sherry
1.25 litres/2¼ pints plus 5
* tablespoons water*
salt and pepper
6 teaspoons sugar
3 medium-thick slices fresh
* root ginger*
2 teaspoons dark soy sauce
2½ teaspoons cornflour
1 teaspoon sesame oil
175 g/6 oz loin of pork, sliced
2 shallots, grated
1 clove garlic, crushed
100 ml/4 fl oz chicken stock
1 teaspoon light soy sauce
1 teaspoon oyster sauce

Cut the broccoli into florets,
then soak these in salt water
for 30 minutes. Heat 2
tablespoons oil in a saucepan.
Add 1 tablespoon sherry and
1.25 litres/2¼ pints of the
water, 1 tablespoon salt, 1
tablespoon sugar and 2 slices
of ginger. Boil. Add the
broccoli and blanch for 2
minutes. Drain and rinse.

Mix the dark soy sauce, 1
teaspoon each of sugar, sherry
and cornflour, a pinch of
pepper, ½ teaspoon sesame oil,
3 tablespoons water and 1
tablespoon oil. Marinate the
pork in this for 30 minutes.

Heat the oil for deep frying
to 190 c/375 f, then fry the
pork for a few minutes, until
just cooked without allowing
it to brown. Drain on
absorbent kitchen paper and
set aside. Grate the remaining
ginger.

Heat 2 tablespoons oil in a
wok or frying pan. Sauté the
ginger, shallots and garlic,
then stir in the broccoli to fry
for a while. Put in the pork
and mix thoroughly. Stir in
the remaining sherry, stock,
seasoning to taste, final 2
teaspoons sugar, light soy
sauce, oyster sauce and
remaining sesame oil. Bring to
the boil. Mix the cornflour
with the water, stir into the
pork and simmer for 2
minutes. Serve hot.
Serves 4–6

Shredded Pork in Hot Sauce

2 teaspoons light soy sauce
2 teaspoons cornflour
1½ teaspoons sugar
1½ teaspoons dry sherry
pinch of pepper
5 tablespoons water
3 tablespoons oil plus oil for
  deep frying
175 g/6 oz loin of pork, cut
  into strips
7 g/¼ oz black fungus
2 teaspoons grated fresh root
  ginger
2 cloves garlic, crushed
10 canned water chestnuts,
  shredded
2 tablespoons hot broad bean
  paste
1 teaspoon sesame oil
1 teaspoon vinegar
strips of red and green pepper
  to garnish

Mix 1 teaspoon each of light
soy sauce and cornflour,
½ teaspoon each of sugar and
sherry, a pinch of pepper,
2 tablespoons water and
1 tablespoon oil. Pour this
over the pork, mix well and
marinate for 20 minutes.

Soak the black fungus in
water for about 30 minutes.
Drain and shred, then blanch
in boiling water for a few
minutes. Refresh and drain.

Heat the oil for deep frying,
then add the pork and fry
until just cooked but not
browned. Drain on absorbent
kitchen paper.

Heat 2 tablespoons oil in a
wok or frying pan. Sauté the
ginger and garlic until
fragrant. Drop in the black
fungus and water chestnuts
then stir-fry for a few seconds.
Add the broad bean paste and
strips of pork and stir-fry until
browned. Pour in the
remaining sherry and sugar,
the remaining light soy sauce,
sesame oil, 2 tablespoons
water, the vinegar and
pepper. Bring to the boil.
Blend the cornflour with the
remaining water and stir into
the sauce. Simmer for 2
minutes, toss well and serve
hot, sprinkled with red and
green pepper. *Serves 4*

Sautéed Pork with Snow Peas

100 g/4 oz loin of pork, cut
  into strips
2 teaspoons light soy sauce
1 teaspoon sugar
½ teaspoon cornflour
2 teaspoons dry sherry
salt and pepper
3 tablespoons water
2 tablespoons oil plus oil for
  deep frying
25 g/1 oz preserved turnip or
  fresh white radish
½ teaspoon grated fresh root
  ginger
2 cloves garlic, crushed
150 g/5 oz snow peas or mange
  tout peas, trimmed
75 g/3 oz leeks, trimmed and
  shredded

Mix the pork with 1 teaspoon
light soy sauce, a generous
½ teaspoon each of sugar,
cornflour and sherry, a pinch
of pepper and 2 tablespoons
water. Marinate for 20
minutes. Heat the oil for deep
frying to 190 c/375 f. Add the
pork and fry until half cooked
but not browned.

Soak the preserved turnip,
if used, in cold water for 30
minutes, then drain and shred.
Alternatively shred the white
radish.

Heat 2 tablespoons oil in a
wok or frying pan, then sauté
the ginger and garlic until
fragrant. Put in the snow
peas, salt to taste and
remaining sugar, then stir-fry
rapidly. Add the pork and
preserved turnip or radish,
stirring thoroughly. Pour in
the remaining sherry, soy
sauce and water. Bring to the
boil then stir in the leeks and
mix well. Serve hot. *Serves 4*

Chop Suey with Shredded Pork

175 g/6 oz loin of pork,
  shredded
2 teaspoons light soy sauce
1 teaspoon sugar
salt and pepper
½ teaspoon cornflour
100 g/4 oz canned bamboo
  shoots or parboiled carrots
1 teaspoon dry sherry
3 tablespoons water
generous 3 tablespoons oil plus
  oil for deep frying
4 Chinese dried mushrooms
15 g/½ oz black or white fungus
150 g/5 oz Chinese cabbage
50 g/2 oz bean thread
150 g/5 oz bean sprouts
½ teaspoon sesame oil
1 teaspoon white vinegar
2 eggs

Marinate the pork for 20
minutes in a mixture of
1 teaspoon light soy sauce,
¼ teaspoon sugar, a pinch of
pepper, the cornflour,
½ teaspoon dry sherry, the
water and 1 tablespoon oil.
  Heat the oil for deep frying
to 190 c/375 f, then add the
pork and fry until just cooked
but not well browned. Drain
on absorbent kitchen paper
and set aside.
  Soak (separately), drain and
shred the mushrooms and
black fungus. Shred the
cabbage and soak the bean
thread until soft. Steam the
mushrooms with a little salt,
sugar and oil for 10 minutes
over boiling water.
  Heat 2 tablespoons oil in a
wok or frying pan. Add the
cabbage and stir-fry for a
while. Add the black fungus
and bean sprouts; mix well.
Stir in all the remaining
ingredients apart from the
eggs and sesame oil. Stir-fry
for a few minutes.
  Beat the eggs with salt to
taste. Heat the remaining oil
in a wok or frying pan, then
pour in the eggs. Stir lightly
until the eggs begin to set,
then leave until browned.
  Transfer the chop suey to a
serving dish and invert the
omelette on top. Serve at
once. *Serves 4*

Sautéed Lotus Root with Pork

100 g/4 oz shoulder of pork,
  sliced
2 teaspoons light soy sauce
1 tablespoon sugar
2 teaspoons cornflour
2 teaspoons dry sherry
salt and pepper
100 ml/4 fl oz plus 3
  tablespoons water
2 tablespoons oil
2 shallots, sliced
2 cloves garlic, sliced
2 tablespoons ground bean
  paste
450 g/1 lb lotus root or carrots,
  peeled and sliced
3 spring onions, shredded
GARNISH
1 tomato, sliced
1 lemon, sliced

Marinate the pork with
1 teaspoon each of light soy
sauce, sugar, cornflour and
sherry; ¼ teaspoon pepper and
2 tablespoons of the water for
30 minutes. Parboil for 1
minute and drain.
  Heat the oil in a wok or
large frying pan. Put in the
shallots and garlic, and sauté
until fragrant. Stir in the bean
paste and lotus root or carrots
and fry for a while. Gradually
add the pork, then pour in the
remaining sherry, the 100 ml/
4 fl oz water, salt to taste, the
remaining sugar and light soy
sauce. Heat through to boiling
point.
  Blend the remaining
cornflour with the remaining
water, stir the mixture into
the sauce and simmer for 2
minutes or until thickened.
  Lastly mix in the spring
onions and transfer the
mixture to a heatproof serving
plate. Add a garnish of halved
tomato and lemon slices and
serve at once. *Serves 4*

Chopsticks Stir-fry

*thickly peeled rind of 3
   oranges*
50 g/2 oz dried shrimps
3 Chinese dried mushrooms
*1 small carrot, sliced and
   blanched*
*50 g/2 oz canned water
   chestnuts*
*1 green pepper, deseeded and
   halved*
1 red chilli, deseeded
150 g/5 oz belly pork, diced
1¾ teaspoons light soy sauce
1¼ teaspoons cornflour
1 teaspoon sugar
1½ teaspoons dry sherry
3 tablespoons water
pinch of pepper
2 tablespoons oil
2 shallots, grated
1 clove garlic, crushed
*1 tablespoon grated fresh root
   ginger*
*1½ teaspoons ground bean
   paste*
½ teaspoon sesame oil
½ dessert apple to garnish

Scrape the pith off the orange peel, then soak it in hot water for 2 days, changing the water daily. Blanch the peel twice in boiling water for 2 minutes each time, draining it thoroughly between each blanching. Rinse and dry, cut the peel into diamond shapes.

Wash and soak the dried shrimps for 1 hour, then drain thoroughly and chop them. Soak the mushrooms in cold water for 10 minutes, then drain and steam them for 15 minutes. Discard the woody stalks.

Cut the carrot, water chestnuts, mushrooms, green pepper and red chilli into diamond shapes.

Marinate the pork for 20 minutes with ¾ teaspoon each of light soy sauce and cornflour, ½ teaspoon each of sugar and sherry, 2 tablespoons water and a pinch of pepper. Cook the pork very briefly in boiling water, then drain it thoroughly.

Heat the oil in a wok or frying pan. Stir in the shallots, garlic, ginger and bean paste and stir-fry until fragrant. Add the pork, orange peel and all the remaining ingredients apart from the rest of the cornflour and remaining water. Stir-fry until the pork is cooked. Blend the cornflour with the water, stir into the ingredients and simmer for 2 minutes.

For the garnish, cut the piece of apple in half, then into fine slices. Arrange the slices from the two wedges in an overlapping pattern as shown in the picture. To prevent the apples from discolouring, then first dip them in lemon juice.

Transfer the cooked stir-fry to a heated serving dish and add the garnish, then serve at once. *Serves 4*

Note: This dish can be garnished with orange slices, cut in half and arranged in a similar way to the apples. Additional garnishing ingredients can be added round the edge of the plate if you like. For example, try sprigs of flat-leafed parsley or a few spring onion curls (page 34).

It is important with any stir-fry cooking that all the ingredients are prepared in advance. And this means the ingredients which are to be used for the garnish as well as those which are to be cooked as part of the dish.

Roasted Spare Ribs

1 kg/2 lb meaty pork spare ribs
(in one piece)
red food colouring
25 g/1 oz ground bean paste
25 g/1 oz sweet paste
15 g/½ oz sesame paste
75 g/3 oz sugar
75 ml/3 fl oz dark soy sauce
1 teaspoon Spicy Salt (page 229)
1 teaspoon sesame oil
2 cloves garlic, crushed
2 shallots, grated
1 teaspoon dry sherry
50 g/2 oz honey

Score a criss-cross pattern on the meat.

Put all the ingredients apart from the honey in a bowl and mix thoroughly. Pour this mixture over the meat, rubbing it in well. Cover and set aside to marinate for 1 hour.

Rest the pork on a roasting rack over a roasting tin. Cook the ribs in a hot oven (230 c, 450 f, gas 8) for 15 minutes. Brush with honey and return them to the oven for another 10 minutes. Coat with more honey and bake for the final 5–10 minutes. Remove and chop the ribs into serving pieces. *Serves 4–6*

To weigh honey: The easiest way to measure honey by weight, is to place a small light-weight container on the scales (a plastic basin or empty margarine container) and adjust the scales back to the zero position.

Warm a metal spoon over a gas flame or by dipping it in boiling water (dry it quickly), then spoon the honey into the container until the required amount is measured. Warming the spoon will prevent the honey from sticking.

Deep Fried Spicy Ribs

450 g/1 lb pork spare ribs
2 teaspoons grated fresh root ginger
2 teaspoons grated shallot
4 cloves garlic, crushed
cayenne pepper to taste
½ teaspoon salt
2 teaspoons light soy sauce
1 tablespoon sugar
1½ teaspoons dry sherry
1 tablespoon cornflour
¼ teaspoon pepper
4 tablespoons water
1 teaspoon sesame oil
oil for deep frying
GARNISH
2 carrot flowers
parsley sprigs

Chop between the spare ribs to separate them (your butcher will probably do this for you if you ask him), then chop them across in half to make short pieces. Place the pieces in a dish. Mix all the remaining ingredients and pour the mixture over the ribs, rubbing it in well to coat them completely. Set aside to marinate for 1 hour.

Heat the oil for deep frying to 190 c/375 f, then fry the spare ribs until well browned. Drain them on absorbent kitchen paper, then arrange the ribs on a warmed serving plate.

Garnish with the carrot flowers, and parsley sprigs. Serve at once. *Serves 2–4*

Tomato roses: These are not as difficult to make as you may think. Thickly peel the tomatoes, keeping the peel in one piece. If you work slowly, then you are less likely to break the skin.

Use a small sharp knife, cut a scalloped edge on the skin, then roll it up to form a flower shape. Secure the flower at the base with a cocktail stick. This can be concealed in the garnish by adding parsley sprigs.

Spare Rib and Chestnut Casserole

275 g/10 oz fresh chestnuts
175 g/6 oz pork spare ribs (separated)
½ teaspoon sugar
2 teaspoons dry sherry
1 teaspoon light soy sauce
1 teaspoon cornflour
pepper
a few drops of sesame oil
300 ml/½ pint plus 1 tablespoon water
2 tablespoons oil plus oil for deep frying
3 tablespoons grated fresh root ginger
4 shallots
3 cloves garlic
¼ teaspoon salt
1 teaspoon dark soy sauce
3 spring onions, shredded, to garnish

Cook the chestnuts in boiling water for 10 minutes then peel them.

Chop the spare ribs into bite-sized pieces and marinate these for 30 minutes in a mixture of ½ teaspoon sugar, 1 teaspoon each of sherry, light soy sauce and cornflour, a pinch of pepper, a few drops of sesame oil and 1 tablespoon water.

Heat the oil for deep frying to 190 c/375 F, add the ribs and fry until lightly cooked but not browned. Drain on absorbent kitchen paper and set aside.

Heat the 2 tablespoons oil in a flameproof casserole. Sauté the ginger, shallots and garlic in the oil until fragrant. Stir in the spare ribs and fry for a while. Add the chestnuts, mix thoroughly, then pour in the remaining sherry and 300 ml/½ pint water. Bring to the boil, reduce the heat, cover and simmer for 30 minutes.

Stir in the salt, dark soy sauce and a pinch of pepper. Cook for a further 10 minutes, or until the pork is tender.

Sprinkle with the spring onions and serve hot. *Serves 4–6*

Spicy Spare Rib Casserole

350 g/12 oz pork spare ribs
1 teaspoon light soy sauce
2 teaspoons sugar
a pinch of monosodium glutamate
2 tablespoons dry sherry
4 teaspoons fermented red bean curd
½ teaspoon ground mixed spice
2 teaspoons cornflour
red food colouring
1 teaspoon sesame oil
2 tablespoons oil plus oil for deep frying
2 medium-thick slices fresh root ginger, shredded
2 shallots, sliced
2 cloves garlic, sliced
250 ml/8 fl oz chicken stock
pinch of pepper
1 crisp lettuce to serve

Chop the spare ribs into chunks. Marinate these for 1–2 hours with a mixture of ½ teaspoon light soy sauce, the sugar, a pinch of monosodium glutamate, 1 tablespoon sherry, half the fermented red bean curd, the mixed spice, the cornflour, a few drops of red food colouring and the sesame oil.

Heat the oil for deep frying to 190 c/375 F. Add the spare ribs and fry until golden brown. Drain on absorbent kitchen paper.

Heat the 2 tablespoons oil in a flameproof casserole. Sauté the ginger, shallots and garlic until fragrant, then stir in the remaining fermented bean curd and the spare ribs. Pour in the last of the sherry and the stock. Bring to the boil, reduce the heat, cover the pan and simmer for 30 minutes.

Stir in a pinch of pepper and the remaining light soy sauce. Arrange the lettuce leaves in a bowl, pour in the pork and serve hot. *Serves 4*

Pork

Braised Spare Ribs with Chestnuts

225 g/8 oz fresh chestnuts
175 g/6 oz pork spare ribs
2 teaspoons light soy sauce
2 teaspoons dry sherry
1 teaspoon sugar
salt and pepper
1 teaspoon cornflour
250 ml/8 fl oz water plus 1
 tablespoon
2 tablespoons oil
3 tablespoons grated fresh root
 ginger
2 shallots, grated
2 cloves garlic, crushed
1 teaspoon oyster sauce
1 teaspoon sesame oil
parsley sprigs to garnish

Cook the chestnuts in boiling salted water for 10 minutes, then drain and peel them.

Chop the spare ribs into bite-sized pieces. Marinate these for 30 minutes with a mixture of 1 teaspoon of the light soy sauce and sherry, ½ teaspoon sugar, a pinch of pepper, the cornflour and 1 tablespoon water. Parboil and drain; set aside.

Heat the oil in a flameproof casserole. Sauté the ginger, shallots and garlic until fragrant. Add the spare ribs and chestnuts and stir-fry until the pork is browned. Pour in the remaining sherry, 250 ml/ 8 fl oz water, seasoning to taste, the remaining sugar and light soy sauce and the oyster sauce. Bring to the boil, then cover and simmer over a low heat for 20–30 minutes.

Sprinkle the sesame oil over the spare ribs just before serving, garnished with parsley sprigs. *Serves 2–4*

Hot and Sour Pork Chop

350 g/12 oz pork chops
2 teaspoons dry sherry
2 teaspoons light soy sauce
1 teaspoon cornflour plus extra
 for dusting
1½ teaspoons sugar
pepper
2 tablespoons water
7 teaspoons oil
2 medium-thick slices fresh
 root ginger, chopped
2 cloves garlic, sliced
1 onion, chopped
1 green pepper, deseeded and
 diced
50 g/2 oz red chillies, deseeded
 and diced
100 g/4 oz tomatoes, peeled
 and chopped
100 ml/4 fl oz chicken stock
50 g/2 oz carrots, diced and
 parboiled
2 slices fresh or canned
 pineapple, diced
50 g/2 oz shelled peas
50 ml/2 fl oz tomato ketchup
2 teaspoons hot broad bean
 paste
1 teaspoon sesame oil

Marinate the pork with 1 teaspoon each of sherry, light soy sauce and cornflour; ½ teaspoon sugar; a pinch of pepper and the water for 20 minutes. Mix in 1 teaspoon of the oil and continue to marinate for a further 20 minutes.

Heat the remaining oil in a wok or frying pan. Dust the pork chops with a little cornflour then fry them until both sides are golden. Remove from the pan and drain the meat on absorbent kitchen paper.

Add the ginger and garlic to the fat in the pan. Stir in the onion, green pepper, chillies and tomatoes and fry until the oil turns red. Return the pork chops to the pan, pour in the remaining sherry and the stock. Simmer, covered, for about 10–15 minutes or until the chops are cooked through.

Add all the remaining ingredients, including the 1 teaspoon soy sauce. Stir them into the sauce, heat through and serve at once. *Serves 4*

Pork Chops with Rice

4 pork chops
3 tablespoons oil plus oil for
 deep frying
1 carrot, diced
1 onion, chopped
1 celery stick, diced
225 g/8 oz tomatoes, peeled
 (page 32) and chopped
100 g/4 oz shelled peas
150 ml/¼ pint chicken stock
½ teaspoon sugar
1 teaspoon light soy sauce
1 teaspoon sesame oil
pinch of pepper
2 teaspoons cornflour
2 tablespoons water
1 egg, beaten
225 g/8 oz long-grain rice,
 boiled or steamed
MARINADE
¼ teaspoon garlic salt
¼ teaspoon celery salt
1 teaspoon sugar
1 teaspoon Worcestershire
 sauce
1 teaspoon dry sherry
½ teaspoon soy sauce
2 tablespoons water
1 tablespoon oil

Pour the mixed marinade
ingredients over the chops, set
aside for 30 minutes.

Heat 2 tablespoons oil in a
wok or saucepan. Sauté the
vegetables until soft, then stir
in the next eight ingredients
and boil. Blend the cornflour
with the water, stir into the
sauce and simmer for 2
minutes.

Heat the oil for deep frying
to 190 c/375 F. Deep fry the
chops until browned. Drain
thoroughly.

Heat the remaining oil in a
wok. Cook the egg until it
begins to set, then stir in the
rice. Put in an ovenproof
casserole; top with the chops.
Pour the sauce over and bake
in a hot oven (230 c, 450 F,
gas 8) for 15 minutes. *Serves 4*

Steamed Pork with Salted Eggs

2 canned water chestnuts
   (optional)
350 g/12 oz lean minced pork
3 salted egg yolks (page 226)
2 teaspoons grated fresh root
   ginger
salt and pepper
1 teaspoon light soy sauce
1 teaspoon dry sherry
1 teaspoon sugar
1 teaspoon cornflour
2 tablespoons water
1 teaspoon sesame oil
GARNISH
2 parsley sprigs
1 spring onion, shredded

Finely chop or mince the
water chestnuts (if used), and
mix them into the pork. Cut
the salted egg yolks in half.
Set four of these halves aside
for the garnish, then chop the
remainder.
   Mix the chopped salted egg
yolk into the meat with the
ginger. Add seasoning to
taste, the light soy sauce,
sherry, sugar, cornflour, and
water. Pound the meat

mixture thoroughly until all
the ingredients are well
combined. Stir in the sesame
oil and set the mixture aside
for 20 minutes.
   Transfer the mixture to a
heat-proof bowl and steam the
pork over boiling water for 30
minutes.
   To serve, spoon the meat
on to a warmed serving plate,
then add a garnish of the
reserved egg halves, parsley
and the shredded spring
onion. Serve at once.
Serves 4–6

Note: If you do not have a
steamer, the pork can be
cooked on a fairly large,
shallow dish or plate over a
large saucepan of boiling
water. Cover the plate or dish
completely with cooking foil
and make sure it fits neatly
over the pan of simmering
water. Keep the water topped
up during cooking as
necessary.

Minced Pork with Dried Squid

50 g/2 oz dried squid
1 sprig parsley, chopped
1 teaspoon grated fresh root
   ginger
2 spring onions, chopped
350 g/12 oz minced pork
¼ teaspoon salt
1 teaspoon sugar
1 teaspoon dry sherry
1 teaspoon light soy sauce
pinch of pepper
a few drops of sesame oil
1 teaspoon cornflour
1 tablespoon oil plus oil for
   greasing
GARNISH
1 tablespoon finely shredded
   fresh root ginger
flat-leafed parsley sprigs

Soak the squid in plenty of
cold water for 30 minutes,
then drain thoroughly and
dice it finely.
   Mix the chopped parsley,
grated ginger and spring
onions into the minced pork.
Add all the remaining
ingredients and set aside to
marinate for 15 minutes.

Transfer the pork to a
greased platter, then cook it
in a steamer over boiling
water for 30–40 minutes. Top
up the boiling water under the
steamer if necessary during
cooking.
   Serve hot, garnished with
the shredded ginger and
parsley. *Serves 4*

Note: If you like you can use
fresh squid in this recipe
instead of the dried seafood.
   Follow the instructions on
page 16 for preparing the
squid, then chop all the edible
parts finely and quickly sauté
them in a little oil before
stirring into the pork.
Continue to cook as in the
main recipe.

Braised Meatballs

450 g/1 lb minced pork
salt and pepper
2 teaspoons light soy sauce
2 teaspoons sugar
1 teaspoon cornflour plus extra
  for coating
1 teaspoon dry sherry
300 ml/½ pint plus 2
  tablespoons water
3 tablespoons oil plus oil for
  deep frying
175 g/6 oz peeled cooked
  shrimps
1 teaspoon grated fresh root
  ginger
1 tablespoon chopped spring
  onion
1 shallot, sliced
1 clove garlic, sliced
2 teaspoons oyster sauce
½ teaspoon sesame oil
1 crisp lettuce to serve

Place the pork in a bowl, then add ¼ teaspoon salt, 1 teaspoon each of light soy sauce, sugar, cornflour and sherry, 2 tablespoons water, a little pepper and 1 tablespoon oil. Mix thoroughly, then set aside to marinate for 20 minutes.

Mash the shrimps, then add them to the minced pork with the ginger and spring onion. Pound the mixture until firm and thoroughly bound together. Shape the meat into small balls about the size of walnuts. Coat these with cornflour.

Heat the oil for deep frying to 190 c/375 f, then add the meatballs and cook until golden brown. Drain on absorbent kitchen paper.

Heat the remaining 2 tablespoons oil in a flameproof casserole, then add and sauté the shallot and garlic until fragrant. Stir in the meatballs and fry for a few minutes.

Pour in the remaining sherry, water, remaining soy sauce, the oyster sauce, remaining sugar and the sesame oil. Bring to the boil, then simmer, uncovered, for 8–10 minutes.

Arrange the lettuce in a serving dish and pile the meatballs on top. Pour over the cooking juices and serve at once. *Serves 4*

Taro Croquettes

275 g/10 oz taro
2–3 tablespoons boiling water
25 g/1 oz cornflour
50 g/2 oz dried shrimps
3 Chinese dried mushrooms
225 g/8 oz lean boneless pork
2 spring onions, chopped
1 tablespoon chopped parsley
1 teaspoon salt
1 teaspoon sugar
2 teaspoons soy sauce
½ chicken stock cube, crumbled
½ teaspoon pepper
½ teaspoon sesame oil
flour for coating
oil for deep frying

Peel and wash the taro, then steam the vegetable over boiling water until soft – about 30 minutes. Pour the boiling water into the cornflour, then stir and mix into a soft dough. Wash and soak the dried shrimps and mushrooms for 30 minutes. Chop both finely. Mince the taro with the pork and cornflour dough. Stir all the remaining ingredients into this minced mixture and shape it into small rounds. Coat these generously in flour.

Heat the oil for deep frying to 190 c/375 f, then deep fry the croquettes until golden brown. Drain on absorbent kitchen paper and serve hot. *Serves 6*

Note: The taro vegetable is a root vegetable which is similar to the potato. If you are unable to obtain taro, then substitute sweet potato or ordinary potatoes.

Meat Patties with Water Chestnuts

3 Chinese dried mushrooms
1 (227-g/8-oz) can water
* chestnuts, drained*
2 spring onions, chopped
450 g/1 lb minced pork
salt and pepper
¼ teaspoon monosodium
* glutamate*
½ teaspoon light soy sauce
½ teaspoon sesame oil
2 teaspoons cornflour plus
* extra for coating*
3 tablespoons oil
1 shallot, chopped
1 clove garlic, crushed
225 g/8 oz fresh spinach,
* trimmed and washed*
1 teaspoon dry sherry
100 ml/4 fl oz chicken stock
2 tablespoons water

Soak the mushrooms in cold water for 30 minutes, then remove their stalks and chop them. Grate the water chestnuts. Mix these ingredients with the spring onions and meat in a bowl. Add seasoning to taste, the monosodium glutamate, light soy sauce, sesame oil and 1 teaspoon cornflour. Pound the meat firmly to make sure all the ingredients are thoroughly combined, then shape it into 24 small patties. Coat the patties with cornflour.

Heat the oil in a large frying pan. Add the shallot and garlic and fry until fragrant, then discard.

Add the patties to the pan, as many as you can fit in, and fry them until well browned underneath. Turn and cook the second side until well cooked. Drain on absorbent kitchen paper and arrange on a serving dish. Keep hot and continue frying the patties until they are all cooked.

Add the spinach to the fat remaining in the pan and sauté it quickly until just cooked. Arrange the leaves with the patties. Keep hot.

Pour the sherry and stock into the pan and bring to the boil. Blend the remaining 1 teaspoon cornflour with the water. Stir this into the sauce and simmer for 2 minutes. Pour the sauce over the patties and serve. *Serves 4–6*

Pork and Sweet Corn Patties

1 (312-g/11-oz) can creamed
* sweet corn*
salt and pepper
½ teaspoon sugar
2 teaspoons light soy sauce
½ teaspoon sesame oil
3 Chinese dried mushrooms
50 g/2 oz preserved mustard
100 g/4 oz minced pork
1 teaspoon sherry
1 teaspoon cornflour
1 tablespoon water
1 large clove garlic, crushed
1 tablespoon chopped parsley
1 teaspoon chopped shallot
50 g/2 oz plain flour
oil for cooking
parsley sprig to garnish

Pour the sweet corn and seasoning to taste into a bowl and mix well. Add the sugar, half the light soy sauce and the sesame oil and mix thoroughly.

Soak the mushrooms and preserved mustard for 15 minutes, then drain. Cook the mushrooms over boiling water for 10 minutes. Dice the mustard. Drain and dice the cooked mushrooms, removing their stalks.

Mix the pork with the remaining light soy sauce, the sherry and cornflour. Stir in the water and a pinch of pepper. Set aside for 10 minutes to allow the flavours to mingle. Stir the garlic, chopped parsley, shallot and flour into the meat.

Heat a little oil in a frying pan. Add a spoonful of the meat mixture, flatten it slightly and cook until golden on the underneath. Turn and cook the second side until golden. Continue cooking the mixture in this way, adding more oil to the pan as necessary, until all the patties are cooked. Serve hot, garnished with a sprig of parsley. *Serves 4*

Meat and Vegetable Won Tons

2 teaspoons light soy sauce
1 teaspoon cornflour
2 teaspoons dry sherry
salt and pepper
½ teaspoon sugar
175 g/6 oz minced pork
175 g/6 oz Chinese cabbage or
    Swiss chard
1 teaspoon finely grated fresh
    root ginger
275 g/10 oz (about 40 squares)
    won ton dough
1 egg white, lightly whisked
2 tablespoons oil
1 medium-thick slice fresh root
    ginger
1 shallot, sliced
1.15 litres/2 pints chicken stock
1 chicken stock cube
1 teaspoon sesame oil

Mix 1 teaspoon each of light soy sauce, cornflour and sherry, seasoning to taste and the sugar into the pork. Leave to marinate for 10 minutes.

Blanch the Chinese cabbage or Swiss chard in boiling water. Drain, squeeze out all the water and chop half the vegetable finely. Mix the chopped cabbage with the minced pork. Add the grated ginger and pound well.

Place a square of won ton dough on the palm of your hand. Put 1 teaspoon filling on to the dough, then roll up and seal with egg-white, folding the end corner in to keep the won tons neat.

Cook the won tons in plenty of boiling water until they float. Add about 300 ml/½ pint of cold water and bring to the boil again. Drain, refresh under cold water and drain.

Heat the oil in a wok or frying pan and sauté the sliced ginger and shallot; discard. Pour in the stock, remaining sherry and soy sauce, crumbled stock cube and sesame oil. Bring to the boil. Drop the won tons and remaining cabbage into the stock, heat for a minute, then serve. *Serves 6*

Pork Slice in Hot Broad Bean Sauce

175 g/6 oz loin of pork
2 teaspoons light soy sauce
2 teaspoons cornflour
2 teaspoons dry sherry
1 teaspoon sugar
pepper
1 generous teaspoon sesame oil
4 tablespoons water
2 tablespoons oil
2 medium-thick slices fresh
  root ginger, shredded
2 shallots, sliced
2 cloves garlic, sliced
1 onion, quartered
1 large green pepper, deseeded
  and roughly chopped
50 g/2 oz chillies, deseeded and
  roughly chopped
2 tablespoons hot broad bean
  paste
50 ml/2 fl oz chicken stock
1 teaspoon vinegar
GARNISH
2 spring onions, shredded
chilli tassel (page 45)

Slice the pork. Mix half the light soy sauce, cornflour, sherry and sugar; a little

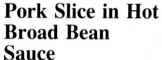

pepper, a few drops of the sesame oil and 2 tablespoons of the water. Pour this mixture over the pork, then mix well and leave to marinate for 30 minutes.

Heat the oil in a wok or large frying pan. Sauté the ginger, shallots and garlic until fragrant, then stir in the onion, pepper and chillies and fry for a while. Mix in the broad bean paste and pork, then fry until browned.

Pour the remaining sherry into the pan and add the rest of the light soy sauce, the stock, remaining sugar and sesame oil. Heat through to boiling point. Blend the remaining cornflour and water to a smooth paste, stir into the sauce and simmer for 2 minutes or until thickened.

Lastly sprinkle in the vinegar, then serve, garnished with the spring onions.
Serves 4

Pork and Offal with Spring Onion

100 g/4 oz pig's liver
100 g/4 oz pig's kidney
100 g/4 oz loin of pork
1 tablespoon light soy sauce
2 teaspoons sugar
7–8 teaspoons dry sherry
1 teaspoon sesame oil
salt and pepper
3–4 tablespoons water
3 tablespoons oil plus oil for
  deep frying
1 tablespoon ginger juice
2 teaspoons cornflour
2 cloves garlic, sliced
12 spring onions, shredded
1 teaspoon dark soy sauce
¼ teaspoon monosodium
  glutamate

Rinse and slice the liver. Trim and slice the kidney. Slice the pork.

Mix 1 teaspoon of the light soy sauce, ½ teaspoon each of sugar, sherry and sesame oil, a pinch of pepper, 2–3 tablespoons of the water and 1 tablespoon of the oil. Marinate the pork in this

mixture for 20 minutes.

Heat the oil for deep frying to 190 C/375 F, then add the pork and fry until half cooked. Drain the meat on absorbent kitchen paper.

Blanch the liver and kidney for 1 minute in boiling water. Drain and wipe dry. Marinate the offal with the ginger juice, 1 tablespoon of the sherry and 1 teaspoon of the cornflour for about 5–10 minutes, then deep fry the slices for 1–2 minutes. Drain them on absorbent kitchen paper.

Heat the 2 tablespoons oil in a wok or frying pan; sauté the garlic and spring onions until fragrant. Add the pork and stir-fry for a short while. Add the liver and kidney, then sprinkle in the remaining sherry. Stir in the dark soy sauce, remaining light soy sauce and monosodium glutamate, then sprinkle in the remaining sesame oil. Blend the last of the cornflour with 1 tablespoon water, stir the mixture into the juices and simmer for 2 minutes to thicken the liquid. Serve at once. *Serves 4–6*

Sweet and Sour Meatballs

450 g/1 lb minced pork
1 medium-thick slice fresh root
   ginger, chopped
1 small egg
2 spring onions, finely
   chopped
salt and pepper
generous pinch of sugar
1 teaspoon light soy sauce
½ teaspoon plus a few drops
   sesame oil
1½ teaspoons dry sherry
2 teaspoons cornflour
1 tablespoon black fungus
1 small carrot, parboiled
2 tablespoons oil plus oil for
   deep frying
1 green pepper, deseeded and
   roughly chopped
300 ml/½ pint Sweet and Sour
   Sauce (page 227)
1 tablespoon water
2 slices fresh or canned
   pineapple, cut into chunks

Mix the minced pork with the ginger, egg, spring onions and seasoning to taste. Add the sugar, light soy sauce, a few drops of sesame oil,

1 teaspoon each of the sherry and cornflour. Pound the mixture firmly then shape it into small meatballs. Soak the black fungus in water for 15 minutes. Dice the carrot.

Heat the oil for deep frying to 190 c/375 F, then add the meatballs and deep fry them until browned. Drain on absorbent kitchen paper.

Heat the 2 tablespoons oil in a saucepan, add the diced carrot, fungus and the green pepper, then sauté for a few minutes. Pour in the sweet and sour sauce and remaining sherry and bring to the boil.

Blend the remaining cornflour with the water, stir this into the sauce with the remaining sesame oil and the pineapple. Simmer for 2 minutes before stirring in the meatballs. Reheat and serve.
Serves 4

Note: The meatballs can be served in one or two scooped-out pineapple halves and garnished extravagantly with sliced quartered apples, cucumber and cherries, sliced peaches and oranges as shown.

Stewed Trotters with Mushrooms

100 g/4 oz Chinese dried
   mushrooms or large open
   mushrooms
6 tablespoons oil
salt and pepper
¼ teaspoon sugar
4 pig's trotters
2 medium-thick slices fresh
   root ginger
4 spring onions
1 shallot, chopped
1 clove garlic, chopped
3 tablespoons fermented bean
   curd
2 teaspoons dry sherry
½ teaspoon sesame oil
1 small crisp lettuce, trimmed
   and separated into leaves
1 carrot, sliced and blanched,
   to garnish

Wash the dried mushrooms, then soak them in water for 10 minutes. Drain thoroughly. Discard the stalks, then marinate the caps with 2 tablespoons oil, ¼ teaspoon salt and the sugar for 10 minutes. Steam these over boiling water for 10 minutes.

Thoroughly clean the trotters, then cook them in boiling water with the ginger and spring onions for 20 minutes. Drain thoroughly.

Heat 2 tablespoons of the remaining oil in a wok or heavy-based saucepan. Add the shallot and garlic and fry for a while. Stir in the fermented bean curd and the trotters. Fry quickly, then add the sherry and pour in enough water to cover the trotters. Bring to the boil, reduce the heat and cover the pan. Simmer for 1–1½ hours or until the trotters are tender.

Heat the remaining 2 tablespoons oil in a large frying pan and add the whole mushrooms. Cook for a while, then stir in the drained trotters and cook for 10 minutes. Add seasoning to taste and the sesame oil.

Blanch the lettuce briefly in boiling water, then drain it thoroughly and arrange the leaves on a warmed serving platter.

Spoon the trotters on to the lettuce, then add a garnish of carrot slices and serve at once.
Serves 4

Pork

Jumbo Meatball Casserole

4 Chinese dried mushrooms
2 tablespoons dried shrimps
10 canned water chestnuts
1 tablespoon roasted peanuts
450 g/1 lb minced pork
2 eggs, beaten separately
50 g/2 oz plus 4 tablespoons
  plain flour
salt and pepper
¼ teaspoon monosodium
  glutamate
2 teaspoons dry sherry
2 teaspoons light soy sauce
2 tablespoons oil plus oil for
  deep frying
1 teaspoon finely chopped
  fresh root ginger
1 teaspoon chopped spring
  onion
1 small Chinese cabbage
  (about 350 g/12 oz in weight)
  or Swiss chard, separated
  into leaves
450 ml/¾ pint chicken stock

Soak the mushrooms and dried shrimps together, then drain. Finely chop the mushrooms, removing their woody stalks, then chop the shrimps too. Chop the water chestnuts and peanuts. Mix all these ingredients into the minced pork. Add one egg and 1 tablespoon flour, then pound the meat thoroughly to make sure that all the ingredients are combined. Stir in seasoning to taste, the monosodium glutamate, 1 teaspoon each of sherry and light soy sauce.

Sift the 50 g/2 oz flour into a bowl, then beat in the remaining egg and enough water to make a thin batter. Coat the meatballs in the remaining 3 tablespoons flour, then coat them as thoroughly as possible in the batter.

Heat the oil for deep frying to 190 c/375 f, add the meatballs and fry until their coating is crisp. Using a draining spoon, lift the meatballs out of the oil and make a small slit in each – it should be deep enough to just crack through the batter. Replace them in the hot oil and continue to fry until golden brown, then drain the meatballs on absorbent kitchen paper.

Heat the 2 tablespoons oil in a saucepan. Add the ginger and spring onion and fry until fragrant. Stir in the Chinese cabbage and cook for a few minutes, then pour in the remaining sherry, light soy sauce and the stock. Bring to the boil and add seasoning to taste, then arrange the meatballs in the sauce. Reduce the heat, cover the pan and simmer for 20 minutes before serving.
Serves 4

CHINESE TITLE

This is a traditional Chinese dish which could well be served as part of a celebration feast. It is, like many recipes which have been handed down over the centuries, representative of good will and good fortune.

The alternative title for the meatball casserole is Lion's Head. This name is used because the large meatballs are meant to represent the heads of lions and the Chinese cabbage which surrounds them is seen as the mane.

The four meatballs represent felicity – a skilful faculty – prosperity, longevity – long life – and happiness.

Jumbo Egg Sheet Rolls

1 teaspoon dark soy sauce
½ teaspoon sugar
1 teaspoon dry sherry
about 5 tablespoons cornflour
salt and pepper
50 ml/2 fl oz plus 4–6 tablespoons water
about 4 tablespoons oil plus oil for deep frying
225 g/8 oz loin of pork, shredded
6 Chinese dried mushrooms
1 clove garlic, sliced
350 g/12 oz bean sprouts
1 (227-g/8-oz) can bamboo shoots, drained and shredded
1 teaspoon light soy sauce
a few drops of sesame oil
6 eggs
GARNISH
cucumber slices
parsley sprigs

TO SERVE
soy sauce
Spicy Salt (page 229)

Mix the dark soy sauce, sugar, ½ teaspoon sherry, 1 teaspoon of the cornflour, a pinch of pepper, 50 ml/2 fl oz water and 1 tablespoon oil. Toss the pork in this mixture and set aside to marinate for 10 minutes.

Wash and soak the mushrooms in cold water for 15 minutes. Then cut off and discard their stalks and shred the mushroom caps finely. Add ½ teaspoon oil and steam for 10 minutes over boiling water.

Heat 2 tablespoons oil in a wok or frying pan. Sauté the garlic until fragrant. Stir in the bean sprouts and bamboo shoots, then add the pork and mushrooms and sauté until thoroughly cooked. Sprinkle in the remaining sherry, the light soy sauce, sesame oil and seasoning to taste.

Blend the cornflour with 1 tablespoon of the water, then stir it into the pork mixture and bring to the boil. Simmer for 2 minutes and set aside to cool.

Beat the eggs with ½ teaspoon salt and 1 tablespoon cornflour. Heat a little oil in a large frying pan and pour in one-third of the beaten egg. Cook until set and lightly browned, then turn the egg over and cook the second side until lightly browned. Remove from the pan. Repeat twice more with the remaining egg to give three egg sheets.

Blend the remaining cornflour with the remaining water. Divide the filling between the egg sheets. Brush the edges with the cornflour mixture, then roll them up, tucking the ends in neatly.

Heat the oil for deep frying to 190 c/375 f. Brush the egg rolls all over with a little of the remaining cornflour mixture, then deep fry them until golden.

Slice through the rolls to give diagonal slices. Arrange the slices on a warmed serving plate and garnish with the cucumber and parsley. Serve at once, with a small dish each of soy sauce and spicy salt.
Serves 6

Note: These egg sheet rolls can be served as an accompaniment for a congee. This will make a light meal, suitable for lunch or supper.

Ham with Mushrooms and Bamboo Shoots

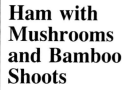

225 g/8 oz cooked ham, sliced
1 (227-g/8-oz) can bamboo
  shoots, drained
50 g/2 oz Chinese dried
  mushrooms
3 tablespoons oil
1 teaspoon sugar
salt
225 g/8 oz broccoli
1 teaspoon dry sherry
a few drops of sesame oil
pinch of pepper
1 teaspoon light soy sauce
1 teaspoon oyster sauce
100 ml/4 fl oz chicken stock
1 teaspoon cornflour
1 tablespoon water
GARNISH
2 tablespoons finely shredded
  fresh root ginger
a few flat-leafed parsley sprigs

Cut the ham into oblong pieces or use a biscuit cutter to cut out fluted circles. Slice and cut the bamboo shoots into the same shape as the ham. Soak the mushrooms until softened, then squeeze out the excess water. Season with 2 tablespoons oil, ½ teaspoon sugar, and a pinch of salt. Steam over boiling water for 10 minutes. Slice the cooked mushrooms into halves.

Arrange the ham, mushrooms and bamboo shoots alternately in two rows on an oval platter. Sprinkle with salt and the remaining sugar and steam for 10 minutes. Drain off and reserve the liquid. Keep the ham hot.

Blanch the broccoli in boiling water for 2 minutes, then drain and arrange round the ham.

Heat the reserved stock with the sherry, 1 tablespoon oil, remaining sugar, sesame oil, pepper, light soy sauce, oyster sauce and chicken stock. Blend the cornflour with the water. Stir into the sauce and simmer for 2 minutes.

Pour the sauce over the ham, garnish with the ginger and parsley to serve. *Serves 4*

Ham in Honey

450 g/1 lb Chinese ham or
  gammon, in one piece
50 g/2 oz lotus seeds
1 (225-g/8-oz) can crushed
  pineapple
75 g/3 oz demerara sugar
3 tablespoons honey
1 tablespoon dry sherry
parsley sprigs to garnish

Cook the ham or gammon in boiling water for 30 minutes. Drain and remove any bones if necessary, then cut the meat into long slices.

Arrange the sliced ham neatly in a bowl. Put the untidy pieces on top. Pour in enough boiling water to cover the meat, then steam over boiling water for 20 minutes. Remove from the steamer and pour away the stock.

Wash and drain the lotus seeds, then place them on top of the ham. Pour the pineapple on top. Mix the sugar, honey and sherry, then pour this over the pineapple. Steam over boiling water for 2 hours.

Top up the water in the saucepan below the steamer as necessary during cooking. Arrange the ham on a serving plate, pour over the juices and serve, garnished with parsley. *Serves 4*

CHINESE TITLE

Many of the recipes in this book have great meaning in their Chinese titles. This traditional recipe for Ham in Honey, for example, has a Chinese title which means 'Affection and Intimacy.'

Stewed Tongue with Black Moss

2 pig's tongues
6 tablespoons oil
4 spring onions
4 medium-thick slices fresh
    root ginger
1 tablespoon dry sherry
1 tablespoon star anise
cayenne pepper
25 g/1 oz black moss
100 ml/4 fl oz chicken stock
1 large carrot, cooked and
    sliced
1 tablespoon oyster sauce
2 tablespoons light soy sauce
2 tablespoons dark soy sauce
1 teaspoon sugar
¼ teaspoon monosodium
    glutamate
salt and pepper
1 teaspoon cornflour
2 tablespoons water
parsley sprigs to garnish

Thoroughly wash the tongues,
then boil them for a few
minutes. Drain and soak in
cold water until cooled, then
scrape them with a small knife
to remove the outer skin.
Heat 2 tablespoons of the

oil in a saucepan, add half the
spring onions and ginger and
sauté to bring out their
aromas. Add the tongues,
sprinkle in half the sherry
then add water to cover, star
anise, and cayenne to taste.
Bring to the boil. Season and
simmer for 1½ hours. Remove
and leave to cool.
Soak the black moss. Cook
it in boiling water for a while,
then drain and rinse. Heat
another 2 tablespoons oil in a
saucepan. Add the remaining
ginger and spring onion.
Sprinkle in the remaining
sherry, then pour in the stock
and bring to the boil. Add the
black moss and simmer for 5
minutes.
Slice the tongues, arrange
the slices on a dish with the
sliced carrot. Add the black
moss in the centre. Heat the
remaining oil in a saucepan,
add the oyster sauce, light and
dark soy sauce, sugar,
monosodium glutamate and
seasoning. Blend the cornflour
with the water, pour it into
the sauce and simmer until
thickened. Pour over the
tongue and serve garnished
with parsley. *Serves 4–6*

Assorted Meat in Sauce

50 g/2 oz pig's liver, trimmed
½ pig's kidney, trimmed
1 fresh squid
1 tablespoon dry sherry
2 teaspoons Ginger Juice (page
    227)
3 tablespoons cornflour
1 teaspoon sugar
1 tablespoon light soy sauce
50 g/2 oz lean pork, sliced
½ egg white
50 g/2 oz uncooked boneless
    chicken, sliced
2 Chinese dried mushrooms
2 tablespoons oil
2 medium-thick slices fresh
    root ginger, chopped
2 spring onions, chopped
450 ml/¾ pint chicken stock
1¼ teaspoons salt
1 tablespoon dark soy sauce
pinch of pepper
½ teaspoon sesame oil
50 g/2 oz gammon, sliced
1 piece canned bamboo shoot,
    sliced
1 canned abalone, sliced
2 tablespoons water

Slice the liver and kidney.
Prepare the squid (page 16)
and cut it into pieces. Mix
these ingredients with 1
teaspoon each of sherry and
ginger juice, and a little
cornflour. Set aside for 20
minutes.
Mix the sugar, light soy
sauce and a little cornflour
with the pork; set aside for 20
minutes. Mix the remaining
ginger juice with ½ teaspoon
sherry, the egg white and a
little cornflour. Mix in the
chicken; set aside for a while.
Soak the mushrooms for 10
minutes, then slice them.
Blanch all the marinated
ingredients, then drain them.
Heat the oil in a wok and add
the ginger and spring onions.
Add the remaining sherry and
stock, then boil. Stir in the
salt, dark soy sauce, pepper
and sesame oil. Add the
blanched ingredients,
gammon, bamboo shoot,
abalone and mushrooms.
Simmer for 30 minutes.
Mix the remaining cornflour
with the water, pour into the
sauce and cook for 2 minutes.
Serves 4

Stewed Pork

1(1.5-kg/3-lb) shoulder of
pork joint
4 tablespoons oil
4 medium-thick slices fresh
root ginger
3 shallots, sliced
2 tablespoons dry sherry
3 star anise
2 teaspoons dark soy sauce
1 tablespoon red bean curd
1 teaspoon salt
4 teaspoons sugar
2 teaspoons light soy sauce
1 chicken stock cube
1 Iceberg lettuce, trimmed and
separated into leaves
1 radish, cut to resemble a
flower, to garnish

Singe any hairs off the skin of
the pork. Heat half the oil in
a large flameproof casserole or
heavy-based saucepan. Add
the ginger and shallots and fry
until fragrant. Sprinkle in the
sherry, then carefully pour in
enough water to one-third fill
the pan. Add the pork and
the star anise and bring to the
boil. Cover and simmer for 1
hour.
  Lift the cooked pork out of

the pan, draining it
thoroughly. Brush the rind all
over with the dark soy sauce.
  Heat the remaining oil in a
large frying pan. Add the
joint of pork and fry it
thoroughly until it is golden
brown on all sides. You will
have to turn the pork several
times during frying and you
may even have to hold it in
position for the skin to brown
all over.
  Add the red bean curd to
the stewing liquid, then stir in
the salt, sugar and light soy
sauce. Crumble in the stock
cube, then replace the
browned pork in the pan and
simmer it gently, covered, for
a further 2 hours.
  Remove the pork from the
pan and keep it hot. Quickly
blanch the lettuce in the
sauce, then transfer it to a
serving platter. Place the pork
on the lettuce and ladle a little
of the cooking liquid over the
top. Add a radish flower to
garnish and serve at once,
with the reserved stewing
liquid. *Serves 6–8*

Bean Curd Casserole with Assorted Meat

75 g/3 oz pig's kidney, trimmed
and cut into chunks
3 teaspoons Ginger Juice (page
227)
2 teaspoons dry sherry
3 teaspoons cornflour
8 Chinese dried mushrooms
75 g/3 oz squid
4 fresh scallops, cleaned
2 tablespoons oil plus oil for
deep frying
675 g/1½ lb bean curd
2 medium-thick slices fresh
root ginger
2 shallots
50 g/2 oz peeled cooked
prawns
50 g/2 oz canned abalone,
sliced
50 g/2 oz cooked ham, sliced
100 ml/4 fl oz chicken stock
a few drops of dark soy sauce
1 teaspoon oyster sauce
salt and pepper
1 teaspoon sugar
1 teaspoon sesame oil
1 spring onion, finely
shredded, to garnish

Marinate the kidney with 1
teaspoon each of ginger juice,
sherry and cornflour for 30
minutes.
  Soak the mushrooms in cold
water for 15 minutes, then
drain and steam them for 10
minutes. Slice the mushroom
caps. Prepare the squid
according to the instructions
on page 16. Mix with 1
teaspoon each of ginger juice
and cornflour, then set aside
for 30 minutes. Marinate the
scallops for 10 minutes with 1
teaspoon each of ginger juice
and cornflour.
  Heat the oil for deep frying
to 190 c/375 F. Fry the
kidney, squid and scallops
separately until just cooked.
Drain. Blanch the bean curd
in boiling water for 1 minute,
then rinse and drain.
  Heat the 2 tablespoons oil
in a wok or frying pan; add
and sauté the ginger and
shallots. Add the bean curd,
kidney, squid, scallops,
prawns, abalone and ham.
Cook for a while, then stir in
all the remaining ingredients.
Boil, simmer for a few
minutes, then serve, garnished
with spring onion. *Serves 4*

Scrambled Eggs with Cha Shiu and Bean Sprouts

2 Chinese dried mushrooms
5 eggs
½ teaspoon salt
¼ teaspoon sugar
pinch of pepper
½ teaspoon sesame oil
25 g/1 oz Cha Shiu (page 225),
    shredded
25 g/1 oz bean sprouts,
    trimmed
1 spring onion, shredded
1 medium-thick slice fresh root
    ginger, shredded
oil for cooking
parsley sprigs to garnish

Soak the mushrooms in cold water for 10 minutes, then drain and steam them over boiling water for 10 minutes. Remove the stalks and slice the mushroom caps.

Beat the eggs with the salt, sugar, pepper and sesame oil. Mix the cha shiu, bean sprouts, onion and ginger into the beaten egg and whisk thoroughly.

Heat a wok or saucepan and add a little oil. Swirl the pan to make sure that it is thoroughly coated in oil, then pour in the egg mixture and cook over low heat, stirring continuously until just set. Serve at once, garnished with parsley sprigs. *Serves 4*

Sautéed Beef with Spring Onions

175 g/6 oz frying steak
2 teaspoons light soy sauce
2 teaspoons sugar
2 teaspoons dry sherry
2 teaspoons cornflour
½ teaspoon bicarbonate of soda
pinch of pepper
50 ml/2 fl oz plus 2 tablespoons
* water*
4 tablespoons oil plus oil for
* deep frying*
2 shallots, sliced
2 cloves garlic, sliced
2 medium-thick slices fresh
* root ginger*
1 bunch spring onions,
* shredded*
50 ml/2 fl oz beef stock
1 tablespoon oyster sauce
½ teaspoon dark soy sauce
½ teaspoon sesame oil

Cut the steak into small, thin slices. Marinate these with a mixture of the light soy sauce, 1 teaspoon each of sugar, sherry and cornflour; ½ teaspoon bicarbonate of soda, a pinch of pepper, 50 ml/2 fl oz water and 2 tablespoons oil for 2 hours.

Heat the oil for deep frying to 190 c/375 F, then add the beef and fry for just a few minutes. Drain on absorbent kitchen paper and set aside.

Heat the 2 tablespoons oil in a wok or frying pan, add the shallots, garlic and ginger and fry until fragrant. Stir in the spring onions and beef and stir-fry for a few minutes.

Pour in the stock, remaining sherry, the oyster sauce, remaining sugar, the dark soy sauce, pepper to taste and the sesame oil. Bring to the boil. Blend the remaining cornflour to a smooth paste with the remaining 2 tablespoons water, stir this into the sauce and simmer for 2 minutes.

Transfer to a heated serving dish and serve at once.
Serves 4

Sautéed Beef with Celery

100 g/4 oz frying steak
1 teaspoon light soy sauce
1 teaspoon sugar
2 teaspoons cornflour
2 teaspoons dry sherry
salt and pepper
50 ml/2 fl oz plus 2 tablespoons water
3 tablespoons oil plus oil for deep frying
150 g/5 oz celery
1 carrot, sliced
a few pieces fresh root ginger, grated
1 shallot, sliced
1 clove garlic, sliced
2 tablespoons beef stock
a few drops of dark soy sauce
1 teaspoon sesame oil

Cut the steak into small, thin slices. Mix the light soy sauce, sugar, half each of the cornflour and sherry, a pinch of pepper and 50 ml/2 fl oz water. Add 1 tablespoon oil, mix thoroughly, then pour this marinade over the steak and set aside for about 30 minutes.

Heat the oil for deep frying to 190 c/375 f. Add the beef and cook for a few minutes. Drain on absorbent kitchen paper and set aside.

Trim the celery and cut it into 3.5-cm/1½-in pieces. Blanch these with the carrot for 1 minute. Drain and rinse under cold water.

Heat the remaining oil in a wok or frying pan. Add the ginger, shallot and garlic and fry until fragrant. Stir in the celery and carrot and stir-fry for a few minutes. Add the beef to the pan, pour in the remaining sherry, the stock, dark soy sauce and sesame oil. Stir in salt to taste and heat through.

Blend the remaining cornflour with the 2 tablespoons water, stir this into the sauce and simmer for 2 minutes. Transfer to a heated serving dish and serve at once.
Serves 4

Sautéed Beef with Cucumber

1 cucumber
175 g/6 oz fillet steak
2 teaspoons light soy sauce
2 teaspoons dry sherry
2 teaspoons cornflour
½ teaspoon sugar
a pinch of pepper
50 ml/2 fl oz water
4 tablespoons oil plus oil for deep frying
15 g/½ oz black fungus
1 medium-thick slice fresh root ginger, shredded
1 shallot, sliced
1 clove garlic, sliced
1 small onion, quartered
50 ml/2 fl oz beef stock
1 teaspoon oyster sauce
1 teaspoon sesame oil

Remove thin strips of peel from the cucumber to give a striped effect. Cut into thick slices or triangular pieces.

Slice and marinate the steak for 30 minutes with 1 teaspoon each of the light soy sauce, sherry and cornflour; ½ teaspoon sugar, a pinch of pepper and the water. Stir in 2 tablespoons of the oil, then continue to marinate for a further 30 minutes.

Heat the oil for deep frying to 190 c/375 f. Add the beef and fry until very lightly cooked. Drain on absorbent kitchen paper and set aside.

Soak the black fungus in boiling water until soft. Trim and wash thoroughly, then cut it into small pieces.

Heat the remaining 2 tablespoons oil in a wok or frying pan. Sauté the ginger, shallot and garlic until fragrant, then add the onion and black fungus and fry for a while. Stir in the cucumber and beef and fry until thoroughly cooked.

Mix all the remaining ingredients together, then pour the mixture into the pan and bring to the boil. Simmer for 2 minutes before serving hot. *Serves 4*

Black Pepper Beef

450 g/1 lb braising steak
3 tablespoons light soy sauce
4 teaspoons sugar
4 teaspoons dry sherry
2 teaspoons cornflour
1 teaspoon meat tenderiser (or monosodium glutamate)
150 ml/¼ pint water
5 tablespoons oil plus oil for deep frying
1 teaspoon ground black pepper
450 g/1 lb potatoes, peeled and cut into chunks
3 shallots
3 cloves garlic
1 teaspoon finely grated fresh root ginger
750 ml/1¼ pints beef stock
½ teaspoon salt

Cut the steak into 2.5-cm/1-in cubes. Marinate these for 30 minutes in a mixture of 2 teaspoons each of the light soy sauce, sugar, sherry and cornflour; the meat tenderiser, water and 3 tablespoons oil. Add the pepper and marinate for another 20 minutes.

Heat the oil for deep frying to 190 c/375 f. Add the drained steak and fry for a few minutes. Drain on absorbent kitchen paper and set aside. Deep fry the potatoes until golden brown, then drain on absorbent kitchen paper and set aside.

Heat the remaining oil in a flameproof casserole or heavy-based saucepan. Add the shallots, garlic and ginger and fry for a few minutes. Stir in the beef and stir-fry for a while, then pour in all the remaining ingredients apart from the potatoes. Bring to the boil, reduce the heat and simmer for 1 hour.

Lastly, add the potatoes, stir well, then re-cover and continue to cook for another 30 minutes before serving.
Serves 4

Beef Fillet with Bean Sprouts

225 g/8 oz fillet steak
1 teaspoon light soy sauce
1½ teaspoons dry sherry
½ teaspoon bicarbonate of soda
pinch of pepper
a few drops of sesame oil
2 teaspoons cornflour
150 ml/¼ pint water
4 tablespoons oil plus oil for deep frying
2 cloves garlic, crushed
2 shallots, grated
225 g/8 oz bean sprouts
2 red chillies, deseeded and shredded
½ teaspoon salt
½ teaspoon sugar
100 ml/4 fl oz chicken stock
1 teaspoon oyster sauce
white part from 1 small leek, shredded

Cut the steak into fine shreds. Mix the light soy sauce, ½ teaspoon of the sherry, the bicarbonate of soda, a pinch of pepper, a few drops of sesame oil, 1 teaspoon of the cornflour, the water and 2 tablespoons of the oil. Pour this over the steak and set aside to marinate for 2 hours.

Heat the oil for deep frying to 190 c/375 f. Drain the beef of marinade, then deep fry the strips until lightly cooked. Drain on absorbent kitchen paper and set aside.

Heat the remaining oil in a wok or frying pan. Sauté half the garlic and 1 shallot long enough to bring out their flavour, then add the bean sprouts and fry over a high heat. Remove and set aside. Add the remaining shallot and garlic clove to sauté for a while. Add the beef, bean sprouts and chillies and stir-fry quickly until cooked.

Mix the remaining cornflour with all the other ingredients, including the leek. Pour this into the pan and heat through to boiling point. Simmer for 2 minutes before serving.
Serves 4

Shredded Beef with Preserved Vegetables

100 g/4 oz fillet steak, shredded
3 teaspoons light soy sauce
2 teaspoons dry sherry
2 teaspoons cornflour
1 teaspoon sugar
¼ teaspoon bicarbonate of soda
salt and pepper
50 ml/2 fl oz plus 2 tablespoons
* water*
3 tablespoons oil plus oil for
* deep frying*
100 g/4 oz preserved mustard
* cabbage*
150 ml/¼ pint Sweet and Sour
* Sauce (page 227)*
2 shallots, sliced
2 cloves garlic, sliced
1 medium-thick slice fresh root
* ginger, shredded*
1 green pepper, deseeded and
* sliced*
2 red chillies, deseeded and
* sliced into rings*
½ teaspoon sesame oil

Marinate the steak for 30 minutes with 1 teaspoon each of the light soy sauce, sherry and cornflour; ½ teaspoon sugar, the bicarbonate of soda, a pinch of pepper, 2 tablespoons water and 1 tablespoon oil.

Heat the oil for deep frying to 190 c/375 F. Drain the steak of marinade (reserve the marinade for later use). Deep fry for a few minutes. Drain on absorbent kitchen paper.

Soak the preserved mustard cabbage in salted water for 1 hour. Drain, cut into shreds, then dry these out in a hot pan. Put in a bowl and marinate for 30 minutes in the sweet and sour sauce.

Heat the remaining 2 tablespoons oil in a wok or frying pan. Sauté the shallots, garlic and ginger until fragrant, then stir in the green pepper, chillies, and drained preserved mustard cabbage. Add the beef and fry for a while. Pour in all the remaining ingredients, simmer for 2 minutes, then serve.
Serves 4

Beef and Mushroom Casserole

25 g/1 oz Chinese dried
    mushrooms
3 tablespoons oil plus oil for
    deep frying
salt and pepper
1½ generous teaspoons sugar
7 g/¼ oz black fungus
25 g/1 oz dried lily flowers
350 g/12 oz frying steak
2 teaspoons light soy sauce
2 teaspoons cornflour
1 tablespoon dry sherry
5 tablespoons water
4 medium-thick slices fresh
    root ginger
2 shallots, sliced
150 ml/¼ pint beef stock
¼ cucumber to garnish

Soak the mushrooms in cold water for 2 hours. Drain and marinate them with a little oil, salt and sugar for a few minutes, then steam over boiling water for 10 minutes.

Soak and trim the black fungus then blanch, refresh and drain it. Mix the fungus with a little oil.

Wash and trim the dried lily flowers. Tie the pieces in pairs to make knots. Cut the beef into small thin slices. Marinate these with 1 teaspoon each of the light soy sauce, cornflour and sherry: ½ teaspoon sugar and 3 tablespoons water for 30 minutes.

Prepare the cucumber garnish at this stage. Cut the piece of cucumber in half horizontally. Lay one half, cut side down, on a board, then use a sharp knife to cut it crossways into very fine slices. Leave all the slices lightly attached at one side. Fold alternate slices to form decorative loops as shown in the picture. Place the garnish on a plate, cover the cucumber and set aside until the meat is cooked.

Heat the oil for deep frying to 190 c/375 f, add the beef and cook for a few minutes. Drain on absorbent kitchen paper and set aside.

Heat the remaining oil in a flameproof casserole or heavy-based saucepan. Drop in the ginger and shallots and sauté for a while. Add the lily flowers, fungus and mushrooms and sauté thoroughly. Stir in the steak and fry rapidly.

Pour in the remaining sherry. Blend the remaining cornflour with all the remaining ingredients, pour the mixture over the beef and bring to the boil. Simmer for 2 minutes, then serve at once, garnished with cucumber.
Serves 4

Dried Lily Flowers: These are dried, elongated lily buds which are about 5–7.5 cm/2–3 in long. They are very fragile and light in weight, with a pale golden colour (or sometimes lighter). In terms of taste, they are delicate, slightly musty and are used to enhance various meat or fish dishes. They can be used in stir-fried dishes or in braised foods. If the dish is not a moist one, then the lily flowers may require soaking before cooking. The flowers can be used either whole, or cut up into shreds. Available from Chinese supermarkets and oriental stores.

Sliced Beef with Satay Sauce

225 g/8 oz frying steak
2 teaspoons soy sauce
2 teaspoons cornflour
1 teaspoon sugar
½ teaspoon bicarbonate of soda
pinch of pepper
50 ml/2 fl oz plus 1 tablespoon
    water
4 tablespoons oil plus oil for
    deep frying
2 shallots
1 clove garlic, crushed
2 tablespoons satay paste (page
    228)
1 large onion, cut into chunks
2 green or red peppers, or 1 of
    each, deseeded and roughly
    chopped
2 red chillies, deseeded and
    roughly chopped
1 teaspoon dry sherry

Cut the steak into small, thin
slices. Mix 1 teaspoon each of
the soy sauce and cornflour,
the sugar, bicarbonate of
soda, a pinch of pepper,
50 ml/2 fl oz water and 2
tablespoons of the oil. Pour
this over the meat and

marinate for 30 minutes.
    Heat the oil for deep frying
to 190 c/375 f, add the
drained beef and deep-fry
until lightly cooked. Drain on
absorbent kitchen paper and
set aside.
    Heat the remaining oil in a
wok or frying pan, add the
shallots and garlic and fry
until fragrant. Stir in the satay
sauce, onion, peppers and
chillies. Stir-fry for a while,
then add the beef.
    Mix all the remaining
ingredients, then pour the
mixture into the pan and
simmer for 2 minutes. Serve
at once. *Serves 4*

Brisket in Ground Bean Sauce

1 kg/2 lb brisket
5 star anise
3 tablespoons dry sherry
small piece of tangerine peel
3 tablespoons oil
50 g/2 oz sliced fresh root
    ginger
3 cloves garlic, sliced
5 tablespoons ground bean
    paste
2 tablespoons sugar
1 tablespoon light soy sauce
¼ teaspoon pepper
2 teaspoons cornflour
2 tablespoons water
1 teaspoon sesame oil
GARNISH
2 spring onions, shredded
red chilli tassel (page 45)

Put the brisket in a
flameproof casserole with
water to cover, the star anise
and 2 tablespoons of the
sherry. Bring to the boil, then
reduce the heat and cover the
pan. Simmer for 2 hours, then
leave for 1 hour in the
casserole. Remove, reserve

the stock and cut the meat
into large chunks. Soak the
tangerine peel in cold water
for 30 minutes.
    Heat the oil in a flameproof
casserole. Sauté the ginger,
garlic and ground bean paste
until fragrant. Add the meat
and mix well. Pour in the
remaining sherry, add the
tangerine peel and reserved
meat stock, adding just
enough to cover the brisket.
Bring to the boil, then simmer
over medium heat for 1 hour.
    Stir in the sugar, light soy
sauce and pepper, then cook
for another 20 minutes. Blend
the cornflour to a smooth
paste with the water. Stir this
into the sauce and simmer for
2 minutes, or until thickened.
Add the sesame oil, stir well
and serve, garnished with the
spring onions and chilli tassel.
Serves 4–6

Beef and Lamb

Lamb Stew

1 kg/2 lb lean boneless lamb
175 g/6 oz sugar cane
4 leeks
1 small piece tangerine peel
2 tablespoons oil plus oil for
* deep frying*
50 g/2 oz bean curd sticks
* (optional)*
100 g/4 oz fresh root ginger,
* sliced*
2 shallots, sliced
2 cloves garlic, sliced
1 tablespoon ground bean
* paste*
50 ml/2 fl oz fermented red
* bean curd*
1 tablespoon dry sherry
750 ml/1¼ pints beef stock
2 tablespoons sugar
1 tablespoon light soy sauce
1 teaspoon cornflour
2 tablespoons water
2 spring onions, cut into
* chunks*
1 small crisp lettuce to serve

Cut the lamb into bite-sized
pieces. Peel, wash and cut the
sugar cane into thin, 3.5-cm/
1½-in pieces. Cut the leeks
into strips. Soak the peel until
soft, drain and shred.

Heat the oil for deep frying
to 190 c/375 F. Add the bean
curd sticks and cook until
golden. Drain on absorbent
kitchen paper and break into
short pieces. Set aside.

Heat the 2 tablespoons oil
in a flameproof casserole.
Sauté the ginger, shallots and
garlic until fragrant. Add the
ground bean paste and
fermented red bean curd and
stir-fry for a few minutes.

Add the meat and leeks to
the pan and sauté until lightly
browned. Pour in the sherry
and stock and bring to the
boil. Reduce the heat, add the
sugar cane and tangerine peel,
then cover and simmer for
1½–2 hours.

Stir in the sugar and light
soy sauce. Blend the cornflour
to a smooth paste with the
water, pour into the sauce and
simmer for 2 minutes or until
thickened. Stir in the spring
onions.

Arrange the lettuce in a
serving dish and ladle the stew
on top. Serve at once.
Serves 4–6

Beef and Taro Casserole

225 g/8 oz frying steak
2 teaspoons light soy sauce
1 tablespoon dry sherry
1 teaspoon cornflour
1 teaspoon sugar
½ teaspoon bicarbonate of soda
salt and pepper
100 ml/4 fl oz water
5 tablespoons oil plus oil for
* deep frying*
3 medium-thick slices fresh
* root ginger*
1 shallot, grated
1 clove garlic, crushed
450 g/1 lb taro or potato, sliced
100–250 ml/4–8 fl oz beef stock
1 tablespoon oyster sauce
½ teaspoon sesame oil
parsley sprigs to garnish

Cut the steak into small, thin
slices, then marinate these for
1 hour with 1 teaspoon each
of light soy sauce and sherry,
the cornflour, ½ teaspoon
sugar, the bicarbonate of
soda, a pinch of pepper, the
water and 2 tablespoons oil

Heat the remaining oil in a
flameproof casserole or heavy-
based saucepan. Sauté the
ginger, shallot and garlic until
fragrant. Arrange the sliced
taro or potato in the
casserole. Add enough stock
to cover the vegetable and
simmer for 20 minutes. Stir in
seasoning to taste, the
remaining sugar, light soy
sauce, the oyster sauce,
sesame oil and remaining
sherry. Top up with extra
stock if necessary, re-cover
and simmer for another 10
minutes.

Heat the oil for deep frying
to 190 c/375 F, add the beef,
drained of marinade, and
deep fry until lightly cooked.
Drain on absorbent kitchen
paper and arrange on top of
the vegetable. Cover and
simmer for a further 5
minutes.

Serve hot, straight from the
casserole if you like, garnished
with parsley. *Serves 2–4*

Casseroled Veal

175 g/6 oz thick veal escalopes
3 teaspoons light soy sauce
4 teaspoons dry sherry
2 teaspoons cornflour
2 teaspoons sugar
pinch of pepper
½ teaspoon cayenne pepper
1 teaspoon sesame oil
50 ml/2 fl oz plus 3 tablespoons
 water
3 tablespoons oil plus oil for
 deep frying
2 medium-thick slices fresh
 root ginger, grated
2 shallots, grated
2 cloves garlic, crushed
2 tablespoons hot broad bean
 paste
1 green pepper, deseeded and
 cut into chunks
2 red chillies, deseeded and cut
 into chunks
1 large onion, quartered

Cut the veal into small, thin
slices. Mix 2 teaspoons each
of the light soy sauce and
sherry, the cornflour, 1
teaspoon of the sugar, a pinch
of pepper, the cayenne,
½ teaspoon of the sesame oil,
50 ml/2 fl oz water and

1 tablespoon oil. Marinate the
veal in this mixture for 30
minutes.
   Heat the oil for deep frying
to 190 c/375 f. Drain the veal
of marinade, then deep fry the
pieces until lightly cooked.
   Heat the remaining
2 tablespoons oil in a
flameproof casserole. Sauté
the ginger, shallots and garlic
until fragrant. Stir in the
broad bean paste, green
pepper, chillies and onion and
fry for a while. Add the veal
and immediately pour in the
remaining sherry.
   Stir in the remaining soy
sauce, sugar and sesame oil,
making sure the meat is well
coated in sauce. Heat through
and serve. *Serves 2–4*

Lamb with Water Chestnuts

1 kg/2 lb lean boneless lamb
1 turnip
a little dried mandarin or
 tangerine peel
2 tablespoons oil
100 g/4 oz fresh root ginger,
 sliced
4 leeks, shredded
2 tablespoons fermented bean
 curd
1 tablespoon ground bean
 paste
1 tablespoon dry sherry
750 ml/1¼ pints beef stock
10 canned water chestnuts
salt
GARNISH
flat-leafed parsley sprigs
2 spring onions, chopped

Cut the lamb into bite-sized
pieces. Cut the turnip into
similar-sized chunks. Soak and
shred the mandarin or
tangerine peel.
   Heat the oil in a flameproof
casserole or heavy-based
saucepan. Add the ginger,
leeks, fermented bean curd
and ground bean paste and

stir-fry for a few minutes. Add
the lamb and sauté for a
while. Pour in the sherry and
stock, then bring to the boil.
Add the water chestnuts and
mandarin or tangerine peel,
reduce the heat and cover the
pan.
   Simmer for 40 minutes,
then add the turnip and cook
for another 30 minutes.
Season to taste, and serve hot,
garnished with the parsley and
spring onions. *Serves 4–6*

Cantonese Hot Pot

175 g/6 oz fillet steak
100 g/4 oz pig's liver
4 teaspoons Ginger Juice (page 227)
2 teaspoons dry sherry
175 g/6 oz loin of pork
175 g/6 oz Chinese fish cake (optional)
100 g/4 oz fresh squid
pepper
100 g/4 oz mung bean thread
1 quantity Fish Balls (page 224)
350 g/12 oz bean curd
225 g/8 oz fresh spinach
225 g/8 oz Chinese cabbage
6 eggs
3 litres/5 pints water
100 ml/4 fl oz light soy sauce
50 g/2 oz sugar
1 teaspoon sesame oil
1 tablespoon chopped parsley
50 ml/2 fl oz sesame paste

Cut the steak across the grain into thin slices. Wash, trim and finely slice the liver. Arrange the slices on a plate and sprinkle over half the ginger juice and the sherry. Finely slice the pork.

Slice the fish cake, if used. Prepare the squid according to the instructions given in the recipe for Hot and Sour Soup on page 16. Marinate the pieces with the remaining ginger juice and a pinch of pepper for a while.

Break the bean thread into pieces, then soak these in cold water until soft. Drain and arrange on a platter to serve.

Prepare the fish balls according to the recipe instructions, then arrange them on a serving plate.

Slice the bean curd and arrange it on a plate. Wash the spinach and Chinese cabbage, drain thoroughly and arrange in a serving dish.

Wash the egg shells and arrange them in a basket or bowl. Make sure that all the ingredients are attractively arranged on serving platters and garnished.

Soak charcoal in methylated spirits, then place it in the base of the hot pot. Set alight and leave it until the flames die down.

Pour the water into the pan. Add the soy sauce, sugar, sesame oil, remaining pepper and the parsley. Bring to the boil.

The ingredients are chosen and cooked by individuals at the table. Serve the sesame paste to accompany the cooked food. *Serves 6*

Cantonese Hot Pot: Known by other names such as firepot or chrysanthemum pot, this hot pot is in fact a type of oriental fondue.

The large moat-shaped vessel surrounds a chimney which comes from a base designed to hold a small charcoal fire. The hot coals are put in the base and these cook the liquid which is poured into the pot, forming a ring around the central chimney.

All the raw ingredients are prepared and arranged attractively on serving platters and these are taken to the table.

The stock or soup in the hot pot may be very rich, made from liquid boiled with many ingredients. The hot pot is taken to the dining area and the diners select the raw food which they are going to eat. Small, long-handled metal baskets are used to lower the pieces of food into the boiling soup and to lift the items out again when they are cooked.

Assorted Meat Combination

6 large Chinese dried
   mushrooms
pinch of sugar
salt
2 teaspoons oil
225 g/8 oz cooked ham
450 g/1 lb roast beef
100 g/4 oz cooked tongue
1 (454-g/1-lb) can abalone,
   drained
½ cooked chicken (preferably
   poached)
GARNISH
1 tomato, sliced
a few green glacé cherries,
   halved

Wash the mushrooms, then soak them in cold water for 10 minutes. Drain and place the mushrooms on a plate. Season with a little sugar, salt and oil, then steam over boiling water for 12–15 minutes. Slice the cooked mushrooms into thin pieces.

Cut the ham, beef and tongue into small, thin slices. Slice the abalone and chop the chicken into pieces.

Arrange the prepared ingredients as shown in the picture, with the chicken in the middle and the other sliced ingredients arranged in leaf shapes at the sides. Garnish with tomato slices and halved cherries and serve lightly chilled. *Serves 4–6*

Tongue with Assorted Vegetables

1 kg/2 lb uncooked ox tongue
5 medium-thick slices fresh
   root ginger
3 star anise
4 tablespoons oil
350 g/12 oz tomatoes, peeled
   and quartered
225 g/8 oz onions, quartered
225 g/8 oz carrots, sliced
3 green or red peppers,
   deseeded and cut into
   chunks
3 red chillies, deseeded and cut
   into chunks
10 cloves garlic, crushed
3 tablespoons dry sherry
1½ teaspoons salt
2 tablespoons sugar
1 tablespoon light soy sauce
¼ teaspoon pepper

Thoroughly wash the tongue and soak it in boiling water for 30 minutes. Drain and scrape the tongue, then rinse clean. Place the tongue in a large saucepan with the ginger and star anise. Pour in enough water to cover, then bring to the boil, removing any scum. Cover and simmer for 4 hours, topping up the water with fresh boiling water as necessary.

Drain the tongue, reserving the stock, allow it to cool enough to handle then remove all the skin and tiny bones. Slice the meat.

Heat 2 tablespoons of the oil in a casserole, sauté the tomatoes, onions, carrots, peppers and chillies for a while. Remove, and add the remaining oil. Sauté the garlic in the oil, then add the tongue and sprinkle in the sherry; mix well. Stir in the vegetables and pour in 600 ml/1 pint of the reserved stock.

Bring to the boil, reduce the heat and simmer for 30 minutes or until the liquid is reduced to a fairly thick sauce.

Stir in the salt, sugar, soy sauce and pepper. Stir well and serve. *Serves 6*

Shredded Lamb in Hot Sauce

175 g/6 oz lean boneless lamb
3 teaspoons light soy sauce
2 teaspoons Ginger Juice (page 227)
2 teaspoons sugar
2 teaspoons cornflour
2 teaspoons dry sherry
pepper
5 tablespoons water
3 tablespoons oil plus oil for deep frying
7 g/¼ oz black fungus
12 canned water chestnuts
2 teaspoons grated fresh root ginger
2 large cloves garlic, crushed
2 tablespoons hot broad bean paste
1 teaspoon sesame oil
1 teaspoon vinegar
parsley sprigs to garnish

Shred the lamb and marinate the strips for 30 minutes with 2 teaspoons of the light soy sauce and the ginger juice, 1 teaspoon each of the sugar, cornflour and dry sherry, a pinch of pepper, 3 tablespoons water and 1 tablespoon oil.

Heat the oil for deep frying to 190 c/375 f, drain the meat of marinade, then deep fry until lightly cooked. Drain on absorbent kitchen paper and set aside.

Soak the black fungus in cold water for 30 minutes. Drain and shred. Blanch in boiling water for a while. Refresh and drain. Shred the water chestnuts.

Heat the remaining 2 tablespoons oil in a wok or frying pan. Sauté the ginger and garlic until fragrant. Drop in the black fungus and water chestnuts, then stir-fry for a few seconds. Add the broad bean paste and shredded lamb and sauté thoroughly. Pour in the remaining sherry, sugar, light soy sauce, a pinch of pepper and the sesame oil. Blend the remaining cornflour with the remaining water, stir this into the sauce and simmer for 2 minutes. Lastly, add the vinegar and serve the lamb, garnished with the parsley sprigs. *Serves 2–4*

Minced Lamb Patties

2 teaspoons dry sherry
1 tablespoon light soy sauce
1 teaspoon sugar
pinch of black pepper
1 tablespoon cornflour
50 ml/2 fl oz water
1 teaspoon sesame oil
450 g/1 lb lean minced lamb
50 g/2 oz canned water chestnuts
1 onion
15 g/½ oz fresh root ginger
small piece of dried tangerine peel
2 small leeks
50 g/2 oz sesame seeds
1 egg, beaten
oil for deep frying

Mix the sherry, light soy sauce, sugar, pepper, cornflour, water and sesame oil together to make a paste. Mix this paste into the minced lamb and pound the ingredients until they are thoroughly bound together.

Mince the water chestnuts with the onion and ginger. Wash the tangerine peel, then soak it in boiling water for 1 hour. Drain and mince or finely chop the tangerine peel. Finely chop the leeks. Mix all these prepared ingredients into the lamb and stir in the beaten egg to bind the ingredients together firmly.

Take small portions of the meat mixture and roll them into balls. Coat these all over with the sesame seeds, then flatten them in the palm of your hand to make little cakes.

Heat the oil for deep frying to 190 c/375 f. Add the meat cakes a few at a time and fry until they are golden brown. Drain the cakes on absorbent kitchen paper and arrange on a warmed serving platter. Serve hot. *Serves 4*

Note: The picture illustrates a fine example of a carved vegetable. If you do not want to attempt this garnish, then substitute parsley sprigs.

Minced Lamb with Assorted Vegetables

2 teaspoons Ginger Juice (page 227)
2 teaspoons dry sherry
3 teaspoons light soy sauce
3 teaspoons cornflour
1½ teaspoons sugar
100 ml/4 fl oz beef stock
2 tablespoons oil plus oil for deep frying
350 g/12 oz lean minced lamb
25 g/1 oz preserved mustard cabbage
40 g/1½ oz vermicelli
1 medium-thick slice fresh root ginger, grated
1 shallot, grated
1 clove garlic, crushed
2 celery sticks, diced
25 g/1 oz red chillies, deseeded and diced
2 spring onions, chopped
¼ teaspoon pepper
4 tablespoons water

Mix the ginger juice and sherry, 2 teaspoons each of light soy sauce and cornflour; 1 teaspoon of the sugar, half the stock and 1 teaspoon oil in a bowl. Marinate the minced lamb in this liquid for 2 hours.

Soak the preserved mustard cabbage in water for about 30 minutes, then drain, dry and dice. Heat the oil for deep frying to 190 c/375 F, add the vermicelli and deep fry until puffed and golden. Drain on absorbent kitchen paper and press flat on a platter.

Heat the remaining oil in a wok or frying pan. Sauté the ginger, shallot and garlic together until fragrant, then stir in the diced ingredients, spring onions and minced lamb. Cook until browned, then pour in the remaining stock and sugar, and the pepper.

Blend the remaining cornflour with the water. Stir this into the sauce and simmer for 2 minutes. Pour the lamb over the vermicelli and serve at once. *Serves 4*

Beef with Pickled Ginger and Pineapple

175 g/6 oz fillet steak
2 teaspoons dry sherry
3 teaspoons light soy sauce
2 teaspoons cornflour
1½ teaspoons sugar
pinch of pepper
4 tablespoons water
4 tablespoons oil plus oil for deep frying
2 shallots, sliced
2 cloves garlic, sliced
1 green pepper, deseeded and roughly chopped
2 chillies, deseeded and roughly chopped
50 g/2 oz Pickled Ginger (page 226)
2 slices fresh or canned pineapple, cut into chunks
50 ml/2 fl oz beef stock
a few drops of dark soy sauce
2 spring onions, shredded, to garnish

Thinly slice the beef. Marinate it for 30 minutes with 1 teaspoon each of the sherry, light soy sauce and cornflour; ½ teaspoon of the sugar, a pinch of pepper, half the water and 2 tablespoons oil.

Heat the oil for deep frying to 190 c/375 F, drain the beef and deep fry it until lightly cooked. Drain on absorbent kitchen paper and set aside.

Heat the remaining 2 tablespoons oil in a wok or frying pan. Sauté the shallots, garlic, green pepper and chillies until fragrant. Add the ginger and pineapple and stir-fry for a while. Add the beef, toss well, then add the remaining sherry, the stock and remaining cornflour mixed to a paste with the soy sauce. Simmer for 2 minutes until thickened, then serve at once, garnished with the spring onions. *Serves 4*

Crispy Vegetarian Roll

2 teaspoons cornflour
2 tablespoons water
4 eggs, beaten
2 tablespoons oil
FILLING
4 Chinese dried mushrooms
2 tablespoons oil
100 g/4 oz bean sprouts
10 canned water chestnuts, cut
   into fine strips
1 small carrot, cut into fine
   strips
1 teaspoon dry sherry
100 ml/4 fl oz vegetable stock
¼ teaspoon salt
½ teaspoon sugar
1 teaspoon light soy sauce
pinch of pepper
a few drops of sesame oil
1 teaspoon cornflour
2 tablespoons water

BATTER
100 g/4 oz plain flour
4 tablespoons cornflour
3 teaspoons baking powder
250 ml/8 fl oz water
4 tablespoons oil
oil for deep frying
carrot flowers to garnish
   (optional)

First make the egg sheets: blend the cornflour with the water, then beat this into the eggs. Heat 1 tablespoon of the oil in a large frying pan, then pour in half the egg mixture and fry until crisp and golden on the underside. Turn and cook the second side. Remove this thin omelette from the pan to drain on absorbent kitchen paper. Cook the remaining egg mixture in the same way.

For the filling, soak the mushrooms in cold water for 15 minutes, then drain and steam them over boilinng water for 15 minutes. Remove the stalks and cut the mushroom caps into fine strips. Heat the 2 tablespoons oil in a wok or frying pan. Add the bean sprouts and cook for a few seconds. Stir in the mushrooms, water chestnuts and carrot and fry for a few seconds. Pour in the sherry and stock, salt, sugar, light soy sauce, pepper and sesame oil. Blend the cornflour with the water, stir into the ingredients and bring to the boil. Cook for 2 minutes to thicken the sauce. Set aside to cool slightly.

Lay the omelettes on a flat surface. Divide the filling between them and roll up to enclose the ingredients completely, brushing a little of the sauce on the edges to make sure they seal together. Tuck the ends in neatly.

For the batter, sift the flour, cornflour and baking powder into a bowl. Make a well in the middle of these dry ingredients. Gradually add the water and oil, beating all the time, to make a smooth batter.

Heat the oil for deep frying to 190 c/375 f. Dip the rolls in the batter to coat them completely, then deep fry them until golden brown and very crisp. Drain on absorbent kitchen paper and serve hot, cut into slices. Arrange the slices on a serving platter and garnish with the carrot flowers, if used. *Serves 4*

Egg Roll with Minced Water Chestnuts

1 (230-g/8-oz) can water chestnuts, drained
5 Chinese dried mushrooms
2 celery sticks, diced
1 small carrot
2 tablespoons chopped spring onion
1 tablespoon chopped preserved mustard
salt and pepper
pinch of sugar
1 teaspoon soy sauce
½ teaspoon sesame oil
2 tablespoons cornflour plus 1 teaspoon
2 eggs
2 tablespoons oil
GARNISH (optional)
1–2 spring onions, shredded
½ small cucumber

Mince the water chestnuts. Soak the mushrooms in cold water for 10 minutes, then drain and steam them for 15 minutes. Dice the mushrooms.

Mix the water chestnuts, celery, carrot, mushrooms, spring onion and chopped preserved mustard in a bowl. Stir in seasoning to taste, a pinch of sugar, the soy sauce, sesame oil and 2 tablespoons cornflour. Mix thoroughly until firmly bound.

Beat the eggs with the remaining cornflour, salt and pepper to taste. Heat 1 tablespoon of the oil in a large frying pan, then pour in half the egg, tilting the pan to make a thin omelette. Cook until brown and crisp on both sides, turning once. Repeat with the remaining egg. Dust a little cornflour on both egg sheets then spread half the filling evenly on each. Roll the sheets from both sides to meet in the middle and enclose the filling. Place on a greased plate and steam the rolls over boiling water for 8 minutes. Slice and serve hot.

Garnish, if you like, with shredded spring onions and cucumber. Cut long lengths of cucumber, slice each in half, then thinly slice almost through, leaving the pieces lightly attached at one side, and arranged in a fan as shown. *Serves 4–6*

Diced Mushrooms with Walnuts

100 g/4 oz shelled walnuts
2 tablespoons oil plus oil for deep frying
8 Chinese dried mushrooms
1 (425-g/15-oz) can straw mushrooms
1 (200-g/7.05-oz) can button mushrooms
75 g/3 oz carrots
2 pieces Spicy Bean Curd (page 137)
1 shallot, sliced
1 clove garlic, sliced
1 teaspoon cornflour
1 tablespoon water
1 teaspoon dry sherry
3 tablespoons vegetable stock
½ teaspoon salt
½ teaspoon sugar
1 teaspoon soy sauce
pinch of pepper
a few drops of sesame oil
4 small broccoli spears to garnish (optional)

Cook the walnuts in boiling salted water for 1–2 minutes, then drain them thoroughly and rub off as much of their skins as possible.

Heat the oil for deep frying to 190 c/375 f, then deep fry the walnuts until lightly browned. Soak the dried mushrooms in cold water for 10 minutes, then steam them over boiling water for 15 minutes. Remove the stalks and dice the caps. Dice the straw mushrooms and button mushrooms, carrots and bean curd.

Heat the 2 tablespoons oil in a wok or frying pan. Add the shallot and garlic and sauté until fragrant. Add the carrot, straw mushrooms and button mushrooms and stir-fry for a few minutes. Stir in the steamed mushrooms and bean curd and cook for a few minutes.

Blend the cornflour to a smooth paste with the water, then stir in all the remaining ingredients apart from the walnuts. Pour this mixture into the pan and bring to the boil. Simmer for 2 minutes, then stir in the walnuts and serve at once, garnished with the broccoli if you like. *Serves 4*

Vegetarian Dishes

Stuffed Mushrooms

24 Chinese dried mushrooms
salt and pepper
1 teaspoon sugar
3 tablespoons oil
1 piece Spicy Bean Curd (page 137)
1 small carrot
1 (227-g/8-oz) can water chestnuts, drained
350 g/12 oz potatoes
¼ teaspoon monosodium glutamate
generous ½ egg white
2 tablespoons cornflour
24 shelled peas
1 shallot, sliced
1 clove garlic
1 teaspoon dry sherry
150 ml/¼ pint vegetable stock
1 tablespoon water
1 teaspoon soy sauce

Wash and soak the mushrooms for 10 minutes. Drain, then marinate them with a little salt, sugar and oil. Steam over boiling water for 12 minutes, then set aside.

Mince the spicy bean curd and carrot, then place in a mixing bowl. Grate the water chestnuts and potatoes, squeeze dry and add to the carrot mixture. Stir seasoning into the carrot mixture, add the remaining sugar, the monosodium glutamate, egg white and enough of the cornflour to bind the mixture together.

Dust the inside of the mushrooms with a little cornflour and place some filling on each one. Top each one with a pea. Place the stuffed mushrooms on a greased plate and steam over boiling water for 10 minutes.

Heat the remaining oil in a wok or frying pan, sauté the shallot and garlic until fragrant, then discard. Pour in the sherry and stock and arrange the stuffed mushrooms in the pan. Simmer for 2 minutes.

Arrange the mushrooms on a serving dish. Blend the remaining cornflour with the water, then stir it into the sauce remaining in the pan. Add the soy sauce and simmer for 2 minutes, then pour over the mushrooms and serve at once. Serves 6

Vermicelli with Preserved Vegetables

225 g/8 oz vermicelli
4 Chinese dried mushrooms
75 g/3 oz preserved vegetables
4 tablespoons oil
50 g/2 oz Pickled Ginger (page 227), diced
1 large carrot, diced
2 pieces Spicy Bean Curd (page 137)
1 teaspoon dry sherry
750 ml/1¼ pints vegetable stock
1 teaspoon salt
1 teaspoon sugar
1 shallot, sliced
1 green pepper, deseeded and diced
1 clove garlic, sliced
2 teaspoons cornflour
1 teaspoon sesame oil
½ teaspoon dark soy sauce
50 g/2 oz roasted peanuts, chopped
parsley sprigs to garnish

Blanch, drain and rinse the vermicelli. Drain thoroughly. Soak the mushrooms in cold water for 10 minutes, then drain and steam them over boiling water for 15 minutes. Clean and dice the preserved vegetables. Mix with a little oil and the pickled ginger. Blanch the carrot, then mix it with the bean curd and mushrooms.

Heat 2 tablespoons of the oil in a saucepan. Add the sherry, then pour in all but 150 ml/¼ pint of the stock, the salt and sugar and bring to the boil. Add the vermicelli and simmer for 1 minute, then transfer to a large bowl.

Heat the remaining oil in a wok or frying pan. Add the shallot, green pepper and garlic and cook until fragrant, then discard. Stir in the preserved vegetable and the other prepared ingredients and fry well. Pour in the remaining stock. Blend the cornflour with all the remaining ingredients, apart from the peanuts, and pour into the pan. Bring to the boil, then simmer for 2 minutes and stir in the peanuts before serving, garnished with the parsley. Serves 4

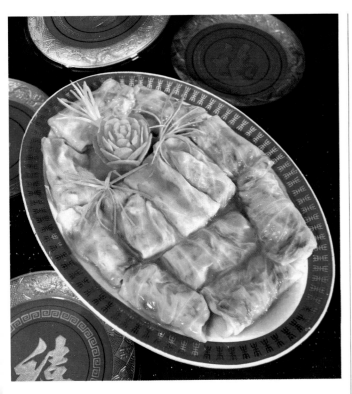

Cabbage Roll

3 Chinese dried mushrooms
6 button mushrooms
6 canned water chestnuts
50 g/2 oz Gluten Balls (page 225)
1 carrot
12 winter cabbage leaves
2 teaspoons cornflour
4 tablespoons water
100 ml/4 fl oz vegetable stock
salt and pepper
2 tablespoons oil
50 g/2 oz bean sprouts
pinch of sugar
a few drops of sesame oil
GARNISH
spring onion curls (page 34)
carrot flower (optional)

Soak the mushrooms in cold water for 10 minutes, then drain and steam them over boiling water for 15 minutes. Remove the stalks and shred the mushroom caps.

Shred the button mushrooms, water chestnuts, gluten balls and carrot.

Blanch the cabbage leaves in boiling salted water until soft. Drain, rinse under cold water and dry on absorbent kitchen paper. Blend half the cornflour with 2 tablespoons of the water. Stir in half the stock and seasoning to taste.

Heat the oil in a wok or frying pan. Add all the prepared ingredients and the bean sprouts and stir-fry until well mixed and lightly cooked. Pour in the prepared liquid and bring to the boil. Simmer for 2 minutes or until thickened, then remove from the heat.

Open out the cabbage leaves and divide the filling between them. Roll up, folding in the sides to form neat packages, then arrange the leaves on a greased plate. Steam them over boiling water for 5 minutes.

Heat the remaining stock with seasoning to taste, the sugar and sesame oil. Blend the remaining cornflour with the remaining water, stir into the sauce and simmer for 2 minutes. Pour this sauce over the cabbage leaves and serve, garnished with spring onion curls and a carrot flower.
Serves 6

Stuffed Aubergines in Black Bean Sauce

3 Chinese dried mushrooms
1 (230-g/8-oz) can water chestnuts, drained
25 g/1 oz preserved mustard
2 pieces Spicy Bean Curd (page 137)
2 tablespoons chopped spring onion
pepper and salt
½ teaspoon sugar
2 teaspoons cornflour
350 g/12 oz long, thin aubergines
4 tablespoons oil
2 cloves garlic
1 teaspoon dry sherry
150 ml/¼ pint vegetable stock
2 tablespoons fermented black bean paste
2 tablespoons water

Soak the mushrooms in cold water for 10 minutes, then drain and steam them over boiling water for 15 minutes. Grate the water chestnuts. Dice the preserved mustard, mushrooms and bean curd.

Put all these ingredients in a mixing bowl together with the spring onion. Add seasoning to taste, the sugar and half the cornflour. Pound until firm, then chill for 30 minutes.

Cut the aubergines into 1-cm/½-in thick slices. Cut horizontally through the slices to make a slit which can be stuffed. Dust the inside of the cuts with cornflour, then fill with the water chestnut mixture.

Heat 3 tablespoons oil in a large frying pan. Sauté the garlic then add the stuffed aubergine slices and fry, turning once, until both sides are golden. Remove from the pan. Add the remaining oil, then sprinkle in the sherry and pour in the stock. Add the fermented black bean paste and replace the aubergines in the pan. Simmer for a few minutes to heat through, then transfer to a serving plate. Blend the remaining cornflour with the water. Stir into the sauce and bring to the boil. Simmer for 2 minutes, then pour over the aubergines and serve. *Serves 6*

Vegetarian Hotpot

75 g/3 oz Chinese dried
    mushrooms
3 tablespoons oil
salt and pepper
1½ teaspoons sugar
1 (230-g/8-oz) can bamboo
    shoots
275 g/10 oz Deep Fried Gluten
    Balls (page 225)
2 medium-thick slices fresh
    root ginger
1 shallot, sliced
1 clove garlic, crushed
1 teaspoon dry sherry
1 teaspoon light soy sauce
1 teaspoon cornflour
2 tablespoons water
½ teaspoon sesame oil
a few lettuce leaves
GARNISH
2 red chillies
flat-leafed parsley sprigs

Soak the mushrooms in cold
water for 10 minutes, then
drain them, reserving the
liquid, and remove the stalks.
Marinate with a little of the
oil, salt and sugar for about 30
minutes. Steam the marinated
mushrooms over boiling water
for 10 minutes.

Cut the bamboo shoots into
thick pieces. Cut the gluten
balls into chunks.

Heat the remaining oil in a
flameproof casserole. Sauté
the ginger, shallot and garlic
until fragrant. Stir in the
bamboo shoots and gluten
balls and fry for a while, then
add the mushrooms and mix
thoroughly. Pour in the
sherry, add the mushroom
water, light soy sauce,
remaining salt and sugar, and
the pepper. Cover and simmer
for 20 minutes.

Blend the cornflour with the
water, stir into the casserole
and simmer for a further 2
minutes. Stir in the sesame
oil. Arrange the lettuce in a
dish, pour the hotpot over and
serve, garnished with the
chillies and parsley. *Serves 4*

Vegetable Curry

100 g/4 oz dried split peas
100 g/4 oz French beans
100 g/4 oz cabbage
100 g/4 oz aubergines
salt and pepper
225 g/8 oz potatoes
100 g/4 oz Spicy Bean Curd
    (page 137)
1½ teaspoons curry powder
6 tablespoons oil plus oil for
    deep frying
1 onion, sliced
2 red chillies, deseeded and
    sliced
450 ml/¾ pint vegetable stock
1 teaspoon sugar
2 teaspoons light soy sauce
¼ teaspoon monosodium
    glutamate
a few whole red chillies to
    garnish (optional)

Wash and soak the split peas
in cold water for 6 hours.
Drain. Cut the French beans
and cabbage into bite-sized
pieces. Cut the aubergines
into chunks. Place these in a
colander and sprinkle with
salt, then leave for 30
minutes, rinse and dry. Cut
the potatoes into chunks.

Heat the oil for deep frying to
190 c/375 F. Add the potato
and cook until lightly
browned. Drain on absorbent
kitchen paper and set aside.
Cut the bean curd into
chunks.

Mix the curry powder with
2 tablespoons oil to make a
paste. Heat the remaining oil
in a flameproof casserole. Put
in the onion and chillies and
cook until transparent. Add
the curry paste and cook until
fragrant. Stir in the drained
split peas, potatoes and stock.
Bring to the boil, cover and
simmer for 10 minutes.

Stir in all the remaining
ingredients and serve,
garnished with a few whole
red chillies if you like.
Serves 4

Deep Fried Egg White with Peas

100 g/4 oz shelled peas
8 egg whites
1 tablespoon oil plus oil for deep frying
1 teaspoon finely grated fresh root ginger
1 teaspoon dry sherry
salt and pepper
½ teaspoon sugar
pinch of monosodium glutamate
150 ml/¼ pint vegetable stock
1 teaspoon cornflour
1 tablespoon water
1 teaspoon sesame oil

Lightly mash the peas, then mix them with the lightly whisked egg whites.

Heat the 1 tablespoon oil in a small saucepan. Add the ginger and sauté for a few minutes, then stir in the sherry, seasoning, sugar, monosodium glutamate and stock. Heat through to boiling point. Blend the cornflour with the water, stir this mixture into the sauce and simmer for 2 minutes. Stir in the sesame oil and leave over a very low heat to keep hot.

Heat the oil for deep frying to 190 c/375 f. Slowly pour the egg whites into the hot oil and deep fry until set. Use a draining spoon to remove the egg white from the pan. Drain it thoroughly, then transfer to a heated serving plate and pour the prepared sauce over. Serve at once. *Serves 6*

Quails' Eggs in Mushrooms

20 large Chinese dried mushrooms
a little oil
salt and pepper
sugar
20 quails' eggs
20 shelled peas
100 ml/4 fl oz vegetable stock
1 teaspoon dry sherry
1 teaspoon soy sauce
½ teaspoon sesame oil
1 teaspoon cornflour
2 tablespoons water
carrot flowers to garnish (optional)

Clean and soak the mushrooms in cold water for 10–15 minutes. Drain and remove the stalks. Squeeze out all the excess water and marinate the mushroom caps with a little oil, salt and sugar. Stand the mushrooms on a plate and steam them over boiling water for 12 minutes.

Break one quail's egg into each mushroom, top each with a pea and steam for a further 3–5 minutes, or until the eggs are cooked. Heat the stock and sherry in a saucepan. Bring to the boil and season to taste. Add the soy sauce, a pinch of sugar and the sesame oil. Blend the cornflour with the water, stir the solution into the sauce and simmer for 2 minutes.

Pour the sauce over the mushrooms. If you like add a garnish of carrot flowers and serve immediately. *Serves 4*

Note: Elaborate garnishes are a traditional feature of authentic Chinese cuisine, however you could substitute simple parsley sprigs, watercress sprigs or cucumber slices.

Stewed Gluten with Mushrooms

50 g/2 oz Chinese dried
  mushrooms
50 g/2 oz dried lily buds
25 g/1 oz hard black fungus
350 g/12 oz Deep Fried Gluten
  Balls (page 225)
2 tablespoons oil
2 medium-thick slices fresh
  root ginger
2 shallots
1 clove garlic
1 teaspoon dry sherry
1 teaspoon cornflour
salt and pepper
1 teaspoon sugar
1 teaspoon soy sauce
½ teaspoon sesame oil

Wash and soak the
mushrooms for 10 minutes.
Drain, reserving the stock,
then steam the mushrooms
over boiling water for 15
minutes. Soak the lily buds
until soft, then trim and clean
them. Tie the pieces in pairs
into knots. Soak, trim and
clean the black fungus, then
cut it into pieces. Blanch for a
minute, then rinse and drain.

Cut the gluten balls into small
pieces.
  Heat the oil in a wok or
frying pan. Sauté the ginger,
shallots and garlic until
fragrant, then add the fungus
and gluten and stir-fry for a
while. Add the mushrooms
and lily buds and mix well.
Sprinkle in the sherry and
pour in the reserved
mushroom water. Bring to the
boil, then cover and simmer
for 5 minutes. Blend the
cornflour with all the
remaining ingredients. Stir this
mixture into the sauce,
simmer for 2 minutes, then
serve. Serves 4

Stuffed Gluten Balls

20 Deep Fried Gluten Balls
  (page 225)
4 Chinese dried mushrooms
6 canned straw mushrooms or
  button mushrooms
6 ginkgo nuts
10 canned water chestnuts,
  diced
2 tablespoons diced peas
5 tablespoons oil
2 tablespoons grated carrot
2 tablespoons minced or finely
  chopped preserved mustard
½ teaspoon dry sherry
2 tablespoons vegetable stock
salt and pepper
¼ teaspoon sugar
a few drops of sesame oil
½ teaspoon cornflour plus extra
  for dusting and coating
1 tablespoon water
1 (439-g/15½-oz) can chestnut
  purée
parsley sprigs to garnish

Blanch the gluten balls very
briefly in boiling water. Drain
thoroughly. Soak the dried
mushrooms in cold water for
10 minutes, then steam them
over boiling water for 15
minutes. Dice the mushroom
caps, straw mushrooms or
button mushrooms and ginkgo
nuts.
  Heat 2 tablespoons oil in a
wok or frying pan. Add all the
prepared ingredients, the
grated carrot and preserved
vegetable, and stir-fry until
well cooked.
  Stir in the sherry, stock,
seasoning to taste, sugar and
sesame oil. Blend the
cornflour with the water, stir
into the sauce and boil, then
simmer for 2 minutes. Stir in
the chestnut purée and cool.
  Slit each gluten ball open.
Dust the inside with cornflour
and press in the filling. Close
and coat with cornflour.
  Heat the remaining oil in a
large frying pan. Add the
stuffed gluten balls and
shallow fry, until golden
underneath. Turn and cook
the second side until golden.
Arrange on a heated serving
platter with any pan juices,
and serve garnished with
parsley. Serves 6

Spicy Bean Curd

450 g/1 lb bean curd
SEASONINGS
3 tablespoons Spicy Salt (page 229)
2 tablespoons sugar
1 teaspoon ground pepper
2 tablespoons grated shallot or onion
oil for deep frying
parsley sprigs to garnish

Cut the bean curd into 5-cm/2-in squares measuring about 2.5/1 in thick. Place these pieces on a fairly large plate and set aside.

Mix the spicy salt with the sugar, pepper and shallot, then carefully spread this mixture over the bean curd, turning the pieces to cover them thinly but evenly. Set aside for about 30 minutes so that the flavour of the seasonings has time to penetrate the bean curd.

When you are ready to cook the bean curd, heat the oil for deep frying to 180 c/375 F. Carefully add a few pieces of bean curd to the hot oil and fry them until they are golden. Drain these pieces on absorbent kitchen paper and continue cooking the remaining bean curd in the same way.

Arrange the cooked bean curd pieces on a warmed serving dish and add a garnish of parsley sprigs, then serve at once.

Alternatively, the bean curd can be used in many recipes – particularly vegetarian dishes. It can be cooled completely, then stored in an airtight container in the refrigerator for several days. It can also be deep frozen for longer storage if necessary.

Sweet and Sour Bean Curd

1 (230-g/8-oz) can water chestnuts
1 tablespoon diced mushroom
1 teaspoon minced or grated carrot
2 egg whites
salt and pepper
about 50 g/2 oz cornflour
350 g/12 oz bean curd
¼ teaspoon sugar
¼ teaspoon monosodium glutamate
½ teaspoon sesame oil
2 spring onions, chopped
150 ml/¼ pint Sweet and Sour Sauce (page 227)
1 teaspoon dry sherry
1 pickled gherkin, chopped

Mince the water chestnuts, then place them in a bowl. Add the diced mushroom, minced carrot, 1 egg white, seasoning and a little cornflour. Mix thoroughly to make a paste, then pound until firm.

Mash the bean curd and stir it into the paste with the second egg white. Add the sugar, monosodium glutamate, sesame oil and spring onions. Press the mixture into a well-greased, oblong cake tin and steam it over boiling water for 10 minutes. Set aside to cool. Cut into pieces when cold.

Coat the pieces of bean curd generously with cornflour. Gently heat the sweet and sour sauce with the sherry and gherkin. Heat the oil for deep frying to 190 c/375 F. Add the pieces of bean curd a few at a time and deep fry until golden brown.

Drain on absorbent kitchen paper and arrange on a warmed serving plate. Pour over the sauce and serve immediately. *Serves 4–6*

Stewed Bean Curd with Assorted Vegetables

225 g/8 oz bean curd
salt and pepper
2 tablespoons oil plus oil for
    deep frying
5 Chinese dried mushrooms
1 teaspoon sugar
15 g/½ oz black fungus
8 ginkgo nuts
1 large carrot, sliced
½ cucumber
1 (230-g/8-oz) can water
    chestnuts, drained
1 clove garlic, sliced
5 canned straw mushrooms or
    button mushrooms
1 teaspoon dry sherry
50 ml/2 fl oz vegetable stock
¼ teaspoon monosodium
    glutamate
a few drops of sesame oil
½ teaspoon dark soy sauce
1 teaspoon cornflour
2 tablespoons water

Slice the bean curd and season it with salt. Heat the oil for deep frying to 190 c/375 F, add the bean curd and deep fry until golden brown. Drain on absorbent kitchen paper and set aside. Soak the dried mushrooms in cold water for 10 minutes. Drain and marinate the mushroom caps with a little oil, salt and sugar then steam them over boiling water for 10 minutes.

Soak the black fungus until soft. Blanch the ginkgo nuts, carrot, and soaked black fungus in boiling water for 2 minutes. Drain, rinse under cold water and drain thoroughly. Slice the cucumber and water chestnuts.

Heat the 2 tablespoons oil in a wok or frying pan until smoking hot. Sauté the garlic until fragrant, then add all the assorted vegetables (including the two sorts of mushrooms and black fungus) and stir well.

Pour in the sherry and stock, seasoning to taste, the remaining sugar, the monosodium glutamate, sesame oil and dark soy sauce.

Blend the cornflour with the water, stir into the sauce and bring to the boil. Add the bean curd and cook for 2 minutes, then serve.
Serves 4–6

Note: You can include any other vegetables in this dish, for example, canned whole baby corn, French or runner beans or bamboo shoots can all be used. If you want to arrange the vegetables in neat separate piles on the serving platter, then add them individually to the cooking pan and do not mix them together as they cook. Then they can be arranged neatly as shown in the picture. Serve plain steamed or boiled rice as an accompaniment.

Spicy Bean Curd with Courgettes

350 g/12 oz courgettes
3 pieces Spicy Bean Curd
   (page 137)
6 canned water chestnuts
15 g/½ oz black fungus
4 Chinese dried mushrooms
2 tablespoons oil
1 shallot, sliced
2 medium-thick slices fresh
   root ginger
1 teaspoon cornflour
2 tablespoons water
1 teaspoon dry sherry
50 ml/2 fl oz vegetable stock
½ teaspoon salt
pinch of sugar
1 teaspoon light soy sauce
a few drops of sesame oil
a few drops of dark soy sauce
1 carrot, sliced and blanched

Lightly peel the courgettes
and cut them into triangles.
Slice the bean curd and water
chestnuts. Soak the black
fungus until soft, then trim
and blanch it in boiling water.
Drain, rinse under cold water,
then cut it into pieces.
   Soak the mushrooms in cold
water for 10 minutes, then
drain and steam them over
boiling water for 15 minutes.
Remove the stalks and slice
the mushroom caps.
   Heat the oil in a wok or
frying pan, then sauté the
shallot and ginger. Stir in the
fungus, courgettes and water
chestnuts and fry thoroughly.
   Blend the cornflour to a
smooth paste with the water,
then stir in the sherry, stock,
salt, sugar, light soy sauce,
sesame oil and dark soy sauce.
Add the carrot, bean curd and
mushrooms to the courgette
mixture, then pour in the
liquid and bring to the boil.
Simmer for 2 minutes before
serving, transferred to a
warmed serving dish. *Serves 4*

Mixed Vegetable Crisp

25 g/1 oz Chinese dried
   mushrooms
salt
1 teaspoon sugar
a little oil plus oil for deep
   frying
3 dried bean curd sheets
8 canned water chestnuts
450 g/1 lb soft bean curd
2 pieces Spicy Bean Curd
   (page 137)
25 g/1 oz preserved mustard
2 spring onions, chopped
1 tablespoon chopped parsley
1 teaspoon soy sauce
pinch of pepper
a few drops of sesame oil
4 tablespoons cornflour
6 tablespoons water

Soak the dried mushrooms in
cold water for 10 minutes,
then drain and marinate them
with a pinch of salt, and a
little of the sugar and oil.
Steam over boiling water for
10 minutes, then dice the
mushrooms and put them in a
mixing bowl. Soak the bean
curd sheets until soft, then
drain and dry them.
   Grate the water chestnuts,
mash the soft bean curd and
spicy bean curd, then add
these ingredients to the
mushrooms with the preserved
mustard, spring onions and
parsley. Stir in a pinch of salt,
the remaining sugar, the soy
sauce, pepper and sesame oil,
then pound the mixture well
to make a firm paste.
   Cut the bean curd sheets in
half. Blend the cornflour with
the water, then brush a little
over each piece of bean curd
and press the halves together
to give four, double-thickness
pieces. Spread a thin layer of
filling on two pieces, then
brush the edges with cornflour
mixture and top with the
remaining sheets. Press well to
seal in the filling.
   Heat the oil for deep frying
to 190 c/375 f. Brush the bean
curd sheets all over with the
remaining cornflour mixture,
then deep fry them until crisp
and golden.
   Drain on absorbent kitchen
paper and serve at once.
Serves 4

Braised Bean Curd Balls with Mushrooms

25 g/1 oz Chinese dried
  mushrooms
350 g/12 oz winter melon or
  marrow
100 g/4 oz bean curd
1 teaspoon cornflour plus extra
  for coating
3 tablespoons oil plus oil for
  deep frying
2 medium-thick slices fresh
  root ginger
1 shallot, sliced
1 clove garlic, sliced
1 teaspoon dry sherry
50 ml/2 fl oz vegetable stock
½ teaspoon salt
¾ teaspoon sugar
pinch of pepper
½ teaspoon sesame oil
2 tablespoons water

Soak the mushrooms in cold
water for 10 minutes, then
drain them and steam the
mushrooms over boiling water
for 12 minutes. Peel the
winter melon or marrow, then
cut it into chunks (cut
attractive shapes using a

biscuit cutter if you like).
  Cut the bean curd into
cubes, coat these thoroughly
in cornflour. Heat the oil for
deep frying to 190 c/375 f,
then deep fry the bean curd
until golden brown. Drain on
absorbent kitchen paper.
  Heat the 3 tablespoons oil
in a wok or frying pan. Sauté
the ginger, shallot and garlic
until fragrant. Add the winter
melon or marrow and bean
curd cubes and stir-fry for a
while. Stir in the mushrooms
and sprinkle in the sherry.
Pour in the stock, salt, sugar,
pepper and sesame oil. Blend
the 1 teaspoon cornflour to a
smooth paste with the water.
Stir into the sauce and simmer
for 2 minutes.
  Serve, if you like, on a bed
of lightly-cooked broccoli.
Serves 4

Braised Bean Curd

6 Chinese dried mushrooms
175 g/6 oz bean curd
3 tablespoons oil
1 clove garlic, crushed
1 teaspoon shredded ginger
1 large piece canned bamboo
  shoot, cut into strips
1 teaspoon dry sherry
50 ml/2 fl oz vegetable stock
salt
½ teaspoon sugar
a few drops of sesame oil
½ teaspoon cornflour
2 tablespoons water

Soak the mushrooms in cold
water, then drain and steam
them over boiling water for 15
minutes. Cut off and discard
the mushroom stalks, then cut
the caps into quarters or
halves.
  Cut the bean curd into
1-cm/½-in thick oblong pieces.
Heat the oil in a frying pan.
Add the bean curd and fry
until golden underneath, then
turn and fry the second side.
Remove from the pan and set
aside.

Add the garlic and fry until
fragrant. Stir in the ginger,
mushrooms and bamboo shoot
and fry for a while. Add the
bean curd, sprinkle in the
sherry and pour in the stock.
Stir in the salt, sugar, and
sesame oil. Heat gently until
the sauce is just boiling.
  Blend the cornflour with the
water, stir this mixture into
the sauce, then simmer for a
further 2 minutes. Serve
immediately. Serves 4

Note: If you like you can cut
the bamboo shoot to achieve a
decorative edge. To do this
score small V-shaped strips
from the edge of the shoot
before you cut it into strips.

Vegetables in Red Bean Curd Sauce

50 g/2 oz Chinese dried
*   mushrooms*
salt and pepper
1 teaspoon sugar
3 tablespoons oil plus oil for
*   deep frying*
25 g/1 oz black moss
25 g/1 oz black fungus
50 g/2 oz mung bean thread
100 g/4 oz bean curd
2 medium-thick slices fresh
*   root ginger*
2 shallots, sliced
3 tablespoons fermented red
*   bean curd*
1 teaspoon dry sherry
1 (227-g/8-oz) can bamboo
*   shoots, drained and sliced*
100 g/4 oz carrots, sliced
50 g/2 oz mange tout peas
2 teaspoons light soy sauce
1 teaspoon sesame oil
1 lettuce, broken into leaves

Soak the mushrooms in cold water for 10 minutes. Drain, reserving the stock. Cut off the stalks; marinate the caps with salt, sugar and oil. Steam them for 10 minutes.

Soak the moss and fungus until soft, then trim, blanch and rinse it. Cut the bean thread into 5-cm/2-in lengths. Wash, soak until soft and drain. Cut the bean curd into 2.5 × 3.5-cm/1 × 1½-in pieces and sprinkle with a little salt. Heat the oil for deep frying to 190 c/375 f. Fry the bean curd until golden brown. Drain.

Heat the remaining oil in a flameproof casserole. Add the ginger and shallots and fry until fragrant. Stir in the red bean curd, mushrooms, black moss and fungus.

Pour in the sherry and reserved mushroom stock, then boil for 10 minutes. Add the bamboo shoots, carrots, softened bean thread, snow peas and bean curd, then simmer for 10 minutes. Stir in the remaining sugar, the soy sauce, pepper and sesame oil, then serve, on lettuce leaves if you like. *Serves 4–6*

Vegetarian Chicken with Celery

1 small head celery
6 pieces Spicy Bean Curd (page 137)
75 g/3 oz carrots
3 Chinese dried mushrooms
3 spring onions
2 tablespoons oil
1 clove garlic, crushed
1 teaspoon dry sherry
½ teaspoon Ginger Juice (page 227)
50 ml/2 fl oz vegetable stock
salt and pepper
½ teaspoon sugar
a few drops of sesame oil
1 teaspoon cornflour

Cut the celery into 3.5-cm/ 1½-in fingers. Blanch these in boiling salted water for 1 minute. Drain thoroughly. Cut the bean curd and carrots into similar-sized pieces to the celery. Blanch and drain the carrots. Soak the mushrooms in cold water for 10 minutes, then drain and steam them for 15 minutes. Cut off the stalks and shred the mushroom caps.

Shred the spring onions.
Heat the oil in a wok or frying pan then sauté the garlic until fragrant. Add the celery, bean curd, mushrooms, spring onions, and carrots and stir-fry for a while.
Blend all the remaining ingredients together, pour the mixture into the pan and bring to the boil. Simmer for 2 minutes, then serve at once. *Serves 4*

Deep Fried Milk Custard

50 g/2 oz cornflour
350 ml/12 fl oz soya milk
50 ml/2 fl oz coconut milk
½ teaspoon dry sherry
½ teaspoon salt
¼ teaspoon pepper
½ teaspoon sesame oil
BATTER
100 g/4 oz plain flour
2 teaspoons cornflour
1 teaspoon baking powder
about 250 ml/8 fl oz water
2 tablespoons oil plus oil for deep frying
Spicy Salt (page 229) to serve

Blend the cornflour with a little of the soya milk to make a smooth paste. Heat the remaining soya and coconut milk with the sherry, salt and pepper and sesame oil. Pour the hot liquid on to the cornflour, stir well, then return the sauce to the pan and bring to the boil stirring continuously. Pour into a greased, oblong cake tin and allow to cool, then chill thoroughly.

To make the batter, sift the flour, cornflour and baking powder into a bowl, then beat in the water and 2 tablespoons oil to make a smooth batter. Heat the oil for deep frying to 190 c/375 f.
Cut the custard mixture into squares, then dip them into the batter and deep fry until crisp and golden. Drain on absorbent kitchen paper and serve at once, with the spicy salt. *Serves 4–6*

Vegetarian Bean Curd Sheet Roll

50 g/2 oz Chinese dried mushrooms
1 (227-g/8-oz) can bamboo shoots
175 g/6 oz carrots, parboiled
4 tablespoons oil
1 teaspoon shredded fresh root ginger
1 teaspoon shredded spring onion
2 teaspoons dry sherry
salt and pepper
2 teaspoons cornflour
4 tablespoons water
7 dried bean curd sheets
250 ml/8 fl oz vegetable stock
1 teaspoon plus 50 g/2 oz sugar
a few drops of sesame oil
dark soy sauce for brushing
a little red food colouring
about ½ cup China tea leaves

GARNISH
1 orange, sliced
¼ cucumber, sliced
1–2 glacé cherries

Wash and soak the mushrooms in cold water for 10 minutes. Drain, reserving the mushroom water, then remove the stalks and steam the mushroom caps over boiling water for 15 minutes. Shred finely. Shred the bamboo shoots and carrots.

Heat half the oil in a wok or frying pan. Sauté the ginger and spring onion until fragrant. Stir in the shredded mushroom, carrots and bamboo shoots. Sprinkle in half the sherry, add the reserved mushroom stock and bring to the boil, then season to taste. Blend half the cornflour with half the water, stir into the pan and bring to the boil. Simmer for 2 minutes, remove from the heat and set aside to cool.

Soak the bean curd sheets until soft. Drain and tear three of the sheets into small pieces. Heat the remaining 2 tablespoons oil in a wok or frying pan. Sprinkle in the remaining sherry and the stock. Mix in seasoning to taste, the 1 teaspoon sugar and the sesame oil. Blend the remaining cornflour with the water and stir into the pan. Add the torn bean curd sheets and simmer for 2 minutes, stirring all the time.

Lay two of the remaining bean curd sheets flat in a double thickness. Spread half the cooked bean curd and half the vegetable mixture on top, then roll up tucking in the ends neatly. Brush the outside of the roll very lightly with a little dark soy sauce and red food colouring. Repeat with the remaining bean curd sheets and filling.

Place the tea leaves and sugar in the base of a steamer or in a wok if you are using a bamboo steamer. Dry cook these ingredients over a very low heat until they become smoky. Place the bean curd rolls in a steamer and cover closely, then leave to smoke for 5 minutes. Turn the rolls over and continue to cook for a further 5 minutes.

Slice and serve, garnished with an arrangement of halved orange and cucumber slices and glacé cherries.
Serves 4–6

Note: This is an authentic Chinese smoking technique. Take great care not to burn the tea leaves and sugar too fiercely and do not leave the pan unattended.

Vegetarian Fried Rice

100 g/4 oz shelled peas
100 g/4 oz carrots, diced
100 g/4 oz sweet corn
4 tablespoons oil
1 clove garlic
1 shallot, sliced
¼ teaspoon salt
¼ teaspoon sugar
pinch of pepper
1 egg white
450 g/1 lb cooked long-grain
  rice
50 g/2 oz button mushrooms,
  diced
1 piece Spicy Bean Curd (page
  137), diced
1 tablespoon light soy sauce

Blanch the peas, carrots and corn together in boiling salted water for 1 minute. Drain thoroughly, then rinse under cold water and drain again.

Heat half the oil in a wok or frying pan. Sauté the garlic and shallot until fragrant, then discard these ingredients. Pour in the mixed vegetables and stir-fry for a while. Sprinkle in the salt, sugar and pepper.

Remove from the pan.

Add the remaining oil to the pan and heat it through. Pour in the egg white and stir-fry quickly until it is beginning to set. Add the rice and mix well. Gently stir in all the other ingredients taking care not to break up the rice grains and make them sticky. Stir the rice mixture frequently over low heat until all the ingredients are hot.

Transfer the cooked rice to a large warmed serving bowl, or to small individual bowls, and serve at once.

Vegetarian E-Fu Noodles

350 g/12 oz Chinese egg
  noodles
25 g/1 oz Chinese dried
  mushrooms
salt and pepper
¾ teaspoon sugar
4 tablespoons oil
1 (200-g/7.05-oz) can button
  mushrooms, drained
1 shallot, grated
1 clove garlic, crushed
100 g/4 oz bean sprouts
1 teaspoon dry sherry
100 ml/4 fl oz vegetable stock
1 teaspoon light soy sauce
½ teaspoon dark soy sauce
¼ teaspoon monosodium
  glutamate
1 teaspoon sesame oil
spring onion curl to garnish
  (page 34)

Blanch the noodles in boiling water for 1 minute, just to soften them, then drain and rinse under running water. Drain thoroughly. Soak the Chinese dried mushrooms in cold water for 10 minutes, then drain and marinate them with a little salt, sugar and oil. Steam for 10–12 minutes, remove the stalks and shred the mushroom caps. Halve the button mushrooms.

Heat 2 tablespoons of the oil in a wok or frying pan. Sauté the shallot and garlic, then discard. Add the bean sprouts and stir-fry for a few seconds. Remove from the pan and set aside.

Heat another 2 tablespoons oil in the pan. Add the noodles and toss well until heated through. Stir in both types of mushroom and the bean sprouts. Pour in the sherry, stock and soy sauces. Season to taste and add the remaining sugar, monosodium glutamate and sesame oil. Heat through, then serve at once, garnished with the spring onion curl. *Serves 4–6*

Broccoli in Mock Crabmeat Sauce

100 g/4 oz bean curd
350 g/12 oz broccoli
4 tablespoons oil
1 shallot
2 thin slices fresh root ginger
2 teaspoons dry sherry
salt and pepper
100 ml/4 fl oz vegetable stock
1 teaspoon sugar
¼ teaspoon monosodium glutamate
½ teaspoon sesame oil
2 teaspoons cornflour
2 tablespoons water
1 egg white
1 teaspoon grated carrot

Dice the bean curd finely. Blanch very briefly in boiling water, drain and set aside. Cut the broccoli into small florets. Blanch the pieces in boiling water for 2 minutes, then drain and rinse in cold water; drain thoroughly.

Heat 2 tablespoons oil in a wok or frying pan. Sauté the shallot and ginger until fragrant, then discard. Add the broccoli and fry for a while. Sprinkle in half the sherry and seasoning to taste. Heat through and transfer to a warmed serving dish, then set aside to keep hot.

Heat the remaining oil in the pan. Stir in the remaining sherry and the stock, then add the bean curd and bring to the boil. Add seasoning to taste, the sugar, monosodium glutamate and sesame oil. Blend the cornflour with the water. Stir the egg white and cornflour mixture into the bean curd and cook, stirring until set.

Spoon the bean curd neatly over the broccoli and sprinkle with the grated carrot. Serve immediately. *Serves 4*

Crackling Balls

225 g/8 oz fresh lotus root, peeled and grated
1 (312-g/11-oz) can cream style corn
1½ teaspoons Spicy Salt (page 229)
1 teaspoon sugar
2 teaspoons soy sauce
pinch of pepper
1 teaspoon sesame oil
3 tablespoons cornflour
50 g/2 oz shelled peas
100 g/4 oz button mushrooms, diced
2 tablespoons diced preserved mustard
1 tablespoon chopped spring onion
about 3 eggs, beaten
100 g/4 oz stale bread, cubed
oil for deep frying
a few crisp lettuce leaves to serve

Mix the lotus root and cream-style corn in a large bowl. Add the spicy salt, sugar, soy sauce, pepper to taste, sesame oil and cornflour and mix thoroughly. Stir in the peas, mushrooms, mustard, spring onion and 1 beaten egg.

The mixture should be stiff enough to shape into balls, but not too dry, so add more egg if necessary.

Shape the mixture into small balls, then dip these in beaten egg, then press the bread cubes firmly around each one.

Heat the oil for deep frying to 190 c/375 f, then cook the crackling balls until crisp and golden. Drain on absorbent kitchen paper and serve on a bed of lettuce. *Serves 4–6*

Shredded Cabbage with Minced Shrimp

50 g/2 oz dried shrimps
350 g/12 oz celery cabbage or
 Chinese lettuce
50 g/2 oz mung bean thread
2 tablespoons oil
1 teaspoon finely shredded
 fresh root ginger
1 shallot, sliced
1 clove garlic, sliced
1 teaspoon dry sherry
150 ml/¼ pint water
½ teaspoon salt
1 teaspoon sugar
1 teaspoon cornflour
½ teaspoon sesame oil
1 teaspoon light soy sauce

Wash and drain the dried shrimps then soak them in hot water for 30 minutes. Drain thoroughly and mash or finely chop them. Wash and shred the celery cabbage. Wash and drain the mung bean thread then soak it in cold water until soft.

Heat the oil in a wok or frying pan. Sauté the ginger, shallot and garlic until fragrant. Stir in the dried shrimps and fry thoroughly.

Add the cabbage and stir-fry for a while, then pour in the sherry, most of the water, the salt and sugar. Bring to the boil, then reduce the heat. Cover and simmer over a low heat for 5 minutes. Stir in the bean thread and cook for a few minutes.

Blend the cornflour to a smooth cream with the remaining water, the sesame oil and the soy sauce. Stir this into the pan and cook for 2 minutes. Transfer the cooked mixture to a warmed serving platter or dish and serve at once. *Serves 4–6*

Winter Melon with Dried Shrimp

450 g/1 lb winter melon or
 marrow
175 g/6 oz leeks or 1 bunch
 spring onions
25 g/1 oz dried shrimps
5 tablespoons oil
2 cloves garlic, crushed
½ teaspoon grated shallot
½ teaspoon grated fresh root
 ginger
1 teaspoon dry sherry
150 ml/¼ pint water
salt and pepper
¾ teaspoon sugar
1 teaspoon light soy sauce
1 teaspoon cornflour
2 red chillies, deseeded and
 shredded

Peel and cut the winter melon or marrow into chunks. Thoroughly wash and shred the leeks or spring onions. Soak the dried shrimps in hot water for 30 minutes, then drain and mash or finely chop them.

Heat 3 tablespoons oil in a wok or frying pan. Sauté the garlic, shallot, ginger and dried shrimps until fragrant. Add the winter melon or marrow and sprinkle in the sherry. Pour in most of the water and seasoning to taste. Add the sugar and soy sauce, then cover and simmer for 5–10 minutes. Blend the cornflour with the remaining water, pour into the pan and simmer for 2 minutes to thicken. Transfer to a warmed serving dish.

Heat the remaining oil in the pan and sauté the leeks and chillies for a few minutes. Pour this over the winter melon or marrow and serve at once. *Serves 4–6*

Stuffed Mushroom in Batter

24 Chinese dried mushrooms
225 g/8 oz lean minced pork
6 canned water chestnuts,
   diced
2 spring onions, chopped
salt and pepper
2 teaspoons dry sherry
2 teaspoons light soy sauce
1 teaspoon sugar
1 tablespoon cornflour
a few drops of sesame oil
½ beaten egg
100 g/4 oz plain flour
250 ml/8 fl oz water
50 ml/2 fl oz chicken stock
oil for deep frying
100 g/4 oz shelled peas

Wash and soak the mushrooms until thoroughly softened – about 1 hour. Drain and squeeze dry. Mix the pork with the water chestnuts, spring onions, seasoning, half the sherry, half the light soy sauce, the sugar, cornflour and a few drops of sesame oil. Mix in enough beaten egg to bind the mixture together.

Remove the stalks from the mushrooms. Divide the meat filling between half the mushrooms and press the other 12 mushrooms on top.

Sift the flour into a bowl, beat in the water to form a coating batter. Pour the stock into a saucepan with the remaining sherry and soy sauce. Bring to the boil, then simmer gently until reduced to a small amount of liquid.

Meanwhile, heat the oil for deep frying to 190 c/375 f. Dip the mushrooms in the batter to coat them completely, then deep fry them until golden. Drain on absorbent kitchen paper and arrange on a warmed serving dish.

Stir the peas into the sauce, heat through and pour over the mushrooms. Serve at once. *Serves 4–6*

Stuffed Courgettes

4 large courgettes
1 tablespoon dried shrimps
3 Chinese dried mushrooms
225 g/8 oz minced pork
1 tablespoon chopped spring
   onion
salt and pepper
1 teaspoon cornflour plus extra
   for dusting
1 tablespoon oil
1 clove garlic, crushed
1 shallot, sliced
1½ teaspoons dry sherry
150 ml/¼ pint chicken stock
1 teaspoon oyster sauce
1 teaspoon cornflour
1 tablespoon water
1 teaspoon light soy sauce
½ teaspoon sesame oil

Thoroughly wash the courgettes, and cut them into 2.5-cm/1-in thick slices. Cut out the middle of each slice to form a hollow. Blanch the courgette rings in boiling water for 1 minute; drain. Soak the shrimps for 30 minutes, drain and chop them.

   Soak the mushrooms in cold water for 10 minutes, drain and steam over boiling water for 15 minutes. Remove the stalks and finely dice the mushroom caps.

   Mix the minced pork with the diced shrimps and mushrooms. Add the spring onion and seasoning to taste.

   Dust the inside of the courgettes with cornflour and stuff with the pork mixture. Arrange on a greased plate then steam over boiling water for about 20 minutes.

   Heat the oil in a small saucepan and sauté the garlic and shallot until fragrant. Discard. Pour in the sherry, stock and oyster sauce. Bring to the boil. Blend the cornflour with the water and light soy sauce. Stir the mixture into the sauce, then simmer for 2 minutes. Stir in the sesame oil.

   Arrange the courgettes on a serving plate, pour over the sauce and serve. *Serves 4*

Sautéed Corn with Mixed Vegetables

100 g/4 oz lean boneless pork
2 teaspoons light soy sauce
2 teaspoons cornflour
2 teaspoons dry sherry
½ teaspoon sugar
salt and pepper
1 teaspoon sesame oil
3 tablespoons water
2 tablespoons oil
1 medium-thick slice fresh root ginger, finely chopped
2 shallots, sliced
1 clove garlic, sliced
1 (195-g/7-oz) can sweet corn, drained
1 green pepper, deseeded and chopped
50 g/2 oz red chillies, deseeded and chopped
6 canned water chestnuts, diced
50 g/2 oz carrots, diced and blanched
2 large open mushrooms, diced
¾ teaspoon oyster sauce
a few drops of dark soy sauce

Marinate the pork for 30 minutes with 1 teaspoon each of light soy sauce, cornflour and sherry, the sugar, a pinch of pepper, a few drops of sesame oil and 1 tablespoon water.

Heat the oil in a wok or frying pan. Add the ginger, shallots and garlic and fry until fragrant. Stir in the sweet corn, green pepper, chillies, water chestnuts, carrots, mushrooms and salt. Stir-fry until thoroughly heated.

Blend the remaining cornflour with the remaining sherry, soy sauce, sesame oil, water, the oyster sauce, and dark soy sauce. Pour in to the pan and bring to the boil, Simmer for 2 minutes, then serve. *Serves 4*

Yam with Minced Pork

175 g/6 oz minced pork
1 tablespoon light soy sauce
1 tablespoon sugar
2 teaspoons dry sherry
2 teaspoons cornflour
salt and pepper
600 ml/1 pint water
3 tablespoons oil
25 g/1 oz dried shrimps
2 medium-thick slices fresh root ginger
2 cloves garlic
2 shallots
2 tablespoons ground bean paste
450 g/1 lb yams, peeled and cut into chunks
a few drops of sesame oil
1–2 spring onions, shredded, to garnish

Marinate the pork for 30 minutes with 2 teaspoons of the light soy sauce, 1 teaspoon each of the sugar, sherry and cornflour, a pinch of pepper, 2 tablespoons water and 2 teaspoons oil. Wash, soak and dice the dried shrimps.

Heat 2 tablespoons oil in a wok or frying pan. Add the ginger, garlic, shallots and pork with its marinade. Stir-fry until browned. Stir in the dried shrimps and stir-fry for a while. Add the ground bean paste and yams, then sprinkle in the remaining sherry and pour in most of the water. Bring to the boil, cover and simmer for 20 minutes or until cooked.

Season to taste, then blend the remaining cornflour with the remaining water, stir into the sauce with the sesame oil and simmer for 2 minutes. Serve hot, garnished with spring onions. *Serves 4*

Stewed Aubergine with Shredded Pork

450 g/1 lb aubergines
salt and pepper
100 g/4 oz lean boneless pork, shredded
1 tablespoon light soy sauce
1 teaspoon sugar
1 teaspoon cornflour
1 teaspoon sherry
50 ml/2 fl oz plus 2 tablespoons water
3 tablespoons oil plus oil for deep frying
1 shallot, sliced
2 cloves garlic, sliced
8–12 large open mushrooms, sliced
100 g/4 oz shelled peas
1 tablespoon dark soy sauce
1 teaspoon vinegar
1 teaspoon sesame oil

Wash, trim and cut the aubergines into chunks. Place in a colander, sprinkle with salt and set aside for 30 minutes. Rinse thoroughly, then dry the pieces.

Marinate the pork with 1 teaspoon of the light soy sauce, ¼ teaspoon sugar, half the cornflour, half the sherry, 2 tablespoons water and 1 tablespoon oil.

Heat the oil for deep frying to 190 c/375 F, then deep fry the aubergines until golden brown. Drain on absorbent kitchen paper.

Heat the 2 tablespoons oil in a wok or frying pan. Add the shallot and garlic and fry until fragrant. Stir in the mushrooms, then stir in the pork and fry until browned. Add the aubergines, peas and remaining sherry. Pour in the water and remaining sugar and simmer for 5 minutes.

Blend the last of the cornflour with all the other ingredients, pour into the pan and simmer for 2 minutes to thicken. Serve at once.
Serves 4

Sautéed Vegetables with Ham

450 g/1 lb Chinese green vegetable or broccoli
2 tablespoons oil
2 medium-thick slices fresh root ginger, finely chopped
2 shallots, finely chopped
2 cloves garlic, finely chopped
50 g/2 oz gammon, shredded
1 teaspoon dry sherry
4 tablespoons water
1½ teaspoons sugar
2 teaspoons light soy sauce
pinch of pepper
a few drops of sesame oil
½ teaspoon cornflour

Wash and trim the Chinese vegetable or broccoli, then blanch it in boiling water, drain thoroughly and set aside.

Heat the oil in a wok or frying pan, then sauté the ginger, shallots and garlic until fragrant. Add the gammon and cook until browned, then remove and keep hot. Sprinkle in the sherry and pour in half the water. Add the sugar, light soy sauce, pepper and sesame oil. Stir well, then blend the cornflour with the remaining water and stir into the sauce. Simmer for 2 minutes, add the vegetables and reheat thoroughly.

Arrange the vegetables on a platter, then pour over the pan juices and sprinkle the gammon on top. Serve at once. *Serves 4*

Note: Chinese broccoli is very similar to some home-grown broccoli. The stalks are long and thin, with small heads at the top or sometimes at the sides. Down their length, the stalks have a few small leaves which are not usually trimmed off before cooking.

Diced Sausages with Vegetables

100 g/4 oz Chinese dried
   sausages
50 g/2 oz dried shrimps
50 g/2 oz mushrooms
50 g/2 oz pickled mustard
50 g/2 oz Spicy Bean Curd
   (page 137)
50 g/2 oz carrrot
50 g/2 oz canned water
   chestnuts
50 g/2 oz cucumber
2 tablespoons oil
½ teaspoon finely grated fresh
   root ginger
1 shallot, sliced
1 clove garlic, sliced
2 red chillies, deseeded and
   diced
1 green pepper, deseeded and
   diced
1 teaspoon dry sherry
50 ml/2 fl oz plus 2 tablespoons
   stock or water
salt and pepper
1 teaspoon sugar
1 teaspoon light soy sauce
½ teaspoon sesame oil
1 teaspoon cornflour
parsley sprigs to garnish

Briefly blanch and dice the
Chinese sausages. Wash and
soak the shrimps in hot water,
then drain and dice them.
Dice the mushrooms; wash and
dice the pickled mustard. Dice
the spiced bean curd, carrot,
water chestnuts and cucumber.

   Heat the oil in a wok or
frying pan. Sauté the ginger,
shallot and garlic until
fragrant. Stir in the dried
shrimps and fry for a while.
Add the chillies, green
pepper, carrot, water chestnut
and cucumber and sauté
thoroughly. Pour in all the
remaining prepared
ingredients and stir-fry for a
few minutes. Pour in the
sherry, 50 ml/2 fl oz stock or
water and season to taste.
Add the sugar, light soy sauce
and sesame oil.

   Blend the cornflour to a
paste with the 2 tablespoons
water. Stir this into the
ingredients and simmer for 2
minutes. Serve, garnished with
parsley. *Serves 4*

Vegetables in White Sauce

1 small cauliflower
225 g/8 oz broccoli
salt and pepper
2 tablespoons oil
1 shallot, grated
1 clove garlic, crushed
2 medium-thick slices fresh
    root ginger, grated
2 teaspoons dry sherry
1 teaspoon sugar
100 ml/4 fl oz stock
100 ml/4 fl oz milk
1 teaspoon cornflour
1 teaspoon sesame oil
¼ teaspoon monosodium
    glutamate

Break the cauliflower and broccoli into small florets, then cook each of these vegetables separately in boiling salted water until they are just tender. Drain thoroughly.

Heat the oil in a wok or frying pan. Sauté the shallot, garlic and ginger until fragrant, then stir in the blanched vegetables and fry for a while. Pour in half the sherry and sprinkle in the sugar with seasoning to taste. Toss the vegetables well to make sure they are thoroughly coated in the seasonings, then transfer them to a warmed serving dish and keep hot.

To make the coating sauce, pour the remaining sherry into a saucepan. Pour in the stock and most of the milk, then heat through almost to boiling point. Blend the cornflour with the cold milk, pour a little of the hot liquid on to it, stirring all the time. Return this mixture to the sauce in the saucepan and bring to the boil, stirring continuously to prevent lumps from forming.

Stir in the sesame oil and monosodium glutamate, taste and adjust the seasoning, then pour this sauce over the vegetables and serve hot.
Serves 4

Dry-cooked French Beans

450 g/1 lb French beans
25 g/1 oz dried shrimps
50 g/2 oz Szechuen preserved
*   mustard*
2 tablespoons oil plus oil for
*   deep frying*
3 tablespoons chopped spring
*   onion*
1 tablespoon chopped fresh
*   root ginger*
1 teaspoon dry sherry
50 ml/2 fl oz water
1 tablespoon sugar
1 tablespoon light soy sauce
¼ teaspoon monosodium
*   glutamate*
salt and pepper
1 tablespoon sesame oil

Choose tender young French beans. Trim the beans and cut them into 3-cm/1¼-in lengths. Soak the dried shrimps in warm water until softened, then chop them finely. Wash and mince the preserved mustard.

Heat the oil for deep frying to 190 c/375 f, then add the beans and cook for a few minutes. Drain on absorbent kitchen paper and set aside.

Heat the 2 tablespoons oil in a wok. Sauté the spring onion and ginger until fragrant. Add the dried shrimps, preserved mustard and French beans. Pour in the sherry, add the water, sugar, light soy sauce, monosodium glutamate and seasoning to taste. Stir-fry until almost dry, add the sesame oil and serve. *Serves 4*

Broccoli in Ginger Stock

1 kg/2 lb Chinese broccoli or
*   other broccoli*
50 g/2 oz fresh root ginger
2 shallots, grated
3 tablespoons oil
3 tablespoons light soy sauce
1 tablespoon dry sherry
2 tablespoons sugar
salt

Wash and trim the broccoli. Peel and slice the ginger, then place it in a saucepan with the shallots and pour in plenty of water. Bring to the boil then add the broccoli and cook for a few minutes. Drain thoroughly. Arrange on a platter and keep hot.

Heat the oil in a wok or frying pan. Add the light soy sauce, sherry, sugar and salt to taste. Boil until the sugar dissolves, then pour on to the vegetables and serve. *Serves 4*

To peel fresh root ginger: The fresh ginger root is quite tough. If you can find juicy, tender, young ginger, then you will not find it too difficult to peel.

Use a good potato peeler and carefully cut all the peel off the knobbles of ginger. Remember that if you do not succeed in removing the peel thinly, then you may have reduced the weight of ginger required quite considerably. So if you do have a very tough root allow a little extra weight.

Mushrooms in Oyster Sauce

100 g/4 oz Chinese dried
    mushrooms
3 tablespoons oil
salt
1 teaspoon sugar
1 Iceberg lettuce
1 small carrot
2 medium-thick slices fresh
    root ginger
1 shallot, sliced
1 clove garlic, sliced
√ teaspoon dry sherry
50 ml/2 fl oz stock
1 tablespoon oyster sauce
½ teaspoon dark soy sauce
½ teaspoon sesame oil
1 teaspoon cornflour
2 tablespoons water

Wash and soak the
mushrooms for 30 minutes,
then season them with a little
oil, salt, and a little of the
sugar. Steam for 12–15
minutes over boiling water.

Wash the lettuce, then
blanch it very briefly in boiling
salted water. Drain thoroughly
and place on a warmed
serving dish. Keep hot.

Slice the carrot and cut the
slices into patterns. Blanch,
rinse under cold water and
drain.

Heat the remaining oil in a
wok or frying pan, then sauté
the ginger, shallot and garlic
until fragrant. Discard. Stir in
the mushrooms and fry for 1
minute. Add the carrot and
mix well. Sprinkle in the
sherry, then pour in the stock,
salt, sugar, oyster sauce, dark
soy sauce and sesame oil.

Blend the cornflour with the
water, stir it into the sauce
and simmer for a few minutes
before serving, poured over
the blanched lettuce. *Serves 4*

Stewed Potato Balls

1 (230-g/8-oz) can water
    chestnuts
2 pieces Spicy Bean Curd
    (page 137)
25 g/1 oz preserved mustard
15 g/½ oz Chinese dried
    mushrooms
350 g/12 oz cooked potatoes,
    mashed
1 small carrot, chopped
2 medium-thick slices fresh
    root ginger, finely chopped
25 g/1 oz plain flour
1 clove garlic, crushed
salt and pepper
1 tablespoon dark soy sauce
1 teaspoon sugar
½ teaspoon sesame oil
cornflour for coating
oil for deep frying
a few crisp lettuce leaves
SAUCE
1 teaspoon cornflour
1 teaspoon dry sherry
150 ml/¼ pint stock
1 teaspoon soy sauce
¼ teaspoon monosodium
    glutamate

Grate the water chestnuts,
mash the bean curd and chop
the preserved mustard. Soak
the mushrooms, then steam
them over boiling water.
Remove the stalks and chop
the mushroom caps.

Mix all the ingredients
together, apart from those
required for the sauce. Shape
the potato mixture into small
balls and coat them
generously with cornflour.

Heat the oil for deep frying
to 190 c/375 F, then deep fry
the potato balls until golden
brown. Drain on absorbent
kitchen paper and arrange on
a few lettuce leaves in a
serving dish.

Mix all the ingredients for
the gravy, stirring to give a
smooth sauce. Heat gently to
boiling point, simmer for 2
minutes and pour over the
potato balls. Serve at once.
Serves 4–6

Cauliflower in Brown Sauce

1 cauliflower
salt and pepper
25 g/1 oz Chinese dried
 mushrooms
2 tablespoons oil
½ teaspoon sugar
1 clove garlic, crushed
1 shallot, grated
a few pieces of cooked carrot
1 teaspoon dry sherry
1 teaspoon cornflour
1 teaspoon light soy sauce
1 tablespoon oyster sauce
a few drops of sesame oil
1 teaspoon dark soy sauce

Separate the cauliflower into small florets. Blanch these in boiling salted water. Drain, rinse and drain again.

Soak the mushrooms for 30 minutes. Steam them with a little oil, salt and sugar over boiling water for 15 minutes.

Heat the oil in a wok or frying pan. Sauté the garlic and shallot until fragrant. Stir in the cauliflower, carrot and mushrooms and sauté well. Sprinkle in the sherry and

seasoning. Blend the cornflour with all the remaining ingredients, stir into the pan and bring to the boil. Simmer for 2 minutes, then serve at once. *Serves 4–6*

Note: Many Chinese dishes contain vegetables which are cut in a decorative fashion. Some vegetables are carefully carved before they are sliced so that each piece of vegetable is perfect when cut.

However there are easier ways of adding decorative vegetables to most dishes. If the vegetables are blanched first, they are easier to cut. You can cut shapes out of the sides of the whole vegetable, or individual slices can be cut into simple shapes with a small pointed knife or by using aspic cutters. With a little imagination you can present an attractive array of different vegetable shapes in any dish.

Shredded Vegetable Combination

100 g/4 oz preserved vegetable
salt and pepper
6 Chinese dried mushrooms
3 tablespoons oil
1 clove garlic, crushed
½ teaspoon sugar
½ carrot, shredded
1 piece canned bamboo shoot,
 shredded
2 spring onions, shredded
½ teaspoon cornflour
2 tablespoons water
1 teaspoon dry sherry
1 teaspoon soy sauce
a few drops of sesame oil

Soak the preserved vegetable in salted water for 2 hours. Drain, refresh under cold running water and drain again. Cut into 2.5-cm/1-in sections. Soak the mushrooms in water for 30 minutes, then steam them over boiling water for 15 minutes. Discard the mushroom stalks and shred the caps.

Heat the oil in a wok or frying pan. Sauté the garlic

until fragrant. Add the preserved vegetable and sugar and stir until well mixed. Add the remaining vegetables and stir-fry thoroughly. Blend the cornflour with all the remaining ingredients, pour into the pan and simmer until thickened. Serve at once. *Serves 4*

Braised Mushrooms with Bamboo Shoots

*50 g/2 oz Chinese dried
   mushrooms
1 teaspoon sugar
salt
2 tablespoons oil plus oil for
   deep frying
1 (227-g/8-oz) can bamboo
   shoots, drained
2 cloves garlic, crushed
1 teaspoon finely grated ginger
1 teaspoon chopped spring
   onion
100 ml/4 fl oz stock
1 teaspoon dry sherry
1 teaspoon cornflour
1 tablespoon light soy sauce
2 teaspoons dark soy sauce
½ teaspoon sesame oil*

Remove the stalks from the
mushrooms. Wash, soak and
slice the mushroom caps,
squeezing out any excess
water. Mix well with a little
sugar, salt and oil. Steam for
10 minutes. Cut the bamboo
shoots into wedges.

Heat the oil for deep frying
to 190 c/375 f, then add the
bamboo shoots and cook for a
few minutes. Add the
mushrooms and continue deep
frying until the bamboo shoots
turn golden brown. Drain on
absorbent kitchen paper.

Heat the remaining 1
tablespoon oil in a wok or
frying pan, stir in the garlic,
ginger and spring onion and
sauté for a while. Pour in the
stock and sherry and bring to
the boil. Add the mushrooms
and bamboo shoots and
simmer for 5 minutes.

Blend the cornflour to a
smooth paste with the light
and dark soy sauces. Stir this
into the sauce and simmer for
2 minutes. Stir in the sesame
oil and serve. *Serves 4*

Bean Thread with Minced Vegetables

*100 g/4 oz bean thread
2 tablespoons oil plus oil for
   deep frying
5 Chinese dried mushrooms
½ teaspoon finely grated fresh
   root ginger
1 shallot, sliced
1 red chilli, deseeded and
   shredded
100 g/4 oz shelled peas
4 canned water chestnuts,
   chopped
25 g/1 oz carrot, chopped
2 pieces Spicy Bean Curd
   (page 137)
25 g/1 oz preserved mustard,
   chopped
2 tablespoons broad bean paste
1 teaspoon dry sherry
250 ml/8 fl oz stock
salt and pepper
1 teaspoon soy sauce
¼ teaspoon monosodium
   glutamate
½ teaspoon sesame oil*

Divide the bean thread into
three portions. Heat the oil
for deep frying to 190 c/375 f,
then deep fry the bean thread

until puffed and golden. Drain
on absorbent kitchen paper.
Soak the mushrooms in cold
water for 15 minutes, drain
and steam over boiling water
for 10 minutes. Drain and
chop finely.

Heat the 2 tablespoons oil
in a wok or frying pan. Sauté
the ginger, shallot and chilli
until fragrant. Stir in all the
vegetables, including the
water chestnuts, the bean curd
and preserved mustard. Fry
for a while. Add the bean
paste, mix well, then pour in
the sherry and stock and add
seasoning. Mix in all the
remaining ingredients,
including the fried bean
thread. Cook for a few
minutes, then serve. *Serves 4*

Assorted Vegetables in Oyster Sauce

175 g/6 oz broccoli
175 g/6 oz cauliflower
salt and pepper
1 (425-g/15-oz) can whole
  baby corn
a few pieces of carrot
2 tablespoons oil
1 clove garlic
1 shallot
½ teaspoon cornflour
1½ teaspoons sugar
1 teaspoon dry sherry
1 tablespoon Ginger Juice
  (page 227)
2 tablespoons oyster sauce
a few drops of sesame oil
50 ml/2 fl oz stock

Trim and cut both the broccoli and cauliflower into small florets. Blanch these separately in boiling salted water until tender. Arrange on a warmed serving dish and keep hot. Heat the corn and add to the vegetable arrangement with the carrot. Keep hot.

Heat the oil in a saucepan. Sauté the garlic and shallot until fragrant. Blend the cornflour with all the remaining ingredients, pour into the pan and bring to the boil. Simmer for 2 minutes, then pour the sauce over the vegetables and serve. *Serves 6*

Assorted Vegetables with White Fungus

25 g/1 oz white fungus
a few large carrots
salt and pepper
175-g/6-oz piece choco (the
  green gourd-like vegetable in
  the picture; buy from
  Chinese supermarkets) or
  marrow
4 tablespoons oil
2 medium-thick slices fresh
  root ginger
2 shallots
2 cloves garlic
2 teaspoons dry sherry
300 ml/½ pint stock
1 (425-g/15-oz) can straw
  mushrooms, drained
½ teaspoon cornflour
1 teaspoon sugar
1 teaspoon light soy sauce
½ teaspoon sesame oil
½ teaspoon dark soy sauce

Soak the fungus until soft,
then trim, blanch and rinse it
under cold running water.
Leave to soak in cold water
until you are ready to use it.
Cook the carrots in boiling
salted water until just tender.

Drain and use a melon baller
to shape the carrots. Use the
melon baller to shape the
choco or marrow, then blanch
these in boiling water for 2
minutes. Drain thoroughly.

Heat 2 tablespoons of the
oil in a wok or frying pan.
Add half the ginger, shallots
and garlic, then fry until
fragrant and remove these
ingredients from the pan.
Drain the white fungus and
add it to the pan, then fry
thoroughly. Stir in half the
sherry, 150 ml/¼ pint of the
stock and seasoning to taste.
Simmer gently for a while.

Heat the remaining oil in a
separate pan, sauté the
remaining ginger, shallots and
garlic, then add the carrots,
choco or marrow and straw
mushrooms. Stir-fry for a
while, then add the rest of the
sherry and stock. Blend the
cornflour with all the
remaining ingredients, pour
into the pan and bring to the
boil. Simmer gently for a few
minutes. Spoon the fungus on
to a plate, then top with the
vegetables and serve. *Serves 4*

Assorted Vegetables in Turmeric Sauce

175 g/6 oz potatoes, cut into
  cubes
100 g/4 oz carrots, cut into
  cubes
100 g/4 oz button mushrooms
2 tablespoons oil
1 shallot, sliced
1 clove garlic, sliced
2 medium-thick slices fresh
  root ginger
4 tablespoons plain flour
100 ml/4 fl oz stock
100 ml/4 fl oz milk
100 ml/4 fl oz coconut milk
salt and pepper
1 teaspoon sherry
½ teaspoon sugar
¼ teaspoon monosodium
  glutamate
1 tablespoon turmeric
175 g/6 oz broccoli to serve

Cook the potatoes and carrots
together in boiling salted
water until just tender. Drain
and mix with the mushrooms.

Heat the oil in a flameproof
casserole. Add the shallot,
garlic and ginger and fry until

fragrant. Stir in the mixed
vegetables and stir-fry for a
while. Stir in the flour, then
pour in the stock, milk and
coconut milk and bring to the
boil. Stir in the seasoning,
sherry, sugar, monosodium
glutamate and turmeric.

Transfer the casserole to a
hot oven (230 c, 450 f, gas 8)
for about 10–15 minutes.
Blanch the broccoli while the
vegetables are cooking, then
drain thoroughly and arrange
it around the edge of the
casserole and serve at once.
Serves 4

Chopsticks Salad

1 cucumber
salt
1 carrot
100 g/4 oz Chinese cabbage
100 g/4 oz Pickled Ginger
   (page 226)
100 g/4 oz celery
100 g/4 oz mung bean sheet
2 tablespoons oil
2 cloves garlic
100 g/4 oz bean sprouts
1 green pepper, deseeded and
   shredded
1 red chilli, deseeded and
   shredded
DRESSING
1 tablespoon sugar
4 tablespoons sesame paste
1 teaspoon sesame oil
½ teaspoon chilli oil
1 tablespoon soy sauce
4 tablespoons stock

Shred the cucumber, place it in a colander and sprinkle with salt, then leave for 30 minutes. Squeeze out the excess water. Dry the cucumber on absorbent kitchen paper. Shred and blanch the carrot and cabbage. Shred the pickled ginger and celery. Soak the mung bean sheet in warm water for 30 minutes, then shred and quickly blanch it.

Heat the oil in a wok or frying pan, add the garlic and fry until fragrant. Quickly sauté the bean sprouts, remove them from the pan and sauté the cabbage, celery and green pepper in the same way, keeping all the ingredients separate. Arrange these ingredients on a serving platter with the mung bean sheet, ginger and chilli.

Mix all the dressing ingredients and sprinkle the dressing over the salad just before serving. *Serves 6*

Ham in Winter Melon or Marrow

450 g/1 lb winter melon or
   marrow, peeled
100 g/4 oz gammon, sliced
½ teaspoon sugar
½ teaspoon salt
50 ml/2 fl oz plus 1 tablespoon
   water
2 tablespoons oil
1 medium-thick slice fresh root
   ginger
1 shallot, grated
1 teaspoon dry sherry
1 teaspoon sesame oil
pinch of monosodium
   glutamate
½ teaspoon cornflour

Peel the winter melon or marrow and remove any seeds. Cut the vegetable into slices, then cut these into small, oblong pieces about 1 cm/½ in thick.

Cut the rind off the gammon and thinly slice it, then cut the slices into small oblong pieces about the same size as the melon or marrow. Blanch these slices of meat in boiling water for 2 minutes then drain them thoroughly.

Carefully cut a slit in each piece of melon or marrow to make an opening. Do not cut right through the vegetable.

Place a piece of gammon in each piece of vegetable and arrange them in a heatproof bowl. Sprinkle half the sugar and salt over and pour in the 50 ml/2 fl oz water. Steam for 20 minutes.

Heat the oil in a wok or large frying pan, then add and sauté the ginger and shallot. Fry until fragrant, then remove from the pan and discard. Pour in the sherry, cooking liquid from the melon or marrow and gammon, remaining salt and sugar. Stir in the sesame oil and monosodium glutamate. Bring to the boil. Blend the cornflour with the water, then pour this mixture into the stock and simmer for 2 minutes or until thickened.

To serve, turn the melon and gammon onto a serving dish or bowl and pour the sauce over. Serve hot, garnished with parsley sprigs. *Serves 4–6*

Black and White Mushrooms in Oyster Sauce

50 g/2 oz Chinese dried
mushrooms
1 teaspoon sugar
salt
3 tablespoons oil
1 lettuce
1 clove garlic
1 shallot
1 (213-g/7½-oz) can button
mushrooms
1 teaspoon cornflour
1 teaspoon dry sherry
3 teaspoons oyster sauce
100 ml/4 fl oz stock

Wash and soak the dried
mushrooms in boiling water
for 1 hour. Drain and season
with a little of the sugar, salt
and a little oil, then steam
over boiling water for 12
minutes. Remove the stalks
and slice the mushroom caps.

Wash and very briefly
blanch the lettuce in boiling
salted water. Drain and
arrange in the middle of a
serving dish.

Heat the remaining oil in a
wok or frying pan. Sauté the
garlic and shallot with the
button mushrooms for a few
minutes. Transfer just the
mushrooms to one side of the
serving plate.

Add the Chinese
mushrooms to the pan. Mix
the cornflour with the sherry,
oyster sauce, stock, remaining
sugar and salt. Pour this
mixture into the pan and bring
to the boil. Simmer for 2
minutes, then scoop the
mushrooms on to the serving
plate and pour the sauce over
all the ingredients. Serve at
once. *Serves 4–6*

Shredded Courgettes with Minced Shrimps

50 g/2 oz dried shrimps
450 g/1 lb courgettes
50 g/2 oz bean thread
4 tablespoons oil
1 teaspoon finely shredded
fresh root ginger
1 shallot, sliced
1 clove garlic, sliced
1 teaspoon dry sherry
175 ml/6 fl oz water
½ teaspoon salt
1 teaspoon sugar
1 teaspoon light soy sauce
½ teaspoon dark soy sauce
1 teaspoon cornflour
½ teaspoon sesame oil

Wash, soak, then mash the
dried shrimps. Wash and very
thinly peel the courgettes (if
they are young there is no
need to peel them), then cut
them into matchstick pieces.

Wash the bean thread, then
soak it in cold water until soft.
Heat half the oil in a wok or
large frying pan, then add half
the ginger, half the shallot and
half the garlic. Fry until
fragrant. Stir in the dried
shrimps and fry thoroughly.
Remove these from the pan
and add the remaining oil.
Heat through, then add the
rest of the ginger, shallot and
garlic and cook until fragrant.
Add the courgettes and stir-
fry for a while, then replace
the shrimps and mix well.

Pour in the sherry and all
but 2 tablespoons of the
water. Stir in the salt and
sugar. Bring to the boil, then
cover and simmer for 5
minutes. Stir in the drained
bean thread and light and
dark soy sauces. Blend the
cornflour with the reserved
water and stir this mixture
into the courgettes. Simmer
for 2 minutes and sprinkle in
the sesame oil before serving.
Serves 6

Sautéed Beans with Assorted Vegetables

175 g/6 oz French beans
50 g/2 oz dried shrimps
75 g/3 oz loin of pork
1½ teaspoons light soy sauce
1½ teaspoons sugar
1 teaspoon cornflour
salt and pepper
4 tablespoons water
3 tablespoons oil
6 Chinese dried mushrooms
75 g/3 oz preserved turnip
½ teaspoon finely grated fresh root ginger
2 shallots, sliced
1 clove garlic, sliced
100 g/4 oz sweet corn
1 teaspoon dry sherry
50 ml/2 fl oz chicken stock
½ teaspoon sesame oil

Cut the beans into short lengths. Wash and soak the shrimps, then drain and mash. Dice the pork. Mix ½ teaspoon each of the light soy sauce, sugar and cornflour, a pinch of pepper, 2 tablespoons water and 1 tablespoon oil. Pour this over the pork and marinate for 20 minutes.

Soak the mushrooms in cold water for 10 minutes, then drain and steam them over boiling water for 15 minutes. Remove the mushroom stalks and dice the mushroom caps. Wash and dice the preserved turnip.

Heat the remaining oil in a wok or large frying pan, then add the pork and sauté for a few minutes, to lightly seal, but not completely cook the meat. Remove the meat from the pan, then add the ginger, shallots and garlic and fry these ingredients until they are fragrant. Stir in the dried shrimps and cook for a while, then add the French beans and cook them vigorously for a few minutes.

Replace the pork in the pan. Add the preserved turnip, sweet corn and mushrooms. Stir in the sherry, stock, seasoning, remaining sugar and soy sauce and the sesame oil. Boil. Blend the remaining cornflour and water, stir into the vegetables and simmer for 2 minutes before serving. *Serves 4*

Braised Courgettes in Scallop Sauce

450 g/1 lb courgettes
25 g/1 oz dried scallops
3 tablespoons oil
1 medium-thick slice fresh root ginger, shredded
1 shallot, shredded
1 clove garlic, chopped
1 teaspoon dry sherry
100 ml/4 fl oz chicken stock or vegetable stock
1 teaspoon light soy sauce
½ teaspoon salt
pinch of pepper
½ teaspoon sesame oil
½ teaspoon cornflour
2 tablespoons water

Trim, very thinly peel and wash the courgettes. Cut large ones lengthways into quarters, smaller ones in half. Blanch in boiling water for 1 minute, then drain thoroughly.

Wash and soak the dried scallops for 1 hour, then drain and steam them over boiling water for 20 minutes.

Heat the oil in a wok or large frying pan and add the ginger, shallot and garlic. Cook until fragrant, then stir in the drained scallops and the courgettes. Pour in the sherry, stock and light soy sauce. Add the salt, pepper and sesame oil. Heat through to boiling point, then simmer gently for 20 minutes.

Blend the cornflour with the water and stir this mixture into the sauce surrounding the courgettes. Simmer for 2 minutes, then transfer to a warmed serving dish and serve. *Serves 4–6*

Lettuce in Oyster Sauce

1 large Iceberg lettuce
2 medium-thick slices fresh
*   root ginger*
salt
1½ teaspoons sugar
5 tablespoons oil
1 shallot
½ teaspoon dry sherry
50 ml/2 fl oz chicken stock
3 tablespoons oyster sauce
1 teaspoon light soy sauce
½ teaspoon sesame oil
½ teaspoon cornflour

Separate the lettuce into leaves, then wash and thoroughly drain them. Bring a large saucepan of water to the boil, add the ginger, 2 tablespoons salt, 1 teaspoon of the sugar and 3 tablespoons of the oil.

Lower the lettuce leaves into this water and simmer for 1 minute, then drain thoroughly and transfer the leaves to a large warmed serving platter and keep hot. Roughly chop the shallot.

Heat 1 tablespoon of the remaining oil in a wok or large frying pan, then add the shallot and fry until browned. Remove from the pan and discard. Pour in the sherry and stock and bring to the boil.

Blend the oyster sauce, light soy sauce, 2 tablespoons of water and sesame oil with the cornflour, then stir this mixture into the sauce in the wok. Simmer for 2 minutes or until thickened. Stir the remaining 1 tablespoon of oil into the sauce to make it glossy. Pour the sauce over the lettuce and serve at once.
Serves 4–6

Note: Various dishes of lightly cooked lettuce served in a sauce are traditional in Chinese cooking. It is important to select a crisp variety of lettuce, otherwise the result could be slightly slimy and unpalatable. Iceberg lettuce gives the best result but a Cos lettuce or Webbs lettuce can also be used.

To ensure a successful result, make certain that the water is boiling quite rapidly before adding the lettuce, then bring the water back to the boil as quickly as possible so that the vegetable can be simmered for just 1 minute. Drain the cooked lettuce thoroughly – use a large Chinese draining scoop if you have one, otherwise use a colander or sieve. Have ready a warmed platter and keep the lettuce hot once it is drained. Prepare the sauce as quickly as possible so that the lettuce does not spoil. Serve immediately the dish is completed.

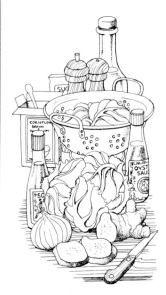

Bundled Bean Curd with Mushrooms

1 bean curd sheet
2 tablespoons oil plus oil for
  deep frying
50 g/2 oz mushrooms
175 g/6 oz bean curd, cut into
  small pieces
1 teaspoon finely shredded
  fresh root ginger
1 tablespoon chopped chives
1 shallot, sliced
1 clove garlic, sliced
1 teaspoon dry sherry
100 ml/4 fl oz vegetable stock
2 tablespoons oyster sauce
½ teaspoon sesame oil
½ teaspoon salt
1 teaspoon sugar
pinch of pepper
a few drops of dark soy sauce
1 teaspoon cornflour
2 tablespoons water
cooked broccoli to serve

Cut the bean curd sheet into pieces measuring about 20 × 2.5-cm/8 × 1-in. Heat the oil for deep frying to 190 c/375 F, then add the pieces of bean curd sheet and cook until they are golden brown. Drain on absorbent kitchen paper and soak in cold water for a while.

Halve the mushrooms. Deep fry the bean curd in the hot oil until golden brown, then drain the pieces on absorbent kitchen paper.

Put a piece of bean curd, a mushroom half and a little of the shredded ginger on each piece of soaked bean curd sheet. Add a little chopped chive and fold up neatly to make a small package. Continue until all the ingredients are used up. Arrange these packages on a heatproof platter.

Heat the 2 tablespoons oil in a wok or frying pan, add the shallot and garlic and sauté until fragrant. Pour in the sherry, stock, oyster sauce and sesame oil. Add the salt, sugar, pepper and dark soy sauce. Blend the cornflour and water, stir into the sauce and simmer for 2 minutes.

Pour the sauce over the bundles and place the platter in the steamer. Cook for 10 minutes. Serve garnished with cooked broccoli. *Serves 4–6*

Mushroom Shiu My

100 g/4 oz lean minced pork
1 teaspoon finely chopped
  parsley
100 g/4 oz peeled cooked
  prawns
1 teaspoon cornflour
½ teaspoon dry sherry
1 teaspoon soy sauce
½ teaspoon sugar
salt and pepper
1 egg white
2 teaspoons oil
1 (200-g/7.05-oz) can button
  mushrooms, drained
parsley sprigs to garnish

Mix the minced pork with the parsley. Mash the prawns, then add them to the pork with the cornflour. Mix in the sherry, soy sauce, sugar and seasoning to taste. Add the egg white and the oil and pound the mixture with the back of a wooden spoon until it binds together firmly. Chill for 30 minutes.

Make sure the mushrooms are thoroughly drained and dry them lightly with absorbent kitchen paper. Place them open side upwards on a clean surface, then divide the pork mixture between them. Use your fingers to neatly press the stuffing into the mushroom caps. The filling should be moulded into a dome shape.

Arrange the mushrooms on a heatproof platter and put them in a steamer. Cook the shiu my over boiling water for 10 minutes.

Transfer the cooked stuffed mushrooms to small serving bowls and garnish each shiu my with a little parsley before serving. *Serves 4–6*

Rice with Shrimps and Eggs

2 tablespoons oil
1 teaspoon dry sherry
100 ml/4 fl oz chicken stock
100 g/4 oz peeled cooked
  shrimps
salt and pepper
½ teaspoon sugar
½ teaspoon sesame oil
1 teaspoon cornflour
1 tablespoon water
1 egg, beaten
1 tablespoon chopped spring
  onion
350 g/12 oz freshly cooked rice

Heat the oil in a wok or large frying pan. Add the sherry and stock and bring to the boil, then stir in the shrimps, seasoning, sugar and sesame oil. Blend the cornflour with the water, stir into the sauce and bring to the boil, then simmer for 2 minutes.

Finally, stir in the beaten egg and spring onion; cook lightly. Pour on to the hot rice and serve at once. *Serves 3–4*

To cook rice: Cooked rice can be prepared in two ways: the rice can be cooked in boiling water as you would prepare it for any recipe. Allow 600 ml/1 pint cold water to each 225 g/8 oz rice. Put the rice and water in a saucepan and add a generous pinch of salt. Bring to the boil, then cover the pan closely and reduce the heat so that the rice simmers gently. Allow about 20–25 minutes cooking time. Fluff up the grains with a fork before serving.

Alternatively the rice can be steamed; this is the traditional method for preparing rice for Chinese dishes. The easy-cook varieties of rice are not suitable for steaming. Wash the rice and pat it dry with absorbent kitchen paper. Place the rice in a basin or bowl and add a little water – about 175 ml/6 fl oz water to each 225 g/8 oz rice. Place the container in a steamer and cook over boiling water for 25–30 minutes. Turn the heat off and stand the rice in the covered steamer for 10 minutes.

Fried Rice with Prawns and Pork

2 eggs, beaten
salt and pepper
a few drops of sesame oil
2 tablespoons oil
450 g/1 lb cooked rice
100 g/4 oz Roast Belly Pork
  (page 88), finely diced
75 g/3 oz peeled cooked
  prawns
1 tablespoon light soy sauce
3 spring onions, chopped, to
  garnish

Season the eggs with a little salt, pepper and the sesame oil.

Heat the oil in a wok. Add the eggs and cook for a short while, until they begin to set. Stir in the cooked rice and sauté until heated through. Add the pork, prawns, seasoning to taste and light soy sauce then cook, stirring, until heated through. Serve at once, sprinkled with the spring onions. *Serves 3–4*

Note: When you are trying to work out the quantities of uncooked rice to prepare for a dish which requires a weight of cooked rice, think in terms of the rice generously doubling its weight during cooking.

For example, 175 g/6 oz uncooked rice will yield about 450 g/1 lb cooked rice; 225 g/8 oz will yield approximately 575 g/1¼ lb and 350 g/12 oz will give about 1 kg/2 lb. The amount you need depends on the other dishes which are being served. If you allow about 50 g/2 oz uncooked rice per person, then the servings will be quite generous. Allow slightly less if you are preparing lots of other dishes.

Rice with Red and White Sauce

175 g/6 oz chicken, shredded
1 teaspoon Ginger Juice (page 227)
3 teaspoons dry sherry
3 teaspoons cornflour
3 teaspoons soy sauce
6 tablespoons water
5 tablespoons oil
50 g/2 oz shelled peas
salt and pepper
225 g/8 oz tomatoes
1 onion, shredded
350 ml/12 fl oz chicken stock
1 teaspoon sugar
50 ml/2 fl oz tomato ketchup
100 ml/4 fl oz milk
175 g/6 oz peeled cooked shrimps (defrosted if frozen)
2 eggs, beaten
450 g/1 lb freshly cooked rice

Marinate the shredded chicken for 30 minutes with the ginger juice, 1 teaspoon each of sherry, cornflour and soy sauce, 2 tablespoons water, and 1 tablespoon oil.

Blanch the peas in boiling salted water, then drain thoroughly. Peel the tomatoes (page 32), then chop finely.

Heat 2 tablespoons oil in a wok or small saucepan. Sauté the onion and tomatoes for 5 minutes. Add the chicken and fry for a while. Sprinkle in half the remaining sherry, then pour in two-thirds of the stock and bring to the boil. Season to taste, add half the sugar and remaining soy sauce and the ketchup. Blend 1 teaspoon of the remaining cornflour with 2 tablespoons of the water, stir this into the sauce and simmer for 2 minutes. Leave over a very low heat to keep hot.

Heat the remaining sherry with the rest of the stock, the milk, shrimps and peas. Blend the last of the cornflour with 2 tablespoons water, stir into the sauce, simmer for 2 minutes.

Heat 2 tablespoons oil in a wok or large frying pan. Stir in the eggs and cook until they are just setting, then stir in the rice. Cook quickly; transfer to a serving dish. Pour the red sauce over one side of the rice and the white sauce over the other. Serve at once. *Serves 4*

Rice Casserole with Chicken and Salted Fish

75 g/3 oz salted fish or cooked ham, diced
5 tablespoons oil
1 tablespoon finely grated fresh root ginger
350 g/12 oz chicken thighs
1 tablespoon Ginger Juice (page 227)
1 tablespoon dry sherry
salt
1 teaspoon sugar
1 teaspoon cornflour
1 tablespoon light soy sauce
pinch of pepper
a little sesame oil
225 g/8 oz long-grain rice
600 ml/1 pint water
1 tablespoon chopped spring onion to garnish

Wash and finely dice the salted fish or ham. Marinate for 20 minutes with 2 tablespoons oil and the grated ginger. Cut the chicken meat off the bones and dice it finely.

Marinate the chicken for 15 minutes with the ginger juice and sherry, ¼ teaspoon salt; the sugar, cornflour, 1 teaspoon of the light soy sauce, a pinch of pepper and a few drops of sesame oil.

Wash and thoroughly drain the rice. Add 2 teaspoons salt and 2 tablespoons oil to the grains and mix well. Pour into a saucepan and add the water. Bring to the boil, cover, then cook over a low heat for 10 minutes. Spread the diced, salted fish or ham on top and re-cover, then cook for another 10 minutes.

Add the diced chicken and continue to cook for 10 minutes. When the cooking time is up, leave the ingredients to stand in the pan, covered, for 10 minutes.

Loosen the cooked rice and ingredients with chopsticks or a fork, then gradually mix in the remaining light soy sauce, oil, pepper and a few drops of sesame oil. Sprinkle with chopped spring onion and serve. *Serves 4–6*

Steamed Rice with Chicken and Mushrooms

350 g/12 oz long-grain rice
5 teaspoons oil
salt and pepper
350 ml/12 fl oz boiling water
½ chicken
1 teaspoon sugar
1 teaspoon dry sherry
1 teaspoon cornflour
1 tablespoon light soy sauce
  plus extra for serving
1 teaspoon Ginger Juice (page 227)
1 tablespoon finely shredded fresh root ginger
6 Chinese dried mushrooms
GARNISH
1 tablespoon finely shredded spring onion
parsley sprigs

Wash, drain and dry the rice by patting it with a large pad of absorbent kitchen paper. Mix it with 2 teaspoons oil and a little salt.

Divide the rice between three heatproof dishes or small basins. Add 100 ml/4 fl oz boiling water to each container, then stand the dishes in a steamer over a pan of boiling water. Cook for 15 minutes.

Meanwhile, chop the chicken into bite-sized pieces. Marinate these with seasoning, the sugar, sherry, cornflour, soy sauce, ginger juice and shredded ginger for 10 minutes.

Soak the mushrooms until soft (about 30 minutes), remove their stalks, then mix the caps with a little oil.

Loosen the rice with chopsticks or a fork, then arrange the chicken and mushrooms on top. Cover and continue to steam for 10 minutes. Turn off the heat and leave the rice in the covered steamer for 10 minutes before serving. Top with a little soy sauce and oil. Garnish with spring onion and parsley. *Serves 6*

Rice with Roasted Duck

salt and pepper
¼ teaspoon sugar
1 teaspoon soy sauce
a few drops of sesame oil
1 egg, beaten
½ fresh roast duck (page 83)
450 g/1 lb freshly cooked rice
1 small spring onion, chopped
2 tablespoons oil

Beat seasoning, the sugar, soy sauce and sesame oil into the egg. Prepare the duck according to the recipe instructions. Cook the rice following the instructions on page 164. Add the spring onion to the beaten egg.

Heat the oil in a wok or large frying pan, then add the egg. Tilt the pan a little so the egg spreads out, then stir in the cooked rice as soon as the egg is three-quarters set. Break the egg up and stir-fry together with the rice. Transfer to a serving dish.

Chop the duck into pieces, then arrange it on top of the rice and serve. *Serves 4*

Note: When you are cooking any stir-fry rice with egg make sure that you use a pan which does not readily stick. A well-seasoned wok is ideal or use a good non-stick frying pan. If you use a pan which is likely to stick, the combination of starch from the rice and the beaten eggs can form a coating which is difficult to wash off.

Rice with Diced Pork and Sweet Corn

1 teaspoon soy sauce
¼ teaspoon sugar
¼ teaspoon dry sherry
1½ teaspoons cornflour
5 tablespoons water
1 tablespoon oil plus oil for
    deep frying
salt and pepper
175 g/6 oz loin of pork, diced
1 (312-g/11-oz) can cream
    style corn
250 ml/8 fl oz chicken stock
1 egg, beaten
450 g/1 lb freshly cooked rice
spring onion curl to garnish

Mix the soy sauce, sugar, sherry, ½ teaspoon of the cornflour, 3 tablespoons water, 1 tablespoon oil and seasoning to taste. Pour this over the pork and set aside to marinate for 10 minutes.

Heat the oil for deep frying to 190 c/375 f, add the pork and fry until just browned. Drain on absorbent kitchen paper, then place in a saucepan with the sweet corn and stock. Bring to the boil, then reduce the heat and simmer for 1 minute. Blend the remaining cornflour with the remaining water, stir this into the corn mixture and simmer for 2 minutes. Stir in the beaten egg.

Turn the cooked rice on to a warmed serving dish. Pour the sweet corn over and top with the spring onion. Serve at once. *Serves 4–6*

Glutinous Rice with Preserved Meat

225 g/8 oz glutinous rice or
  round-grain rice
1 teaspoon salt
generous 4 tablespoons oil
300 ml/½ pint cold water
4 Chinese dried mushrooms
25 g/1 oz dried shrimps
3 dried squid
1 clove garlic, sliced
4 Chinese dried sausages,
  diced
a little sugar
2 teaspoons dark soy sauce
2 spring onions, chopped

Wash, drain and dry the rice,
then place it in a saucepan
with the salt and half the oil.
Pour in the water, then bring
just to the boil and leave over
a low heat to simmer,
covered, for 20 minutes.
  Soak the mushrooms, dried
shrimps and squid in boiling
water for about 30 minutes.
Drain and dice all these
ingredients.
  Heat most of the remaining
oil in a wok or frying pan.

Sauté the garlic, then stir in
the shrimps, squid and
sausages.
  Season the mushrooms with
a little oil and sugar, then
steam them over boiling water
for 5 minutes. Pour into the
pan and sauté well with the
other ingredients. Add this
mixture to the cooked
glutinous rice and mix well
with a pair of chopsticks or a
fork. Cover and leave over a
very low heat for 10 minutes.
Sprinkle in the dark soy sauce
and spring onion, then serve.
Serves 4

Fried Rice with Shredded Meat

75 g/3 oz cooked chicken
75 g/3 oz cooked ham
1 egg
salt and pepper
3 tablespoons plus 2 teaspoons
  oil
1 small onion, shredded
350 g/12 oz cold cooked rice
1 tablespoon light soy sauce
½ teaspoon sugar
1 teaspoon sesame oil
parsley sprigs to garnish

Shred the chicken and ham,
beat the egg with a pinch of
salt and 2 teaspoons oil. Heat
1 tablespoon oil in a frying
pan, add the egg, tilting the
pan to spread it out evenly,
and cook until set, turn and
cook the second side. Remove
from the pan and shred the
omelette.
  Heat the remaining 2
tablespoons oil in a wok or
large frying pan. Add the
onion and cook over a low
heat until transparent. Add
the rice and stir-fry quickly,
then add the shredded meats,

omelette and seasoning to
taste. Stir in the soy sauce,
sugar and sesame oil, then
serve at once, topped with the
parsley. *Serves 4*

Note: To quickly shred an
onion first cut it into thin
slices, then cut these in half.
Separate the rings in the
onion halves and they will
form fine strips.

Garlic Rice

50 g/2 oz glutinous rice or
round-grain rice
225 g/8 oz long-grain rice
2 tablespoons oil
15 g/½ oz garlic, crushed
1 teaspoon dry sherry
1 teaspoon Ginger Juice (page
227)
2 teaspoons salt
500 ml/17 fl oz chicken stock

Mix both types of rice together in a bowl or basin. Pour in enough cold water to cover the grains, then gently stir the rice with your fingers. Do not handle the rice roughly or the grains will be damaged. Drain off the water, add fresh water and continue washing the rice in this way until the water runs clear. Finally, drain the rice thoroughly in a sieve or colander.

Heat the oil in a saucepan, add the garlic and cook, stirring occasionally, for 1 minute, then pour in the sherry and ginger juice. Add the rice and salt, stir-fry for a while then pour in the stock.

Bring to the boil, give the rice a stir and reduce the heat to the lowest setting. Cover the saucepan. Leave to simmer very gently for 30 minutes, turn off the heat and allow the rice to stand for a further 10 minutes. Transfer the cooked rice to a heated serving dish and gently fluff up the grains with a fork. Serve immediately. *Serves 4–6*

Fried Rice with Diced Pineapple

1 large fresh pineapple
3 Chinese dried mushrooms
2 tablespoons oil
1 egg, beaten
350 g/12 oz cold cooked rice
50 g/2 oz peas (defrosted if
frozen)
a few pieces sweetened red
ginger, diced
1 tablespoon chopped spring
onion
5 teaspoons light soy sauce
pinch of pepper
½ teaspoon sesame oil

Cut the top off the pineapple and hollow out the fruit. Dice the pineapple flesh. Soak the mushrooms for 15 minutes, then steam them over boiling water for 15 minutes. Dice the cooked mushrooms, discarding the stalks if they are tough.

Heat the oil in a saucepan, stir in the egg and cook, stirring continuously, until it is just set, then stir in the rice and fry for a while.

Add all the remaining ingredients to the saucepan

and season to taste. Make sure the rice mixture is thoroughly combined. Spoon the rice into the scooped-out pineapple and serve at once. *Serves 4*

Note: If a fresh pineapple is not available for this dish, use a 227-g/8-oz can of pineapple pieces. Drain off the syrup or juice and cut the pineapple into small dice. Add the fruit to the cooked rice, then transfer it to a heated serving dish instead of putting it in the scooped-out fruit.

Rice Sticks with Shredded Meat

225 g/8 oz rice sticks
2 Chinese dried mushrooms
2 tablespoons oil
2 cloves garlic
100 g/4 oz bean sprouts
100 g/4 oz roasted duck meat
    (page 83), shredded
75 g/3 oz Cha Shiu (page 225),
    shredded
75 g/3 oz chicken, shredded
2 spring onions, shredded
salt and pepper
1 teaspoon sugar
1 teaspoon dry sherry
1 tablespoon dark soy sauce
1 tablespoon oyster sauce
½ teaspoon sesame oil

Blanch the rice sticks in
boiling water until soft. Drain,
separating the sticks.

Soak the mushrooms in cold
water for 30 minutes, then
drain and steam them over
boiling water for 15 minutes.
Remove the mushroom stalks
and shred the caps.

Heat the oil in a pan. Add
the garlic and fry for a few
minutes, stir in the bean

sprouts and cook very quickly,
then remove from the pan.

Add the rice sticks to the
pan with all the remaining
ingredients and fry for a
while. Replace the bean
sprouts, stirring to mix
everything thoroughly. When
all the ingredients are heated,
turn them out on to a warmed
serving dish. *Serves 4*

Note: Rice sticks are flat
noodles, similar to Italian egg
noodles but shorter. They are
obtainable from Chinese
supermarkets but you can use
egg noodles instead if the rice
sticks are not available.

Rice Sticks with Sliced Beef

225 g/8 oz rice sticks
175 g/6 oz frying steak
pinch of bicarbonate of soda
pinch of cornflour
1 tablespoon dark soy sauce
1 teaspoon sugar
50 ml/2 fl oz water
4 tablespoons oil
1 Chinese dried mushroom
1 clove garlic, crushed
225 g/8 oz bean sprouts
1 teaspoon dry sherry
a few drops of sesame oil
salt and pepper
2 teaspoons light soy sauce
white part of 1 leek, shredded

Blanch the rice sticks in
boiling water for a few
minutes to soften them, then
drain thoroughly.

Slice the steak across the
grain into small, thin slices.
Marinate the beef for 10
minutes with a pinch each of
bicarbonate of soda and
cornflour; 1 teaspoon of the
dark soy sauce, ¼ teaspoon of
the sugar, the water and 2
tablespoons oil.

Soak the mushroom for 10
minutes, then drain and steam
it for 15 minutes. Remove the
mushroom stalk and slice the
cap. Heat the remaining oil in
a wok or large frying pan, add
the garlic, fry for a while,
then stir in the bean sprouts.
Stir-fry for just a few seconds,
then remove.

Add the rice sticks to the
pan with the beef and sauté
for a while. Sprinkle in the
sherry, then add the
mushroom and sesame oil,
seasoning, remaining sugar,
and dark soy sauce and the
light soy sauce. Toss all the
ingredients to mix them
thoroughly, then sprinkle in
the leek and serve at once.
Serves 4–6

Rice Sticks with Beef and Pepper

100 g/4 oz frying steak
2 teaspoons soy sauce
½ teaspoon meat tenderiser or monosodium glutamate
1½ teaspoons sugar
2 teaspoons cornflour
1 teaspoon dry sherry
50 ml/2 fl oz plus 1 tablespoon water
5 tablespoons oil plus oil for deep frying
275 g/10 oz rice sticks
1 green pepper, deseeded and cut into chunks
1 red chilli, deseeded and roughly chopped
2 tablespoons preserved black bean paste
100 ml/4 fl oz beef stock
¼ teaspoon salt
½ teaspoon dark soy sauce
chilli tassel to garnish (page 45)

Cut the steak across the grain into small, thin slices. Marinate these for 1 hour in a mixture of 1 teaspoon of the soy sauce, the meat tenderiser, ½ teaspoon each of the sugar, cornflour and sherry; 50 ml/2 fl oz water and 1 tablespoon oil.

Blanch the rice sticks in boiling water until soft, then drain them. Heat 1 tablespoon oil in a wok or frying pan. Add the rice sticks and toss over a medium heat until thoroughly heated. Transfer to a serving dish and keep hot.

Heat the oil for deep frying to 190 c/375 f, add the beef, drained of marinade, and fry for about 1 minute. Drain on absorbent kitchen paper.

Heat the 3 tablespoons oil in a wok or frying pan. Add the green pepper, chilli and black bean paste. Pour in the remaining sherry, the stock, salt, remaining sugar and soy sauces.

Blend the remaining cornflour with the 1 tablespoon water and stir it into the sauce. Bring to the boil, then add the beef and simmer for a few minutes. Pour the beef over the rice sticks and serve at once, garnished with a chilli tassel if you like. *Serves 4*

Noodles with Fish Balls

275 g/10 oz Chinese egg noodles
4 tablespoons oil
1 teaspoon dry sherry
100 ml/4 fl oz stock
salt and pepper
1 tablespoon oyster sauce
a few drops of sesame oil
1 clove garlic, crushed
1 shallot, grated
275 g/10 oz Fish Balls (page 224)
GARNISH
3 tablespoons finely shredded fresh root ginger
3 tablespoons shredded spring onion

Blanch the noodles in boiling water for 1 minute, just to soften them. Drain thoroughly. Heat half the oil in a saucepan with the sherry and stock, bring to the boil, then add seasoning to taste, the oyster sauce and sesame oil. Add the noodles and cook for 2–3 minutes.

Meanwhile, heat the remaining oil in a wok or frying pan, add the garlic and shallot and fry until fragrant, then discard. Stir the fish balls in the pan for about 10 minutes, or until cooked through.

Arrange the noodles and their stock on a serving plate and add the fish balls. Garnish with shredded ginger and spring onion. Serve at once. *Serves 4–6*

Silver Pin Noodles

100 g/4 oz cornflour
pinch of salt
4–5 tablespoons boiling water

Sift the cornflour and salt into a bowl, then mix in enough boiling water to make a dough. Cover and allow to stand for 5 minutes, then knead thoroughly and cut into 24 portions. Roll each piece into a long thin roll (about the size of a chopstick), then cut into short thin noodles and roll the ends into points to resemble short bean sprouts. Steam the noodles on a greased plate over boiling water for 5 minutes, then use as required.

Silver Pin Noodles with Shrimps

100 g/4 oz lean boneless pork,
* shredded*
2 teaspoons soy sauce
1 teaspoon sugar
½ teaspoon cornflour
salt and pepper
2 tablespoons water
5 tablespoons oil
2 eggs, beaten
275 g/10 oz silver pin noodles
* (recipe left)*
175 g/6 oz bean sprouts
100 g/4 oz peeled cooked
* prawns*
4 button mushrooms, shredded
50 g/2 oz shelled peas
* (defrosted if frozen)*
1 teaspoon dry sherry
½ teaspoon sesame oil

Marinate the pork for 20 minutes with 1 teaspoon of the soy sauce, ½ teaspoon of the sugar, the cornflour, a pinch of pepper, 2 tablespoons water and 1 tablespoon oil.

Heat 1 tablespoon oil in a frying pan. Pour in the eggs and cook until set and golden brown. Turn and cook the second side until browned. Remove and cut into short strips, then set aside.

Heat 2 tablespoons oil in a wok or frying pan, then add and fry the noodles. Transfer to a heated serving dish and keep hot.

Heat the remaining oil in a wok or frying pan, then add the pork and fry quickly until cooked. Add the bean sprouts, cook for 1 minute, then stir in all the remaining ingredients and cook for a few minutes to heat through. Stir in the omelette, then serve poured over the noodles.
Serves 4–6

Crabmeat with Noodles

175 g/6 oz Chinese egg noodles
4 tablespoons oil
2 teaspoons dry sherry
350 ml/12 fl oz chicken stock
salt and pepper
75 g/3 oz bean sprouts
½ teaspoon sugar
1 teaspoon sesame oil
3 mushrooms, sliced
75 g/3 oz crabmeat (defrosted if frozen)
1 tablespoon shredded white leek

Blanch the noodles in boiling water for 2 minutes, then drain and rinse them under cold water.

Heat 2 tablespoons oil in a saucepan, then pour in half the sherry and half the stock. Season to taste. Put in the noodles and simmer for 10 minutes.

Heat the remaining oil in a wok until very hot, then sauté the bean sprouts. Pour in the remaining sherry and stock, seasoning, sugar and sesame oil. Stir in the mushrooms,

bring to the oil, then add the crab meat. Blend the cornflour with the water, pour it into the pan and simmer for 2 minutes. Add the leek.

Pour the noodles into a serving bowl, then pour the crab meat mixture over them. Serve at once. *Serves 4*

Note: Crabmeat can be used canned, fresh or frozen. In the frozen form it is available in the form of a block or in sticks. The sticks are sold as crab sticks or they may be sold as ocean sticks.

Fried Noodles with Sliced Beef

175 g/6 oz frying steak
1 teaspoon soy sauce
1 teaspoon sugar
1 teaspoon dry sherry
pinch of bicarbonate of soda
1½ teaspoons cornflour
salt and pepper
50 ml/2 fl oz plus 2 tablespoons water
4 tablespoons oil plus oil for deep frying
275 g/10 oz Chinese egg noodles
1 clove garlic
100 g/4 oz French beans
100 ml/4 fl oz beef stock
1 tablespoon oyster sauce
2 spring onions, shredded

Cut the beef into small, thin slices. Mix the soy sauce, ½ teaspoon each of the sugar and sherry; a pinch of bicarbonate of soda, ½ teaspoon of the cornflour, a pinch of pepper, 50 ml/2 fl oz water, 2 tablespoons oil. Pour this marinade over the beef and set aside for 10 minutes.

Heat the oil for deep frying

to 190 c/375 f. Deep fry the noodles in two batches until both sides are crisp and golden. Drain on absorbent kitchen paper, place on a serving platter and keep hot.

Heat the remaining oil in a wok or frying pan. Add the garlic, steak, beans and salt to taste, then sauté thoroughly. Sprinkle in the remaining sherry, then pour in the stock, oyster sauce and remaining sugar. Blend the remaining cornflour with the 2 tablespoons water, then stir this mixture into the sauce and simmer for 2 minutes. Stir in the spring onions.

Pour the beef over the noodles and serve at once. *Serves 4–6*

Spaghetti with Shredded Beef

100 g/4 oz fillet steak, shredded
3 tablespoons dark soy sauce
2 tablespoons sugar
¼ teaspoon bicarbonate of soda
1 teaspoon dry sherry
salt and pepper
1 teaspoon sesame oil
1 teaspoon cornflour
50 ml/2 fl oz water
3 tablespoons oil
225 g/8 oz spaghetti
1 clove garlic, sliced
1 onion, shredded

Marinate the beef for 30 minutes in a mixture of 1 teaspoon of the soy sauce, ½ teaspoon of the sugar, the bicarbonate of soda, ½ teaspoon of the sherry, a pinch of pepper, a few drops of sesame oil, the cornflour, the water and 1 tablespoon oil.

Cook the spaghetti in boiling salted water for 15 minutes, until tender but not too soft. Drain, rinse under cold water, then drain thoroughly.

Heat the remaining oil in a wok or frying pan, then sauté the garlic and onion for a few minutes. Add the beef and fry until cooked, then stir in the remaining sherry, soy sauce, sugar, pepper and sesame oil.

Heat the sauce before adding the spaghetti, then cook until reheated and serve at once. *Serves 4*

Macaroni Chopsticks

350 g/12 oz macaroni
4 tablespoons oil
salt and pepper
2 eggs, beaten
1 clove garlic, sliced
1 onion, shredded
1 green pepper, deseeded and
   cut into strips
75 g/3 oz carrots, shredded
100 g/4 oz Cha Shiu (page
   225), shredded
100 g/4 oz peeled cooked
   prawns
2 large open mushrooms,
   sliced
1 chilli, deseeded and cut into
   strips
225 g/8 oz bean sprouts
100 g/4 oz cucumber, shredded
50 g/2 oz pickled vegetables,
   shredded
225 g/8 oz tomatoes, peeled
   and roughly chopped
2 tablespoons sugar
1 teaspoon dry sherry
2 tablespoons tomato ketchup
1 tablespoon soy sauce
1 teaspoon sesame oil

Cook the macaroni in boiling
salted water until tender, then
drain and rinse under cold
water. Drain thoroughly.

Heat 2 tablespoons of the
oil in a frying pan. Season the
eggs, then pour them into the
pan and cook until set and
browned underneath. Turn
the omelette and cook the
second side, then remove and
shred it into pieces.

Heat the remaining oil in a
wok or frying pan. Sauté the
garlic until fragrant, then
remove and discard it. Stir-fry
the onion, green pepper and
carrots for a few minutes.

Add the cha shiu, prawns,
mushrooms, chilli and all the
other vegetables. Stir-fry for a
while, then add the macaroni.
Stir in seasoning, the sugar,
sherry, ketchup, soy sauce and
sesame oil. Heat through and
serve. *Serves 4–6*

Noodle with Braised Brisket

450 g/1 lb brisket
2 tablespoons oil
2 large cloves garlic, crushed
50 g/2 oz fresh root ginger,
   sliced
3 tablespoons ground bean
   paste
1 tablespoon dry sherry
600 ml/1 pint plus 2
   tablespoons water
2 star anise
1 piece of tangerine peel
1 tablespoon dark soy sauce
2 tablespoons sugar
½ teaspoon sesame oil
salt and pepper
1 tablespoon cornflour
275 g/10 oz Chinese egg
   noodles
GARNISH
¼ cucumber, sliced diagonally
3 spring onions, sliced

Trim the brisket and cut it
into bite-sized pieces. Heat
the oil in a flameproof
casserole, add the garlic,
ginger and bean paste, then
sauté thoroughly. Stir in the
meat and fry for a while, then
pour in the sherry, 600 ml/
1 pint water, star anise and
tangerine peel.

Bring just to the boil,
reduce the heat and cover
closely, then simmer very
gently for 1½ hours or until the
meat is tender. Stir the soy
sauce, sugar and sesame oil
into the beef with seasoning to
taste. Blend the cornflour with
the 2 tablespoons water, stir
the mixture into the beef and
continue to cook for
5 minutes.

Cook the noodles in boiling
salted water for about 2
minutes or until tender. Drain
and place on a serving plate.
Serve the beef poured over
the noodles, or in a separate
bowl, then garnish with the
cucumber and spring onions.
Serves 4

Noodles with Spicy Tongue

1 calf's tongue (about
   1 kg/2 lb)
4 star anise
1 teaspoon ground cumin
small piece of tangerine peel
2 thick slices fresh root ginger
4 spring onions, shredded
350 ml/12 fl oz light soy sauce
250 ml/8 fl oz dry sherry
25 g/1 oz demerara sugar
¼ teaspoon monosodium
   glutamate
1 tablespoon cornflour
2 tablespoons water
450 g/1 lb Chinese egg noodles
1 crisp lettuce
a few glacé cherries, sliced, to
   garnish

Thoroughly wash the tongue, blanch it in boiling water, then drain and scrape the skin.

Place the cleaned tongue in a large saucepan with the star anise, cumin, tangerine peel, ginger, spring onions and enough water to cover the meat. Add the soy sauce, sherry, sugar and monosodium glutamate, then bring to the boil and reduce the heat. Cover the pan and simmer the tongue for 1½–2 hours or until tender.

Lift the tongue out of its cooking liquid and remove all the skin and bones, then cut the meat into slices. Pour about 300 ml/½ pint of the cooking stock into a small saucepan. Blend the cornflour with the water, stir the mixture into the reserved stock, then bring to the boil and simmer until thickened. Place the sliced tongue in the sauce and simmer for a few minutes.

Cook the noodles in boiling salted water for 1–2 minutes, just long enough to soften them. Drain and transfer to a serving bowl. Top with the lettuce, then arrange the tongue slices on top and pour over the sauce. Garnish with glacé cherries if you like.
Serves 6

Fried Noodles with Shredded Pork

100 g/4 oz pork fillet, shredded
1½ teaspoons dark soy sauce
1 teaspoon sugar
2 teaspoons cornflour
salt and pepper
4 tablespoons water
3 tablespoons oil plus oil for
   deep frying
175 g/6 oz Chinese egg noodles
175 g/6 oz bean sprouts
2 Chinese dried mushrooms
1 teaspoon dry sherry
100 ml/4 fl oz chicken stock
1 teaspoon light soy sauce
½ teaspoon sesame oil
2 spring onions, shredded, to
   garnish

Marinate the pork with 1 teaspoon of the dark soy sauce, ½ teaspoon each of the sugar and cornflour, a pinch of pepper, 2 tablespoons water and 1 tablespoon oil for 15 minutes.

Blanch the noodles in boiling salted water for 1 minute, drain and rinse under cold water, then drain again.

Heat the oil for deep frying, add the noodles and cook until golden brown. Drain on absorbent kitchen paper, place on a serving dish and keep hot.

Heat the remaining 2 tablespoons oil in a wok or frying pan. Add the bean sprouts, toss quickly, then remove from the pan. Add the pork and cook until lightly browned.

Replace the bean sprouts in the pan, then add the mushrooms. Blend the remaining cornflour with the rest of the water and all the remaining ingredients, then add to the pork and simmer for 2 minutes or until thickened.

Pour the pork over the noodles, sprinkle with spring onions and serve immediately.
Serves 4

Cold Noodles with Assorted Meat

50 g/2 oz dried shrimps
450 g/1 lb cooked noodles
2 tablespoons oil
1 green pepper, deseeded and
　cut into fine strips
1 red chilli, deseeded and cut
　into fine strips
100 g/4 oz bean sprouts
1 small carrot, cut into fine
　strips
50 g/2 oz pickled gherkin,
　shredded
2 large open mushrooms,
　shredded
100 g/4 oz Cha Shiu (page
　225), shredded
DRESSING
salt and pepper
2 tablespoons sugar
2 tablespoons soy sauce
4 tablespoons sesame paste
1 teaspoon sesame oil
½ teaspoon chilli oil
2 tablespoons chicken stock

Soak the shrimps in hot water until soft, then drain and mash them.

Rinse the noodles under warm water, then drain them thoroughly.

Heat the oil in a wok or frying pan. Add the green pepper, chilli and bean sprouts, then cook them quickly for a few seconds.

Mix in the noodles and all the other ingredients, then chill lightly. Place all the dressing ingredients in a bowl, whisk them together until well mixed and pour over the noodles just before serving.
Serves 6

Macaroni with Shredded Meat

225 g/8 oz macaroni
1 chicken thigh
1 teaspoon Ginger Juice (page 227)
2 teaspoons dry sherry
1⅓ teaspoons salt
2 tablespoons oil
100 g/4 oz shelled peas
1 carrot, diced
1.15 litres/2 pints water
1 teaspoon sugar
1 teaspoon soy sauce
pinch of pepper
1 chicken stock cube
a few drops of sesame oil
100 g/4 oz cooked ham, shredded
1 (454-g/1-lb) can abalone, drained and shredded

Cook the macaroni in boiling salted water for 8 minutes. Drain thoroughly, rinse and drain again.

Marinate the chicken thigh in the ginger juice, 1 teaspoon of the sherry and a little salt for 10 minutes.

Cook the chicken with its marinade, over boiling water for 10 minutes, then remove the meat from the bones and cut into fine shreds.

Heat the oil in a wok or frying pan, then stir in the peas and carrot. Pour in the water and remaining sherry and bring to the boil. Add the remaining salt, the sugar, soy sauce, pepper, stock cube and macaroni. Stir in the sesame oil, chicken, ham and abalone, then bring to the boil, reduce the heat and simmer for 5 minutes. Ladle into bowls and serve at once. *Serves 4–6*

Rice with Sweet and Sour Prawns

4 tablespoons oil
2 eggs, beaten
salt and pepper
450 g/1 lb freshly cooked rice
2 green peppers, deseeded and cut into strips
1 red chilli, deseeded and cut into strips
1 tablespoon dry sherry
150 ml/¼ pint Sweet and Sour Sauce (page 227)
1 teaspoon cornflour
2 tablespoons water
1 tablespoon sugar
450 g/1 lb peeled cooked prawns

Heat half the oil in a wok or large frying pan. Pour in the eggs and add seasoning to taste, then cook, stirring continuously, until they begin to set. Stir in the rice and cook for a few minutes, then transfer to a warmed serving plate and keep hot. If you like, the rice can be packed into a ring mould before turning out on to a warmed serving plate.

Add the remaining oil to the pan and sauté the green peppers and chilli for a few minutes. Stir in the sherry, then pour in the sweet and sour sauce. Blend the cornflour with the water, pour into the sauce, add the sugar and the prawns. Simmer for a few minutes, then serve on the rice or poured into the rice ring. *Serves 4–6*

Fried Rice with Minced Beef

¼ teaspoon bicarbonate of soda
2 teaspoons light soy sauce
½ teaspoon cornflour
2 tablespoons water
salt and pepper
a few drops of sesame oil
3 tablespoons oil
100 g/4 oz minced beef
2 eggs, beaten
450 g/1 lb cooked rice
225 g/8 oz shelled peas
1 teaspoon chopped spring
   onion
GARNISH
a few strips of red pepper
parsley sprigs

Mix the bicarbonate of soda, 1 teaspoon of the light soy sauce, the cornflour, 2 tablespoons water, a pinch of pepper, a little of the sesame oil and 1 tablespoon oil. Stir this into the minced beef, then set aside to marinate for 10 minutes.

Heat the remaining oil in a wok or large frying pan, then add the beef and fry until browned. Remove the meat from the pan, then add the eggs. Stir in seasoning to taste, the remaining soy sauce and a few more drops of sesame oil. Continue to cook until the eggs begin to set.

Stir in the rice, peas and spring onion and cook for a few seconds. Return the beef to the pan and continue to cook until the rice is completely heated. Transfer the cooked mixture to a warmed serving dish or pile it on to individual plates. Add a garnish of short red pepper strips and parsley sprigs. Serve at once. *Serves 4*

Macaroni with Diced Chicken

225 g/8 oz boneless uncooked
   chicken
1 teaspoon Ginger Juice (page
   227)
2 teaspoons dry sherry
1 teaspoon soy sauce
1 teaspoon cornflour
salt and pepper
a few drops of sesame oil
275 g/10 oz macaroni
4 tablespoons oil
1 teaspoon sugar
1 onion, shredded
100 g/4 oz button mushrooms,
   sliced
25 g/1 oz plain flour
350 ml/12 fl oz chicken stock
parsley sprigs to garnish

Dice the chicken meat and marinate it for 10 minutes with the ginger juice, 1 teaspoon of the sherry, the soy sauce and cornflour, a little pepper and the sesame oil.

Cook the macaroni in boiling salted water until tender – about 15 minutes, then drain thoroughly.

Heat half the oil in a wok or frying pan, then stir-fry the macaroni. Add salt to taste and half the sugar. Mix well and transfer to a baking dish.

Heat the remaining oil in the pan, then sauté the onion. Mix in the diced chicken and fry briefly before adding the mushrooms. Sprinkle in the remaining sherry, seasoning to taste, the flour and remaining sugar. Stir in the stock and bring to the boil.

Pour the chicken mixture over the macaroni and cook in a moderately hot oven (200 c, 400 F, gas 6) for 10–15 minutes, then serve at once, garnished with parsley sprigs. *Serves 4–6*

Noodles with Shredded Pork and Pickled Vegetables

2 teaspoons soy sauce
1 tablespoon sugar
2 teaspoons cornflour
2 teaspoons dry sherry
salt and pepper
5 tablespoons water
3 tablespoons oil
175 g/6 oz loin of pork
600 ml/1 pint chicken stock
275 g/10 oz Chinese ribbon noodles, trimmed and shredded
1 clove garlic, sliced
75 g/3 oz pickled vegetable
1 small carrot, cut into thin strips
3 large open mushrooms, sliced
a few drops of sesame oil

Mix 1 teaspoon of the soy sauce, $\frac{1}{2}$ teaspoon of the sugar, cornflour and sherry, a pinch of pepper, 3 tablespoons water and 1 tablespoon oil. Pour this over the pork and marinate for 10 minutes.

Heat three-quarters of the stock to boiling point. Cook the noodles in boiling salted water until just tender, then drain, rinse under hot water and drain again. Place the noodles in a serving bowl, then pour the stock over them. Set aside to keep hot while the pork is cooked.

Heat the remaining oil in a wok or frying pan. Stir in the garlic, pickled vegetable and sugar. Mix well, then add the pork, carrot and mushrooms. Sauté until the meat is cooked. Sprinkle in the remaining sherry, add the remaining stock, then season to taste. Blend the remaining cornflour with the remaining soy sauce and water. Stir this mixture into the pork with the sesame oil and simmer for 2 minutes, or until thickened. Serve the pork at once, with the noodles. *Serves 4–6*

Noodles with Shredded Pork and Cabbage

275 g/10 oz Chinese egg noodles
salt and pepper
1 teaspoon soy sauce
$\frac{1}{2}$ teaspoon sugar
1 generous teaspoon cornflour
1 teaspoon dry sherry
4 tablespoons water
4 tablespoons oil plus oil for deep frying
100 g/4 oz lean boneless pork, shredded
1 clove garlic, sliced
1 shallot, sliced
225 g/8 oz cabbage, shredded
150 ml/$\frac{1}{4}$ pint chicken stock
1 tablespoon oyster sauce
$\frac{1}{2}$ teaspoon sesame oil

Cook the noodles in boiling salted water for 1–2 minutes until tender. Drain thoroughly and set aside.

Mix the soy sauce, $\frac{1}{4}$ teaspoon of the sugar, a pinch of cornflour, $\frac{1}{2}$ teaspoon of the sherry, a pinch of pepper, 3 tablespoons water and 1 tablespoon oil. Pour this over the pork and set aside to marinate for 10 minutes.

Heat the oil for deep frying to 190 C/375 F. Deep fry the noodles until crisp and golden brown. Drain on absorbent kitchen paper and transfer to a serving dish. Keep hot.

Heat the remaining oil in a wok or frying pan, then add the garlic and shallot and fry until fragrant, then discard. Add the shredded cabbage and pork, stir-fry for a few minutes to brown the meat, then sprinkle in the remaining sherry, the stock, oyster sauce, sesame oil, remaining sugar and seasoning. Bring to the boil. Blend the remaining cornflour with the remaining water, stir it into the sauce and simmer for a few minutes.

Pour the pork and cabbage over the noodles, then serve immediately. *Serves 4–6*

Spinach Noodles with Shredded Pork

225 g/8 oz spinach
salt and pepper
1 egg white
225 g/8 oz plain flour
2 teaspoons light soy sauce
1 teaspoon sugar
½ teaspoon cornflour
½ teaspoon plus a few drops of
  sesame oil
350 ml/12 fl oz plus 2
  tablespoons water
4 tablespoons oil
175 g/6 oz loin of pork,
  shredded
2 spring onions
1 clove garlic, sliced
2 teaspoons shredded fresh
  root ginger
225 g/8 oz cabbage
1 teaspoon dry sherry

Wash and thoroughly drain the spinach, then blend it in a liquidiser or food processor and press the pulp through a sieve to obtain just the juice.

Measure the juice – you need about 150 ml/¼ pint. Then mix it with ½ teaspoon salt and the egg white.

Sift the flour into a bowl and make a well in the middle. Pour the spinach juice into it, then slowly stir in the flour to make a soft dough. Knead thoroughly until smooth, then set aside. Mix 1 teaspoon of the light soy sauce, ½ teaspoon of the sugar, the cornflour, a pinch of pepper, a few drops of sesame oil, 2 tablespoons water and 1 tablespoon oil. Pour this marinade over the pork and set aside for 5 minutes.

Heat 2 tablespoons of the remaining oil in a wok or frying pan. Add the pork and spring onions, stir-fry for a while, then stir in the garlic, ginger and cabbage. Continue to cook until the pork is thoroughly fried. Pour in the sherry and water, season to taste, then stir in the remaining soy sauce and sesame oil. Leave over a low heat while the noodles are cooked.

Cut the noodle dough into four portions. Knead each one separately, then roll out on a floured surface to about 3 mm/⅛ in thick. Cut long fine strips off the dough and dust lightly with flour to prevent them sticking together. Cook these noodles in plenty of boiling salted water, with a little oil added, for 2–5 minutes until just cooked. Do not overcook the noodles or they break.

Drain the noodles and toss them with a little oil, then transfer them to a serving dish and pour the pork mixture on top. Serve at once. *Serves 4–6*

Note: If you own a pasta machine, then you can use it to make these noodles – use a narrow cutting blade to cut the dough.

Rice Sheet with Shredded Meat

1 teaspoon Ginger Juice (page 227)
2 teaspoons dry sherry
1 teaspoon cornflour
salt and pepper
½ teaspoon plus a few drops of sesame oil
3 tablespoons water
1 boneless chicken breast, shredded
1 teaspoon light soy sauce
½ teaspoon sugar
5 tablespoons oil
100 g/4 oz loin of pork
450 g/1 lb dried rice sheets (about 6 sheets)
175 g/6 oz broccoli
600 ml/1 pint chicken stock
1 clove garlic, crushed
100 g/4 oz bean sprouts

Mix the ginger juice, ½ teaspoon each of the sherry and cornflour, ¼ teaspoon salt, a pinch of pepper, ½ teaspoon sesame oil and 1 tablespoon water. Pour this over the chicken and set aside to marinate for 10 minutes.

Mix the light soy sauce, a pinch of sugar, the remaining cornflour, 2 tablespoons water and 1 tablespoon oil. Pour this marinade over the pork and set aside for 10 minutes.

Soak the rice sheets in cold water until soft, then cut them into ribbon strips. Blanch the broccoli in boiling salted water for a few minutes, then drain thoroughly.

Heat half the remaining oil in a wok or saucepan, then pour in the stock and seasoning to taste. Add the strips of rice sheet, then simmer for a few minutes until tender. Transfer to one large bowl or individual serving bowls and set aside to keep hot.

Heat the remaining oil in the pan, then sauté the garlic and discard. Add the chicken and pork and stir-fry until browned, then stir in the broccoli and bean sprouts and sauté until cooked. Stir in seasoning to taste, the remaining sherry, sugar and sesame oil. Bring to the boil, then pour this mixture over the strips of rice sheet and serve at once. *Serves 4–6*

Spaghetti with Prawns

350 g/12 oz frozen uncooked king prawns, peeled and deveined
1 teaspoon cornflour
1 egg white
salt and pepper
2 tablespoons oil plus oil for deep frying
225 g/8 oz spaghetti
1 clove garlic, sliced
2 onions, quartered
350 g/12 oz tomatoes, peeled (see page 32)
1 teaspoon sugar
2 teaspoons dry sherry
parsley sprigs to garnish

Coat the prawns in a mixture of the cornflour, the egg white and pepper.

Heat the oil for deep frying to 190 c/375 f, then add the prawns and fry for a few minutes. Drain on absorbent kitchen paper.

Cook the spaghetti in boiling salted water for 15 minutes. Drain thoroughly and transfer to individual plates.

Heat the oil in a wok or frying pan. Fry the garlic and onion for a while, then stir in the tomatoes, sugar and sherry, and cook until soft. Mix in the prawns and seasoning, then serve poured over the spaghetti, garnished with parsley. *Serves 4*

Noodles with Stewed Pork

2 pork trotters (about 675 g/
   1½ lb in weight)
2 tablespoons oil
2 cloves garlic, sliced
2 medium-thick slices fresh
   root ginger, grated
3 tablespoons mashed
   fermented red bean curd
1 tablespoon dry sherry
1 teaspoon light soy sauce
1 tablespoon dark soy sauce
2 tablespoons sugar
½ teaspoon sesame oil
salt
a few lettuce leaves
275 g/10 oz Chinese egg
   noodles

Soak the trotters in cold water
for several hours.

Heat the oil in a large
saucepan, then sauté the garlic
and ginger for a while. Stir in
the red bean curd and add the
drained trotters. Sprinkle in
the sherry, then pour in
enough water to cover the
pork. Add the soy sauces,
sugar and sesame oil. Bring to
the boil, reduce the heat and

simmer for 1½ hours.

Cook the noodles in plenty
of boiling salted water, then
drain thoroughly and transfer
to a warmed serving dish. Top
with the lettuce. Ladle the
trotters, with as much of their
cooking liquid as you would
like, over the lettuce and
noodles. Serve at once.
Serves 4

Noodles with Shredded Ham

6 Chinese dried mushrooms
100 g/4 oz cooked ham
100 g/4 oz Chinese cabbage
2 tablespoons oil
1 shallot
1 clove garlic, sliced
275 g/10 oz Chinese egg
   noodles
½ teaspoon dry sherry
2 teaspoons light soy sauce
½ teaspoon sesame oil
¼ teaspoon salt
1 teaspoon sugar

Soak the mushrooms in water
for 10 minutes, then drain and
steam them over boiling water
for 15 minutes. Thinly slice
the cooked mushrooms,
discarding the stalks if they
are woody.

Shred the ham and the
cabbage, then wash and
thoroughly drain the cabbage.
Heat the oil in a wok or large
frying pan. Add the shallot
and garlic and fry until
fragrant.

Meanwhile, cook the
noodles in boiling water for

2 minutes, drain them
thoroughly and rinse them
under cold water. Drain any
water off the noodles and set
them aside.

Add the cabbage to the
garlic and shallot and stir-fry
for a while. Add the noodles,
mushrooms and ham and
cook, tossing the ingredients
all the time, until thoroughly
heated.

Pour the sherry, soy sauce
and sesame oil into the pan.
Add the salt and sugar, then
mix thoroughly. When all the
ingredients are hot and well
mixed transfer them to a
serving dish and serve at once.
Serves 4–6

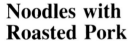

Noodles with Roasted Pork

275 g/10 oz Chinese egg
   noodles
salt and pepper
100 ml/4 fl oz chicken stock
1 teaspoon dry sherry
1 teaspoon soy sauce
½ teaspoon sugar
a few drops of sesame oil
225 g/8 oz freshly roasted Cha
   Shiu (page 225)
GARNISH
2 tablespoons shredded fresh
   root ginger
2 tablespoons shredded spring
   onion

Blanch the noodles in boiling
salted water for 1 minute,
drain and rinse them, then
drain again.

Heat the stock, sherry, soy
sauce, seasoning, sugar and
sesame oil in a wok or
saucepan. Add the noodles
and cook, turning the noodles
occasionally, until all the stock
is absorbed.

Transfer the cooked noodles
to a heated serving dish,
arranging them neatly. Slice

the roasted pork and arrange
the slices attractively on the
noodles.

Add a garnish of ginger and
spring onions on the noodles
surrounding the pork and
serve at once before the
noodles are cold. *Serves 4–6*

Note: Chinese egg noodles are
thin, slightly yellow noodles
made from a paste of flour
and egg. They are available
both fresh and dried from
Chinese supermarkets, or dried
varieties can be found in most
supermarkets or delicatessens.
The noodles must be cooked
briefly in boiling water before
use in any number of moist
dishes; they can also be fried
to achieve a crisp texture.

Fried Noodles with Mixed Vegetables

3 Chinese dried mushrooms
½ carrot, sliced
100 g/4 oz mange tout peas,
   trimmed
generous 2 tablespoons oil plus
   oil for deep frying
1 teaspoon salt
1 teaspoon sugar
pinch of monosodium
   glutamate
275 g/10 oz Chinese egg
   noodles
100 g/4 oz bean sprouts
1 teaspoon dry sherry
100 ml/4 fl oz chicken stock
1 (425-g/15-oz) can straw
   mushrooms (optional)
1 (213-g/7½-oz) can button
   mushrooms
1 piece canned bamboo shoot,
   sliced
1 teaspoon cornflour
1 tablespoon oyster sauce
½ teaspoon sesame oil
1 tablespoon water

Soak the dried mushrooms for
15 minutes, then drain them.
Cook the carrot, mange tout

peas and soaked mushrooms
for 5 minutes in boiling water
seasoned with a little of the
oil, salt, sugar and the
monosodium glutamate.

Blanch the noodles in
boiling water until soft, then
drain them thoroughly. Heat
the oil for deep frying to
190 c/375 f, then add the
noodles and cook until they
are crisp and golden brown.
Drain on absorbent kitchen
paper, arrange on a serving
dish and keep hot.

Heat the 2 tablespoons oil
in a wok or large frying pan,
then add the bean sprouts and
toss them quickly over a high
heat. Remove from the pan.
Add the sherry and stock to
the pan, then stir in all the
mushrooms, the bamboo
shoot and carrot. Bring to the
boil.

Blend the cornflour with the
oyster sauce, sesame oil and
water, then stir the mixture
into the vegetables and add
the remaining salt and sugar.
Simmer for 2 minutes, then
pour over the noodles and
serve. *Serves 4–6*

Fried Rice Yang Chow

*75 g/3 oz peeled cooked
    shrimps or prawns*
1 teaspoon cornflour
salt and pepper
100 g/4 oz Cha Shiu (page 225)
3 spring onions
2 eggs
about 575 g/1¼ lb cooked rice
1 tablespoon light soy sauce
a few drops of sesame oil

Coat the shrimps or prawns in the cornflour and a little pepper, then set them aside for a while.

Dice the cha shiu. Chop the spring onions and beat the eggs with a little salt and pepper. Heat the oil in a wok or heavy-based frying pan or saucepan (it must be large enough to hold all the rice). Add the shrimps or prawns and fry for a while, then remove them from the pan. Stir in the eggs and cook, stirring all the time, until they just begin to set.

Add all the rice to the pan and toss it quickly to coat all the grains in egg. Cook, stirring occasionally, until the rice is hot, then add the cha shiu and shrimps or prawns. Sprinkle in the light soy sauce, pepper to taste and the sesame oil. Toss well until the ingredients are hot, then transfer the rice mixture to a warmed serving dish.

Sprinkle the chopped spring onions over the rice and serve at once, to accompany a main dish. *Serves 4–6*

Macaroni in White Sauce

225 g/8 oz macaroni
salt and pepper
4 tablespoons oil
1 teaspoon sugar
100 g/4 oz shelled peas
1 carrot, diced
*1 green pepper, deseeded and
    diced*
*1 red pepper, deseeded and
    diced*
2 tablespoons flour
250 ml/8 fl oz milk
100 ml/4 fl oz chicken stock
1 teaspoon sesame oil
2 large open mushrooms
100 g/4 oz cooked ham

Cook the macaroni in boiling salted water for 12–15 minutes. Drain and rinse under cold water, then drain again.

Heat half the oil in a wok or frying pan. Stir in the macaroni and fry it with a little salt and sugar. Mix well, then transfer to an ovenproof dish.

Blanch the peas, carrot and peppers in salted water for a few minutes, then drain and rinse in cold water.

Heat the remaining oil in a saucepan, stir in the flour, then gradually stir in the milk, stock and seasoning to taste. Add the remaining sugar, the sesame oil, vegetables (including the mushrooms) and ham. Pour over the macaroni and cook in a hot oven (230 c, 450 f, gas 8) for 15–20 minutes. Serve at once. *Serves 4*

Curried Vermicelli

275 g/10 oz vermicelli
salt and pepper
1 egg, beaten
3 tablespoons oil
225 g/8 oz bean sprouts or
  cabbage, shredded
1 onion, shredded
1 green pepper, deseeded and
  shredded
1 red chilli, deseeded and
  shredded
4 large open mushrooms,
  shredded
100 g/4 oz cooked ham,
  shredded
100 g/4 oz peeled cooked
  prawns (defrosted if frozen)
2 tablespoons curry paste
1 teaspoon sugar
1 teaspoon soy sauce
½ teaspoon sesame oil

Cook the vermicelli in
simmering salted water for 20
minutes, then drain. Cook the
egg in a little oil in a frying
pan until set, then remove and
shred it.

Heat the remaining oil in a
wok until hot, then add the
bean sprouts and toss over a
high heat for a few seconds.
Remove. Add the onion,
pepper, chilli and mushrooms
and cook for a few minutes.
Stir in all the prepared and
remaining ingredients and
cook for a few minutes until
thoroughly heated and mixed.
Serve at once. *Serves 4*

Noodles with Mushrooms

40 g/1½ oz Chinese dried
  mushrooms
350 g/12 oz Chinese egg
  noodles
3 tablespoons oil
1 clove garlic, crushed
1 (213-g/7½-oz) can sliced
  mushrooms, drained
1 teaspoon dry sherry
100 ml/4 fl oz chicken stock
½ teaspoon salt
½ teaspoon sugar
1 teaspoon soy sauce
1 teaspoon dark soy sauce
1 tablespoon oyster sauce
pinch of pepper
½ teaspoon sesame oil
carrot flower to garnish
  (optional)

Soak the Chinese mushrooms
for 10 minutes, then drain and
steam them for 10 minutes.
Remove their stalks and slice
the mushroom caps.

Blanch the noodles in
boiling water for 1 minute,
then drain and rinse them.
Drain again.

Heat the oil in a wok or
large frying pan. Add the
garlic and fry it for a while,
then discard it. Add all the
mushrooms, sauté for a while,
then mix in the noodles.
Sprinkle in the sherry, then
add all the remaining
ingredients and cook for a few
minutes. Serve at once, with
some of the mushrooms
picked out and arranged in a
neat garnish. Add a carved
carrot flower if you like.
Serves 4

Noodles with Prawns

450 g/1 lb Chinese egg noodles
25 g/1 oz dried shrimps
50 g/2 oz cucumber
50 g/2 oz carrot
4 Chinese dried mushrooms
100 g/4 oz bean sprouts
2 tablespoons oil
1 shallot, sliced
1 clove garlic, sliced
175 g/6 oz peeled cooked
  prawns (defrosted if frozen)
salt
2 tablespoons sugar
2 tablespoons soy sauce
3 tablespoons sesame paste
3 tablespoons chicken stock
1 teaspoon sesame oil
½ teaspoon chilli oil

Bring a large saucepan of water to the boil. Add the noodles, bring the water back to the boil and reduce the heat. Simmer for 2 minutes, then drain the noodles and rinse them under cold water. Set these aside to drain thoroughly.

Wash the dried shrimps, then soak them in cold water to cover until they are soft. Mash the shrimps almost to a paste. Finely peel and shred the cucumber and the carrot.

Soak the mushrooms in enough hot water to cover for 10 minutes, then steam them over boiling water for 15 minutes. Shred the cooked mushrooms, discarding any tough, woody stalks, and set aside. Wash and trim the bean sprouts, discarding any which are discoloured or soft. Pick out any small green skins which covered the unsprouted beans and discard these.

Heat the oil in a wok or large frying pan and add the shallot with the garlic. Sauté these ingredients until they are fragrant, then add the bean sprouts and toss well. Stir in the prawns and dried shrimps then add the cucumber, carrot, mushrooms, salt to taste, the sugar and soy sauce, sesame paste, stock and both types of oil.

Stir well, then remove the pan from the heat and stir in the noodles. Toss the noodles thoroughly to make sure the ingredients are well mixed, then transfer the prepared noodles with prawns to a serving dish and serve cold.
Serves 4–6

Note: Serve this dish of cold noodles as part of a menu, with a selection of other hot dishes.

Shrimp Dumplings in Soup

DOUGH
150 g/5 oz strong white flour
pinch of bicarbonate of soda
1 teaspoon water
2 eggs, beaten
cornflour for dusting
FILLING
oil for deep frying
1 dried plaice fillet (optional)
25 g/1 oz Chinese dried
  mushrooms
225 g/8 oz peeled cooked
  shrimps, diced
175 g/6 oz lean, boneless pork,
  finely diced
50 g/2 oz canned bamboo
  shoots, finely diced
1 egg, beaten, plus extra for
  brushing
salt and pepper
a few drops of sesame oil
1 teaspoon cornflour

1 teaspoon sugar
TO SERVE
1.15 litres/2 pints good chicken
  stock
2 tablespoons light soy sauce
225 g/8 oz Chinese cabbage or
  leeks, shredded

Sift the flour into a bowl and make a hollow in the centre. Stir the bicarbonate of soda into the water, then stir this solution into the beaten eggs and pour them into the well in the flour. Slowly work the flour into the eggs and knead to make a soft dough.

Sift a little cornflour on a work surface. Roll the soft dough into a thin pastry, dust with more cornflour, fold and roll out until very thin. Repeat several times, dusting the dough with cornflour, folding it and rolling it thinly. Finally cut the thinly rolled dough into 6-cm/2½-in squares.

Heat the oil for deep frying to 190 c/375 f, add the plaice fillet (if used) and deep fry until lightly browned. Drain and mince the fish.

Soak the mushrooms in hot water for 30 minutes, then drain them and remove their stalks. Finely chop the mushroom caps. Mix in the diced shrimps, pork, bamboo shoots and minced plaice. Stir in the beaten egg, seasoning to taste, a few drops of sesame oil, cornflour and sugar. Mix the ingredients to make sure they are thoroughly combined.

To make the dumplings, place a little filling in each pastry square. Brush the edge with a little beaten egg, then fold in half to make a triangle shape. Pinch the edges together firmly, gathering them up slightly, to thoroughly seal in the filling. Continue until all the dough

and filling is used. Cook the dumplings in simmering water for 20 minutes, drain and place the cooked dumplings in a bowl of cold water.

Heat the stock with the light soy sauce and Chinese cabbage or shredded leeks. Season to taste, then add the drained dumplings and cook for a few minutes before serving. *Makes 30*

Congee with Scallop

100 g/4 oz rice
1 tablespoon oil
2½ teaspoons salt
2 bean curd sheets (optional)
10 ginkgo nuts, shelled
  (optional)
2.25–3 litres/4–5 pints water
50 g/2 oz dried scallops
finely shredded fresh root
  ginger to garnish

Wash and drain the rice, then mix it with 1 tablespoon oil and 1 teaspoon salt. Wash and tear the bean curd sheets into small pieces.

Soak the ginkgo nuts in hot water for 10 minutes, then rub off their skins.

To make the congee, pour 2.25 litres/4 pints of the water into a large saucepan and bring to the boil. Add the bean curd sheets, nuts and rice, then boil for 30 minutes, stirring occasionally.

Wash the scallops then soak them in hot water for 1 hour. Drain and shred them finely, then add to the congee with the remaining salt. Continue to boil the congee for 30 minutes, then add the remaining water. Cook for a further 30 minutes, until smooth and all the ingredients are tender. Press the soup through a sieve if it is not smooth. Serve topped with a little finely shredded ginger. *Serves 6*

Congee: A congee is a rice soup which may be thin or thick. A small quantity of rice is cooked in a large amount of water, until a soft, smooth mixture is formed.

The congee can be eaten for breakfast or supper, as a snack or as a dish for anyone who is unwell. The congee can be served plain or with the addition of other ingredients – in this case dried scallops.

Most usually, a congee is served with a selection of other savoury dishes. When served the congee must be very hot indeed.

Har Kow (Shrimp Dumplings)

DOUGH
100 g/4 oz strong white flour
1 teaspoon cornflour
100 ml/4 fl oz boiling water
1 teaspoon lard
FILLING
275 g/10 oz peeled cooked
  shrimps
50 g/2 oz carrots
1–2 egg whites
¼ teaspoon salt
½ teaspoon sugar
pinch of pepper
½ teaspoon sesame oil
1 teaspoon cornflour

First make the dough: sift the flour and cornflour into a mixing bowl. Pour in the boiling water stirring rapidly to mix in the flour. Cover and leave to stand for 2 minutes. Knead thoroughly to make a smooth, soft dough. Add the lard and knead well.

Roughly chop the shrimps and shred or dice the carrots. Place these ingredients in a bowl with the egg white, salt, sugar and pepper, sesame oil and cornflour. Pound the mixture until it binds together. Chill for 30 minutes.

Cut the dough in half, then cut each piece into 20 small portions. Roll out a piece of dough to give a thin circle. Place a little filling in the middle, then fold the dough over and pinch one side into 5 pleats as shown in the picture. Make sure the filling is thoroughly sealed in the dough.

Thoroughly grease a steamer then place the dumplings in it, making sure they do not touch. Cook over boiling water for 10 minutes. Serve at once. *Makes 40*

Cabbage Dumplings

FILLING
*350 g/12 oz peeled cooked
    shrimps
½ teaspoon salt
½ teaspoon sugar
pinch of pepper
1 teaspoon cornflour
75 g/3 oz carrots, parboiled
    and finely diced
a few drops of sesame oil
1 tablespoon chopped parsley*
DOUGH
*150 g/5 oz strong white flour
15 g/½ oz cornflour
¼ teaspoon salt
200 ml/7 fl oz boiling water
7 g/¼ oz lard
a few drops of green food
    colouring*

First make the filling. Roughly chop the shrimps. Add the salt, sugar, pepper and cornflour. Stir in the carrots, sesame oil and parsley; mix to bind the ingredients together. Chill for 30 minutes.

For the dough, sift the flour, cornflour and salt into a large bowl. Pour in the boiling water and stir quickly, then knead the mixture with the lard on to a lightly floured surface until smooth.

Roll the dough into a cylinder, then cut it into 40 equal portions. Flatten a portion of dough, then roll it out thinly to give a round or oval shape. Put a little filling in the middle, then enclose it in the dough, pressing the edges together to make a three-sided seam as shown in the picture. Some of the dumplings can be folded in half and the edges pinched into a frilly pattern. Alternatively, the top of the dumplings can be left open as shown. Brush the very edge of the pastry with a little food colouring as shown. Continue until all the dough and filling is used. Arrange the dumplings in a greased steamer and cook over boiling water for 8 minutes. Serve at once. *Makes 40*

Pan Stickers with Minced Beef

DOUGH
275 g/10 oz plain flour
75 ml/3 fl oz cold water
salt and pepper
100 ml/4 fl oz boiling water
FILLING
2 teaspoons soy sauce
½ teaspoon sugar
½ teaspoon bicarbonate of soda
½ teaspoon dry sherry
1 teaspoon cornflour
100 ml/4 fl oz water
2 tablespoons oil plus extra for
*   shallow frying*
350 g/12 oz minced beef
5 canned water chestnuts,
*   minced or finely chopped*
25 g/1 oz pickled mustard
*   cabbage, minced or finely*
*   chopped*

To make the dough, sift the flour then divide it into two equal portions. Mix one portion with the cold water, then knead the dough until smooth. Add salt to the other portion and mix it with the boiling water. Combine both mixtures and knead into a soft dough. Cover with cling film while you prepare the filling.

For the filling, mix the soy sauce, sugar, bicarbonate of soda, sherry, cornflour, pepper, water and 2 tablespoons oil into the minced beef, then set aside to marinate for 30 minutes. Add the minced water chestnuts and pickled mustard and mix well. Knead the dough into a long roll, then cut it into 24 equal portions. Roll a piece of dough into a round, place 2 teaspoons filling on top and fold over to seal in the filling in a crescent shape.

Heat a little oil in a large non-stick frying pan. Add the crescents and cook for 2 minutes. Pour in a little water – just less than 150 ml/¼ pint – and a pinch of salt, boil and reduce the heat. Cover, then simmer for 10 minutes. Uncover, add a little oil and cook for 3 minutes, until the liquid has dried up and the pan stickers are golden. Cook any remaining pan stickers and serve. *Makes 24*

Crackling Triangles

100 g/4 oz spring roll pastry, in
*   one sheet*
175 g/6 oz minced beef
1 teaspoon soy sauce
1 teaspoon sugar
2 teaspoons dry sherry
3 tablespoons water
2 tablespoons oil plus oil for
*   deep frying*
1 tablespoon grated shallot
2 cloves garlic, crushed
3 tablespoons chopped onion
1 teaspoon chopped red chilli
1 teaspoon finely grated fresh
*   root ginger*
1 teaspoon five spice powder
1 teaspoon paprika
salt and pepper

Cut the spring roll sheet into long strips about 3–3.5 cm/1¼–1½ in wide.

Marinate the minced beef with the soy sauce, ½ teaspoon of the sugar, 1 teaspoon of the sherry and 2 tablespoons water for 30 minutes. Heat the 2 tablespoons oil in a wok or frying pan and sauté the shallot, garlic and onion until fragrant. Add the chilli, ginger and beef and fry until dry, stirring frequently to prevent the meat from burning.

Pour in the remaining sherry, sugar, water, the five spice powder, paprika and seasoning to taste, then set aside to cool. Place a generous teaspoonful of the mixture on to a strip of pastry, then fold over the end corner to enclose the meat in a triangle of dough. Fold this again from the opposite side, then continue folding the dough over and over until completely enclosed to make a triangular shaped pasty. Tuck the end in neatly. Continue until all the filling and pastry is used.

Heat the oil for deep frying to 190 c/375 F and deep fry the triangles until crisp and golden. Drain on absorbent kitchen paper and serve. *Makes 34*

Sesame Prawn Triangles

4 medium-thick slices white
  bread
25 g/1 oz pork fat
450 g/1 lb peeled cooked
  prawns
2 tablespoons chopped parsley
2 spring onions, chopped
5 teaspoons cornflour
salt and pepper
½ teaspoon sugar
a few drops of sesame oil
100 g/4 oz sesame seeds
oil for deep frying
a few whole cooked prawns to
  garnish

The bread slices should be
dry. If they are not, then put
them under a low grill to
become crisp without
browning.

Blanch the pork fat in
boiling water, then drain it
thoroughly and chop the fat
finely. Roughly chop, then
mash the prawns in a basin.
Add the pork fat, parsley and
spring onions, then mix in the
cornflour, seasoning, sugar
and sesame oil. Make sure
that all the ingredients are
thoroughly combined.

Spread the prawn mixture
on to the bread in a thick,
even layer, moulding it with
your fingers. Press the sesame
seeds on to the prawn mixture
to make an even coating.

Heat the oil for deep frying
to 190 c/375 f. Add the
sesame-coated slices, a few at
a time, and fry them until
they are golden brown. Drain
on absorbent kitchen paper.
Cut the slices into small neat
triangles, then serve them hot.
Garnish with a few whole
cooked prawns if you like.
Makes 16

Beef Shiu My

FILLING
small piece dried tangerine peel
225 g/8 oz minced beef
salt and pepper
1 teaspoon sugar
¼ teaspoon bicarbonate of soda
50 g/2 oz canned water
  chestnuts, finely diced
1 spring onion, finely chopped
½ teaspoon finely grated fresh
  root ginger
1½ teaspoons light soy sauce
1 teaspoon cornflour
2 tablespoons water
1 tablespoon oil
DOUGH
100 g/4 oz strong plain flour
100 ml/4 fl oz boiling water
1 teaspoon lard
parsley sprigs to garnish

Soak the tangerine peel in hot
water until soft, then mince or
finely chop it. Mix the minced
beef with salt to taste, the
sugar and the bicarbonate of
soda. Set aside to marinate for
30 minutes. Add all the
ingredients to the beef, apart
from those required for the
dough. Then pound the meat
mixture thoroughly.

For the dough, sift the flour
and ¼ teaspoon salt into a
mixing bowl. Pour in the
boiling water and stir
vigorously then cover and
allow to stand for 3 minutes.
Add the lard and knead well
to give a smooth dough.

Roll the dough into a thin
long cylinder and cut it into
35–40 equal portions. Roll
out a portion of dough until
quite thin. Put a generous
teaspoonful of the meat
mixture in the middle and fold
the dough around the filling,
pleating it neatly. The filling
should not be completely
enclosed but the dough should
form a small 'basket' for the
meat. Continue until all the
dough and filling is used.

Flatten the top of the meat
with a knife, then garnish
each with a tiny sprig of
parsley and place the shiu my
in a greased steamer. Cook
over boiling water for 15–20
minutes, then serve at once.
Makes 35–40

Savoury Sesame Balls

DOUGH
350 g/12 oz potatoes
salt and pepper
50 g/2 oz sugar
100 ml/4 fl oz water
225 g/8 oz glutinous rice flour
   or rice flour

FILLING
4 Chinese dried mushrooms
100 g/4 oz loin of pork
1 teaspoon soy sauce
1 teaspoon sugar
1 teaspoon dry sherry
25 g/1 oz dried shrimps
2 tablespoons oil plus oil for
   deep frying
½ teaspoon grated shallot
1 tablespoon chopped chives
50 g/2 oz canned water
   chestnuts, diced
2 tablespoons water
1 teaspoon five spice powder
1 teaspoon oyster sauce

¼ teaspoon sesame oil
1 teaspoon cornflour
100 g/4 oz sesame seeds for
   coating

Cook the potatoes in boiling salted water until tender, then mash them until they are quite smooth. Dissolve the sugar in the water in a saucepan over a fairly low heat.

Sift the rice flour into a large bowl. Make a well in the centre, then add the mashed potatoes and sugar solution. Gradually stir in the rice flour, then knead the mixture into a soft dough. Cover with cling film or a tea towel and chill. Prepare the filling.

Soak the mushrooms in cold water for 15 minutes, then drain and steam them over boiling water for 15 minutes. Remove the mushroom stalks, then finely dice the caps.

Finely dice the pork and marinate it with the soy sauce,

½ teaspoon of the sugar and ½ teaspoon of the sherry for 10 minutes. Soak and dice the dried shrimps.

Heat the 2 tablespoons oil in a wok or frying pan. Add the pork, shallot and shrimps and fry for a while, then stir in all the remaining filling ingredients.

Roll the dough into a cylinder shape, then cut it into 32 equal portions. Press the pieces of dough into flat circles and place a little filling in the centre of each. Draw up the edges of the dough, working it around the filling to seal it in and make neat balls. Coat these completely in sesame seeds.

Heat the oil for deep frying to 190 c/375 f, then add the sesame balls and deep fry them until golden brown. Drain and serve. *Makes 32*

Dim Sum

Spring Rolls

*225 g/8 oz spring roll pastry
 squares or circles*
1 egg, beaten
FILLING
3 Chinese dried mushrooms
*50 g/2 oz carrot or canned
 bamboo shoot*
*75 g/3 oz Cha Shiu (page 225)
 or cooked ham, shredded*
salt and pepper
*75 g/3 oz uncooked boneless
 chicken, shredded*
*75 g/3 oz uncooked lean
 boneless pork, shredded*
1 teaspoon sugar
1 teaspoon light soy sauce
1 teaspoon dry sherry
¼ teaspoon sesame oil
2 teaspoons cornflour
2 tablespoons water
*2 tablespoons oil plus oil for
 deep frying*
225 g/8 oz bean sprouts

First prepare the filling: soak
the mushrooms in cold water
for 10 minutes, then drain and
steam them for 15 minutes
over boiling water. Cook the
carrot in boiling salted water,
then drain and shred it.
Alternatively shred the

bamboo shoot. Shred the
mushrooms.
 Season the shredded
chicken and pork to taste. Mix
these ingredients and add a
pinch of sugar, a few drops of
soy sauce, sherry and sesame
oil; and ½ teaspoon of the
cornflour. Blend the
remaining cornflour with the
water.
 Heat the oil in a wok or
frying pan, then add the
shredded meats. Cook until
browned. Add the
mushrooms, carrot, bean
sprouts, cha shiu or ham and
all the remaining filling
ingredients, including the
cornflour mixture. Bring just
to the boil and simmer for 2
minutes. Cool.
 Lay a piece of pastry flat on
the work surface and place a
little filling in the middle.
Brush the edges with egg,
then fold the sides over and
roll up from one end to seal.
Make sure the edges are well
sealed.
 Heat the oil for deep frying
to 190 c/375 F. Cook the rolls
until golden, drain and serve
hot. *Makes 12*

Shiu My

DOUGH
50 g/2 oz plain flour
50 g/2 oz strong white flour
1 egg, beaten
cornflour for dusting
2 Chinese dried mushrooms
*175 g/6 oz peeled cooked
 prawns*
225 g/8 oz lean boneless pork
50 g/2 oz pork fat
*50 g/2 oz canned bamboo
 shoot, diced*
1 teaspoon salt
1 teaspoon sugar
1 teaspoon light soy sauce
pinch of pepper
1 teaspoon cornflour
1 tablespoon water
GARNISH
*small shapes cut out of carrot
 or radish*
parsley sprigs

Sift the flours into a large
bowl and make a hollow in
the centre. Pour in the eggs
and work in the flour, then
knead into a smooth, soft
dough. Shape the dough into
a long thin roll and cut it into
24 small pieces.
 Soak the mushrooms in cold

water for 10 minutes, then
drain and steam them for 15
minutes. Remove the stalks
and dice the mushroom caps.
 Finely dice the prawns.
Wash and finely dice or mince
the lean pork and pork fat.
 Mix all the filling
ingredients in a bowl and
pound them together until
firm.
 On a clean surface lightly
dusted with cornflour, roll out
a piece of dough into a thin
round and put a small
spoonful of the filling in the
middle. Fold up the dough to
surround and support the
filling without enclosing it on
top. Press the filling into the
dough, then continue until all
the dough and filling is used.
 Place the shiu my in a
greased steamer and cook
them over boiling water for 20
minutes. Serve at once, with
cut out vegetable shapes and
parsley sprigs. *Makes 24*

Crispy Meat Pies

DOUGH
275 g/10 oz strong white flour
½ teaspoon salt
300 ml/½ pint boiling water
FILLING
350 g/12 oz lean boneless pork,
    diced
350 g/12 oz peeled cooked
    prawns, diced
100 g/4 oz canned bamboo
    shoot, diced
2 spring onions, chopped
½ teaspoon salt
½ teaspoon sugar
1 teaspoon light soy sauce
2 teaspoons cornflour
pinch of pepper
½ teaspoon sesame oil
BATTER
175 g/6 oz plain flour
1½ teaspoons baking powder
¼ teaspoon salt
3 tablespoons cornflour
250 ml/8 fl oz water
3 tablespoons oil plus oil for
    deep frying
GARNISH
parsley sprigs
chrysanthemum flowers
    (washed)

First make the dough: sift the
flour and salt into a bowl.
Pour in the boiling water and
stir vigorously.
  Mix all the ingredients for
the filling, making sure they
are thoroughly combined.
  Divide the dough into four
equal portions, then roll one
into a long strip and cut it into
ten small pieces. Roll these
pieces of dough into small
rounds.
  On half the rounds, pile a
little of the filling, then cover
them with the remaining
circles, pinching the edges
together thoroughly to seal in
the filling. Continue cutting,
shaping and filling the
remaining three-quarters of
the dough in this way.
  Place the filled circles in a
greased steamer, then cook
them over boiling water for 5
minutes.
  For the batter: sift the
flour, baking powder, salt and
cornflour into a bowl, then
beat in the water and oil until
smooth. Heat the oil for deep
frying to 190 c/375 F. Dip the
pies in batter, then deep fry
until golden. Drain and
garnish, then serve. *Makes 20*

Four-colour Shiu My

FILLING
175 g/6 oz minced pork
1 teaspoon light soy sauce
1 teaspoon dry sherry
1 teaspoon cornflour
½ teaspoon sugar
salt and pepper
2 tablespoons water
1 tablespoon oil
175 g/6 oz peeled cooked
    shrimps, diced
1 teaspoon finely grated fresh
    root ginger
1 teaspoon chopped spring
    onion
225 g/8 oz winter melon or
    courgettes, grated
a pinch of monosodium
    glutamate
DOUGH
450 g/1 lb plain flour
175 ml/6 fl oz boiling water
150 ml/¼ pint cold water
GARNISH
2 tablespoons peas
2 tablespoons diced carrot
2 tablespoons minced black
    fungus
2 tablespoons sieved hard-
    boiled egg yolk

Marinate the pork with the
light soy sauce, sherry and
cornflour, the sugar, a pinch
of pepper, the water and oil
for 20 minutes. Mix in the
shrimps ginger, chopped
spring onion, winter melon or
courgettes, seasoning and
monosodium glutamate. Chill
for 1 hour.
  To make the dough, sift the
flour and divide it in half. Mix
the boiling water into one
portion and knead well. Mix
the cold water into the second
portion. Knead thoroughly.
Combine both doughs and
knead until smooth. Roll into
a cylinder and cut into 50
equal portions. Roll these into
thin rounds. Fold them in
half, pinch the middle
together, then open the dough
to form a bow. Pinch opposite
ends of the bow together in
the middle to make four neat
pockets. Press filling into each
pocket; top with peas, carrot,
black fungus and egg yolk.
Steam the shiu my over
boiling water for 10 minutes.
Serve at once. *Makes 50*

Savoury Rice in Lotus Leaf

4 Chinese dried mushrooms
50 g/2 oz canned straw
  mushrooms or button
  mushrooms
75 g/3 oz Roast Belly Pork
  (page 88)
75 g/3 oz roast duck (page 83)
2 tablespoons oil plus extra for
  greasing
1 egg, beaten
75 g/3 oz peeled cooked
  shrimps
1 tablespoon light soy sauce
1 teaspoon sugar
pinch of pepper
½ teaspoon sesame oil
2 large lotus leaves, soaked
350 g/12 oz cooked rice

Soak the mushrooms in cold water for 10 minutes, then drain and steam them over boiling water for 15 minutes. Remove the stalks and dice the mushroom caps. Dice the straw mushrooms or button mushrooms. Dice the roast pork and roast duck.

Heat the oil in a frying pan, then pour in the egg to make a thin omelette. Cook until golden brown underneath, then turn it over and cook the second side until golden. Remove and dice the omelette.

Mix all the ingredients apart from the lotus leaves; grease these with a little oil. Pour in the savoury rice and fold the leaves around it to enclose the mixture completely in neat packages. Tie the packages, then place in a greased steamer and cook over boiling water for 30 minutes. Serve the rice at once, straight from the leaves. *Serves 4–6*

Steamed Raviolis

DOUGH
100 g/4 oz strong plain flour
¼ teaspoon salt
50 ml/2 fl oz boiling water
½ teaspoon lard or oil
FILLING
2 Chinese dried mushrooms
50 g/2 oz carrots
100 g/4 oz lean boneless pork,
  finely diced
2 teaspoons soy sauce
1 teaspoon sugar
½ teaspoon cornflour
2 tablespoons water
2 tablespoons oil
100 g/4 oz peeled cooked
  shrimps, finely diced
1 teaspoon chopped parsley
1 teaspoon dry sherry
¼ teaspoon salt
pinch of pepper
½ teaspoon sesame oil

Sift the flour into a mixing bowl and add the salt, then stir in the boiling water, making sure the dough is evenly mixed. Cover and set aside for 1–2 minutes. Knead thoroughly to make a smooth, soft dough. Add the oil or lard and knead well. Cover and set aside while you prepare the filling.

Soak the mushrooms in cold water for 10 minutes, then drain and steam them over boiling water for 15 minutes. Remove the stalks and finely dice the mushroom caps.

Blanch the carrot in boiling water for a few minutes, then drain and dice it finely.

Marinate the pork for 10 minutes with 1 teaspoon of the soy sauce, ½ teaspoon of the sugar, the cornflour, 2 tablespoons water and 1 tablespoon soy sauce.

Heat 1 tablespoon oil in a wok, sauté the pork and shrimps. Stir in all the other filling ingredients.

Knead the dough into a long cylinder. Cut into 40 equal portions. Take a portion, roll it into a small, thin circle then place a spoonful of filling in the middle and fold the dough to enclose it completely. Press the edges together well, then place in a greased steamer. Continue until all the dough and filling are used. Boil the ravioli for 4 minutes; serve. *Makes 40*

Rice Dumpling Fritters

450 g/1 lb glutinous rice or
   round-grain rice
2 teaspoons salt
3 tablespoons oil
2 teaspoons sugar
½ teaspoon bicarbonate of soda
225 g/8 oz belly pork, finely
   diced
1 tablespoon mixed spice
1½ teaspoons pepper
1 tablespoon dry sherry
225 g/8 oz haricot beans,
   soaked overnight
about 6 bamboo leaves for
   wrapping
BATTER
225 g/8 oz plain flour
3 teaspoons baking powder
2 tablespoons cornflour
300–350 ml/10–12 fl oz water
100 g/4 oz lard, melted
a little salt
oil for deep frying

Wash and soak the glutinous rice for 30 minutes, then drain and mix it with 1 teaspoon salt, 2 tablespoons oil, 1 teaspoon sugar and the bicarbonate of soda.

Sauté the pork with ½ teaspoon salt, ½ teaspoon sugar, the mixed spice, pepper and sherry.

Drain the haricot beans, then rub off their skins and mix the insides with ½ teaspoon salt, ½ teaspoon sugar and 1 tablespoon oil.

Wash the bamboo leaves and soak them in boiling water until soft. Drain. Place two leaves together and fold them into a cone. Put 2 tablespoons rice, and 1 tablespoon beans in the base of the leaves. Fill the centre with pork, then cover with another tablespoon beans and 2 tablespoons rice. Fold the leaves around the filling and tie them firmly in place to

make sure that the leaves completely enclose the rice mixture, forming a waterproof wrapping. Cook in boiling water for 6 hours, then drain thoroughly.

While the dumplings are cooling slightly, make the batter: sift the flour, baking powder and cornflour into a mixing bowl. Gradually beat in the water, lard and salt to give a smooth batter.

Unwrap the dumplings carefully, then cut them into quarters. Heat the oil for deep frying to 190 c/375 F. Dip the dumplings in batter, then deep fry them until golden brown and crisp. Drain on absorbent kitchen paper and serve at once. *Makes 12*

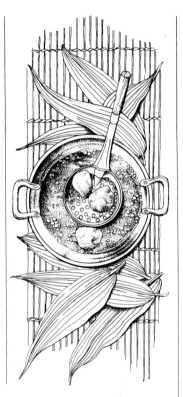

Spare Ribs in Black Bean Sauce

225 g/8 oz pork spare ribs
1 teaspoon finely shredded
  fresh root ginger
2 teaspoons fermented black
  bean paste
1 clove garlic, crushed
salt and pepper
1 teaspoon sugar
1 teaspoon dry sherry
1 teaspoon light soy sauce
a few drops of sesame oil
1 teaspoon cornflour
2 tablespoons water
GARNISH
2 spring onions, chopped, or 1
  red chilli, deseeded and cut
  into fine strips

Chop the spare ribs into small pieces and place them in a heatproof dish or suitable individual dishes.

Mix the shredded ginger with the black bean paste and garlic. Mix in seasoning to taste. Stir in all the remaining ingredients, then pour this sauce over the spare ribs.

Stand the dish or dishes in a steamer and rest it over a wok or saucepan of boiling water. Cook, topping up the water if necessary, for 12 minutes or until the ribs are cooked.

Serve at once, garnished with the spring onions or shredded red chilli. *Serves 4*

Green Leek Swirl

DOUGH
275 g/10 oz strong plain flour
½ teaspoon salt
150–175 ml/5–6 fl oz water
FILLING
pinch of pepper
1 teaspoon light soy sauce
1 teaspoon sherry
1 teaspoon cornflour
½ teaspoon dark soy sauce
½ teaspoon sugar
½ teaspoon sesame oil
275 g/10 oz pork
225 g/8 oz leeks, chopped
1 teaspoon finely grated fresh
  root ginger
1 teaspoon five spice powder
1 teaspoon sweet paste
oil for cooking

Sift the flour into a bowl and make a well in the middle. Add the salt and pour in the water. Slowly stir in the flour, then knead thoroughly to make a soft dough.

Mix a pinch of pepper, the light soy sauce, sherry and cornflour, the dark soy sauce, sugar and sesame oil into the pork and set aside for 10 minutes. Add all the other filling ingredients and mix thoroughly. Divide the dough into six or eight portions. Roll each piece of dough into a thin long triangle. Spread the meat paste evenly over the dough, then roll it up from the narrow end to make a cylinder.

Hold the cylinder vertically in the left hand, then press it firmly with the other hand to flatten it. Twist your hands in opposite directions to flatten the dough and create a swirled effect.

Grease a griddle or heavy-based frying pan with a little oil, then fry the leek swirls until golden brown on the underneath. Turn and cook the second side until well browned. Serve freshly cooked. *Makes 6–8*

Flaky Cakes with Ham and Turnip

OUTER DOUGH
150 g/5 oz plain flour
75 ml/3 fl oz warm water
INNER DOUGH
150 g/5 oz plain flour
75 g/3 oz lard, softened
FILLING
175 g/6 oz cooked ham, minced
225 g/8 oz turnip or carrot, grated
3 tablespoons chopped spring onion
¼ teaspoon salt
½ teaspoon sugar
1 teaspoon five spice powder
pinch of pepper

First prepare the outer dough: sift the flour into a bowl and make a well in the middle. Add the warm water and gradually mix it in, then knead it thoroughly to make a smooth dough.

Sift the flour for the inner dough into a bowl, then gradually knead in the lard to make a soft dough. Mix all the ingredients for the filling,

making sure they are thoroughly combined. Cut both doughs into 12 equal portions. Flatten a piece each of the outer and inner pastry into a circle. Place the inner pastry on top of the outer dough, then fold to enclose the inner dough completely. Shape the dough into a long strip and roll it out fairly thinly. Roll up the dough from the short end, turn it sideways and roll it out again. Repeat this rolling process twice, ending with a roll.

When the pastry is thoroughly rolled, shape it into a circle and place a spoonful of the filling on top. Fold the dough over to enclose the filling completely, then flatten the cakes to make neat, thin circles.

Grease a griddle or heavy-based frying pan and cook the flaky cakes until golden brown on both sides. Serve at once.
Makes 12

Sweet Sour and Curry Gluten Balls

40 Deep Fried Gluten Balls (page 225)
4 tablespoons oil
2 teaspoons shredded fresh root ginger
2 shallots, grated
2 cloves garlic, crushed
150 ml/¼ pint Sweet and Sour Sauce (page 227)
2 teaspoons dry sherry
2 teaspoons soy sauce
2 teaspoons sugar
½ teaspoon monosodium glutamate
pinch of pepper
1 teaspoon cornflour
2 tablespoons water
2 tablespoons curry paste
100 ml/4 fl oz chicken stock
parsley sprigs to garnish

Blanch the gluten balls in boiling water, then drain them thoroughly and divide them into two equal portions.

Heat half the oil in a wok or frying pan and sauté half the ginger, shallot and garlic until fragrant. Pour in the

sweet and sour sauce with half the sherry, soy sauce and sugar, ¼ teaspoon of the monosodium glutamate and a pinch of pepper. Stir in one portion of the gluten balls and simmer for 5 minutes.

Blend the cornflour with the water, pour half into the sweet and sour gluten balls and simmer for 2 minutes, or until thickened.

Heat the remaining oil in a separate pan. Sauté the remaining shallot, garlic and ginger, then pour in the curry paste and add the remaining gluten balls. Mix well. Stir in all the remaining ingredients (including the cornflour mixture) and simmer for 5 minutes.

To serve, ladle the sweet and sour mixture on to one side of a dish and arrange the curried mixture on the other side. Garnish with parsley sprigs. *Serves 4–6*

Red Bean Paste Dumplings

450 g/1 lb glutinous rice or round-grain rice
2 tablespoons water
¼ teaspoon bicarbonate of soda
2 tablespoons oil
6 bamboo leaves
275 g/10 oz red bean paste
golden syrup or caster sugar to serve

Wash and soak the glutinous rice for 30 minutes. Drain thoroughly, then mix with the water, bicarbonate of soda and oil.

Cook the bamboo leaves in boiling water for a few minutes. Drain and wash thoroughly, then dry the leaves with absorbent kitchen paper.

Place three leaves together, overlapping them slightly. Spoon a thin layer of rice on the leaves, then top with bean paste pressing it slightly into an oblong shape. Cover the paste with another thin layer of rice. Draw the leaves together to enclose the rice completely and tie up loosely with clean string. Continue until all the rice and bean paste is used. Put a few bamboo leaves in the base of a deep saucepan, arrange the dumplings on top. Cover with cold water, then bring to the boil. Continue boiling over a medium heat for 6 hours, topping up the water with fresh boiling water as necessary. Unwrap the hot dumplings and serve with a little syrup poured over or sprinkled with sugar. *Makes 2*

Red Bean Paste Buns

YEAST DOUGH
1 teaspoon dried yeast
75 g/3 oz plus ½ teaspoon sugar
175 ml/6 fl oz plus 1 tablespoon lukewarm water
350 g/12 oz strong plain flour
1 tablespoon lard
½ teaspoon bicarbonate of soda
1 teaspoon baking powder
FILLING
65 g/2¼ oz plain flour
40 g/1½ oz lard
225 g/8 oz red bean paste

Prepare the yeast dough 12–15 hours in advance. Dissolve the dried yeast and ½ teaspoon sugar in 175 ml/6 fl oz lukewarm water and set aside for 10 minutes, or until frothy. Sift 225 g/8 oz of the flour into a bowl, then pour in the yeast liquid and work in the flour. Knead thoroughly to make a soft dough, then leave to prove, covered, in a warm place for 12–15 hours.

Mix the 75 g/3 oz sugar, lard, bicarbonate of soda and remaining water into the risen dough. Sift the remaining flour and baking powder into a bowl and make a well in the centre. Add the yeast mixture, then draw in the flour and knead into a smooth dough. Roll into a cylinder shape and cut into 24 equal portions.

Prepare the filling: sift the flour into a bowl, add the lard and knead into a soft dough. Roll into a cylinder and divide into 24 equal portions. Press a portion of the dough into a circle. Add a portion of the flour and lard, then fold the yeast dough around it to enclose it completely.

Roll out the dough into a long strip, roll this up from the short end. Turn the roll and again roll it out into a strip. Repeat the rolling. Press the dough into a small circle on the palm of your hand. Place a little red bean paste on the dough, then fold it round to enclose the paste. Press a small piece of greaseproof paper on the side with the opening, then place the buns in a greased steamer and cook over boiling water for 8 minutes. Serve hot or cold. *Makes 24*

Crackling Egg Roll

4 eggs
100 g/4 oz sugar
50 ml/2 fl oz coconut milk
25 g/1 oz strong plain flour
50 g/2 oz cornflour
pinch of bicarbonate of soda
oil for cooking

Beat the eggs until fluffy. Add the sugar and coconut milk and continue beating the mixture until the sugar dissolves.

Sift the flour, cornflour and bicarbonate of soda together, then gradually add these dry ingredients to the eggs beating continuously to keep the mixture smooth.

Heat a griddle or heavy-based frying pan and grease it with a little oil.

Pour a ladleful of batter on to the hot surface and cook over a moderate heat until the batter sets and is lightly browned on the underneath, then use a spatula or palette knife to turn the pancake and cook the second side until golden. Use a palette knife to roll the soft pancake in the pan, then remove and cool on a wire rack until crisp. *Makes about 8*

Note: It is important to keep the heat under the griddle or pan even. If the pan becomes too hot the pancake will burn. When you are ready to roll the pancake, work fairly quickly before it overcooks. The cooled mixture will not roll, so it has to be rolled while still in the pan.

Sweet Potato Croquettes

225 g/8 oz sweet potatoes
25 g/1 oz lard
175 g/6 oz glutinous rice flour
100 g/4 oz red bean paste
1 egg, beaten
100 g/4 oz sesame seeds
oil for deep frying

Peel the sweet potatoes, then cut them into small pieces. Steam over boiling water for 15 minutes. Mash the cooked sweet potato with the lard.

Mix the glutinous rice flour into the mashed sweet potato, then knead thoroughly to form a soft dough and shape it into a cylinder. Cut the dough into 24 equal portions.

Take a portion of the sweet potato and flatten it slightly in the palm of your hand. Place a small portion of red bean paste in the middle, then fold the sweet potato mixture around it. Shape into a short cylinder, dip in beaten egg and coat thoroughly in sesame seeds, pressing them on well. Continue in this way until all the dough is used.

Heat the oil for deep frying to 190 c/375 f. Add the croquettes and cook until golden brown. Drain on absorbent kitchen paper and serve at once. *Makes 24*

Note: These croquettes can be served to accompany a sweet soup.

Flaky Sweet Paste Triangle

OUTER PASTRY
225 g/8 oz plain flour
100 ml/4 fl oz water
2 tablespoons oil
INNER PASTRY
150 g/5 oz plain flour
75 g/3 oz lard
FILLING
225 g/8 oz red bean paste

First make the outer pastry: sift the flour into a bowl and make a well in the middle. Pour in the water and oil, then gradually mix in the flour from the edges to make a dough. Knead thoroughly until smooth and soft. Cover and set aside.

For the inner pastry, sift the flour into a bowl and add the lard, cut into small pieces. Work the fat into the flour to make a smooth dough. Cover and chill.

On a floured work surface, form both doughs into long rolls. Cut each roll into 28 equal portions. Flatten a portion of the outer dough in the palm of your hand. Take a portion of the inner dough and flatten that too, then place it on top of the piece of outer dough. Fold the outer dough around the inner one to seal it in completely. Press the dough into a small oblong shape, then roll it into a strip. Roll this up from the short end (like a Swiss roll), then turn it so that the end of the roll is facing you. Press the roll flat, then roll it out into a strip again. Roll it up again and flatten the dough. Shape it into a circle and press the dough out thinly on the palm of your hand.

Place a little red bean paste on one side of the dough, then fold it over and press the edges together to seal in the filling. Repeat until all the dough is used.

Heat the oil for deep frying to 190 c/375 f. Add the sweet paste triangles and cook until they are golden brown. Press the triangles down into the oil as they cook and turn them over once or twice to make sure that they are evenly browned.

Drain thoroughly on absorbent kitchen paper then arrange the triangles on a dish and serve hot. *Makes 28*

Note: The cooked triangles should have a crisp, flaky texture similar to deep-fried puff pastry but not as well puffed.

Sweet Corn Soup in Coconuts

225 g/8 oz sweet corn
750 ml/1¼ pints water
1 medium-thick slice fresh root
  ginger
2 large fresh coconuts
50 g/2 oz sugar
300 ml/½ pint coconut milk

Blanch the sweet corn in boiling water for 2 minutes, then drain it thoroughly.

Pour the measured water into a large saucepan and add the ginger. Bring to the boil over a low heat so that the ginger has time to flavour the water. Scoop out the ginger and discard it.

Pour the sweet corn into the water and bring to the boil, then simmer for 10 minutes.

Pierce two of the eyes in the coconut, then drain away the water from inside. Saw off the coconut tops. Stir the sugar and coconut milk into the soup, then ladle it into the coconuts and place them in a steamer. Cook over boiling water for 30 minutes.

Serve the soup straight from the coconuts. If you like, the soup can be cooled, then chilled thoroughly before it is served. *Serves 6–8*

Note: You can use either canned or frozen sweet corn to make this soup. If you are using canned corn, then drain it first; if frozen sweet corn is used, then defrost it and drain off any water before cooking.

White Fungus in Coconuts

25 g/1 oz white fungus (see
  below)
2 medium-thick slices fresh
  root ginger
2 fresh coconuts
750 ml/1¼ pints water
225 g/8 oz sugar
250 ml/8 fl oz coconut milk
4 glacé cherries, halved, to
  garnish

Wash and soak the white fungus in cold water for 2 hours, or until soft. Trim off any hard ends. Cook the fungus with the ginger in boiling water to cover for 5 minutes. Drain, rinse and soak in cold water.

Saw the tops off the coconuts. Drain off the coconut water. Mix the water, sugar and coconut milk, then divide it between both coconuts. Cover and steam for 1 hour over boiling water. Add the drained white fungus and steam for 30 minutes.

To serve, remove the coconuts from the steamer and stand them in small dishes so that they do not fall over. Add a garnish of glacé cherries and serve at once. *Serves 6*

Note: The best quality white fungus should be slightly yellow in colour and it should be crunchy after cooking. It is important to thoroughly blanch the fungus before cooking to remove its slightly unpleasant smell.

Mock Bean Curd in Sweet Red Bean Soup

7 g/¼ oz agar agar
1.15 litres/2 pints water
50 g/2 oz sugar
1 (170-g/6-oz) can evaporated milk
¼ teaspoon almond essence
SOUP
100 g/4 oz red kidney beans
small piece dried tangerine peel (about 2.5-cm/1-in square)
1.75 litres/3 pints plus 2 tablespoons water
100 g/4 oz rock sugar or granulated sugar
2 tablespoons cornflour

Wash the agar agar and soak it in cold water for a while, then drain and add it to the measured water in a saucepan. Stir in the sugar and bring to the boil. Simmer, stirring occasionally, until both the agar agar and sugar have dissolved.

Remove the pan from the heat, stir in the evaporated milk and almond essence. Strain the liquid into a large container (about 25-cm/10-in square) and chill until set. Cut this mock bean curd into small cubes when set.

To make the soup, soak the beans in cold water for several hours or overnight. Soak the tangerine peel until it is soft.

Drain the beans and put them in a large saucepan with the water. Bring to the boil, then *boil hard for 1 minute.* Add the drained tangerine peel, reduce the heat and simmer for 1 hour.

Stir the rock sugar into the soup and continue stirring until it dissolves. Blend the soup in a liquidiser or press it through a sieve and return it to the rinsed-out saucepan.

Mix the cornflour with the 2 tablespoons water and stir this into the soup. Bring to the boil, stirring continuously, then simmer for 2 minutes. Cool and chill the soup.

To serve, ladle the soup into bowls and top each with some of the diced mock bean curd. *Serves 6*

Sweet Potato Fritters

350 g/12 oz sweet potatoes
about 50 g/2 oz cornflour for dusting
BATTER
65 g/2½ oz plain flour
2 tablespoons cornflour
2 teaspoons baking powder
100 ml/4 fl oz water
1 tablespoon oil

First make the batter: sift the flour, cornflour and baking powder into a bowl. Make a well in the middle and pour in the water. Gradually beat in the dry ingredients to make a smooth batter.

Peel, wash and slice the sweet potato. The slices should be about 5 mm/¼ in thick. Soak the slices in salted water for about 10 minutes.

Drain the sweet potato and dry the slices on a clean tea-towel or absorbent kitchen paper. Dust the slices generously with cornflour. Beat the oil into the batter. Heat the oil for deep frying to 190 c/375 f. Dip the sweet potato slices in the batter, then deep fry them until they are crisp and golden brown. Drain the fritters on absorbent kitchen paper and serve hot. You will have to cook the slices a few at a time, so keep the cooked fritters hot while the remainder are frying.
Serves 4–6

Steamed Cabbage Pudding

450 g/1 lb white cabbage
25 g/1 oz Chinese dried
* mushrooms*
75 g/3 oz dried shrimps
5 tablespoons oil
3 shallots, sliced
150 g/5 oz rindless bacon,
* diced*
2 Chinese dried sausages,
* diced*
600 ml/1 pint water
275 g/10 oz rice flour
salt and pepper
1 tablespoon sugar
1 teaspoon sesame oil
1 chicken stock cube
GARNISH *(optional)*
2 spring onions, chopped
2 tablespoons chopped parsley

Thoroughly wash, dry and mince the cabbage, removing any hard central core.

Wash and soak the dried mushrooms for 10 minutes. Drain and steam them over boiling water for 15 minutes. Wash and soak the dried shrimps, then drain and mince them. Drain the cooked mushrooms and remove any woody stalks, then dice the tender part.

Heat 2 tablespoons of the oil in a wok or large frying pan and add half the shallots. Fry until fragrant, then add the shrimps, bacon, Chinese sausages and mushrooms. Fry for a while, then remove these ingredients from the pan and set them aside.

Heat the remaining oil in a saucepan and add the rest of the shallots with the cabbage. Sauté for 3 minutes, then pour in the water and bring to the boil. Simmer, covered for about 15 minutes, or until the cabbage is tender.

Return the shrimps, bacon and mushrooms to the pan and mix well. Stirring all the time, gradually pour in the rice flour. Add seasoning to taste, the sugar, sesame oil and crumbled stock cube. Beat the mixture thoroughly.

Pour this mixture into a greased 25-cm/10-in round cake tin and cook the pudding in a steamer over boiling water for 1½ hours.

Cool the cooked pudding and shallow fry 1-cm/½-in thick slices. Add a garnish of spring onions and parsley.
Serves 10–15

Glutinous Rice Shiu My

450 g/1 lb glutinous or round-grain rice
1 teaspoon salt
4 tablespoons oil
450 ml/¾ pint water
50 g/2 oz dried shrimps
1 teaspoon minced shallot
25 g/1 oz Chinese dried mushrooms
100 g/4 oz dried Chinese sausages
1 tablespoon chopped parsley or spring onion
2 tablespoons light soy sauce
1 teaspoon sugar
pinch of pepper
a few drops of sesame oil
40 pieces Shiu My pastry (page 194)

Wash and drain the glutinous rice, then put it in a saucepan with the salt and half the oil. Mix well and pour in the water. Bring to the boil, reduce the heat and cover the pan, then cook for 30 minutes.

Wash, soak and dice the dried shrimps. Heat the remaining oil in a wok or frying pan. Sauté the shallot and dried shrimps until fragrant. Transfer to a bowl. Soak the mushrooms in cold water for 10 minutes, then drain and steam them over boiling water for 15 minutes. Steam the Chinese sausages for 10 minutes. Dice the mushroom caps and sausages and add them to the shrimps with the rice, parsley or spring onion, soy sauce, sugar, pepper and sesame oil.

Place a piece of shiu my pastry on the palm of your hand and top with a little of the rice mixture. Draw the edges of the pastry around the filling, leaving the top open. Arrange the shiu my in a greased steamer and cook over boiling water for 3–4 minutes. Serve hot. *Makes 40*

Popcorn Patties

275 g/10 oz unsweetened popcorn
50–75 ml/2–3 fl oz water
150 g/5 oz sugar
2–3 tablespoons oil

Grind the popcorn to a powder in a liquidiser or food processor, then place it in a bowl. Pour the water into a saucepan and add the sugar. Heat slowly until the water boils, stirring continuously to make sure the sugar dissolves.

Make a well in the ground popcorn, then pour in the sugar solution and stir thoroughly to bind all the ingredients together. Add the oil and mix well, then turn the mixture out on to a clean surface and knead thoroughly until soft and smooth.

Press the dough into small moulds – the picture shows a Chinese fish-shaped mould. If you do not have a suitable mould, then shape the mixture into small cakes. If you like you can add some sort of colourful decorations to the cakes; the fish-shaped ones in the picture have flat-leafed parsley sprigs and tiny pieces of carrot added to them. *Makes about 18*

Note: If you cannot find unsweetened popcorn, then buy uncooked corn and pop it yourself. To do this, heat a small amount of oil in a large saucepan which has a lid. Add a handful of popping corn and quickly cover the pan. Hold the pan over medium heat, shaking it frequently, until the popping has ceased.

Deep Fried Ravioli

1 quantity dough as for
Steamed Ravioli (page 196)
FILLING
150 g/5 oz peeled cooked
prawns
1 teaspoon cornflour
75 g/3 oz lean boneless pork,
diced
2 teaspoons light soy sauce
1 teaspoon sugar
1 teaspoon sesame oil
1 tablespoon water
1 Chinese dried mushroom
25 g/1 oz carrot, finely diced
1 teaspoon dry sherry
pinch of pepper
1 tablespoon chopped parsley

Prepare the dough according
to the recipe instructions, then
knead it into a long roll and
cut this into 40 equal portions.
Cover with a damp tea-towel
and set aside.

Finely dice the prawns and
mix them with the cornflour.
Mix the prawns with the pork
and add the light soy sauce,
sugar, sesame oil, a little
cornflour and the water. Mix

thoroughly, then set aside for
30 minutes.

Soak the mushroom for 10
minutes, then drain and steam
it for 10 minutes. Remove the
stalk and finely dice the
mushroom cap.

Heat a wok or large frying
pan, add the pork mixture and
fry for a while. Stir in the
carrot and mushroom, sherry
and pepper. Cook for a few
minutes, then remove from
the pan and allow to cool. Stir
the parsley into this filling.

Take a small portion of the
dough and press it out into a
circle. Place a little of the
filling in the middle of the
dough. Fold the dough over
and seal the edges to keep the
filling in. Continue until all
the dough and filling is used.
Place the ravioli in a greased
steamer and cook them over
boiling water for 4 minutes.

Heat the oil for deep frying
to 190 c/375 F. Add the
ravioli, a few at a time, and
cook until golden brown and
crisp. Drain on absorbent
kitchen paper and serve hot.
Makes 40

Crispy Munchies

175 g/6 oz dried broad beans
salt
175 g/6 oz shelled fresh peanuts
175 g/6 oz new potatoes, sliced
175 g/6 oz taro or old potatoes,
sliced
oil for deep frying

Soak the broad beans in hot
water for 24 hours, then drain
them thoroughly and peel off
their skins. Cook in boiling
salted water for 30 minutes,
then drain and cool.

Soak the peanuts in hot
salted water for a few hours,
then drain them and rub off
their skins. Set aside until
quite dry.

Cut the potatoes and taro
into small diamond shapes,
triangles or circles and soak
both vegetables separately in
hot salted water for about 30
minutes. Drain and dry
thoroughly when soaked.

Heat the oil for deep frying
to 190 c/375 F. Deep fry the
beans, nuts and potatoes or
taro separately in several
batches. Drain thoroughly on
absorbent kitchen paper. Then

sprinkle each portion with salt
while still hot. *Serves 4–6*

Note: When absolutely cold
these crunchy cocktail snacks
can be stored successfully in
an airtight container in a cool,
dry place for 2–3 weeks. The
broad beans and peanuts have
a slightly longer storage life
than the potatoes or taro, so it
is best to make the vegetable
snacks when you want to
serve them.

Steamed Meat Pies

1 quantity dough as for
  Steamed Ravioli (page 196)
175 g/6 oz lean boneless pork
¼ teaspoon dry sherry
¼ teaspoon salt
2 teaspoons light soy sauce
1½ teaspoons sugar
1 teaspoon cornflour
pinch of pepper
2 tablespoons water
1 teaspoon sesame oil
100 g/4 oz peeled cooked
  prawns
50 g/2 oz carrots
1 Chinese dried mushroom
1 tablespoon chopped parsley

Prepare the dough according to the recipe instructions. Knead it into a smooth cylinder shape and cut this into four equal portions. Cover these and set aside.

Dice the pork finely and mix it with the sherry, salt, light soy sauce, sugar, cornflour, pepper, water and sesame oil. Set aside for 30 minutes.

Dice the prawns and carrots finely. Soak the mushroom in cold water for 10 minutes, then drain and steam it over boiling water for 15 minutes. Remove the stalk and chop the mushroom cap.

Add the prawns, carrot and mushroom to the marinated pork. Stir in the parsley and pound the mixture thoroughly to combine all the ingredients. Set this aside for 10 minutes.

Cut each portion of dough into 15 equal pieces. Press these flat and roll them into small circles. Place a little filling on a piece of dough and top it with a second circle of dough. Press the edges together well to seal in the filling. Continue to make the little pies in this way until all the dough and filling is used.

Arrange the meat pies in a greased steamer and cook them over boiling water for 8–10 minutes. Remove and serve hot. *Makes 30*

Note: To make a well-sealed, attractive edge on these little pies (as shown in the picture) press the dough together evenly, making the edge quite wide and thin; take care not to break the dough. Fold the edge over, in towards the middle of the pies, and pinch the edge evenly and neatly to give a patterned finish. This edge will form an effective seal as well as offer an attractive appearance.

Sweet Paste Patties

OUTER DOUGH
175 g/6 oz plain flour
generous 50 ml/2 fl oz water
2 tablespoons oil
INNER DOUGH
100 g/4 oz plain flour
65 g/2½ oz lard
FILLING
350 g/12 oz sweet red bean paste
DECORATION
1 egg, beaten
1 tablespoon black sesame seeds

First make the outer dough. Sift the flour into a bowl and make a well in the middle. Pour in the water and oil, then gradually work in the flour and knead to make a smooth dough. Roll the dough into a cylinder shape and cut into 24 equal portions.

For the inner dough, sift the flour into a bowl, then work in the lard and knead thoroughly to make a smooth dough. Again shape this dough into a cylinder and cut it into the same number of equal-sized portions as the first dough.

Take a piece of the outer dough and place a piece of the inner dough on it. Wrap the outer dough to enclose the inner portion completely. Flatten the dough and roll it out into a long thin piece, then roll up from the narrow end. Give the dough a half turn, then roll it out again and repeat the process once more. Press the dough into a thin circle.

Put a little red bean paste in the middle of the pastry, then draw the edges around it to enclose the filling completely. Brush with beaten egg, place on a greased baking tray and sprinkle with sesame seeds. Repeat until all the dough and filling is used.

Bake the patties in a cool oven (150 C, 300 F, gas 2) for 20 minutes. Cool on a wire rack. *Makes 24*

Savoury Crisp

275 g/10 oz strong white flour
½ teaspoon baking powder
¼ teaspoon bicarbonate of soda
1 teaspoon Spicy Salt (page 229)
2 tablespoons fermented bean curd paste
50 ml/2 fl oz water
2 eggs, beaten
1 teaspoon sugar
1 tablespoon black sesame seeds
oil for deep frying

Sift the flour, baking powder, bicarbonate of soda and spicy salt together into a bowl and make a well in the middle.

Mix the fermented bean curd paste with the water then pour this liquid into the well with the eggs, sugar and sesame seeds. Mix thoroughly and knead into a soft dough.

Divide the dough into 12 equal portions, and roll each portion into a paper-thin oblong piece. Cut into small triangles or any other shapes.

Heat the oil for deep frying to 190 C/375 F, add the dough shapes and deep fry until they are crisp and golden. Drain on absorbent kitchen paper. Store in an airtight container. *Makes about 150 (Serves about 20)*

Note: Fermented bean curd paste is mashed fermented bean curd which is available either canned or in jars from Chinese and oriental supermarkets

Spicy Doughnut

DOUGH
1 quantity Yeast Dough (page 211)
200 g/7 oz sugar
250 ml/8 fl oz water
15 g/½ oz bicarbonate of soda
575 g/1¼ lb strong white flour
FILLING
5 tablespoons fermented red bean curd
1 teaspoon five spice powder
1 teaspoon salt
oil for deep frying

Prepare the yeast dough according to the recipe instructions, then allow it to stand for 12–15 hours.

Mix the dough with the sugar and water until the sugar has dissolved. Add the bicarbonate of soda and sift in the flour, then knead the flour into the dough. Continue to knead the dough for 10 minutes, until it is smooth and elastic. Cover the dough and set it aside for 1 hour.

Roll the pastry into a 1-cm/½-in thick rectangle measuring about 25 cm/10 in wide. Mix the filling ingredients and spread them over the dough, then roll up from the long side. Set aside to prove, covered with a tea towel, for 1 hour.

Heat the oil for deep frying to 180 c/350 F. Cut the dough into 1-cm/½-in thick slices, then deep fry these until golden brown. Drain on absorbent kitchen paper and serve warm or cold. *Makes 24*

Twisted Doughnuts

575 g/1¼ lb strong white flour
1 teaspoon bicarbonate of soda
2 teaspoons salt
350 ml/12 fl oz water
oil for cooking

Sift the flour and bicarbonate of soda into a large bowl. Make a well in the centre and put in the salt and water. Mix well, working in the flour to form a smooth dough.

Knead the dough thoroughly for 10 minutes. Cover with a tea-towel and set aside to prove for 30 minutes. Repeat the kneading and proving once more. Roll the dough out into a rectangular sheet, approximately 3-mm/⅛-in thick. Cut into 2.5-cm/1-in wide and about 15-cm/6-in long strips. Sandwich the strips on top of each other in pairs. Press the strips together in the middle, then pull them out to make long strips.

Heat a little oil in a wok, then add the strips of dough and cook, pressing and turning them all the time, until well cooked and golden brown. Drain on absorbent kitchen paper and serve hot. *Makes 24*

Note: These twisted doughnuts are often used as an ingredient in recipes as well as for serving on their own as a crisp snack. They are sometimes served as an accompaniment to soups or congee.

Cha Shiu Buns

DOUGH
1 teaspoon dried yeast
75 g/3 oz sugar
100 ml/4 fl oz plus 2
    tablespoons lukewarm water
350 g/12 oz strong plain flour
1 teaspoon baking powder

FILLING
150 ml/¼ pint chicken stock
2 tablespoons cornflour
4 tablespoons water
225 g/8 oz Cha Shiu, diced
    (page 225)
1 tablespoon oyster sauce
1 teaspoon sugar
1 teaspoon light soy sauce
1 tablespoon chopped spring
    onion

Make the yeast dough 12–15
hours in advance. Dissolve the
dried yeast and ½ teaspoon of
the sugar in the 100 ml/4 fl oz
water. Set aside for 10
minutes, or until frothy. Sift

225 g/8 oz of the flour into a
bowl, pour in the yeast liquid
then mix to form a soft
dough. Knead thoroughly,
replace the dough in the bowl
and set aside, covered, for 12–
15 hours.

Put the yeast dough, and
remaining sugar in a large
bowl. Gradually add the
remaining water and rub it
into the dough to make a stiff
batter. Sift the remaining flour
and baking powder into a
bowl, then pour in the yeast
batter. Gradually work the
flour into the yeast mixture
and knead thoroughly to make
a smooth dough.

Heat the stock in a
saucepan. Blend the cornflour
with the water, then stir it
into the stock together with all
the remaining filling
ingredients. Bring to the boil
then simmer for 2 minutes.
Cool and chill.

Divide the dough into 24

equal portions and flatten
each into a circle. Place a
little filling in the middle of
each, then gather up the edges
of the dough and twist them
together over the filling to seal
it in completely.

Cut out 24 small squares of
greaseproof paper and grease
each piece lightly with oil.
Place each of the buns on a
piece of greaseproof paper,
then stand them in a steamer
and cook them over boiling
water for 8 minutes. If you do
not have a large, two or three
tier steamer, then you will
probably have to cook the
buns in several batches. If so,
try to serve the buns as they
are cooked or keep them hot
on a covered plate over a
saucepan of gently simmering
water. Ideally the buns should
be served at once. *Makes 24*

Sweet Dishes

Lychees in Syrup

450 g/1 lb fresh lychees
250 ml/8 fl oz water
225 g/8 oz sugar
1 slice fresh root ginger
1 slice lemon
a few glacé cherries to decorate

Peel the lychees, then remove
their stones. Do this in the
same way as you would stone
a cherry: by pushing the stone
out from one end to leave a
cavity in the middle of the
fruit.

Wash the stoned lychees,
rinse them under cold water
and drain thoroughly. Dry the
fruit on absorbent kitchen
paper.

Pour the water into a
saucepan and bring it to the
boil, then add the sugar,
ginger and lemon. Heat
gently, stirring continuously,
until the sugar has dissolved
completely.

Arrange the lychees in a
heatproof serving dish, then
pour the syrup over them and
set aside to cool. Lightly chill
the lychees, then add a
decoration of sliced cherries

before you serve the fruit.
Serves 4

Note: Fresh lychees are not
always available but they are
worth the effort involved in
preparing them when they are
in the shops.

If you are unable to obtain
the fresh fruit, you can
prepare a quick and simple
dessert by draining the syrup
from a can of lychees into a
saucepan. Add the slice of
ginger and lemon and heat the
liquid through very gently
until it is almost boiling. This
will give the syrup a chance to
absorb the flavour from the
ginger and lemon.

Pour the hot syrup over the
fruit and allow to cool, then
chill lightly before serving.

Cold Almond Bean Curd

15 g/½ oz agar agar
1.15 litres/2 pints water
100 g/4 oz sugar
100 ml/4 fl oz milk
1 teaspoon almond essence
*1 (410-g/14½-oz) can fruit
cocktail*

Wash, soak and drain the agar
agar. Pour the water into a
large saucepan. Add the sugar
and agar agar, bring to the
boil, stirring occasionally, then
simmer over a low heat until
completely dissolved.

Remove the pan from the
heat. Stir the milk and almond
essence into the dissolved agar
agar, then pour it through a
fine strainer. Pour the liquid
into a large container – a
clean roasting tin or plastic
container, for example – and
allow to set. The mixture
should be about 2.5–5 cm/1–
2 in thick.

When it has solidified, cut
the jelly into cubes or neat
diamond shapes. Serve in a
bowl with fruit cocktail.
Serves 6

Note: Agar agar does not
require chilling in order to set
but leave the jelly in a cool
place. The fruit and almond
mixture does benefit from
being lightly chilled before
serving. If you like, the mock
bean curd can be served in a
home-made fresh fruit salad.

Mango and Sago Pudding

100 g/4 oz sago
2 large ripe mangoes
20 g/¾ oz agar agar
1.4 litres/2½ pints water
225 g/8 oz sugar
250 ml/8 fl oz milk
3 eggs, beaten

Cook the sago in plenty of boiling water until transparent – about 15 minutes. Drain and rinse, then drain thoroughly. Peel and dice the mangoes. Soak the agar agar for about 30 minutes.

Pour the water into a large saucepan and bring to the boil, then stir in the agar agar and sugar. Simmer until dissolved. Remove from the heat and stir in the milk.

Stir in the eggs, sago and mangoes, then stand the saucepan over a bowl of ice and whisk the sago continuously until it is half set. Pour into a mould and chill until set. Turn out to serve. *Serves 6*

Note: If you are unable to obtain fresh mangoes, then substitute drained canned mangoes or canned mango purée. Alternatively you could use fresh or canned peaches or apricots.

If you use fresh mangoes, use a sharp pointed knife and cut the fruit into quarters in as far as the stone. Peel back the skin and the soft flesh can be easily cut off the stone in four pieces.

Coconut New Year Pudding

75 g/3 oz water chestnut flour
50 g/2 oz cornflour
900 ml/1½ pints water
200–250 ml/7–8 fl oz coconut milk
1 (200-g/7-oz) can condensed milk
50 g/2 oz rice flour
75 g/3 oz glutinous rice flour
225 g/8 oz sugar
glacé cherries to decorate

Soak the water chestnut flour and cornflour in 300 ml/½ pint of the water for 10 minutes. Stir in the coconut milk and condensed milk. Sift in the rice flour and glutinous rice flour, then stir until evenly mixed.

Bring the remaining water to the boil. Add the sugar and simmer until dissolved. Leave to cool, then pour into the flour batter and mix thoroughly.

Grease a 15-cm/6-in deep cake tin and place it in a steamer. Pour a thin layer of batter into the tin to steam for 6 minutes. Repeat layer by layer until all the batter is in the tin. As the layers are added the steaming time will have to be increased and the final layers may require lengthy cooking for up to 1½ hours. It is important that all the layers are set. Remove and leave to cool in the tin.

Turn out and serve cold, decorated with glacé cherries. Alternatively, slice the pudding into wedges, dip these in beaten egg and shallow fry them until golden brown on all sides. *Serves 6*

Sago Crystal Cakes

200 /7 oz sago
50 g/2 oz sugar
3 tablespoons milk
100 g/4 oz cornflour
1 tablespoon lard
175 g/6 oz lotus seed paste

Soak the sago for 30 minutes, then drain and cook it in plenty of boiling water for about 3 minutes. Remove from the heat but leave to cool for 15–30 minutes. Drain and rinse under cold water, then drain thoroughly.

Mix the sugar and milk in a mixing bowl, then sift in the cornflour, whisking all the time. Add the sago and mix to a soft paste. Place in a greased bowl and steam over boiling water for 30 minutes. Allow to cool.

Add the lard and knead into a dough.

Knead the dough into a cylinder shape, then divide it into 20 equal portions. Wet your hands and press each piece flat, place a little lotus seed paste in the middle and fold the dough around it to seal it in completely.

Press the dough pieces into a decorative mould (a traditional wooden one is shown in the picture) or place them straight in a greased steamer. Cook over boiling water for 8 minutes, then serve hot. *Makes 20*

Water Chestnut Pudding

2 (225-g/8-oz) cans water
  chestnuts, drained
350 g/12 oz sugar
1.75 litres/3 pints water
275 g/10 oz water chestnut
  flour starch or cornflour

Grate the water chestnuts and place them in a large saucepan with the sugar and 1.15 litres/ 2 pints of the water. Bring to the boil, stirring to dissolve the sugar and cook for a few minutes.

Mix the water chestnut flour or cornflour with the remaining water, then strain it and gradually pour the mixture into the saucepan, stirring all the time to prevent lumps from forming. Pour the mixture into a greased 25-cm/ 10-in square deep cake tin, then stand it in a steamer and cook over boiling water for 40 minutes.

Leave to cool completely, then turn out and cut into small oblong pieces to serve.
Serves 8–10

Note: If you like, a small portion of the water chestnut pudding mixture can be mixed with a little milk and steamed in a small basin. This can then be turned out for serving in the middle of the slices as shown in the picture.

Snow Balls in Banana Leaves

225 g/8 oz glutinous rice flour
  or ordinary rice flour
50 g/2 oz rice flour
250 ml/8 fl oz boiling water
20 g/¾ oz lard
FILLING
100 g/4 oz unroasted peanuts
2 tablespoons sesame seeds
25 g/1 oz desiccated coconut
175 g/6 oz sugar

Sift the glutinous rice flour and the ordinary rice flour into a bowl. Pour in the boiling water, stirring all the time to make a soft dough. Add the lard and knead the dough until it is quite smooth. Cover and set aside while the filling is prepared. For the filling, soak the peanuts in boiling water for 20 minutes, then drain them and toast the nuts under a grill, on a low setting, until crisp and browned. Chop the toasted nuts quite finely.

Place the chopped nuts in a bowl and add the sesame seeds, coconut and sugar. Mix these ingredients thoroughly.

Cut the dough into 24 equal portions. Take a portion of the dough and flatten it into a circle in the palm of your hand. Place a little of the filling in the middle of the dough. Fold the dough around the mixture to enclose it completely. Pinch the edges together to seal in the filling and roll it into a smooth ball. Continue shaping the mixture in this way until all the dough and filling is used.

Place one of the dough balls on a piece of banana leaf, neatly trimmed into an oval shape, then secure it in place with a tooth pick or wooden cocktail stick. Wrap all the balls in this way. If you do not have any banana leaves, then put the balls in small folded pieces of cooking foil.

Arrange the snow balls in banana leaves in a steamer and cook them over boiling water for 5 minutes. Serve warm or cold. *Makes 24*

Coconut Layer Pudding

900 ml/1½ pints coconut milk
175 g/6 oz sugar
¼ teaspoon salt
175 g/6 oz rice flour
40 g/1½ oz cornflour
red food colouring

Heat the coconut milk in a saucepan until just warm. Stir in the sugar and salt, then heat gently, stirring frequently, until completely dissolved.

Sprinkle the rice flour and cornflour into the coconut milk, stirring all the time. Pour the liquid through a fine sieve and divide it into two equal portions.

Grease a 15-cm/6-in square tin. Colour one portion of the liquid pink. Pour a little of the coloured liquid into the tin and cook it in a steamer over boiling water for 10–15 minutes or until set. Pour in a thin layer of white liquid, then steam it for a further 10–20 minutes or until set. Continue steaming and building up the layers in this way until there is a total of nine layers, all cooked. As more layers are added the steaming time will become longer; the final layers may require 1–1½ hours cooking.

Leave the thoroughly cooked pudding to cool completely in the tin before cutting it into small diamond shapes. Arrange these on a serving platter. *Serves 6*

Sweet Paste Buns

OUTER DOUGH
½ quantity yeast dough (page 211)
75 g/3 oz sugar
1 tablespoon lard
½ teaspoon bicarbonate of soda
2 tablespoons water
50 g/2 oz plain flour
1 teaspoon baking powder
INNER DOUGH
50 g/2 oz plain flour
25 g/1 oz lard
FILLING
100 g/4 oz lotus seed paste or red bean paste

Prepare the yeast dough according to the recipe instructions, making it 12–15 hours in advance.

Mix the sugar, lard, bicarbonate of soda, and water into the prepared yeast dough. Sift the flour and baking powder over it and mix thoroughly, then knead until the dough is smooth and soft.

For the inner dough, sift the flour into a bowl and work in the lard until a smooth dough is formed.

Cut both doughs into 20 equal portions, then wrap a portion of the inner dough in a piece of the outer dough and roll it out into an oblong shape. Fold the dough and give it a half turn, then roll it into an oblong. Repeat this rolling once more.

Roll the piece of dough into a small circle and place a little filling in the middle. Fold the dough around the filling, pinching the edges thoroughly. Roll into a smooth ball and place the bun on a small square of greaseproof paper. Continue making the buns in this way until all the dough is used.

Arrange the shaped buns in a steamer and cook them over boiling water for 10–12 minutes. Remove and allow to cool before serving. *Makes 20*

Long Life Buns

DOUGH
300 ml/½ pint warm water
2 teaspoons dried yeast
½ teaspoon sugar
450 g/1 lb plain flour
2 teaspoons baking powder
50 g/2 oz caster sugar
40 g/1½ oz lard
powdered red food colouring
FILLING
225 g/8 oz red bean paste

Pour the warm water into a mixing bowl. Scatter the yeast and sugar over the water, cover the bowl and leave it in a warm place for about 10 minutes or until the liquid is frothy. Stir well.

Sift the flour into a large bowl, make a well in the middle and pour in the yeast liquid. Gradually work in the flour and knead the dough until smooth. Transfer the dough to a greased bowl, cover and set aside in a warm place for about 4 hours.

Turn the risen dough out on to a floured surface. Sprinkle the baking powder and sugar on to the dough, then add the lard. Fold the dough to enclose these ingredients and knead it until smooth. Shape the dough into a long cylinder and cut this into 32–48 equal portions.

Take a portion of the dough and flatten it in the palm of your hand. Place a little filling in the middle, then fold the dough around it to make a ball. Pinch the edges together to seal in the red bean paste. Shape one end of the bun into a point. Press a deep line from the centre of the bun towards the point. Flatten the base of the bun and place it on a small piece of greaseproof paper. Continue shaping the buns in this way until all the dough is used.

Allow the buns to prove in a warm place for 10–20 minutes, then place them in a steamer and cook them over boiling water for 8 minutes.

Remove the cooked buns from the steamer, then sprinkle a little red food powder on each one. *Makes about 32–48*

Sesame Crisps

275 g/10 oz plain flour
40 g/1½ oz lard
½ teaspoon bicarbonate of soda
100 ml/4 fl oz water
100 g/4 oz sugar
1 egg, beaten
sesame seeds for coating

Place the flour in a bowl and place it in a steamer. Cook over boiling water for 10 minutes. Crush the flour with the end of a rolling pin, then sift it into a mixing bowl. Make a well in the flour and put the lard and soda in it.

Bring the water to the boil in a saucepan and add the sugar. Stir until the sugar has dissolved, then pour it into the well with the soda and lard. Gradually work in the flour to make a soft dough. Knead lightly and allow to cool.

Roll out the cooled dough to a thickness of 3 mm/⅛ in and cut out small rounds using a biscuit cutter. Brush both sides of the biscuits with a little beaten egg and coat them completely with sesame seeds. Transfer to greased baking trays and cook in a cool oven (150 c, 300 f, gas 2) for 10 – 15 minutes.

Transfer the cooked sesame crisps to a wire rack to cool, then store them in an airtight container. *Makes about 50*

Date Jam Crisp

275 g/10 oz plain flour
2 teaspoons baking powder
100 g/4 oz lard
100 g/4 oz sugar
2 eggs, beaten
FILLING
225 g/8 oz date jam
50 g/2 oz blanched almonds,
   quartered lengthways, to
   decorate
1 egg, beaten to glaze

Sift the flour and baking powder into a bowl. Make a well in the middle and put in the lard, sugar and beaten eggs. Gradually work in the dry ingredients and knead the mixture to make a smooth dough. Shape the dough into a long cylinder and cut this into 20 equal portions.

Take a portion of the dough and shape it into a ball. Flatten the piece of dough in the palm of your hand and put a little jam filling in the middle. Fold the edges of the dough around the filling and pinch them together to seal in the mixture.

Line two baking trays with rice paper and put the buns on them. Top each with a piece of almond. Brush with a little beaten egg and bake in a moderately hot oven (200 c, 400 F, gas 6) for about 25 minutes or until golden brown.

Lift the cooked buns off the tray, trim the rice paper from round the edges of the buns and transfer them to a wire rack to cool completely. The cooked buns can be stored in an airtight container for several days. *Makes 20*

Flaky Coconut Patties

OUTER PASTRY
275 g/10 oz plain flour
150 ml/¼ pint water
50 ml/2 fl oz oil
INNER PASTRY
175 g/6 oz plain flour
90 g/3½ oz lard
FILLING
50 g/2 oz desiccated coconut
50 g/2 oz unsalted peanuts,
   finely ground
2 tablespoons sesame seeds
225 g/8 oz sugar

First make the outer pastry: sift the flour into a bowl and make a well in the middle. Pour in the water and oil, then gradually mix in the dry ingredients to make a smooth dough. Knead thoroughly, then cover and set aside while you prepare the inner dough.

For the inner dough, sift the flour into a bowl and add the lard. Work it into the flour until a smooth dough is formed.

Shape both doughs into long cylinders and cut each

into 32 equal portions. Flatten a portion of the outer dough in the palm of your hand. Do the same with a piece of the inner dough, then lay this on the piece of outer dough. Fold the outer piece over to enclose the inner dough completely, then roll it into an oblong shape. Fold the dough in half, turn and roll the dough twice more, then shape it into a circle.

Mix all the filling ingredients together and place a little in the middle of the circle of dough. Fold the dough over to make a semi-circular pasty and pinch the edges together to seal in the filling. Alternatively, the filling can be sandwiched between two circles of dough to make a round patty. Continue rolling and shaping the patties until all the dough and filling is used up.

Heat the oil for deep frying to 190 c/375 F. Deep fry the patties until golden brown and drain them on absorbent kitchen paper. *Makes 32*

Chrysanthemum Crisp

OUTER PASTRY
175 g/6 oz plain flour
¼ teaspoon yellow food
   colouring
50 ml/2 fl oz water
50 g/2 oz lard, melted
INNER PASTRY
100 g/4 oz plain flour
65 g/2½ oz lard
FILLING
175 g/6 oz lotus seed paste
1 egg yolk
black sesame seeds or poppy
   seeds to decorate

For the outer pastry: sift the flour into a bowl. Stir the colouring and water into the flour and pour in the lard. Knead to make a smooth dough. Replace the dough in the bowl and cover, then set aside.

For the inner dough, sift the flour into a bowl, add the lard, then gradually work it in until smooth.

Cut both doughs into 24 equal portions. Wrap a portion of the inner pastry in a piece of the outer dough, then roll it into a strip. Roll up from the short end, give it a half turn and roll out again. Repeat twice.

Press the dough into a circle. Place a little lotus seed paste on it. Enclose the filling in dough, then turn the bun over and flatten it. Make 16 cuts from the middle to make the petals, twist each to show the filling. Brush with beaten egg and sprinkle with seeds.

Arrange the crisps on greased baking trays and bake in a moderately hot oven (180 C, 350 F, gas 4) for 15–20 minutes, or until browned. Cool on a wire rack. *Makes 24*

Thousand Layer Pudding

450 g/1 lb plain flour
5 teaspoons baking powder
150 g/5 oz sugar
1 tablespoon corn oil
250 ml/8 fl oz water
FILLING
3 salted eggs
225 g/8 oz mixed candied peel
50 g/2 oz custard powder
75 g/3 oz sugar

Sift the flour and baking powder into a bowl and stir in the sugar. Make a well in the middle of the dry ingredients, then add the oil and water. Gradually stir in the dry ingredients to make a dough and knead until smooth.

Cook the salted eggs in boiling water for 5 minutes, then drain and shell them. Halve the eggs, remove the yolks and reserve these, set aside the whites for another use. Dice the yolks and place them in a basin. Chop the candied peel and add it to the yolks with the custard powder and sugar. Mix thoroughly.

Divide the dough into four equal portions. On a lightly floured surface, roll out a portion of dough into a 15–18-cm/6–8-in square. Lay this on a large sheet of greased cooking foil.

Divide the filling into three equal portions and spread one of these over the dough. Roll out a second piece of the dough and lay it on top of the filling. Spread a second portion of the filling on the dough, then roll out the remaining two portions of dough and layer them in the same way, ending with dough on top.

Wrap the foil around the pudding and lay it on a platter, then cook in a steamer or over boiling water for about 45 minutes. Unwrap and cut into squares or diamonds to serve.
Makes about 40 pieces

Sesame Cookies

4 tablespoons water
50 g/2 oz sugar
1 egg
2 tablespoons oil
275 g/10 oz plain flour
½ teaspoon baking powder
½ teaspoon bicarbonate of soda
sesame seeds for coating
oil for deep frying

Bring the water to the boil in a small saucepan. Remove the pan from the heat and stir in the sugar. Continue to stir until it dissolves completely. Beat the egg with the oil.

Sift the flour, baking powder and bicarbonate of soda into a bowl and make a well in the middle. Pour the sugar solution into the well and stir in the beaten egg with oil. Slowly work the flour into the liquid to make a soft dough then knead it lightly until smooth. Roll the dough into a cylinder and cut it into 32 equal portions. Roll each portion into a ball.

Coat the balls of dough completely in sesame seeds, pressing them on well. Heat the oil for deep frying to 190 C/375 F. Add the cookies and fry them until lightly browned. Reduce the heat and continue to fry until a small crack is formed in the top of each cookie.

Drain the sesame cookies on absorbent kitchen paper and allow them to cool. When thoroughly cooled, they can be stored in an airtight container for up to a month. *Makes 32*

Crystal Date Jam Spirals

225 g/8 oz glutinous rice flour
 or ordinary rice flour
250 ml/8 fl oz boiling water
450 g/1 lb potatoes
225 g/8 oz date jam
oil for deep frying
CARAMEL
250 ml/8 fl oz water
225 g/8 oz sugar

Sift the rice flour into a mixing bowl, then pour in the boiling water, stirring all the time.

Cook the potatoes in boiling water until tender, then drain them thoroughly and mash them until quite smooth. Mix the mashed potatoes into the rice flour mixture until smooth.

Take a small portion of the dough and flatten it in the palm of your hand. Place a little of the date jam in the middle and twist the dough around it to enclose the filling completely in a droplet shape. Continue shaping the spirals until all the dough is used.

Heat the oil for deep frying to 190 C/375 F. Deep fry the spirals until golden brown, then drain them on absorbent kitchen paper. Continue until all the spirals are fried.

Meanwhile, put the sugar and water for the caramel in a saucepan and heat slowly, stirring all the time, until the sugar has dissolved. Bring to the boil and boil hard until the syrup turns a pale golden colour.

Dip the spirals in the caramel and allow all the excess to drain, then place them on a greased plate until crisp. Serve warm. *Makes about 40*

Sweet Dishes

Deep Fried Sesame Balls

275 g/10 oz glutinous rice flour
250 ml/8 fl oz water
125 g/4½ oz sugar
sesame seeds for coating

Sift the rice flour into a bowl and make a well in the middle. Pour in the water and add the sugar. Stir until the sugar has dissolved, then work in the rice flour to make a dough. Knead until smooth.

Roll the dough into a cylinder shape and cut it into 40 equal portions. Roll each of these into a ball and coat thoroughly with sesame seeds, pressing them on well.

Heat the oil for deep frying to 190 c/375 f. Deep fry the sesame balls until golden brown. Use a fish slice, or draining spoon, to press the balls slightly during cooking so that they puff up.

Drain the sesame balls on absorbent kitchen paper and serve them either warm or cold. *Makes 40*

Note: Ordinary rice flour can be used in the above recipe; add the liquid carefully until a workable consistency is obtained. The quantity of water required should be the same as for glutinous rice flour.

Glutinous Rice Balls in Syrup

275 g/10 oz glutinous rice flour
or ordinary rice flour
175 ml/6 fl oz cold water
50 g/2 oz cornflour
50 ml/2 fl oz boiling water
50 g/2 oz lard
40 g/1½ oz sugar
250 ml/8 fl oz golden syrup
100 g/4 oz roasted peanuts,
* roughly chopped*
a few glacé cherries for
* decoration*

Sift 225 g/8 oz of the rice flour into a large bowl and make a well in the middle. Pour in the cold water and mix it in thoroughly to make a soft dough.

Sift the cornflour into a bowl and pour in the boiling water, stirring all the time to make a soft dough.

Press both doughs together and knead them thoroughly until smooth and well combined. Cut the dough in half and divide one portion into eight small pieces. Bring a large pan of water to the boil, then cook the small balls of dough for 10 minutes.

Drain these and knead them with the large piece of uncooked dough, the remaining 50 g/2 oz rice flour, lard and sugar.

Cut the resulting dough into 40 small pieces and roll these into balls. Bring a large saucepan of water to the boil and cook the balls of dough for 3 minutes. Drain thoroughly and transfer to a serving bowl.

Pour the syrup over the balls and sprinkle the nuts on top. Decorate each glutinous ball with a slice of cherry and serve. *Makes 40*

Note: Ordinary rice flour can be used for this recipe but both quantities of water must be reduced: use 150 ml/¼ pint cold water and 3 tablespoons boiling water.

Ma Chai

DOUGH
350 g/12 oz strong white flour
2 teaspoons baking powder
2 tablespoons oil
4 eggs, beaten
oil for deep frying
SYRUP
175 ml/6 fl oz water
350 g/12 oz sugar
175 g/6 oz honey
2 slices lemon
75 g/3 oz desiccated coconut
DECORATION
100 g/4 oz walnut pieces

To make the dough, sift the flour into a bowl with the baking powder and make a well in the middle. Pour the oil into the well and stir in the eggs. Gradually mix in the flour to make a dough, then knead until smooth and soft.

Cut the dough into quarters and roll each piece out quite thinly. Cut the rolled-out dough into short strips. Heat the oil for deep frying to 190 c/375 f. Add the strips and fry until golden brown, then drain them on absorbent kitchen paper and set aside.

To make the syrup, put the water into a saucepan and bring to the boil. Add the sugar and honey and stir until dissolved. Add the lemon, then simmer until enough water has evaporated to make the syrup thick.

Put the deep fried strips into a large bowl and pour in the syrup. Grease a large, oblong tin or roasting tin and coat it thickly with coconut. Press the syrup-coated strips into the tin and press them under a heavy weight. Leave until quite cold.

Decorate the top with walnuts and cut the mixture into squares before serving. *Makes 24*

Glutinous Balls with Sweet Paste

225 g/8 oz glutinous rice flour or ordinary rice flour
175 ml/6 fl oz cold water
50 g/2 oz cornflour
50–75 ml/2–3 fl oz boiling water
2 tablespoons oil
2 tablespoons sugar
FILLING
175 g/6 oz sweet red bean paste
about 75 g/3 oz desiccated coconut for coating

Sift the rice flour into a large bowl and make a well in the middle. Pour the cold water into the middle, then gradually work in the rice flour to make a dough and knead thoroughly until smooth.

Sift the cornflour into a bowl, then pour in the boiling water, stirring rapidly all the time. Add the oil and sugar and knead the dough thoroughly. Press the two doughs together and knead them until they are thoroughly combined.

Cut the dough in half, then place one portion in a steamer and cook it over boiling water for 10 minutes. Remove the hot dough and knead it into the other uncooked portion until smooth.

For the filling, shape the sweet red bean paste into 32 small balls. Cut the dough into 32 equal portions. Flatten one of these and put a ball of sweet paste in the middle. Fold the dough around the paste and roll it between your palms until quite smooth. Continue until all the dough is filled and shaped.

Roll all the balls in coconut, making sure they are well coated. Arrange the balls on a serving plate. *Makes 32*

Chicken Stock

450 g/1 lb boiling bacon
450 g/1 lb lean boneless pork
450 g/1 lb pork bones
1 boiling chicken

Cut the bacon and pork into large chunks and place them in a large saucepan with the bones. Pour in water to cover and bring to the boil. Reduce the heat, then simmer for 10 minutes. Drain and rinse the meat and bones under cold water.

Pull the skin off the chicken, then place the bird in the pan and pour in water to cover, then bring to the boil and simmer for 5 minutes. Drain, then rinse the chicken under cold water. This process of pre-boiling and rinsing the chicken will remove any excess fat.

Put the bacon, pork, bones and chicken in the rinsed-out saucepan and pour in enough water to cover. Bring to the boil, then reduce the heat and cover the pan. Simmer gently for 4 hours.

Allow the stock to cool slightly, then strain it to remove the meat and bones. When the stock is cold, pour it into a large bowl and chill it thoroughly. The fat will rise to the surface and set in a layer; this can be skimmed off easily with a palette knife or spatula.

The stock can be reduced further by rapid boiling. It may be frozen in this concentrated form. Remember to add water before using it.

The drained chicken and meat can be returned to the saucepan and more water added for a second boiling. This should be simmered for a further 4 hours and the stock strained. This stock will be lightly flavoured.

Vegetarian Broth

225 g/8 oz dried straw mushrooms
7 teaspoons oil
100 g/4 oz dried mushroom stalks or mushrooms
1 medium-thick slice fresh root ginger
450 g/1 lb soya bean sprouts (sprouted soya beans)
1 teaspoon dry sherry
1.75 litres/3 pints water
225 g/8 oz carrots, sliced
salt

Wash the straw mushrooms, then soak them in cold water to cover for 15 minutes. Squeeze all the excess water from the soaked mushrooms and sprinkle 1 teaspoon oil over them. Set aside for 15 minutes. Soak the mushroom stalks until softened.

Heat the remaining oil in a heavy-based saucepan. Add the ginger and fry until fragrant, then add the bean sprouts and fry thoroughly. Pour in the sherry and the water. Add the carrots, straw mushrooms and drained mushroom stalks.

Bring to the boil, then reduce the heat and simmer for 1 hour. Allow the stock to cool slightly, then strain it through a fine sieve and press all the liquid out of the ingredients. Add seasoning to the stock and use as required.

Fishballs

Fishballs

1 kg/2 lb mackerel, gutted
25 g/1 oz pork fat (optional)
2 teaspoons cornflour
1 teaspoon salt
¼ teaspoon pepper
4–6 tablespoons water

Ask the fishmonger to fillet the fish. Scrape all the fish off the skin.

Blanch the pork fat (if used) in boiling water for 2 minutes, then drain and dice it. Add this to the fish and mix thoroughly.

Blend the cornflour with the salt, pepper and water to make a smooth paste. Add a little of this to the fish and pound the mixture thoroughly. Add a little more paste and pound the mixture again. Continue to add the paste in small quantities and pound the mixture until all the ingredients are incorporated to give a firm, elastic mixture.

Heat the oil for deep frying to 190 c/375 F. Make sure that your hands are clean, then take a handful of the fish mixture in the palm of your left hand and close your fist. Squeeze your fist shut to extrude some of the fish mixture and form a ball. Scoop this from your hand with a small spoon and drop the fishball into the hot oil.

Continue shaping and frying the fishballs in this way until all the mixture is used, but do not put too many in the oil at once. Cook until browned, then drain on absorbent kitchen paper and use as required. *Serves 6–8*

Gluten Balls

Deep Fried Gluten Balls

1 kg/2 lb strong white flour
600 ml/1 pint water
5 teaspoons baking powder

Sift the flour into a large bowl, then make a well in the middle and pour in the water. Gradually work in the flour, then knead the mixture thoroughly to make a soft dough. Set aside for 20–30 minutes.

Knead the dough for about 45 minutes, until it is smooth and very elastic. This kneading is necessary to develop the gluten in the flour.

Place the dough in a large clean bowl and pour in cold water to cover. Wash the dough with your hands to remove any excess flour, then rinse it thoroughly under clean water. Drain thoroughly.

Knead the baking powder into the dough, folding it over to make sure it is all worked in. Set aside for 6–8 hours to prove.

Cut the dough into 80 equal portions. Heat the oil for deep frying to 190 c/375 f, then fry the pieces of gluten a few at a time until they puff up to several times their original size. Drain on absorbent kitchen paper and use as required.

Gluten Balls

1 kg/2 lb strong white flour
600 ml/1 pint water
2 tablespoons salt

Sift the flour into a large bowl and make a well in the middle. Pour in the water. Gradually work the flour into the water to make a soft dough. Turn out on to a clean surface and knead to make a smooth dough. Set aside in a covered bowl for 30 minutes.

Turn the dough out on to a floured surface and knead it again for 1 hour, until it becomes very elastic. Put the dough in a large bowl of water and wash it thoroughly to remove all the excess flour. Change the water and wash the dough for a second time. Rinse the dough, which should end up firm and clean. Knead it lightly, then cut it into small walnut-sized balls.

Bring a large saucepan of water to the boil and add the salt. Add the gluten balls and boil for a few minutes, then drain and use as required. The gluten balls can be stored in the refrigerator for a few days.

Cha Shiu

1 kg/2 lb pork shoulder
4 shallots, grated
4 cloves garlic, crushed
1 teaspoon Spicy Salt (page 229)
50 g/2 oz sugar
2 tablespoons sherry
3 tablespoons ground bean paste
3 teaspoons sweet paste
5 teaspoons sesame paste
100 ml/4 fl oz light soy sauce
1 teaspoon sesame oil
a little red food colouring
50 ml/2 fl oz water
50 g/2 oz honey

Cut the pork shoulder into four thick strips. Cut a criss-cross pattern on both the rind and the meat.

Mix the shallots and garlic with the spicy salt, sugar, sherry, ground bean paste, sweet paste, sesame paste, light soy sauce, sesame oil and a little red food colouring. Make sure the colour is a true red and not pink. Spread this mixture over the pieces of meat and set aside to marinate for 1 hour, turning the pieces of meat every 15 minutes.

Arrange the marinated pork on a roasting rack over a roasting tin. Cook in a hot oven (230 c, 450 f, gas 8) for 15 minutes.

Meanwhile, bring the water to the boil, then pour in the honey and simmer until the liquid is syrupy.

Brush the pork all over with the honey syrup and replace the meat in the oven for a further 10 minutes. Coat with more of the honey syrup and cook for a final 5–10 minutes.

Serve the pork cut into slices either hot or cold. Alternatively the pork may be required for a particular recipe. *Serves 6–8*

Salted Eggs

Salted Eggs

24 duck or chicken eggs
4 star anise
4 tea bags
1.15 litres/2 pints water
225 g/8 oz sea salt
50 g/2 oz sugar
50 ml/2 fl oz sherry or brandy

Wash the eggs and dry them with a clean tea-towel. Take care not to break them.

Put the star anise and tea bags in a large saucepan with the water. Bring to the boil, then simmer for 10 minutes. Add the salt and sugar, stir until these ingredients have dissolved, then remove the pan from the heat and add the sherry or brandy. Allow to cool completely. Strain the cooled solution.

Carefully place the eggs in large preserving jars, then pour in salt solution to cover them completely. Cover with airtight lids and leave to soak for 30–35 days.

The eggs should be boiled or steamed, then served with rice. Alternatively, they may be required for a particular recipe.

Note: It is most important that the eggs are very fresh if they are to be preserved in this way. Buy them from a farm shop if you can and make sure that they are very clean before they are put into the jars. Also shown in the basket in the picture are dark-coloured thousand year eggs. These can be purchased from Chinese supermarkets.

Pickled Ginger

Pickled Ginger

450 g/1 lb young root ginger
75 g/3 oz salt
600 ml/1 pint white vinegar
450–575 g/1–1¼ lb sugar

When young and at its best, root ginger should have a pale smooth skin. The pieces should be plump and firm – not at all wrinkled or shrivelled. The skin should be thin and when it is peeled off the young ginger should be tender, not fibrous, moist and almost translucent when thinly sliced.

Unfortunately, most ginger sold in greengrocers and supermarkets is fibrous and quite old. The best place to find good ginger is in ethnic markets or busy shops.

Soak the ginger in cold water for 30 minutes, then drain and peel it. Cut the root into thick slices, then place these in a bowl and sprinkle the salt over. Leave for 2 hours, then thoroughly rinse the ginger to remove all the salt, squeezing the pieces as you do so. Dry the ginger on absorbent kitchen paper or in a clean tea-towel.

Pour the vinegar into a saucepan and add the sugar, then bring to the boil, stirring to dissolve the sugar. When the liquid has boiled and all the sugar has dissolved, set it aside to cool.

Put the ginger into jars and pour in the cool vinegar to cover the slices completely. Allow to mature for a few days, then the ginger can be cut into small pieces and served to precede a meal or used in recipes, as required.

Ginger Juice

Ginger Juice

1.75 kg/4 lb fresh root ginger

Thoroughly wash the ginger, then soak it in cold water for 30 minutes.

Thinly peel or scrape the ginger. Cut it into small pieces and process these in a juice extractor to obtain ginger juice.

Alternatively, the ginger can be ground in a liquidiser until it is very fine, or put through a food processor. Squeeze out all the juice, then discard the squeezed-out ginger.

For a weaker ginger juice, the remaining ginger can be soaked in water and squeezed out.

The ginger juice can be stored in an airtight container in the refrigerator for up to two weeks, or it can be frozen for a few months. If the ginger juice is poured into an ice tray, then it will form cubes which can be removed easily when they are required.

Bean Sprouts

Various beans and pulses can be sprouted but mung beans are the most common and are the type which are sold as bean sprouts.

Wash the mung beans, then soak them in cold water for 6–8 hours. Drain the beans and rinse them under cold water. Place them in a large, clean, shallow container and cover with wet muslin. Set aside in a dark place.

Sweet and Sour Sauce

Rinse and drain the bean sprouts four or five times a day, leaving them covered with the rinsed out muslin to keep them moist but not too wet.

It is important that the bean sprouts are washed regularly to clean away any bacteria which may collect round them.

The sprouts will be ready for use in three or four days. They should be washed and some of the loose green shells should be cleaned away.

Sweet and Sour Sauce

450 ml/¾ pint white vinegar
225 g/8 oz brown sugar
100 ml/4 fl oz tomato ketchup
1 tablespoon Worcestershire sauce
¼ teaspoon monosodium glutamate
pinch of salt
a little red food colouring

Pour the vinegar into a large saucepan and add the sugar. Bring to the boil over low heat, stirring to dissolve the sugar. Add the tomato ketchup and Worcestershire sauce, monosodium glutamate, salt and red food colouring. (Make sure that the colour which you use is a true red and not pink.) Simmer the sauce for a few minutes, then leave it to cool.

When the sauce is cold it can be strained into airtight jars and stored for later use. The required quantity should be heated to boiling point, then thickened with a little cornflour blended with water.

Satay Paste

Red Chilli Oil

Satay Paste

100 g/4 oz shallots
50 g/2 oz garlic cloves
25 g/1 oz fresh root ginger
1–2 tablespoons chilli powder
2 teaspoons ground coriander
1 tablespoon cold water
1 tablespoon sugar
1 teaspoon salt
½ teaspoon monosodium glutamate
1½ tablespoons light soy sauce
50 g/2 oz peanut butter
600 ml/1 pint coconut milk
50 ml/2 fl oz boiling water
225 g/8 oz roasted peanuts, ground

Peel and mince the shallots, garlic cloves and ginger. If you have a food processor, then use it to purée these ingredients.

Mix the chilli powder and ground coriander with the 1 tablespoon water.

Heat the oil in a wok or heavy-based saucepan. Add the minced shallot mixture and cook until fragrant. Stir in the chilli and coriander paste and mix thoroughly.

Stir in the sugar, salt, monosodium glutamate and light soy sauce. Add the peanut butter and fry for a while, then pour in the coconut milk and bring to the boil. Simmer until the oil floats to the top of the sauce. Pour in the boiling water and mix thoroughly.

Lastly, sprinkle in the ground peanuts and stir until all the ingredients are evenly mixed. Heat for a few minutes, then serve as required.

Chilli Oil

225 g/8 oz fresh red chillies
4 shallots
4 cloves garlic
450–600 ml/¾–1 pint corn oil

Cut the stalk ends off the chillies, then slit the shells and remove all the seeds from inside. Rinse each chilli to wash away any remaining seeds, then dry them all on absorbent kitchen paper. Mince the prepared chillies, or chop them very finely in a food processor or liquidiser.

Peel and mince the shallots and garlic cloves. These can also be puréed in a food processor or liquidiser if you prefer.

Heat the oil in a large saucepan or pan used for deep frying. Add the shallots and garlic and cook until fragrant. Do not allow the oil to become too hot at any stage of the cooking.

Add the chillies to the oil and fry for a few minutes until the oil changes colour. Remove from the heat and leave to cool.

Strain the cold oil through a fine sieve and store it in a bottle for use as required.

Note: Fresh red chillies produce a red chilli oil. To make black chilli oil, allow 225 g/8 oz each of dried chillies and garlic cloves to 1.15 litres/2 pints oil. Fry the ingredients until brown in the oil, then remove them and pound or grind them to a paste. Pour the cooled oil on to the paste and store for a few days before use.

Spicy Salt

Fermented Black Bean Paste

Garlic Chilli Paste

100 g/4 oz red chillies
75 g/3 oz garlic cloves
250 ml/8 fl oz oil
175 g/6 oz ground bean paste
50 g/2 oz sugar
½ teaspoon monosodium glutamate

Cut the stalk ends off the chillies, slit the green part and scrape out all the seeds. Rinse each chilli to remove any remaining seeds and dry them all on absorbent kitchen paper. Dice the chillies and set aside. Peel the garlic cloves and mince or blend them in a food processor.

Heat the oil in a wok or heavy-based saucepan. Add the garlic and fry until it is fragrant. Stir in the chillies and cook for a while, then add the bean paste, sugar and monosodium glutamate. Stir until thoroughly mixed and cook for 1 minute. Remove from the heat and allow to cool.

This paste is generally served as a dip to accompany certain dishes and it goes particularly well with Chinese noodles.

Fermented Black Bean Paste

450 g/1 lb fermented black beans
25 g/1 oz garlic cloves
1 medium-thick slice fresh root ginger
50 g/2 oz sugar
50 ml/2 fl oz oil

Wash and drain the black beans, then mince them to make a paste. A liquidiser or food processor is ideal for reducing the beans to a purée.

Peel the garlic cloves, then mince or process them to a purée. Mince or finely grate the ginger, and mix it into the black bean paste with the garlic purée.

Pound the paste thoroughly to make sure all the ingredients are combined, then stir in the sugar and oil. Put the paste in a heatproof bowl and steam it over boiling water for 10 minutes.

Allow the cooked paste to cool completely, then transfer it to airtight jars and store for use as required. The paste will keep in the refrigerator for a few months.

Spicy Salt

450 g/1 lb salt
100 g/4 oz five spice powder

Heat a wok or heavy-based frying pan over low heat. Pour in the salt and cook for a while. Stir in the five spice powder and mix thoroughly, then set aside to cool. Store in airtight jars when quite cold. Use as required.

Cooking Utensils

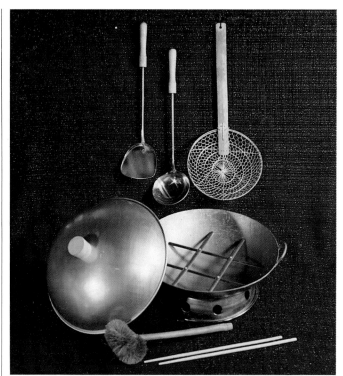

A Chinese wok with steaming rack

Bamboo steamers

Over many thousands of years Chinese cooking equipment has been designed for efficiency and maximum usefulness. The best-known and commonly used cooking pan is the *wok* which is also the most versatile of cooking vessels. For many recipes, *bamboo steamers* are used and for other dishes *earthenware casseroles* are the best pots. Specific cooking techniques may require specialist utensils and the *Mongolian fire pot* is one such piece of equipment. The use of this pot is explained on page 126.

For the preparation of food, a *Chinese cleaver* and *block* is the most effective, but not essential, pair of utensils. Used in the preparation of dishes as well as for eating, *chopsticks* are fun to use if you can tackle them. In addition, *strainers*, *ladles* and *spatulas* feature as common cooking equipment.

As well as this collection of standard Chinese kitchen utensils, special equipment is used for the preparation of bean curd, rice sheets and dim sum. Moulds, strainers and a type of pastry press form part of this group.

Do not let the thought of using unusual equipment put you off Chinese cooking because you do not have to buy any special equipment. However, the following pieces of equipment are those which you are most likely to find useful if you intend investing in any specialist items.

Woks Traditionally made of cast iron, or thin carbon steel, woks are now available in stainless steel, with a non-stick coating or in the form of an independent electric work-top appliance. The cheapest and most effective cooking pan is the carbon steel type. Curved woks are available in different sizes, with different types of handles. They often come complete with a metal stand on which to rest the pan over either a gas or electric hob.

A well-seasoned, traditional wok has a blackened surface. To

clean a carbon steel wok, simply scour it with salt and oil then wipe it out several times with absorbent kitchen paper. A steel wok should rarely be washed. Make sure the surface is always thoroughly oiled to prevent rusting and store the pan in a dry place.

Bamboo Steamers These are designed to sit in the wok, over water in the curved base. They vary in diameter and can be stacked to provide several cooking layers, topped with a bamboo lid. A conventional steamer can be used instead, or the dish of food to be steamed can be rested on an upturned heatproof dish in the base of a large saucepan. Water can be poured in up as far as the base of the dish of food and a close-fitting lid must be placed on the saucepan to keep in the steam.

Earthenware Casseroles These are used quite extensively in Chinese cooking. They can be plain or highly decorated earthenware, with a lid and handle. Any heavy-based flameproof casserole can be substituted if necessary.

Chinese Cleaver (Chopper) and Block For shredding, chopping, slicing and even mincing foods, the Chinese cook uses a heavy, very sharp metal cleaver and a firm, thick, wooden block. Once you master the art of using a cleaver you will probably find that it provides the most effective means of cutting food evenly. However, a good sharp knife and chopping board is quite adequate.

Strainers Used for straining boiled or deep fried foods strainers made of a fine metal mesh usually have long handles. The strainer can be quite small to use for a Mongolian fire pot meal or big enough to remove large items of food from a cooking pan.

A selection of Chinese casseroles

Chopsticks As well as using chopsticks at the table, the Chinese use long chopsticks to turn and move food during cooking. Once you tackle the knack of handling chopsticks you may well find that you prefer eating Chinese food with them rather than with a fork. There are many different ways to use chopsticks but these instructions for holding and manipulating them will give you a starting point from which to perfect the technique.

1 Hold one chopstick in your hand, cushioning the thick end in the curve of flesh between the thumb and forefinger. Let the other end of the chopstick rest on your little finger. Keep this chopstick firm and still.

2 Close your thumb over the chopstick which you are holding to keep it firmly in place. Hold the thick end of the second chopstick parallel to the first one, about 5 mm/¼ inch away from it. Hold this firmly between the end of your thumb and the upper part of your forefinger.

3 Support the second chopstick with your middle finger, to keep it in line with the first chopstick and to facilitate even, controlled movement.

4 Move the second chopstick towards the first one to close the gap between their tips. Keep the ends of the chopsticks level at all times. Tap them vertically on the table to keep them together.

5 Grasp small items of food between the chopsticks, using the mobile one to hold the piece of food, then lift it up.

6 The chopsticks can also be used in a shovelling motion, to pick up several items of food at once. For this technique lift the bowl of food nearer to your mouth to prevent any spillages.

Remember, there is no strict rule about how to hold chopsticks, so practise frequently and develop your own comfortable – and successful – technique.

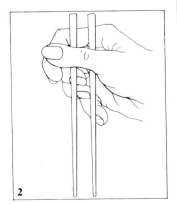

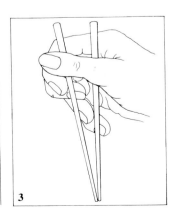

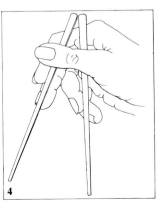

Menus

To Serve Two

Chinese Tea
Beancurd Chop Suey Chowder
Broccoli with Sliced Pork
Sesame Chicken
Plain Steamed Rice

To Serve Four

Chicken and Sweet Corn Chowder
Chicken Wings in Cha Shiu Sauce
Steamed Snapper
Beef fillet with Bean Sprouts
Plain Steamed Rice

To Serve Six

Hot and Sour Soup
Steamed Fish in Blackbean Sauce
Ham in Chinese Cabbage
Poached Chicken
Double Cooked Pork
Fried Rice with Minced Beef

To Serve Eight

Minced Beef Chowder
Szechuen Prawns
Fried Rice Yang Chow
Sautéed Chicken in Preserved Blackbean Sauce
Sautéed Fish with Green Vegetables
Bean Sprouts with Shredded Roast Duck
Duck's Bone and Melon Soup
Peking Duck

To Serve Twelve

Assorted Meat Combination
Sautéed Scallops with Celery
Mushrooms in Oyster Sauce
Dried Scallop Chowder
Salted Baked Chicken Wings
Abalone in Oyster Sauce
Steamed Fish in Soy Sauce
Coconut Consommé
Rice with Red and White Sauce
Noodles with Mushrooms
Glutinous Rice Balls in Sweet Soup
Sweet Paste Buns

Glossary

Abalone This is a shellfish with an oval to round shaped shell which has a pearly lining. The white flesh is tough so it requires thorough beating in order to become tender. Found off the coast of Brittany and the Channel Islands but fished mainly in the warm waters off California, abalone is available canned or dried. The canned type is best as the dried variety needs lengthy soaking for up to several days.

Agar Agar Produced from a red seaweed, this is a very strong setting agent which is similar to gelatine. Agar agar is sold in the form of sheets or thin very light blocks which must be soaked in cold water until soft – about 30 minutes – then simmered in boiling water until dissolved. This is a stronger setting agent than gelatine so it is used in smaller quantities. It sets without being chilled, so it is particularly well suited to hot climates. Available from health food shops and oriental supermarkets.

Bamboo Leaves Narrow, long and fairly thick, these leaves are used to wrap foods before cooking. They can be used to make a waterproof package for small amounts of foods which are to be steamed. Obtainable only from oriental supermarkets, and some ethnic greengrocers, these leaves can be replaced by other suitable wrapping materials, like greaseproof paper or cooking foil.

Bamboo Shoots These are the creamy-coloured shoots of the bamboo plant. They are sold fresh in Chinese supermarkets but are most commonly found canned in water or brine. The fresh shoots must be thickly peeled, then cooked in boiling water until tender. The canned shoots are quite acceptable and they can be stored in fresh water in a covered container in the refrigerator for 1–2 weeks. Change water daily.

Bean Curd Also known as *tofu*, this white curd has a texture similar to a firmly set custard. Prepared from soya beans, the bean curd is bland and it readily absorbs the flavour of other foods; it is also highly nutritious. Sliced or cut into pieces the bean curd can be included in soups, stir-fries or braised dishes. It can also be deep fried until golden before adding to some dishes, or mashed and included as a stuffing ingredient for other recipes. Available from Chinese supermarkets, health food shops and some supermarkets.

Bean Curd, fermented or fermented red Fresh bean curd which is allowed to produce a mould and ferment to encourage a vague wine-like flavour. The fermented curd is cut into cubes and stored in jars. Covered with brine, tightly sealed, the fermented bean curd can be stored for months for use in small quantities as required. Available in cans or jars from Chinese supermarkets.

Bean Curd Sheets Produced from thick bean curd milk and dried to make thin, stiff, sheets which are yellow-cream in colour with a shiny surface. The sheets have to be soaked before use, then cooked to make wrappers for vegetarian dishes or spring rolls which can be deep fried or steamed. Available from Chinese supermarkets; but a very thin omelette can be substituted.

Bean Thread or Mung Bean Thread These are very fine translucent noodles made from mung beans and they are sold wrapped in bundles. After soaking in cold water for a while they become soft and transparent, and are then cooked with other ingredients which have distinct or strong tastes, in dishes with plenty of liquid or sauce. The bean thread absorbs a great deal of liquid and flavour during cooking. Available from oriental supermarkets, the dry bean thread can be stored in a cool dry place for a few months.

Blachan This is a pungent Malaysian paste prepared from dried shrimps, ground to make a thick, dark, strongly flavoured sauce which is used in small quantities. Packed in jars and sold in Indian or Chinese shops or some delicatessens. It is used in Malaysian curries.

Black Beans Small, oval-shaped, dried black soya beans about the size of small peas. They are available from oriental supermarkets or some ethnic shops and they can be stored in an airtight container in a cool, dry place for several months. Before lengthy simmering in plenty of water, the beans must be washed and soaked for several hours, then drained and rinsed.

Black Beans, fermented Sold in cans, jars or plastic vacuum packs, these are preserved and salted black soya beans. They have a very strong, salty taste so they are used in small quantities as a seasoning ingredient. Available from Chinese or Indian supermarkets, delicatessens and some health food shops.

Black Bean Paste A strong pungent paste prepared from fermented black soya beans, used as a seasoning.

Black Moss Dried, fine, black, hair-like shreds, sold in small blocks or packets. Used in very small quantities and soaked before use, black moss is available only from Chinese supermarkets but it is not an essential ingredient.

Black Fungus Also known as *cloud ears*. About the size of large mushrooms, the pieces of fungus are flat or slightly curved in the middle with wavy edges. Black on one side and grey on the other side, black fungus resembles dried mushrooms in colour. The fungus has to be soaked until soft first, then trimmed and shredded or cut up and cooked as required. Available from Chinese supermarkets,

Glossary

the dried product will keep well in an airtight container in a cool, dry place for several months.

Broad Bean Paste A hot and thick, spicy paste available from oriental supermarkets. Brown bean paste prepared from soya beans, mixed with ground chillies can be substituted.

Chinese Broccoli Dark green, with very long stalks and several small florets, Chinese broccoli resembles home-grown broccoli. The broccoli sold in most greengrocers and supermarkets can be substituted.

Chinese Cabbage This vegetable resembles Swiss chard; it has long white stalks with dark green leaves formed in a loose plant. The vegetable sold in many supermarkets as Chinese cabbage is the tall, pale green vegetable with tightly packed, slightly curly leaves. This is also known as celery cabbage or Chinese lettuce and it can be eaten raw in salads as well as cooked. Swiss chard is the best substitute for true Chinese cabbage.

Chinese Dried Sausages These are known as *wind dried sausages*. They are thin, slightly wrinkled and quite dark red or brown in colour, made from pork or liver. Slightly sweet and spicy, the sausages are usually steamed on their own or with rice, then sliced to be eaten with the rice or to be included in stir-fries. Available from oriental supermarkets.

Coconut Milk Coconut milk is prepared from the grated fresh coconut flesh which is soaked in water then squeezed out. The liquid is thick coconut milk, if the squeezed-out coconut is soaked again, then the second batch of liquid is thin coconut milk. Coconut milk is also sold canned, or in a concentrated

form in small blocks to be dissolved in hot water. Desiccated coconut can also be soaked in hot water, then squeezed out to make coconut milk.

Cuttlefish Similar to squid but with a larger head and wider, bigger body, cuttlefish is more tender than squid. It is prepared in the same way as squid and can be replaced by this.

Dried Chinese Mushrooms Dark brown and quite large, dried Chinese mushrooms have rough stems. The mushrooms must be soaked in water until soft, then the stems can be removed if they are still tough. The soaked mushrooms *must* be marinated with salt, sugar and oil, cooked in a steamer, then sliced, chopped or left whole and cooked in stir-fries or braised dishes. These mushrooms have a meaty texture and a distinct flavour. They are available only from oriental supermarkets.

Dried Scallops The white scallop flesh is dried to give small, round, pink-brown coloured dried scallops. These are sold in oriental supermarkets and they are quite expensive, so canned scallops can be substituted.

Dried Shrimps Very small pink-brown dried shrimps are sold in packets in Chinese or Indian shops. They must be washed, then soaked until soft before use. They have a strong flavour so they are used in comparatively small quantities. They will keep for several months packed in an airtight container in a cool, dry place.

Dried Squid Available from Chinese and Indian supermarkets, whole dried squid require fairly lengthy soaking to soften them before cooking. They are then cut up to be included in braised, steamed and stir-fried dishes.

Dried Tangerine Peel Sold in shreds or small squares, the dark brown peel is sold in airtight packets in Chinese and Indian supermarkets. The peel will keep in an airtight container in a cool, dry place for several months. Before use, the pieces must be soaked to soften them.

Five Spice Powder A dark powder made from five different ground spices: star anise, anise pepper, fennel, cloves and cinnamon. Available from oriental stores and delicatessens.

Ginger, fresh root The knobbly ginger root has a smooth beige-brown coloured skin which varies slightly in thickness. Young root ginger has a light, thin skin and smooth, quite juicy, tender flesh. The older more common ginger has a fairly thick skin and slightly fibrous flesh. The root should not be wrinkled even if it is older. Available from greengrocers and supermarkets or Chinese and Indian shops, the ginger can be stored in a plastic bag in the refrigerator for several weeks (check to make sure that any cut ends do not develop a mould) or in a pot of sand. The root can be grated without being peeled or it can be peeled then thinly sliced and cut into fine shreds.

Ginger Juice This is juice which is extracted from fresh root ginger, the recipe is on page 227.

Ginkgo Nuts Small white nuts from the ginkgo tree. They have tough, beige-coloured shells which have to be broken with a strong nut cracker. The nuts are blanched by soaking them in boiling water for 5–10 minutes, then the skins can be removed. They can be purchased fresh or ready prepared in cans from oriental supermarkets. The nuts can be used in sweet soups and congees or other moist dishes.

Glutinous Rice This is a short-grain, opaque pearly-white rice which becomes sticky when cooked. Available from oriental shops, the rice must be washed before use in soup and for making pastries, puddings and dumplings.

Glutinous Rice Flour This is rice flour prepared from glutinous rice. Available from Chinese supermarkets, this rice flour is used for doughs and dumplings, ordinary rice flour can be substituted.

Hoisin Sauce A thick dark brown sauce prepared from soya beans, dried prunes and garlic to give a sweet and spicy result. Used as a seasoning or condiment, this is sweet not hot. Available in jars or cans from Chinese supermarkets or delicatessens and good supermarkets.

Hot Oil Oil flavoured with chillies either fresh or dried. Recipe page 228.

Lemon Grass Similar in appearance to a spring onion, but with reed-like stalks, lemon grass smells and tastes of lemon. Available from good greengrocers or supermarkets and Chinese or Indian shops.

Longan Berries These are a cherry-sized fruit which are available pitted and dried at which stage they resemble large raisins. They have a slightly sweet, delicate yet distinct taste which is slightly unusual.

Lotus Leaves Large, fan-shaped leaves of the water lily, these are very thin and delicate. Used to wrap food before cooking. Available from Chinese supermarkets.

Lotus Root A large potato-like root of the water lily with holes in the flesh. Although the fresh root can be found occasionally in some Chinese supermarkets, lotus root is most commonly available canned or dried in slices. The dried variety requires soaking before it is cooked.

Lotus Seeds Small seeds with a fresh taste, available dried or canned from oriental supermarkets.

Lychees Fresh lychees have a red, knobbly shell which covers the translucent white flesh. Inside there is a large shiny stone. They can be found occasionally in good greengrocers, otherwise the fruit is widely available canned in syrup.

Monosodium Glutamate (MSG) This is a chemical substance which lightens the flavour of savoury foods and acts as a tenderising agent. Used in small quantities, this is an optional ingredient. Available from ethnic shops, some delicatessens and supermarkets.

Mustard Cabbage A dark green vegetable, similar both in size and texture to a small cabbage but with a cool and bitter taste. Available in cans (or sometimes fresh) from oriental shops.

Oyster Sauce A concentrated sauce prepared from oysters, soy sauce and brine, this is a brown liquid which intensifies the flavour of other foods. Easily available in jars and bottles from good supermarkets, delicatessens or oriental shops.

Preserved Mustard Cabbage Available in cans, jars or packets from oriental stores, this is a highly seasoned ingredient normally used in small quantities.

Preserved Turnip or Preserved Vegetables Available in jars, cans or earthenware pots from oriental stores.

Red Bean Paste A sweet paste or purée of red beans, available in cans and jars from oriental supermarkets.

Rice Vermicelli Thin, fine noodles available from oriental stores. Ordinary vermicelli can be substituted if necessary.

Sesame Oil A nutty-flavoured oil which can vary in flavour depending on how refined it is. The very dark sesame oil can be quite overpowering in flavour. Available from health food shops, delicatessens and supermarkets as well as oriental stores.

Soy Sauce This is an essential ingredient in Chinese cookery. Either dark or light, this flavouring ingredient is prepared from soya beans. The dark variety contains caramel and has a stronger flavour than the light soy sauce which is more delicate. Both types are available from supermarkets and delicatessens as well as oriental stores.

Spring Roll Pastry A very fine pastry which is used as a wrapping for spring rolls. Available in large and small squares, frozen or fresh from Indian and Chinese supermarkets. Very thin, partly cooked pancakes or omelettes can be substituted.

Star Anise A star-shaped spice which encloses the distinctly flavoured aniseeds. Used whole, quite sparingly as it

has a strong flavour, this spice is available from Indian and Chinese supermarkets.

Straw Mushrooms Small droplet-shaped mushrooms with a dark top which becomes paler at the droplet end. These mushrooms have a slightly gelatinous texture. Available canned from oriental supermarkets.

Sweet Paste Unless an alternative is offered, this is a name used for hoisin sauce or paste.

Water Chestnuts Available canned from supermarkets as well as specialist shops, these are small, round and white with a crunchy texture. Used sliced or chopped. A dry, ground water chestnut flour is also available from Chinese supermarkets and this is used in the preparation of sweet dishes.

Whole Baby Sweet Corn Immature cobs of corn about 3.5–7.5 cm/1½–3 inches in length. Sold in cans which can be found in supermarkets as well as specialist shops.

Winter Melon A very large, dark green, tough-skinned melon, available only from oriental shops. Marrow can be used instead.

Yellow Bean Paste Also known as brown bean paste or ground bean paste. A salty brown paste prepared from soya beans, this is used to flavour foods or it may be mixed with hoisin paste and served as a dip. Available from oriental shops.

Chinese Wines

In this book sherry has been substituted for Chinese wines which can be expensive and difficult to obtain if you do not live near a good oriental supermarket. However, if you are able to buy Chinese wine the following guide may be of some help.

Different Chinese wines are used in cooking for different purposes. Chinese wines are, in general, much stronger than western cooking wine and they should not be treated in the same manner.

White Rice Wine This is the most common wine used in Cantonese cooking. Chinese rice wine is clear and it is used to add fragrance to a dish. It is added to the edge of the wok so that it sizzles and by the time the liquid slides to the ingredients in the centre of the wok all the alcohol has evaporated and only the fragrance is added to the food. If this wine is sprinkled directly on to the food the flavour will be too strong and the dish will become bitter in taste. Rice wine is also used as a marinade for chicken and pork, to make the flavour of the meat more delicate.

Rose Wine This is a fragrant wine which has a strong taste and it is normally used as an ingredient in Chinese roasts.

Yellow Wine This wine, known as *shiu chau*, is used mostly in the cooking of northern China. It is commonly used in Peking dishes.

237

Index

Index